Mending
BROKEN PEOPLE

3ABN Miracle Stories

THE VISION. THE LIVES. THE BLESSINGS.

KAY KUZMA

Pacific Press® Publishing Association
Nampa, Idaho
Oshawa, Ontario, Canada
www.pacificpress.com

3ABN BOOKS

Cover designed by Kenton Rogers
Photos provided by 3ABN

Unless otherwise noted,
all Scripture quotations are from the King James Version.

Additional copies of this book are available by
calling toll free 1-800-765-6955 or
online at www.abcasap.com
Also available from 3ABN
618-627-4651 or online at www.3ABN.org

Library of Congress Cataloging-in-Publication Data

Kuzma, Kay.
Mending Broken People : the vision, the lives, the blessings / the
miracle stories of 3ABN / Kay Kuzma.
p. cm.
"3ABN books"
ISBN: 0-8163-2066-7
1. 3ABN (Organization) 2. Religious broadcasting. 3. Television in
religion. 4. Radio in religion. 5. Seventh-day Adventists. I.Title

BV655.K89 2005
269'.26–dc22   2004065471

05 06 07 08 09 · 5 4 3 2

Dedication

To God be the glory

"For the Lord God is a sun and shield;
The Lord will give grace and glory;
No good thing will He withhold
From those who walk uprightly.
O Lord of hosts,
Blessed is the man who trusts in You!"
—Psalm 84:11, 12, NKJV.

Contents

Foreword

The Bible describes three angels flying through the heavens calling the people of the world to prepare to meet their God. These angels are symbols of God's messengers, and the message is a message of the final judgment of planet Earth. It is to be carried to the ends of the earth and to reach all people—pleading with them to leave the deceptive evils of the world and turn in true worship to the God of Creation—for it is time for Jesus to return as King of kings and Lord of lords to gather all who will accept Him as Lord of their lives for all eternity.

Counterfeit messages now abound and hold the whole world captive. It is time for undiluted truth to be revealed and for the counterfeit to be unmasked. For this purpose, and this purpose alone, God reached down and tapped Danny Shelton on the shoulder, saying, "Go, build a television station that will reach the world and call the people to come to Me!"

This is the setting for the story of 3ABN as told so beautifully in this book by noted author Kay Kuzma. As you read its pages, your heart will resonate with the heart of God as you learn of His miracle-working grace acting through the lives of those whom He has called to work together to spread the three angels' messages to the world. You will witness a great God doing unfathomable things through these humble servants, seemingly so inadequate by this world's standards. But they have heard His call and have said to Him, "Here am I, send me!"

As you read, let the Spirit of God speak to your heart, too. Not all are called to build television networks to reach the world, but all who hear the good news are called to share the testimony of what God has done for them—be it little or much. The Bible says "God was in Christ, reconciling the world unto himself, . . . and hath committed unto us the word of reconciliation. Now then we are ambassadors for Christ" (2 Corinthians 5:19, 20).

Walter Thompson, M.D.,
Chairman of the Board of Directors of 3ABN.

Introduction

You've heard about the Old Testament miracles that made it possible for Moses to lead millions of people out of slavery and into the promised land of Canaan—stories about how water came out of a rock, how Moses' rod turned into a snake, and how manna fell each day—except on Sabbath.

God's power was also seen in New Testament times as Peter walked on the water, was released from prison by an angel, and raised Dorcas from the dead.

Even in the late nineteenth century, God enabled George Müller to provide for thousands of orphans by faith alone! Müller committed himself to ask only God, not men—and God came through. The orphans never went hungry, even if it meant God woke someone up in the middle of the night to bake bread or a milk truck had to break down in front of the orphanage when the cupboards were bare!

But are you aware of what God is doing today?

The story you are about to read is one of the most incredible sagas of God's miraculous power that has ever been recorded—and it's happening right now. In fact, as you read this book of miracles that have taken place in the last few years, new miracles are happening in the continuing story of Three Angels Broadcasting Network (3ABN), a satellite television and radio ministry dedicated to sharing Bible truth worldwide.

Learn how God called a gospel-singing carpenter to a ministry that touches millions of lives each day.

Marvel at how God pinpointed the site for the uplink satellite equipment and directed the building of the studios in Thompsonville, Illinois, an out-of-the-way coal-mining region—and how this ministry today is mining precious souls from every continent of the world.

Praise God as you read how He . . .

. . . developed the multimillion dollar 3ABN Evangelism Center in Nizhny Novgorod, Russia, so that the Russian people could hear the gospel in their own tongue.

... has made it possible for His message to be on satellites that literally cover the earth, beaming the gospel to the faraway continents of Europe, Asia, Africa, and Australia.

... worked through the Philippine ambassador to Papua New Guinea to have the president of the Philippines grant a construction permit for 3ABN to build a full-power station in the metro-Manila area, which could potentially reach more than twenty million people.

... inspired the governor general of Papua New Guinea to invite 3ABN to build a television station in Port Moresby, which would reach the entire country's population of 4.2 million.

... opened doors so that 3ABN could reach a potential cable television audience of one-quarter of a billion people in India.

If you have ever doubted that God is alive and actively involved with His people today, this book will wash away your doubt. If you have ever questioned whether God can use you for a great work, this book will convince you that God can use anyone who is willing. If you have wondered why we don't see more miracles today, perhaps you're tuned-in to the wrong channel. Let me challenge you to begin watching Three Angels Broadcasting Network and become a part of what is happening "on holy ground," which is what people call the site on which 3ABN is built.

Kay Kuzma, Ed.D.

"Slowly, steadily, surely,
the time approaches when the vision will be fulfilled.
If it seems slow, wait patiently, for it will surely take place.
It will not be delayed"
—Habakkuk 2:3, NLT.

Acknowledgments

To Danny Shelton and the staff, volunteers, and friends of 3ABN who so willingly shared their stories.

To Bobby Davis, a producer and managing editor at 3ABN, who carefully edited this manuscript to make sure it reflects an accurate history of 3ABN.

To my sister, Dianne Affolter, and my friend Tim Jacobsen for their editorial help.

To those who critiqued and proofread the book—Mollie Steenson, Shirley Burton, Shelly Quinn, Barbara Nolen, Mark Finley, and Jim Gilley.

To those who helped me personally during the final phase of writing. Although there are too many to mention by name, I want to especially thank...

My daughter and her husband, Kari and Jeff St. Clair, and their children, Levi and Kristen, who immediately came to stand by my side and by their dad's (and grandpa's) bedside during the darkest hours when my husband, Jan, was in ICU after suffering a stroke while we were at 3ABN where I was working long hours to complete this manuscript.

The kind and competent staff at Herrin Hospital where Jan spent two and a half weeks in the hospital and in rehabilitation, struggling to regain his left-side function. A special thanks goes to our gentle and compassionate 3ABN physician, Dr. Meshach Samuel.

Danny Shelton, John and Angela Lomacang, and John and Rochelle Stanton for the touching anointing service, and to Brad Walker for videotaping the service. Our family was truly blessed by the words, the songs, and the hope for healing.

April Worf, who gave unselfishly of her time to stay with my husband in the hospital when I left his side to continue researching and writing this book.

Hal Steenson, who volunteered to transport Jan back to our daughter's home in Tennessee, allowing me to spend a few more days wrapping up the final details of this manuscript.

And to those who prayed for Jan and for the finishing of this book.

To each of you, *"Thank you so very, very much!"*

What Is Three Angels Broadcasting Network (3ABN)?

Three Angels Broadcasting Network (3ABN) is a nonprofit religious organization with the vision to "mend broken people" through the powerful messages of God's Word broadcast twenty-four hours a day through a television and radio satellite network that encircles the globe. As of January 2005, eight satellites, over 250 television stations, 58 radio stations, more than 250 cable systems, and a global Internet service were carrying 3ABN programming to every inhabited continent. 3ABN television is also available through Sky Angel's satellite subscription service. Since 3ABN's beginning in 1984, Danny Shelton has served as president and visionary leader of this worldwide ministry. The worldwide headquarters, uplink station, and production studios are located in the small township of Thompsonville, Illinois, just ten miles north of West Frankfort, Illinois.

3ABN offers a wide variety of programming including inspirational music, testimonials, weekend church services, nationally syndicated religious programs, and discussions of Bible topics ranging from current Christian concerns to prophecy seminars. Believing a healthy mind and body promote a healthy spiritual life, 3ABN personnel consider health programming to be of particular importance. A variety of family oriented programs address child rearing, marriage relationships, cooking, and gardening. In addition, 3ABN offers programming for children and youth.

God is expanding this ministry on a daily basis; therefore, to obtain the latest information on how you can be blessed by this powerful God-led ministry, visit the Web site at www.3abn.org or call 3ABN's worldwide headquarters in the United States at 618-627-4651. For a free newsletter subscription or catalog of 3ABN books and music, send an email message to 3ABN at mail@3abn.org or write 3ABN, P.O. Box 220, West Frankfort, IL 62896. In Canada, the address is Three Angels Christian Communications, P.O. Box 2369, Abbotsford, BC V2T 4X3. For information about 3ABN activities in other countries, call 3ABN's worldwide headquarters.

The Board of Directors

I speak for 3ABN's vast worldwide audience when I say, "Thank you, board members. May God bless you for your leadership, support, and prayers for the 3ABN ministry."—Kay Kuzma

God has used a dedicated group of people behind the scenes of 3ABN's global ministry to assist, advise, enable, finance, encourage, support with prayer power, and promote 3ABN's mission to take the gospel to a lost and dying world. Because of the board of directors, 3ABN is a worldwide, vibrant, stable, respected, and influential ministry.

Although it is impossible to name everyone who has given time, resources, and administrative savvy to guiding this organization over the years, we thank each one of you. May God bless you abundantly for what you have done to support God's work.

A special word of thanks goes to those board members who have served for almost the entire history of 3ABN: May Chung, Bill Hulsey, Ellsworth McKee, Walter Thompson, Owen Troy, and Larry Welch. If you were to look at a list of the names of current 3ABN board members, you would notice that two members have the same last name—Thompson. Neither had anything to do with the naming of the township of Thompsonville, Illinois, where 3ABN is located, nor are they related—other than being brothers in the Lord!

In addition to Danny Shelton, the following longtime board members continue to serve in 2004 as 3ABN celebrates twenty years of miracles.[1]

---

[1] On September 21, 2004, Merlin Fjarli, Nicholas Miller, Wintley Phipps, Mollie Steenson, and Carmelita Troy were asked to join the 3ABN Board of Directors. Carmelita took the place of her father, Owen Troy.

May Chung makes her home in San Bernardino, California, although she isn't there very often because of traveling for the Lord and supporting various projects. May is a philanthropist, but she is also a dynamic, dedicated, and energetic worker for God. She has had two special lifelong missions. The first is to spread the knowledge of the Ten Commandments to those who are ignorant of God's will. Her message is that God's law starts with God declaring His relationship with man, "I am the Lord your God," followed by ten ways

May Chung

humans can respond to God's love. As of 2004, May had personally carried this message to fourteen current leaders of nations. May's second mission is to reach the world with the gospel. This is what inspired her to support 3ABN from the very beginning. She wanted to make sure that the cost of transponder fees would not be an excuse for 3ABN to hold back from reaching the world. May's encouragement and support have helped make 3ABN a worldwide satellite network.

Kenneth A. Denslow is the president of the Illinois Conference of Seventh-day Adventists. From the beginning, 3ABN has always had the president of the Illinois Conference on its board. Over the years, the following presidents have served: Everett Cumbo, B. J. Christiansen, and Wayne Coulter. Ken is somewhat different from the others because his parents, Al and Bernie Denslow, spend approximately eight months each year volunteering for 3ABN. Ken is incredibly dedicated and supportive of the 3ABN mission. He has a

Kenneth A. Denslow

tremendous vision for evangelism; his encouragement has been worth his weight in gold.

Bill Hulsey, retired CEO of Collegedale Wood Products, not only lives in Collegedale, Tennessee, but also holds the honor of being the mayor of that city. God has gifted Bill with incredible

Bill Hulsey

business savvy and ethics. Plus, he has a generous heart for the Lord. Often, Bill's role on the board is to form motions and policies into just the right words to represent the will of the group. In a way, you might say, the board gives Bill the last word! In addition to his love of the Lord and his mission for evangelism, Bill has a heart for the community that surrounds 3ABN. Whenever there is a special community need, Bill steps in and makes it possible for 3ABN to meet that need. Because of his generosity, 3ABN has become a highly respected organization in West Frankfort, the closest town to 3ABN's headquarters.

Ellsworth McKee, from Ooltewah, Tennessee, served as chairman of the board of directors during the 1990s. During Ellsworth's leadership, 3ABN experienced an amazing growth spurt, obtaining new satellites, constructing new stations, and reaching new countries. When Ellsworth isn't busy with 3ABN matters, he is the chairman of the board of McKee

Ellsworth McKee

Foods, Inc., the company known for Little Debbie snack cakes as well as for its support of global evangelism in the Seventh-day Adventist Church. Because Ellsworth is so highly respected among church leadership, he has at times acted as a buffer for 3ABN by deflecting friendly fire. Danny Shelton considers Ellsworth one of his best friends.

G. Ralph Thompson has recently moved from Silver Spring, Maryland, to Naples, Florida. He was serving as undersecretary of the General Conference of Seventh-day Adventists when he joined the 3ABN board in 1991. He is a true friend, supporter, and worldwide ambassador for the ministry. In the early days of 3ABN, before Ralph was a board member, he attended a meeting discussing whether the Seventh-day Adventist Church should endorse 3ABN because it wasn't a part of the organized work. Elder Thompson finally stood and said, "Gentlemen, last night in my hotel room, I watched 3ABN for the first time, and I was so excited about seeing Adventist preachers and musicians come on one after another that I could hardly sleep. My buttons almost popped on my shirt. I said, 'This guy [Danny Shelton] is doing something right.' 3ABN is not using church finances to take the Adventist message to the world. 3ABN doesn't cost the church a dime, and it is not in debt. Because of

G. Ralph Thompson

3ABN, new members are coming into the church and paying tithe. It's a win-win situation. There is no question but that we should support them. Watch their programming, and I think you will say, 'Praise God for 3ABN.' "

Walter Thompson is a retired surgeon who spent most of his career at Hinsdale Hospital in Chicago, Illinois. He has always had a heart for people. Through the years, he established his own ministry and went into the slums of Chicago to give free medical service. In addition to being a physician, he is the author of numerous books and has a passion to reach the world with the benefits of living a healthy lifestyle. Through his influence and financial support, 3ABN has been able to produce excellent quality health program-

Walter Thompson

ming. For over seventeen years, Dr. Walt has been advising, counseling, encouraging, and supporting the mission of 3ABN. He now carries the leadership role as chairman of the board of directors. He has written a beautiful foreword for this book. Be sure to read it!

Owen Troy is both multitalented and internationally talented. His love has always been the media ministry because he has seen the potential of reaching people through television and radio. After he retired from his work at the North American Division of the

Owen Troy

Seventh-day Adventist Church, where he held the position of director of communications, he became 3ABN's director of international development, with his daughter, Carmelita, working as his assistant. Owen has been an important liaison between 3ABN and church entities in many foreign countries. His special interest, however, is Africa. Because of his contacts and influence there, 3ABN is known throughout the continent. Owen has an incredible desire to get the gospel and the message of Revelation 14 to the world. He truly is 3ABN's ambassador to the world.

Larry Welch

Larry Welch has the distinction of being involved with 3ABN from the very beginning—when Danny first had the dream. It was Larry's ministry to Mrs. Fonda Summers that resulted in her coming to the prayer meeting where she heard about Danny's dream for a worldwide television ministry. She was impressed to give a section of her land for the original uplink building that housed a production studio and offices. Larry has given twenty years of friendship, enthusiasm, and leadership skills to this ministry. He has not only carried board responsibilities but also worked for 3ABN much of the time. He is currently construction manager at 3ABN. When you visit and see the beautiful buildings that house 3ABN, think of Larry and the hours he has given to this ministry. Larry is not at all surprised about the phenomenal growth of 3ABN. One of the things that inspired him to move his family back to southern Illinois from California was the dream he had in which he saw southern Illinois as the center of the universe, with beams emanating out to the rest of the world. Larry says, "I had a distinct impression that this was where God was concentrating His power."

Section I
How It All Began

"I am Your servant;
Give me understanding,
That I may know Your testimonies.
It is time for You to act, O Lord,
For they have regarded Your law as void.
Therefore I love Your commandments
More than gold, yes, than fine gold!
Therefore all Your precepts concerning all things
I consider to be right;
I hate every false way"
—Psalm 119:125-128, NKJV.

Some have compared Danny Shelton (the singer) to King David (the psalmist)—not for David's fiascos but for his fearlessness and for his faith. No one can doubt that David and God were mighty close—as are Danny and the Lord. One of the things that amazed Linda, when she and Danny first got married, was waking in the middle of the night and seeing Danny kneeling by the side of their bed, hands folded and head bowed, talking things over with his Friend in heaven.

God called David "a man after His own heart" because of their close relationship. For that same reason, one might say that Danny is a "man after God's own heart." Not only can we hear Danny pray the words of David in Psalm 119:125-128, but we can hear him sing the lilting melodies that mend our broken hearts and call us back to a closer relationship to God—as did David so many years ago.

And just as God called David to the special work of preparing for the building of His temple, God has called Danny to facilitate the development of a work that prepares people for His coming. This is the story that you're about to read.

1
The Calling of a Gospel-Singing Carpenter

"I heard the voice of the Lord, saying:
'Whom shall I send,
And who will go for Us?'
Then I said, 'Here am I! Send me.'
And He said, 'Go...'"
—Isaiah 6:8, 9, NKJV.

How it all began

It was November 14, 1984, in the tiny Midwest town of West Frankfort, Illinois. And it was late—probably too late to turn on the TV. But in the two years since his wife had been killed in a tragic automobile accident, Danny Shelton had sometimes watched TV during the lonely hours of the night. After he said Good Night to his friend, Linda, and her two little ones who had stopped by for a visit, and after he gave his thirteen-year-old daughter, Melody, her usual bedtime hug and kiss, he stretched out on the couch and picked up the remote. He watched a little news then flipped to a Christian channel, where a program caught his attention.

As he adjusted the volume, he couldn't believe what he was hearing. The speaker, on a religious network beaming a signal to literally millions around the world, was saying, "When the rapture comes, we will be leaving our television equipment behind for Jesus and all the disciples and all the prophets to use to win the souls of all the wicked that will be left behind on this earth."

Danny was incensed. How could the producers of a well-meaning Christian network say such things when the Bible's account of Christ's second coming was so different? (See Matthew 24; 1 Thessalonians 4.) The way Danny read the Bible, Christ's coming will be no secret. Sure, a lot of people will be surprised. They won't expect it any more than they would a thief in the night. But they certainly won't miss seeing Christ and all His angels coming in the clouds of heaven—not with the trumpets blasting, lightning flashing, and Christ giving a shout loud enough to wake the righteous dead! The Bible is clear about what happens next: All God's people are going to be caught up together to meet the Lord in the air and go to heaven. What about the wicked people? The brightness of Christ's coming kills them (see 2 Thessalonians 2:8). That's it for life here on this old world! There will be no need for television equipment to be left behind, because there won't be anyone left to evangelize.

Danny wouldn't have been so upset if it had been atheists spouting their theories about God not existing. Those wanting to know Bible truth would question atheistic beliefs. But these people were Christian leaders! How many people would be led astray because they believed everything this Christian network presented? Danny sighed and muttered to himself, "If only there were a Christian television station to expose these false theories and broadcast Bible truth!"

That thought continued spinning around in his head as he knelt and prayed for God to do something about this deplorable situation. He crawled into bed, but he couldn't seem to press the pause button on his thoughts. *Why doesn't my Bible-believing church have a television station to beam truth around the world? Why?*

He tossed and adjusted his pillow as he began to think of the disastrous personal lives of so many of the television preachers who were almost worshiped by their viewers. It brought a sense of righteous indignation to his soul. Television had such a powerful influence on people. Once again, he questioned, *Why couldn't someone broadcast Bible truth twenty-four hours a day? The hurting and brokenhearted need the comfort of God's saving truth.*

Immediately, Danny's mind flitted back to almost a year before, when he and Melody had been asked to appear on *Nightline,* a religious call-in program on a television station in North Carolina. The experience made him realize just how powerful the influence of television could be on people's lives.

After Melody finished singing on the program, the *Nightline* host asked Danny to tell about his family. As a part of his testimony, Danny mentioned that his wife had died in a terrible automobile accident. The host asked, "Didn't you get mad at God for taking your wife?"

That was Danny's chance! Impulsively, he replied, "God didn't take my wife. That's not biblical. God isn't like that. Besides, people don't immediately go to heaven when they die." And then, Danny began to rattle off Bible texts that he had been reading ever since a Baptist lady in West Frankfort had tried to console him the day Kay died by saying, "You can feel comforted that God needed another voice in His angel choir, and He chose your wife. She had such a beautiful voice." In horror, he asked the woman where she got that idea.

"Well," she said, "that's what I've been taught since I was a little girl."

Danny was disturbed to think people would believe that God would take someone's life, leaving behind a grieving husband and three daughters, just because He thought His choir didn't sound quite right! What a misrepresentation of God's loving character! If that's what people thought God was like, no wonder they hated Him!

So when the host asked Danny the question about God taking his wife, he quoted Ecclesiastes 9:5, "The dead know not anything," and Psalm 146:4, "His breath goeth forth, he returneth to his earth; in that very day his thoughts perish," biblical confirmation that death is an unconscious state.

Then Danny made the point that God isn't the one who is going around killing our loved ones. That's the work of a thief, the devil. "In John 10:10, Jesus says, 'The thief cometh not, but for to steal, and to kill, and to destroy: I am come that they might have life, and that they might have it more abundantly.'"

"And God certainly doesn't burn you in hell forever," Danny continued. "How cruel to tell a child, 'Johnny, you be careful. Jesus loves you more than anything. But if you're not good, Jesus will burn you forever.' Even Hitler didn't do that! God is not a God of vengeance. He doesn't torture people. The Bible says that Sodom and Gomorrah suffered the vengeance of eternal fire, but are they still burning today? No way! They burned until they were destroyed. And that's exactly what's going to happen to the wicked in the end." (See chapter 3 for Bible references on these points.)

Danny went on and on. The ten minutes he was supposed to be on the air stretched into thirty, then sixty, and still the phones kept ringing.

One man who called said, "I'm sixty-four years old. I've hated God since I was five. My mother died, and I was told God took her. From that moment on, I never wanted to have anything to do with God. When I was flipping through the TV channels, I just happened to stop on this one. I'm so glad I did because what you have said in the last thirty minutes has changed my life!" Then he added, "Is it too late for me to have salvation?"

Danny assured this man that Jesus was saying to him, just as He had said to Zacchaeus, "This day is salvation come to this house" (Luke 19:9).

After that night in 1983, when Danny discovered television's power to meet people's needs, he began to imagine how wonderful it would be to have the opportunity to present, via television, the wonderful Bible truths he had been taught as a child and to hear the phones ring in response.

A little later, this idea was stirred again when Danny was standing around, talking with some other musicians waiting to go on stage on a live TV program in Illinois.

One of them asked Danny, "What church do you go to—the Assemblies?"

"No," Danny replied, "I go to the Adventist Church."

"What church?"

"I'm an SDA."

"Well, I've got a brother whose in-laws are Mormon."

Then Danny had to explain, "I don't know any Mormons."

"Oh, you're a Jehovah's Witness!"

It astonished Danny that these people, right in his own community, had no idea who Seventh-day Adventists were. Even though Adventists have the largest Protestant school system in the world and operate hundreds of hospitals and clinics, most people still don't know what Adventists believe.[1] *Shouldn't we be the head and not the tail?* Danny questioned. *Shouldn't we be on the cutting edge of television technology presenting our beliefs to the world?*

With all these thoughts flooding back into his mind, Danny began to plead with God. *Father,* he asked, *can't You do something about this? You're all powerful. Something needs to be done to get Your truth out to the people who might never step inside the door of an Adventist church! Something needs to be done so Bible truth can be available 24/7, whenever people turn on their TV sets!*

Danny thought about how God had raised up different churches over the centuries to reveal different truths—Lutherans presented the truth that salvation was a free gift; Baptists, the truth about baptism by immersion; Pentecostals, the importance of joyful praise and worship. *Lord,* he asked, *wasn't the Adventist Church raised up to call people back to the Bible and give the end-time warning message to the world?* [Pause] *Yes? Then, where is it being broadcast?*

There was an Adventist television program called *It Is Written,* on which Danny and Melody had been guest artists but Danny had never seen it on television. There were a few other half-hour Adventist programs, that existed and aired on a few stations. *Why doesn't the Adventist Church build a television station to present Bible truth every day, all week long?* his mind agonized. *Either the message I believe is real or it isn't! Why doesn't someone do something to tell people what the Bible really says and warn them to be ready for Jesus' second coming?*

God calls Danny

Danny must have dozed then, but his sleep was shallow as he periodically glanced at the clock, saw the hours slipping away, and continued his monolog of frustration to the Lord. Midnight, one-thirty, two-fifteen. He remembered saying once again, *Lord, can't You do something about this? Can't You find someone to build a television station that could broadcast Bible truth?* Then in the wee morning hours of November 15, it happened.

Danny Shelton in 1984

Suddenly, Danny was struck with the most incredible thought that had ever entered his thirty-three-year-old brain! The words were clear—no fuzzy, mixed-up, middle-of-the-night, sleep-deprived blur. Into his mind blazed the message, *I want you to build a television station that will reach the world with the undiluted three angels' messages; one that will counteract the counterfeit.*

What? Danny's mind shouted in the stillness. He sat bolt upright! Was he dreaming? What had he heard? He knew his own thoughts and wishes, and he had *never* wanted to start a television station.

Danny was beginning to doubt his sanity when God pressed the repeat button. Amazingly, he heard the message once again, just as clear as before: *I want you to build a television station that will reach the world with the undiluted three angels' messages; one that will counteract the counterfeit.*

If Danny was agitated before, you can imagine his agitation now! He reasoned, *There is no way I could build a station! I would be the last person in the world qualified to build one. I know nothing about television, except how to sing in front of the cameras. I have no education in communication, except how to turn on a television set. I have no money. I have no friends of influence.* Later, Danny admitted he didn't even understand the meaning of the words he had heard—". . . the undiluted three angels' messages; one that will counteract the counterfeit." These were certainly not *his* words. If he had been talking to himself, he would have said, "A television station to share the message of Jesus, the seventh-day Sabbath, the state of the dead, and the importance of living a healthy lifestyle."

But "the three angels' messages"? Even though Danny had heard about that phrase since he was a kid, he really didn't understand exactly what these angels were or the significance of their messages. He seldom, if ever, said the word *undiluted.* He might have said, "not watered down," but he wouldn't have used the word *undiluted!* That word just wasn't a part of his southern Illinois upbringing in an uneducated family that worked junkyards and pumped septic tanks. Danny had never before said the phrase, "counteract the counterfeit." It just wasn't him!

Danny has always been a very direct person. He made it very clear to the Lord that He had made a big mistake putting that thought into his mind. But, as Danny lay there wrestling with the Lord, the reality of the calling intensified. *I want you to build a television station that will reach the world with the undiluted three angels' messages; one that will counteract the counterfeit.*

Facing the reality of his qualifications

Danny began to argue with the Lord. "I'm not qualified." Then the Lord brought to his mind the conversation He had with Moses thousands of years ago. Moses had said the same thing. Moses had protested that he was unable to speak well, and God had replied, "Don't worry about that. I will provide."

And provide God did! Not only did God use Moses, a murderer, to lead the people of Israel out of slavery and establish an orderly society based on God's laws, but He used Moses to record the history of the world, a record that has become the first five books of the Bible. Quite an accomplishment for an eighty-year-old man who had a speech impediment!

Then there was Joseph, who was sold into slavery by his own brothers and later ended up in prison. Yet with God's help, Joseph became the prime minister of Egypt and saved hundreds of thousands from famine, including his own family.

Daniel was also a captive. But God made him a great advisor to the kings of two of the greatest nations in the world: Babylon and Media-Persia.

As Danny struggled with his lack of qualifications to do the work God had called him to do, an example came to his mind of a more recent calling when in 1843 God asked a seventeen-year-old girl, Ellen Harmon, to speak for Him. Not only was she handicapped by having only three years of formal schooling, but she had such poor health that many thought she would die soon! But that didn't stop God. With Ellen's willingness, God used her to preach to thousands and to write books. In addition, God used Ellen—known to us today by her married name, Ellen G. White—to help forge a Bible-believing church with its many health institutions, schools, and publishing houses. And all of this took place at a time when it wasn't popular to have women as leaders!

Danny took a deep breath. It all seemed so impossible. Yet there it was again—that strong impression that God was calling him as He had called Moses, Joseph, Daniel, and Ellen White. God was calling him to do what seemed, at the moment, to be an impossible task.

Accepting the challenge

Danny shook his head in disbelief at the wonder of it all. Then the Lord's words, *"Not by might, nor by power, but by my spirit"* (Zechariah 4:6) came to his mind. Danny spoke aloud, "OK, God, if this is from You, I'll go forward, and You supply every need."

Later, he thought about the words of his "acceptance speech." He came to the conclusion they weren't his words. The safe way to proceed would have been to say, "OK, God, You provide every need, and then I'll go forward." But the Holy Spirit led him to turn it around. He had just told God that he would go forward first, knowing that God would come through. This one decision has probably done more than anything else to set the tone and heart-beat for everything that 3ABN ministry has accomplished. Danny merely stepped out in faith, knowing that if it were God's will, he would have nothing to worry about. And if it wasn't God's will, he would know because the resources wouldn't be there.

Looking back over the years, Danny comments, "I have never been disappointed. Many times I muster courage by thinking back to Joshua leading the children of Israel into Canaan and coming upon the Jordan River. How were they to cross? It wasn't until the priests waded in and got their feet wet that the river dried up!"

After Danny committed himself to "wet feet," the thought came: *If there were a station that would indeed reach the world with Bible truth—giving the pure everlasting gospel of Jesus Christ—Satan would be furious. He would try in every way possible to destroy such a ministry either by direct attack or, if necessary, by "friendly fire." The only way to avoid the devil's traps and safeguard the delivery of truth would be to continually apply the Isaiah 8:20 test to everything that went out on the broadcast: "To the law and to the testimony: if they speak not according to this word, it is because there is no light in them."*

Confirmation of the calling

At that point, Danny knew this calling had to be from the Lord. God had challenged His church to be the head and not the tail. The time to act was now! Amazed and ecstatic about the reality of what had just occurred, Danny couldn't wait to tell someone. He had committed himself to moving forward, but like Gideon and Hezekiah he wanted a sign to make sure that what had been imprinted in his brain was really from the Lord. He was well aware that the devil also can plant thoughts in a person's mind. This idea of building a world-wide television ministry was so totally outside the boundary of his own personal reality he knew it was either from God or the devil. But after praying and "trying the spirits" there was no doubt in his mind; it was God. Yet he wondered what his friends would say.

He glanced at the clock. Almost three o'clock in the morning! "I shouldn't call them now," he reasoned. "They would really think

I'm crazy!" But the urgency going on inside drove him either to confirm God's calling or to rebuke the devil just as quickly as possible.

He dialed Linda's number.

"Hello," she drawled, still half asleep.

"Linda!" Danny's excitement rang in his voice. "You won't believe this, but the Lord has impressed me to build a television station to reach the world."

She was speechless. His words penetrated slowly into her sleepy brain.

"Well," she said slowly, "I think that's good." Linda was too stunned and too sleepy to say more. As she hung up the phone, it never occurred to her that this was an insane idea. She never questioned whether God had really called Danny or whether he was qualified. She didn't have any doubt about Danny and God building a television station. If God had called him, then with God's help Danny could do it. If the Lord had parted the Red Sea for Moses, she knew He could do it for Danny. If this was from the Lord, it was going to happen. Period!

At the time of Danny's telephone call, Linda had known Danny for almost two years, and she was deeply impressed that he had a very special relationship with God. "To me," she says, "Dan was a modern-day David. Just as God had called David a man after his own heart [see Acts 13:22], I felt that He could say the same about Dan. I knew the Lord had something very special in store for him. Already, he was serving the Lord in a meaningful way with his gospel singing, and this would be an expansion of that work."

Besides, Linda had already seen miracles that confirmed God's leading in Danny's life. For example, the year before, she had watched him build a fully functioning recording studio in just three weeks. Danny had only a three-sided pole barn when the Lord impressed him to build a recording studio at his home. At the time, he was taping a one-hour local interview program on the radio and taking recording artists to Nashville to record. Acting on the Lord's direction, he announced over the air, "We'll soon be recording in a studio at my home so local artists will be able to record right here in our community for a lot less money." He added, "I'm not asking for money, I just wanted you to know what the Lord is doing."

How would it be possible to build a recording studio without money? Danny never worried about money. His theory was that God expected him to start using what he did have, and when more was needed, God would provide. In other words, "Where God guides, He provides!" So one day, symbolically, Danny took Linda out to his pole barn, picked up a sixteen-foot two-by-four and nailed it across the open end. He had used all he had to build a studio. Now he would wait on the Lord to provide.

At the time, Danny didn't even have any recording equipment. What he did have was a Les Paul Gibson electric guitar that was so special to him that he vowed he would never sell it. That week someone offered to trade him some recording equipment for his guitar. Danny saw the hand of the Lord and made the trade. In three weeks he had converted a bedroom into a studio and begun recording there. As he earned money, he extended the bedroom and built an eight-track recording studio.

After the early morning phone call in which Danny told Linda about building a television station, it occurred to him that he should call his friends, Jim and Ann Greer, in Alexandria, Louisiana. They had a daughter the same age as his daughter, Melody. Ann had offered to promote Danny's and Melody's musical careers. She had already arranged a tour for them through Mississippi, Alabama, and Louisiana. Danny respected the Greers and wondered what they would say about this latest turn of events.

When Danny called them at that unearthly hour and explained that the Lord was asking him to begin a television station, Ann didn't question him as he had anticipated. Instead, she responded, "Praise the Lord! Well, let's see, I'm in classes tomorrow, and Jim is working. He probably can't come, but if I could get my father to help me drive all night Thursday, we could be there Friday morning to help you start the station."

That shocked Danny—and scared him. He hadn't asked her to come to West Frankfort, Illinois. He had accepted God's call only a few minutes before; he hadn't thought that the Lord would want him to start on the station so soon! What would they do on Friday? He wondered if his call at such an early hour might have affected Ann's rational thinking. So he started to explain, "Ann, you *do* realize that I don't have any money, property, equipment, or knowledge about how to start a TV station, don't you? So if you come up here, what are we going to do?"

"I don't know," she replied, "but if the Lord told you to build a station, and I believe He did because there is a great need, then we'd better get started. It's about a twelve-hour drive," she continued. "I think we can be there a little after ten o'clock Friday morning to help you start the station."

Danny hung up the phone in a daze. There was no doubt in his mind now that God really did want him to do this. He felt a little like Hezekiah after God moved the shadow on the sundial backward ten degrees in response to his request for a sign that the words of the prophet were true that he would live another fifteen years (see 2 Kings 20).

Danny fell back on his bed in astonishment at what the Lord had just done. He slept soundly for a couple of hours and was up again at 6:00 A.M., energized and ready to start on this new adventure with the Lord. He decided to call his family, his friends, and anyone he knew who was interested in television, telling them the exciting news.

The fulfillment of the vision begins

On Friday morning Danny heard a car on the gravel drive and glanced at his watch—ten-thirty. Ann Greer and her father were right on time. He went out to meet them. "I know you've been driving all night. Do you and your dad want to go inside and sleep a while before we get started?"

"No," Ann exclaimed, "I didn't come here to sleep. Let's get to work! Do you know anyone who has some television equipment that we can look at and get some ideas?"

"Sure," Danny responded. "I have a good friend, a pastor from a charismatic church, who has a complete studio. His name is Hal Steenson. He produces programs for a local Christian television station."

"Well, let's start by talking to him."

So that's how it began. God has always raised up just the right people at the right time to get the work done. Danny later said he thought God sent Ann to set a fire under him and to impress him that there was no time to lose. And what happened next convinced him that there was absolutely no question that the Lord was in this thing![2]

Danny and Ann immediately got in the car and headed to Hal

Pastor Hal and Mollie
Steenson in 1984

Steenson's church. Danny introduced Ann to Pastor Hal and asked if he would show them his television studio and equipment. Hal graciously took time to show them around.

When they finished, Danny said, "Brother Hal, I want to tell you something I'm hesitant to tell even my own pastor. The night before last, the Lord called me to build a television station that will reach the world with the undiluted three angels' messages; one that would counteract the counterfeit. I'm not sure what all this means. But it's a calling God has put on my life, and it has to do with getting the Seventh-day Adventist message about the Bible to the world."

Pastor Hal called his wife. "Mollie, you've got to come and listen to what Danny just told me."

After Danny repeated the story, Mollie smiled, looked back at Hal, and walked off. Danny knew something was going on between them, but he didn't know what. Then Hal began to tell Danny that a pastor from Indiana had come to see him recently about buying his television equipment. Hal told him he wasn't interested in selling. After the man left, Hal realized he hadn't consulted the Lord about that decision and wondered if he had made a mistake. Pastor Hal prayed, *Should I have sold it, Lord?* And the Lord told him, *No.*

Great, Hal thought, *then I get to keep it.*

The reply was, *Not necessarily.*

What do you mean? Hal questioned the Lord. *You don't want me to sell it, and You don't want me to keep it? What do you want me to do? Give it away?*

Then God said, *There will be a time, a place, and a person to whom you are to give the equipment. When it's time, you'll know.*

At that point in Hal's story, he looked directly at Danny and said, "I'm getting a terrible feeling that this is the time and the place—and that you're the person."

As the sun sank in the west, the happenings of that day ran around inside Danny's head. He and Melody celebrated the beginning of the

Sabbath with Ann Greer and her father. Danny ate a light supper and excused himself to prepare for bed. He and Melody were leaving early the next morning to give a concert in Missouri. Danny had to get some sleep. But there was no way he could sleep until he knew for sure what Pastor Hal meant when he said he was getting a terrible feeling that this was the right time and place, and that Danny was the right person. So a little after eleven o'clock, Danny dialed Pastor Hal's number.

"How are you doing, Brother Hal?" Danny began.

"Danny, what can I do for you?"

"Nothing," Danny said trying to not be too forward.

There was an uncomfortable silence. They talked about inconsequential things, the weather, and finally Hal asked, "What's on your mind, Danny?"

"Well," Danny began, not knowing exactly what to say. "After what you told me today about your television equipment, I'm so excited that I can't sleep. But you never said you'd give the equipment to me. So I figured every hour on the hour while I'm awake, I'd just give you a call because it's your fault I can't sleep."

"Well," said Pastor Hal, "go back to bed, Danny, and get some sleep. Over the course of the day, the Lord has impressed me to give you the equipment. You know we've recently changed the name of our church from Praise Chapel to Praise World Outreach because the Lord showed me in a dream that this area of southern Illinois was like the hub of a wagon wheel with spokes reaching into the whole world. I thought God's message was for me. But now I'm convinced it's for you and that we should support you in the work you have been called to do. So as soon as your building is ready, we'll donate the television equipment to you."

Once Pastor Hal said he would give him the equipment, the last shred of doubt was erased in Danny's mind. This calling had to be from the Lord. From that moment on, he never looked back. God says "Go ye therefore, and teach all nations . . . to observe all things whatsoever I have commanded you," but He doesn't leave it at that. The next phrase says, "and, lo, I am with you alway, even unto the end of the world" (Matthew 28:19, 20).

Danny resolved, "If God has said it, I'll believe it. I will step out in faith, and I know God will be with me!"

In the next few weeks, he told the story of the gift of the television equipment at various churches, and he found many doubting Thomases. "How do you know that Pentecostal pastor is really going to give the equipment to you?" they queried.

"Because he said he was," Danny replied.

"What authority does he have to give away church equipment? What if his church board says No?"

Danny decided the only way to erase the doubts of others was to give his friend another call. So a few weeks later he asked Pastor Hal, "Are you sure you can give us the equipment?"

"Why not?" he replied.

"Well, you haven't even talked to your church board about it," Danny reasoned. "I have a feeling if our pastor would give away a cassette deck without getting permission, we'd tar and feather him and run him out of town."

Pastor Hal replied, "God has sent me the type of people who support me. If I say God has impressed me to do something, they will believe me and go along with me." Later, the Praise World Outreach Church had a board meeting and unanimously voted to donate the television equipment to 3ABN. But interestingly, by the time the 3ABN studio was built, God provided newer and better television equipment from another source, and Pastor Hal's equipment wasn't needed. God merely used this gift as the sign Danny needed to move forward.

Two of Danny's favorite texts are found in Philippians. The first is, "I can do all things through Christ which strengtheneth me" (Philippians 4:13). And the second is, "My God shall supply all your need according to his riches" (Philippians 4:19).

During the next few weeks as Danny reflected on the miracles God was working for 3ABN, he made this observation, "We serve the same God of might and miracles that parted the Red Sea for Moses and the Israelites when they were certain to be slaughtered by the Egyptian army because they had no way of escape. I often wonder what would have happened if Moses hadn't had faith in God and moved forward. That Bible story, coupled with the unexpected gift of television equipment that had been given to me by Pastor Hal that day, gave me the faith I needed to begin stepping into the water. And each time I do, I discover once again that God has counted His resources and is found not wanting."

The trip that changed Danny's life

As Danny was praising the Lord for His incredible gift of television equipment, just two days after his call from the Lord, never in his wildest imagination would he have believed what God would impress him to do as the sun began to rise early the next morning.

Danny was driving down Highway 32 on the way to Farmington, Missouri. The trip would take about three hours. Before dawn, Danny picked up Linda and her children. They tucked in Alyssa, who was five, and Nathan, who was four, beside Melody in the back of the van so that the kids could get a little more sleep, and headed toward Farmington, Missouri, for a concert he and Melody were to give. As Linda was dozing in the passenger seat, Danny was getting a strong impression from the Lord. *Marry her and get your honeymoon over with, because I have a lot of work for you to do.*

Danny began to argue with the Lord, *But we don't have any money!*

God seemed to respond, *How much more evidence do I need to give you in order for you to believe that I can supply all your needs? Wasn't what I did for you this last week enough?*

Suddenly, mind made up, Danny turned to Linda and said, "Let's get married!"

And they did—eight days later!

---

[1] See Appendix 2 to find out more about Seventh-day Adventists.

[2] Ann and Jim Greer continued for a number of years to be very involved with the development of the 3ABN ministry, traveling from Louisiana to Illinois as often as possible. When the 3ABN uplink building was completed and the television signal was being beamed up to the satellite, the Greers even moved to West Frankfort for a time. Ann wrote the first newsletters that kept 3ABN donors informed. 3ABN will always be thankful for individuals who, like the Greers, sensed God's need and were willing to offer their services.

2
The Incredible Miracles
That Started 3ABN

" 'Ask, and it will be given to you;
seek, and you will find;
knock, and it will be opened to you' "
—Matthew 7:7, NKJV.

Danny had no idea what he was getting into when God and he formed their partnership. He felt like David who, as a mere boy, ran to meet Goliath with only a staff, a sling, and five smooth stones because the king's armor wouldn't fit him. Danny ran to meet the giant task of building a television station with only a guitar and a hammer. Not exactly the king's armor!

Because he didn't have the knowledge, skills, or financing to build a television station, Danny took courage in what the Bible said about David. Upset that Goliath was defying God, David boldly faced and slew the giant so "that all the earth may know that there is a God" (1 Samuel 17:46). He was so sure that God wanted a television station proclaiming Bible truth that rightly represented His character that when God called him to build such a network, Danny said, "Yes."

Although Danny never doubted God's calling, he did think about how ill-prepared he was for the task. How could he, a gospel singer from the little town of West Frankfort, build a television station that would reach the world with the three angels' messages? Danny had no rich relatives, he knew no influential people in business that could open doors, nor did he know anyone in the administrative positions of the church that he could count on for support. He didn't think he even knew anyone in the television industry who had the training and experience necessary to tell him what to do.

But he knew he had something far more important going for him. He had the same powerful God that David had when he killed the giant! The Israelites scoffed at David and predicted failure, but that didn't stop him. Danny knew there were many people who thought he was crazy. They were predicting that nothing would come of this. But no amount of criticism and rejection could stop him. He never once doubted his mission because he knew this was God's calling—and with God all things are possible! He believed that one person with God is a majority! Anyone with God is a success!

How the phone bill got paid

Danny never hesitated to share with others what he was doing, because he never considered the possibility of failure. After all, he was partnering with the Lord. In fact, Danny called so many people in those early days to tell them about his plans that he was shocked when he got his first long distance bill. It was for $384, and it might as well have been $384,000, because he didn't have the money. He began saving, but when the date arrived that his telephone service was to be disconnected for nonpayment, he still had only a hundred dollars set aside. He decided he needed to go into the district telephone office in Marion, Illinois, pay what money he had, and ask if the phone company would work with him until he could pay the entire amount.

On the way, Danny decided to stop by Randy Mercer's small buisness because Randy had said he wanted to donate something toward the ministry. This is the story Randy told Danny: "About six weeks ago, I lost my glasses. I kept thinking I'd find them, so I didn't get new ones. But after six weeks without glasses, I gave up and turned the problem over to God. 'Lord,' I said, 'it's a shame to spend a hundred dollars on new glasses if I don't need to do it. If You'll let me find my glasses, I'll give the money to Danny for his new TV ministry.'

"By noon, my wife called. 'Guess what?' she exclaimed. 'I found your glasses!'

"I couldn't believe it. 'Where were they?' I asked.

" 'Right in the middle of the driveway!' she said. We have driven in and out of the driveway three or four times a day for the last six weeks. We should have seen them or they should have been smashed to pieces! It was obvious to me that God protected those glasses. That's why I want to give you this money."

Randy took out his checkbook and began writing, "I'm going to give you a hundred dollars now, but I'm impressed that if the Lord continues to bless, I should be helping you with $300 every month starting next month." Then the strangest thing happened. Instead of writing the check for $100, he wrote $300. Danny was tempted to grab the check and run, but that wasn't necessary. When Randy realized what he had done, he said, "I can't believe I made that mistake." He paused and then said, "I guess it wouldn't hurt to give you $300 starting this month."

And, of course, the $300 check, plus the money Danny had saved, was more than enough to pay the phone bill. With great rejoicing, he drove on to Marion. But this was just the beginning of the miracles!

Learning about a satellite location

A few days after he had promised the Lord to move forward and build a television station, Danny decided it might be a good idea to see what one looked like. So, he asked two of his brothers, Tommy and Kenny, if they wanted to go with him to the television station in Marion and have a look. Danny had been to this station a number of times, but it had always been to sing in front of the cameras. He had never looked at the equipment. He had no idea what it took to operate a television station, and he figured looking around would help. What he didn't know was that God had someone waiting at the station with vital information, someone He had ordained to help Danny build the television network.

When the Shelton brothers walked in, Danny immediately recognized Clarence Larson, whom he'd met before. "Hi, Clarence," he called. "I'm Danny Shelton."

"I know who you are," Clarence responded. "I remember you and your family singing here."

Danny knew Clarence was an engineer, so he wasn't about to tell him that the Lord had impressed him to build a television station that would reach the world. Clarence, of all people, would surely laugh! Danny introduced Clarence to Tommy and Kenny and then asked, "Do you mind showing us around? I want my brothers to see your station, and I'd like to look at the equipment."

So Clarence took them around and showed them the different pieces of equipment. Just as they were about to leave, Clarence led Danny into a partially finished room that was being added to the station. He shut the door and said, "I feel compelled to tell you something. I think of the Shelton brothers as musicians and carpenters, so I don't know why I'm telling you this. I just feel compelled to do so." He paused before continuing. "I believe a satellite uplink station could be built here in southern Illinois—about six to eight miles north of West Frankfort and a few miles east. Out by Thompsonville."

"What's a satellite uplink station?" Danny asked.

Later, Clarence told Danny that when he asked that question, Clarence felt foolish. He had thought perhaps it had been God who was impressing him to tell Danny about the possibility of a satellite uplink station. But if Danny didn't even know what such a station was, he certainly didn't need to know that one could be built in the area. *God must not have been guiding me,* Clarence thought. It wasn't until much later that he began to understand how God was using him, a Baptist engineer at a Pentecostal station, to support Danny in building a television station dedicated to sharing the three angels' messages of Revelation.

"How far will a satellite station reach?" Danny asked. Danny knew the station in Marion reached about eighty miles, so he figured a satellite station would have broader coverage.

"Well," Clarence replied, "how far do you want to reach?"

And just that quick, Danny caught on. How to reach the world had been the biggest problem he had been struggling with for the last few days, and now he knew the answer.

"The world!" Danny exclaimed.

Clarence confirmed it, "Well, that's the way you reach the world—via satellite!"

Just a few days earlier, Pastor Hal had agreed to give him a hundred thousand dollars' worth of television equipment. Now, Danny had just discovered that a satellite station could be built out by Thompsonville. But he still hadn't caught on to the complete picture. "Why can't you just build a satellite station anywhere?"

Clarence explained that satellites work off of microwave signals.

"So?"

"Well, have you heard of companies like AT&T, GTE, and General Bell?"

Danny admitted he corresponded with them monthly when he paid his phone bill.

"These companies also work off microwaves," Clarence explained. "So there are very few places in the United States where you can build a C-band satellite uplink station without microwave interference. And the more satellites that go up into space, the more difficult it will be to find an interference-free east-to-west arc that would allow you to reach them all."

For some time, Clarence told them, he had been playing around at home on his little Apple II computer, exploring the potential of having another satellite uplink station in the area. And he had just discovered this information.

Danny could hardly contain his excitement! He wasn't one to run and jump and shout, but if he ever came close, it was at that moment when he realized that everything that would be necessary to establish a worldwide television ministry could be done just a few miles down the road from his home! It was becoming clearer to him why God had called a person from such an unlikely place as West Frankfort, Illinois.

God must be involved, Danny thought to himself. *This is certainly bigger than one church or one denomination! First of all, God sends me to a charismatic pastor who confirms my calling and commits a hundred thousand dollars' worth of television equipment. Then suddenly, there's a Baptist engineer who works at a Pentecostal station saying, "The Lord's compelling me to tell you this information."* For the first time he began to understand the global nature of the work he was to do. He saw that God was using His people everywhere, from all faiths, to cooperate in this worldwide project. It was exciting!

Meeting the doubting Thomases

Not everyone, however, shared Danny's excitement. A few days later, Danny and his family traveled to California, where Melody was scheduled to sing on the Trinity Broadcasting Network. While the family was on the West Coast, Danny and Melody gave a number of weekend concerts in churches. At one church, between songs, Danny began sharing the miracles that had happened in the last few weeks as God had called him to build a worldwide television network. In the middle of his presentation, the pastor frantically began giving him the cut-off sign from the back of the sanctuary by slicing his hand in front of his neck. Danny couldn't figure out what was wrong but told the audience that they would be taking a short break. Danny then made his way back to the pastor.

"Listen," the pastor said, "I feel very uncomfortable with you standing up there telling people that you're going to build a television station that's going to reach the world. You've already told us enough about your background that I can't understand why you'd even be involved in such a project. And second, I don't want any of my people giving money to something that's never going to happen." He caught a breath and continued, "And besides, how do you know the people that you say are committed to help will really come through—like the charismatic pastor giving the TV equipment?"

This pastor's attitude really surprised Danny. In his excitement, he had no doubt that God was leading, but now he realized that other people could view him as somebody bouncing off the wall. *Lord,* Danny prayed, *how am I going to be able to share this vision You've given me with others so they'll know it's really from You?*

About this same time, Danny attended a meeting for Adventists working in television media. As people introduced themselves, they told what they planned to do in television. When Danny's turn came, he said, "I plan to build a television station that will reach the world with the undiluted three angels' messages; a station that will counteract the counterfeit."

The discussion leader said, "You must be kidding!"

"No," said Danny, "I know God wants me to do this."

"Are you an engineer? What kind of training do you have?"

"No, I'm not an engineer, and I have no experience in television." Then Danny went on to tell them about his background in construction and the gospel music field.

"It will cost a fortune."

"I believe the Lord will supply."

"Don't you know there are only so many pieces to the Adventist financial pie? When people like you come along and take a big share, that just means there will be less for the official ministries who are trying to produce quality programming."

Danny was beginning to get the message that he was about the only one in the group who was excited about building a worldwide television ministry. But never one to shrink when attacked, Danny merely commented, "I believe that if you look in the refrigerator, you'll find that God has many more pies."

The dream of fat cattle

Danny thought about David's brothers and how they were the ones with the most negative attitude when David volunteered to fight the giant. Danny knew his immediate family was supportive, but he wondered how his church family would react. Would they stand behind him? Or would they see God's calling as an impossible dream?

At prayer meeting the next Wednesday night, Danny decided he couldn't keep quiet any longer. He knew he needed property for the project. He had contacted someone with property close to Thompsonville about selling, but the person was reluctant to do so. The burden to find land was weighing on Danny's heart when he stood up in his little West Frankfort church in front of ten or twelve people. He hadn't yet discussed this project with his own pastor. What would he think?

Danny took a deep breath and said, "I want you to really pray for something. We have a special need." Danny then told about God's calling, the miracle of the equipment, and discovering that a satellite station could be built in the area. "We're looking for some property, and I'm talking to a man over by Thompsonville about some land. Maybe I could get you to pray with us that he would sell this property to us, if it's the Lord's will." Then they prayed.

The next Friday night, Danny's mother called. "Danny, doesn't God work in marvelous ways?"

Danny said, "Yes, He does."

She continued, "Danny, do you remember Fonda Summers, a lady in her mid-seventies who was at prayer meeting? She belongs to the First Christian Church. When Larry Welch was a literature evangelist, he sold her the book *The Desire of Ages* and asked me if I'd be willing to give her Bible studies."

"Yes," Danny said, "I know her."

"Well, last Wednesday night was the first time she had ever visited our church, and she was so impressed with what God has called you to do that she went home and began to pray about the television station. And she's just called me. Do you know what God has impressed her to do?"

"What?" Danny asked eagerly.

"She says that God has impressed her to give you some land for your station."

"But," he began to explain to his mother, "you can't just build a satellite uplink station anywhere; there are just a few places in the country left where there isn't any microwave interference." Then he asked, "Where is her land?"

"Well, it's in Thompsonville about six to eight miles northeast of West Frankfort. She said to call her if you're interested."

Danny couldn't believe what he was hearing. Mrs. Summers's land was in the exact location where Clarence said he thought a satellite uplink station could be built—and just a few miles away from the land he was trying to buy! Danny got goose bumps all over. Surely the Spirit of God was in this thing!

Immediately, Danny called Mrs. Summers. She said, "I was so impressed with the story you told at prayer meeting about God asking you to build a television station to reach the world. I went home, knelt down, and said, 'Lord, I'd like to help Danny build this station, but I don't have any money. I don't have anything!' And it was like the Lord asked me the same question He had asked Moses, 'What is this you have in your hand?' I answered, 'I don't have anything, but I wish I did.' The Lord said again, 'What is this in your hand?' Then it came to me. 'I have eight acres of land. But that's all.' The Lord impressed me that I should give some of it to you. I probably should give you the good property up by the road, but I feel impressed to give you the back two acres."

Later, Mrs. Summers told Danny's mother this story: "Forty years ago, my husband and I were going to sell off some of our land. But before we did, I had a dream. I saw a fence encircling our property. The south gate opened, and the most beautiful fat cattle came in from all directions until the back end of the property was filled with them. It seemed to me that the Lord was going to use this property for something special, so we didn't sell it. Ten years ago, I had the same dream. Then three years ago when my husband died, I thought maybe I'd sell and move into town, but I had the dream again, so I didn't.

"Then last night the dream came back, only this time the Lord showed me that those beautiful fatted cattle represented people coming from all over the world, won to Christ by spirit and truth from the back part of my property. So I'm impressed that I should give the land to you for your television station. I just feel God is going to do great and wonderful things."

Checking out God's gift of land

Danny called Clarence to tell him about the land. Clarence told him to contact Comsearch, a frequency protection company that tested for microwave interference, to see if the property could be used for an uplink satellite station.

So he called Comsearch. "We have two acres of land that's being donated to us, and we want to build an uplink station, and ..." Danny sensed after a minute that the company's representative knew this was not his field, so Danny explained, "I'm not an engineer."

The man replied, "Yes, I know!"

Danny continued, "I'm really green at this."

Again, he replied, "Yes, I know!"

Finally, the representative said, "What you're asking me to do is very expensive. It's going to cost you six thousand dollars each time we come out to check a piece of property." Then he explained, "There are hundreds of potential microwave interferences that could make it impossible to build an uplink station. You can't just pick out some land and expect it to be interference-free. So what we'll do is check all of southern Illinois. Then we'll tell you where the interference-free places are, and you can arrange with the owner of the land to buy it for an uplink station."

"No," Danny insisted, "all I want you to do is come out and test this piece of property."

The man argued, "Here is what will happen. We'll probably find interference. So you'll have to go find another piece of property, and that will have interference. You'll end up with an enormous bill! The best way is if we check a wide area first and then tell you where a station could be built."

What this man was suggesting would make sense to any rational person, but what he didn't know was that Danny was absolutely certain that the land that had been given by Mrs. Summers was land that God had ordained should be used for this ministry. Therefore, Danny was certain it had to be interference-free.

Danny replied, "Sir, I hate to sound persistent, but we already have the acreage, and since God has given it to us, I believe it will work."

"Well," the representative said, "it's your money! But if you're not going to listen to our advice, then you need to understand that it's going to cost you six thousand dollars every time we test another piece of property."

After Danny assured the Comsearch representative that he understood, the man finally said he would make arrangements to check out the property. A few months later, Danny received seventeen pages explaining what the company had found. And although the fledgling organization called Three Angels Broadcasting Network didn't have a penny to pay for this service when Danny had requested it months before, by the time the report was finished, God had provided the six thousand dollars.

The report looked like Greek to Danny, so he took it over to Clarence's house for him to decipher. Clarence read it and shook his head in disbelief. "It looks like you got yourself the right property."

Danny knew it was going to be, but it was good to hear Clarence confirm the fact. Then Danny decided it wouldn't hurt to check with the research company just to make sure he and Clarence were reading the report correctly. So, he called Comsearch again. "Can you tell me if we can start an uplink station on the land you checked?"

"We sent you a report giving you our findings."

"Yes, I know," Danny said. "I just wanted to make sure the report says what I think it says."

"Well," the Comsearch representative said, "you're one of the luckiest people I've met in a long time. From your property you can send a signal to any satellite in space. There are over a hundred possible interferences coming into that area and dozens of potential interferences around your property on three sides, but the two acres that you have are interference-free."

The miracle of road money

Immediately, Danny decided that he and his brothers, who were helping him during their spare time, should start building a road back to the property. It would need to be fourteen hundred feet long and twenty-five feet wide. If they didn't get started soon, the fall rains would make it impossible to get back to the site. They used all the money they had to rent a bulldozer and grade a roadway. Some days, they had enough money to buy only five gallons of diesel fuel to run the equipment.

Once the road was graded, they had to get gravel on it immediately, so Danny called the rock company and made arrangements to have the gravel delivered. The only day the company could deliver was a week from Tuesday—and the company representative made it clear that he would be expecting six thousand dollars in payment for the gravel at the time of delivery. "We'll have the money," Danny assured him, although he had no idea where it would come from. He was almost afraid to tell his family that he had gone ahead and ordered the gravel without the money to pay for it. When Linda heard what he'd done, her response was, "I believe God is going to bless."

They had determined they were going to take God at His Word and do whatever He impressed them to do. This meant they had to think and act with boldness, rather than in the more cautious way that might be appropriate in handling their personal affairs. Caution would limit God. So they decided to move forward in faith. They had already seen so many barriers fall that committing themselves to pay for the gravel just meant that they would once more go to their knees and ask God to supply this need. If their timing was off—if God didn't want the road in before the fall rainy season—they would just wait.

Danny checked the mailbox every day that next week, but there were few donations. He was away for the weekend, but when he returned, he rushed to the post office box expecting numerous letters that would bring them the needed money. There were only two. Danny's heart sank—until he opened the first letter. It was from a lady in Chicago who had seen a short article about 3ABN in the May 21, 1985, issue of the *Lake Union Herald,* a church paper. In the envelope was a check for two thousand dollars. Until this time donations had trickled in mostly ten dollars or twenty-five dollars at a time. Occasionally, there would be a check for fifty or one hundred dollars. So Danny wasn't used to getting such a major donation, especially from a stranger who hadn't been there to see the project.

With hopes raised, Danny opened the second letter. He could hardly believe what he saw: a check for four thousand dollars. A total of six thousand dollars—exactly the amount he needed for the gravel that was to be delivered the next day! The interesting thing about the second letter is that it was from a couple in California who had been in the audience at the meeting where the pastor thought Danny shouldn't be telling the people about a project that he considered would never succeed!

Planning the building

As Danny began to see God work miracle after miracle at just the right time with just the right amount of money, his faith soared. On Friday nights and Sabbaths, he and the little group of family and church members would gather at the 3ABN building site to sing "We are standing on holy ground" and to pray. Those were hopeful days. They had so little—and they needed so much. But like pioneers, they had set their sights on the goal ahead instead of on the tremendous hurdles they faced. And they kept moving forward.

The group had no idea how large a building to construct. Danny started out with plans to build a building 40 by 70 feet. Then he enlarged it to 50 by 90. But when he and his brother, Kenny walked out on the land to stake out the building, Danny put a stake in one corner. Then with Kenny holding the tape measure, he started walking in the opposite direction and went a number of yards past the ninety feet he had intended. "Do you think this is big enough?" he called.

"It looks fine to me," Kenny yelled.

But Danny kept walking—almost to the end of the tape and stopped at 150 feet. "What do you think about making it this big?" Danny called.

"OK," Kenny hollered back. So Danny pounded in a stake.

Then they did the same thing to determine the width of the building—and ended up with a building 60 by 150 feet. If they made most of the building two stories, there would be a total of about 16,000 square feet. It looked big to Danny, seeing those stakes in the middle of the empty field.

In those days, none of the little group had any idea as to the magnitude of the work they were beginning, except perhaps Pastor Hal Steenson, who had said he would donate his television equipment. When he looked at the building stakes, he commented, "It's not nearly big enough!" Within a few years, his prediction came true. In 1994, 3ABN began to build a new office and production facility that would be three times larger than the original building. In 1996, when the new building was complete, it became the major production center and worldwide headquarters for 3ABN. The original uplink building, with one production studio, was used for master control. Later, it would house the offices and production equipment for 3ABN Radio. Then in 2000, 3ABN built a large call and fulfillment center, and in 2003 they moved master control to the new production center. The construction hasn't stopped since as 3ABN continues to grow.

The faith gift and the power line miracle

Danny had two hundred dollars in the bank when he and his brothers began to build a road and dig the footings for the original 3ABN uplink building. It was just enough money to rent a bulldozer and backhoe. Their idea was to get the shell of the building completed before winter. Then they could work on the inside when the weather was bad.

The phone rang. A retired couple from Apison, Tennessee, had learned about what God was building in southern Illinois from a

newsletter that Danny had typed himself on a little Commodore 64 computer and sent to two hundred people. Someone had passed the newsletter along to this couple, and they were so impressed that they sent a small donation a few weeks later. Now they were calling to explain, "We're on our way to Newfoundland to see

Danny and Kenny (and Kenny's son, Jeremy) with Marvin and Rosella McColpin

about helping a ministry there, and we thought about stopping by to talk to you about what you're doing. Would that be OK?"

"Sure," Danny said. "We're just getting started, but we would be happy to have you."

Marvin and Rosella McColpin were planning to spend only a day with the Sheltons, but they became so excited about the project that they spent four or five days and ended up canceling their trip to Newfoundland. When they saw Danny and his brothers digging the trenches for the footings, they asked, "How much money do you have to put up the building?"

"We have about two hundred dollars in the bank," Danny replied. "And that will go for renting the construction equipment."

"You mean you don't have enough money to pour the footings?" They were amazed that Danny would start the building project without any money. "What if you get the footings dug and it rains before you get money for the cement?"

"Well," Danny laughed, "maybe the Lord wants three-feet-deep ditches! Besides," he explained, "how can we expect the Lord to give us more money if we haven't used what He has already given us?"

"How much do you think it will cost to put up the shell of the building?" they inquired.

"Maybe fifty thousand dollars," Danny answered, as truthfully as he could. The McColpins were kind people and interested in God's work. But Danny could tell by the simple way they lived and the age and make of the car they drove that they didn't have much to contribute. Marvin had been a school teacher, and now that he and Rosella were retired, they supported themselves by purchasing property, dividing it into five-acre lots, and reselling them.

Three days after the McColpins arrived at the building site, Clarence Larson called. With a sense of panic in his voice, he asked, "Is it too late to stop the building?"

"Yes, it's too late," was Danny's reply.

"We may have made a terrible mistake," Clarence continued, "and I'm feeling very responsible because I'm helping you with this project."

"What's wrong?" Danny wanted to know.

"Well, I just realized that you're going to need three-phase power for your uplink, and I don't believe there are any three-phase power lines near your property. You're going to have to pay half of the costs to get industrial power out to your site. Your property is a mile and a quarter off Highway 34. Do you realize what four large cables, plus the poles, plus the construction is going to cost? Danny, this will bankrupt you!"

"Well, Clarence," Danny replied, "I'm not worried about it. One of two things is going to happen. Either God's already figured out who the person is who will give us the money we need, or we've already got power out by our property, and we just don't know it."

"I don't think it's possible that there would already be three-phase power way out in the middle of a pasture where your property is. I can't believe I didn't think of this sooner."

"Do you know what three-phase power looks like on the pole?" Danny asked.

"Yes," Clarence said, "and I'm not going to rest until I know where the closest power is."

"Well then, if you're worried about it, let's go and check things out right now. Do you have a powerful flashlight?" It was nine o'clock at night.

"Sure."

Danny invited Marvin McColpin to come along with him and Clarence as they went out in the middle of the night looking for the closest pole where three-phase power would be available. They flashed the light on every pole as they came down the road from the highway. No three-phase power. The further they got away from the highway, the more disturbed Clarence became. "I knew it wouldn't be out here. There are only a few farmhouses and a trailer on this road."

Soon they came to a sharp right-hand turn in the road, only a few hundred feet from 3ABN's driveway. Clarence flashed the light up the pole and shouted, "That's it! There is three-phase power right here. This is impossible!" he exclaimed. "There's nothing out here that requires it!"

The next morning, they went back out to make sure they hadn't made a mistake. To their amazement, they found that three-phase power cut through a field off the highway right to their driveway and then made a sharp turn and headed a different direction. There seemed to be no rational reason for it being where it was!

Clarence explained that two electrical companies supplied power to this area. "And," he said, "the way things are going for you, it's probably the cheaper one. Call them and find out why there's three-phase power out here in the middle of the field. And ask them if we can hook up to it."

Danny did, and sure enough, the power lines belonged to the less expensive company. Danny asked the company representative, "Why is there three-phase power out in the middle of the field? My engineer friend can't understand why it's there. It would have seemed a lot more logical to bring it down the road."

"I have no idea," the person from the electric company answered. "You know how the big wheels are. They don't always do things that make sense. The company has lines running east and west. And somewhere along those thirty to forty miles they had to run a cable north and then back west in order to power their own system. So someone—maybe thirty-five or forty years ago—must have decided to take off across the field and cut a path through the trees. I agree they could have more easily gone down the road. All I can say is that you are a very lucky man!"

"I think it's more than luck," Danny replied as he told him about the project and what God was doing. Later, 3ABN was able to hook into this power supply for less than two thousand dollars! Amazingly, God had supplied the power for this project at just about the same time He had first given Fonda Summers the dream about the cattle coming into the back portion of her property! It was no accident, nor a mere coincidence, that the right kind of power was waiting at the 3ABN driveway. Miracles like this have confirmed and strengthened Danny's resolve to take God at His word. He believes that far in advance of asking someone to do a work for Him, God has counted His resources and is never found wanting.

After Marvin and Rosella witnessed what God was doing—climaxed by the three-phase power miracle—they said they wanted to meet with Danny and his family. That night they wrote a check for twenty-five thousand dollars. Danny was shocked! The next morning the McColpins handed him another check, saying that God had impressed them that night to give an additional twenty-five thousand dollars. "But," they warned, "don't cash the checks yet. We have to make arrangements to get the money into the bank."

Danny was surprised by the size of their donation. *Obviously,* he thought, *they must have that much in savings.* Several months later, however, he learned what really happened. When the McColpins gave those checks that made it possible to frame the 3ABN building, Marvin and Rosella *didn't* have any money. But that didn't stop them from giving. They were so impressed that this work was God's work that they went home and mortgaged their house for fifty thousand dollars so that the 3ABN facility could be built before winter!

But that's not the whole story. Marvin later told Danny, "In the next six months, our business of reselling land made more money than we had ever made before. In fact, we made enough money to pay off the mortgage we had put on our house—and still have as much money left over as we had before we gave the fifty thousand dollars to 3ABN!"

Many years later, upon hearing this story in a public presentation, a man stood up and commented, "The McColpins came to our home and earnestly asked us to help with this project. We had the money to do so, but I was worried about the makeup of the board of directors and the organizational structure of 3ABN, so I refused. I've always regretted that decision!" It's easy to let our heads rule out the impressions God is making on our minds. But He is good and will give us another opportunity to experience the blessings of giving—if we are open to His leading.

How God paid for the cement floor

It was now August 1985. The shell of the building was nearing completion. The next major expense—approximately ten thousand dollars—would be pouring the cement floor. Just at this time, Dale McBride called from LaMesa, California. "I heard about what you're doing from Gary Rusk, a friend of mine, and I'd like to invite you to come to the ASI convention in Big Sky, Montana, at the end of August. Gary thinks your story needs to be told."

"I don't even know what ASI is," Danny honestly admitted.

"ASI stands for Adventist-Laymen's Services and Industries. It's an organization of Adventist lay-persons who have businesses or self-supporting ministries. We meet together to discuss ways we can more effectively present Christ in our businesses and help with various worthy projects."

"Well," Danny said, "it sounds interesting, but we don't have the money to fly to Montana. And where would we stay?"

"There are places for you to stay. And we think you should plan to stay all week."

Dale urged him to consider coming until Danny finally said, "We'll pray about it, and if the Lord sends us the money, then we'll go. If He doesn't, we won't." Then he hung up the phone, called Linda into the room, and explained the situation to her. They knelt to pray. "Lord, we're so busy building that we don't see why we should be taking time off to go to this convention. If you want us to go, we'll go. But You will need to provide the necessary funds."

The phone rang. It was Dale again. "I was just thinking," he said. "You need an answer to prayer, right?"

"Yes," Danny replied.

"Well, why don't I be your answer to prayer. I'll sponsor you, buy your plane tickets, pay your hotel bill, and give you money for food while you're there." Once again the impossible was happening! Danny and Linda went to the ASI convention. Rosella McColpin went with them. Rosella was an effective public-relations agent. She was just bubbling over with the miracles 3ABN had experienced—and was telling everyone. People started coming to Danny asking, "Are you going to tell your story here at ASI?" Danny said he was willing, if there was an opportunity. One of the ASI officers overheard this conversation and told Danny that everything on the program had been planned a year in advance. It was ASI policy to not make any last minute additions to the program. He went on to explain that the year before, ASI had allowed someone to speak without adequately checking him out. He had taken an offering of several thousands of dollars, and no one had heard of him since. "So," the official explained, "there won't be any opportunity for you to speak this year."

"I understand," Danny said. He explained that he hadn't come to Montana to speak but was there as a guest of an ASI member. Linda was usually very shy about speaking in public, but she immediately commented, "If the Lord wants my husband to speak while we're here, he'll speak."

The man replied, "Well, I'll guarantee that he won't be speaking this year, because I'm on the committee. This is nothing against you, but we just don't know you." Danny understood.

But God works in mysterious ways. Sometimes He stills the wind and waves, and sometimes He brings the clouds and rain. The weather had been beautiful all week. Friday afternoon no meetings were scheduled so that the people could enjoy golfing, hiking, or taking the ski lift up into the beautiful Montana mountains. But that morning a heavy cloud settled upon the mountain, obscuring the view. Torrents of rain began to fall. By noon, it was obvious that the planned outdoor activities would have to be canceled. What inside activity could be planned for the three or four hundred people who were attending the convention?

During the last meeting of the morning, Henry Martin, the vice president of ASI, beckoned Danny over. "We're in a real predicament here," he said. "We have to plan something for the people since there is nothing for them to do outside. Could I impose on you to tell your story?"

A few minutes later Danny said to Linda, "Honey, let me show you something." He led her to the window and pointed to the cloud that was covering the mountain. "See that cloud? God still uses clouds to lead by day." Then he told her what he had just been asked to do.

That was Danny's introduction to ASI. Danny told his story, and God used that testimony to bring in the resources He needed to give His ministry a major boost forward. People God had blessed with major financial assets were touched by the story, and in the days and months that followed, they began to come forward as a mighty army to carry this work to the ends of the earth.[1] The first fruits came later that afternoon.

There was a booth area where a few ministries and businesses were displaying their products and sharing their stories with those who came by. May Chung, Kay Kuzma, and some other exhibitors immediately saw the need of making a sign for 3ABN and setting up a table for Danny and Linda to put out their gospel music cassettes and a flyer about the television station. All week, Danny and Linda had been praying that God would supply their need for ten thousand dollars so that they could pour the cement floor of the 3ABN building, but they hadn't mentioned it to anyone.

Then it happened. Linda sold two tapes to Bill and Betty Bowers. When she looked at the check that was given to her for the cassettes, she noticed the amount on it and immediately came over to Danny and interrupted the conversation he was having with someone. "You've got to see this," she told him. When he hesitated, she said, "You have to speak to those people who are walking away. They just paid for two cassettes with a check for . . ." Danny looked at the amount of the check she held in front of his eyes—ten thousand dollars! He immediately thanked them for their generous gift. Once more God had taken care of their need. In recalling the incident later, Danny joked, "Either they made a mistake or we were selling our cassettes too cheap!"

Later that afternoon, God sent a beautiful rainbow at the end of the storm that seemed to encircle the building where they were. It seemed a fitting symbol to remind them of God's promise that He would take care of His ministry.

Why does 3ABN get all the miracles?

You might ask, "Why has God blessed, and why does He continue to bless, the 3ABN ministry in such an incredible way?" Let me assure you, it's not because of Danny or any of the staff who have worked so hard. God blesses this work in spite of people—because it is *His* work. If you don't feel the Holy Spirit is alive and well in your life, and you don't see God performing miracles day after day in answer to your prayers, then ask God for a brand-new touch from Him. He has a work for you to do! Step out and do it! God doesn't steer parked cars!

As Danny puts it, "God wants us to do only two things in life—to *come* and to *go*. To *come* to the foot of the Cross and dedicate our lives to Him as our Savior, and then to *go* out and tell the entire world what God has done for us." When you start living life like that, your life will most likely be filled with the same kind of miracles that 3ABN has experienced.

When Danny tells the story of the early miracles at 3ABN, he emphasizes that as wonderful as it is that God worked in such a miraculous way to provide for the location and building of the 3ABN facilities, the real story of miracles has to do with the lives touched by this ministry, the hard hearts that have been softened, and the souls won to God's kingdom. (See Section V.) God is indeed a miracle-working God!

The first uplink center under construction at 3ABN

---

[1] Shirley Burton, who was then communications director of the Pacific Union Conference and later became the communications director of the General Conference, was one of those influential supporters. For a number of years she co-anchored the Adventist World Report. Currently, Shirley is working with the 3ABN Books division.

3
The Dreams That Shaped This Ministry

*"Where there is no vision,
the people perish"*
—Proverbs 29:18.

Once God and Danny formed their partnership of faith—with Danny promising to move forward and the Lord promising to meet all his needs—and once it was clear to him that God was calling him not just to build a television station but to build a television station that would provide programming for a satellite network that would reach the world, Danny said, "We've got to have a name for the network."

The three angels' dream

Danny had thought the name should reflect basic doctrines, such as the importance of the seventh-day Sabbath or Christ's second coming. Perhaps it should be a descriptive name like the name *Seventh-day Adventist,* chosen in 1860 when the church was being organized. Or maybe it should have something to do with counteracting the false messages of Satan that were being preached in the name of Christianity! But of all the names he considered, nothing seemed quite right. One night just before bed, Danny earnestly prayed again that God would help in the choice of the right name for the network.

That's when God gave him the following dream. It was as though he were looking out over the dark universe—far, far out into space—and all he could see were the stars and the planets like bright pinpricks of light on a clear, moonless night. Suddenly, he heard a noise like the mighty rushing wind spoken of in Acts 2 when the Holy Spirit came on the Day of Pentecost. One of the tiny insignificant "stars" began to move toward him, closer and closer, traveling at a tremendous speed. As it spun near enough, he could tell by the oceans and the continents that it was the planet Earth. Then Danny saw an angel begin to circle the earth blowing a trumpet. Another angel followed, and then another, until three angels were circling this planet, blowing their trumpets. It was then that Danny knew the Lord was impressing him to name the ministry Three Angels Broadcasting Network.

He recalled, too, the words of God's calling, *I want you to build a television station that will reach the world with the undiluted three angels' messages.* The three angels' messages? Danny had been an Adventist all his life, so the term "three angels' messages" was familiar to him. The founders of the Seventh-day Adventist Church had felt that their movement had a distinct responsibility to take these messages to the world. Adventist churches often used the symbol of the three angels on their churches or bulletins.

Why are the three angels' messages so important?

What exactly were the three angels' messages that God gave to the apostle John in a dream almost two thousand years ago? And why did God specifically mandate to Danny that these messages should be the basis of whatever programming the station would produce and beam to the world? Danny decided he needed to go back to the Bible.

First, he turned to Revelation 14:6-12, which describes three angels flying through the sky with messages to prepare the earth for Christ's second coming and the time that He will reap the harvest of the earth as outlined in verses 14-16.

As Danny continued to ask questions and search the Scriptures for answers, he learned that the first angel has the everlasting gospel to preach to the world. His message announced that human beings should "fear" God—which means to give Him reverence and glory as the Creator of all things. Danny found an interesting definition in the Bible of the phrase "to fear God." Proverbs 8:13 declares, "The fear of the Lord is to hate evil." And what is the glory of God? It's His goodness and love. That's why all glory goes to Christ and not to erring, sinful men.

The second angel's message proclaims that Babylon has fallen. Babylon represents Satan's kingdom of religious confusion—a false religious system that follows human doctrine rather than God's.

The third angel gives a serious warning about worshiping the beast and its image. Revelation 12:9 names the beast as the great dragon called the devil, and Satan, who "deceives the whole world." He is behind all false systems of religion that exalt man's words above God's Word.

Those who heed the warning and accept the gospel of Jesus Christ are found "in Him" keeping His commandments and revealing His victory in their lives. Revelation 14:12 describes them in these words: "Here are they that keep the commandments of God, and the faith of Jesus." Jesus overcame the devil by faith in His Father's Word. He was obedient to His Father's commandments even unto death. All who are "in Him" reveal in their lives His faith, His victory, His deliverance, and His obedience.

Revelation 14:11 describes those who reject God and follow the beast. It says, "And the smoke of their torment ascendeth up for ever and ever: and they have no rest day nor night." What does this mean? Does this support the idea that hell is a place where people are tortured forever?

As a child, Danny had been taught that God is love. He knew that the Bible teaches that God loves the entire world with an undying love (see John 3:16). He knew, too, that torturing people forever is not an act of love. He had been taught from childhood that because God is love, He will bring an end to sin and all who cling to it. It will be an everlasting end. The *results* of the fire that destroys sin are eternal, not the fire itself. The process of burning doesn't continue forever.

Now, Danny searched for Bible evidence for this teaching. He found that Jude 7 says that Sodom and Gomorrah suffered the vengeance of *eternal* fire. But Sodom and Gomorrah aren't still burning today. Once burned, they were gone forever. The results are eternal.

He found that God will make an eternal end of sin. The wicked will become ashes (see Malachi 4:3), and even death itself will be destroyed (see Revelation 20:14). After sin is destroyed, "there shall be no more death, neither sorrow, nor crying, neither shall there be any more pain: for the former things are passed away" (Revelation 21:4). When sin and sinners are no more, the entire universe will be clean and everything will declare that God is love. "And every creature which is in heaven and on the earth and under the earth and such as are in the sea, and all that are in them, I heard saying:

'Blessing and honor and glory and power
Be to Him who sits on the throne,
And to the Lamb, for ever and ever!' "
(Revelation 5:13, NKJV).

The more Danny studied, the more urgency he felt to warn people
that Christ's second coming is near—even at the doors, as Matthew
24:33 says. No longer can people safely remain lukewarm and expect to make it through the time of terrible trouble that evil will soon
unleash upon this world. *Now* is the time when people must decide
whom to worship. Will it be Christ? Or will it be the devil, that beast,
who is trying so hard to capture lukewarm hearts and mark them
for destruction?

This ministry, to which God had called him, had to be in the business of heating up lukewarm hearts with God's love. It had to be in
the business of showing people that obeying God's commandments
kept their minds and bodies in a correct relationship with their Creator so that they could experience the power of His love in their lives.

Just as angels heralded Christ's first coming, so angels are herald-
ing His second coming. And just as those three angels of Revelation
fly through the air declaring a last warning message to earth, so must
this television programming fly through the airwaves, broadcasting
the message to every nation, language, tongue, and people. Three
Angels Broadcasting! Yes, that was to be the mission—and the name.
This television ministry would be known as the Three Angels Broadcasting Network, or 3ABN.

But the dream of the three angels was not the only dream that
shaped this ministry in the early days. God had some major redirec-
tion to do in Danny's own thinking, and He did it through another
dream.

The apple-tree dream

When God called Danny to begin a television ministry to the
world—one that would counteract the counterfeit—Danny was ready
to make war with the counterfeit. He was so frustrated with the
popular television preachers expounding their nonbiblical theories
as if they were the gospel truth that he felt his mission was to go on
the air and expose them. He would prove them frauds. He would
put them in their place. He would lead a crusade for Bible truth, and

if there were casualties, so be it! But God had other plans for him and this new television ministry. And it didn't take God long to let Danny know!

In his sleep, Danny saw himself in a huge apple orchard. For miles around he couldn't see anything but apple trees, and hanging on each tree were the biggest ripe red apples he had ever seen. He didn't need a ladder to pick them; they were everywhere right within his reach. In his dream, Danny asked, "Lord, what are all these ripe red apples that are hanging on the trees?"

The Lord replied, *It is not your job to go out and expose those preachers who aren't teaching Bible truth as you know it or those who aren't modeling Christlike behavior. These ripe red apples represent the people who have learned of Me and who have given their lives to Me through watching these television ministries—even though the messengers and the messages were sometimes flawed.*

My Word does not return unto Me void. Even though these television evangelists don't preach what you're preaching, My words through them have helped people overcome drugs, alcohol, and tobacco. They have given them the power to change other sinful behaviors. People have learned of Me and have given their lives to Me by watching these programs. They have caught the message of how much I love them. And because of that, they have matured into ripe fruit. Now I have called you to teach them a more complete knowledge of the Bible and to pick them.

I use people (including you, Danny) in spite of themselves! Your job is to give a message they haven't heard yet, the message of the three angels, and the apples that are ripe for My harvest will fall into your hands. There are some playacting preachers out there, but it's the message that's important, not the person.

The Lord's words burned themselves into Danny's mind, waking him from sleep. He didn't get up, but just lay there mulling them over, readjusting his thinking. He realized that it is the power in the Word of God, as it goes forth from human lips, that makes the difference—not the human lips! If an atheist actor read the Bible on television, people would be blessed and saved. "All have sinned, and come short of the glory of God" (Romans 3:23). But that doesn't prevent God from using them. The power to change and transform people is in God's Word.

Adventists have focused on doctrine and the prophetic messages of Daniel and Revelation, but in the process of proving these biblical truths, they have sometimes neglected to emphasize God's grace and salvation. They have forgotten to lead people into a personal relationship with Jesus. While they have been stressing the rules of God, other ministries have been stressing the importance of building a relationship with God. Both types of ministries need to come to an understanding of the full message. Both doctrine and relationship are important. That's what keeps a person balanced and safe in God's lifeboat. Stressing just one tips the boat. And the devil doesn't care out of which side of the boat you fall!

No matter how great the temptation might be to uproot the defective trees on which God's people had grown, Danny determined that, with God's help, he would shape a harvesting ministry to pluck the fruit that was ripe for God's end-time message—the message of the three angels.

Thus it has been since the beginning of the 3ABN ministry. Some presenters may have erred at times in their impulsiveness. But the heart thrust of this ministry is sharing God's love to a dying world rather than criticizing those who believe differently or teach false doctrines. The result has been gratifying. Every day the 3ABN mailbox contains testimonies that convince Danny again and again that God knew exactly what He was doing when He gave him the apple-tree dream.

For example, one woman wrote to say she had been a Sabbath school teacher for forty years but didn't know Jesus until she began watching 3ABN. A pastor for thirty-four years confessed he emphasized the "do's" and "don'ts," until what he heard on 3ABN began to convict him of his error. An eighty-four-year-old viewer wrote, "I've learned more about how to have a relationship with Christ in the last four years since I've been watching 3ABN than in all my eighty years before!"

So Danny gained confidence to move forward as he came to realize that God had the power to redirect his faulty thinking into new paths through dreams. He knew as never before that this was God's work, God's ministry. Danny was but the passionate, inexperienced vehicle God had chosen to use modern-day technology to get the three angels' messages out to the world. Now was the time. Calamities were about to fall on the earth. And Danny knew full well, if he didn't do what God had called him to do, that God had the power to use His angel forces—or even the rocks—to cry out this warning message to the world (see Luke 19:40).

God's calling

So, on weekends, Danny began to use his family's musical ministry as the vehicle to share with people the vision of 3ABN. If he had taken time to seriously consider the magnitude of the task, he probably would have been scared into silence. If he had more knowledge of what it takes to beam a signal to the world, he might not have been so bold. In fact, at times even he began to wonder why God had chosen him, an inexperienced gospel-singing carpenter. But when this happened, God raised up people who affirmed Danny's calling and encouraged him to move forward.

One of the first was Dr. Walter Thompson, of Hinsdale, Illinois, who became an influential 3ABN board member. He helped fund the production of many of the early health programs on 3ABN and donated the stained glass windows of the three angels at the entrance of the original 3ABN building. When Danny questioned Walt about how it might be possible to do all that God seemed to be asking him to do, Walt replied, "Do you think God would have said 'go into all the world' if He hadn't counted His resources in advance and found He wasn't wanting?"

In Danny's travels, he learned that he was not the only person whom God had called to start a worldwide television network. In Chicago a lady told him, "I know what you have said today is true because a year ago the Lord impressed me to build a television station that would reach the world. I wanted to do it, so I went to friends and church family to get counsel. They convinced me that I didn't know enough to start such a thing. They told me that it was impossible. So I gave up. I felt I needed to learn more, so right now I'm studying video technology. I decided to put off what God called me to do until I felt I was sufficiently trained by experts to successfully accomplish the task. When I heard what you said tonight, I was shaken. I now realize it was God calling me, and it should have been me doing this work."

Two months later in Indianapolis, Danny told the story of his calling. A man came up after church, shaking with emotion. He related almost the same story. "About a year ago," he said, "I was impressed at night when I couldn't sleep that I was to build a television network that would take the three angels' messages to the world. I tried, but I didn't have the money, or the education, or the communication skills, so I let the dream go."

There was also someone in California whom the Lord impressed to build a station. But the devil discouraged him by causing him to focus on the size of the task. It seemed impossible to him, so he gave up. When he heard Danny's story, he pounded his fist on the table and lamented, "I should have done it!" In 2004, Danny learned that Jim Gilley, who was vice president for evangelism of the North American Division of the Seventh-day Adventist Church, felt that God had called him in 1975 as an evangelist to begin a worldwide television network broadcasting Adventist truth. After failing to convince church media professionals, and after hearing what was happening in a cornfield of southern Illinois, Pastor Gilley gave his support to 3ABN. (See chapter 11.)

The prophecy of the rocks crying out

These stories reaffirmed to Danny that what he had experienced during the early morning hours of November 15, 1984, was indeed a calling from the Lord. He determined that, by God's grace, he would be faithful to the calling no matter what. God wanted this message to go to the entire world. And, if necessary, He would cause the stones to cry out. In fact, He's already been doing just that!

Several years ago, Danny was asked to speak in the Southwest. The doctor who was supposed to meet him at the airport had an emergency. Instead, a farmer picked Danny up in a decrepit vehicle that required him to stop every so often to add a quart of oil. As they slowly drove along, the man asked, "Doesn't the Bible say that if we don't give the message, even the stones will cry out to proclaim the name of Jesus?"

"Yes, it does," Danny agreed.

"Well, what do you suppose those stones are? Did you ever hear of any rocks crying out?" he asked.

"I've seen people talking to pet rocks," Danny joked, not under-standing where the farmer was going with his questioning. "But, I've really never heard of rocks talking."

"I can't believe you're saying that. You of all people should know about the rocks crying out. Aren't you into TV?"

"Yes, I am, but what does that have to do with rocks?"

"Well, actually, it was radio I was thinking about. You know how those early radio sets worked?"

"Not really."

"Well, it was a crystal that made talking through the air possible. And what's a crystal?"

"A rock," Danny answered, finally understanding the farmer's line of reasoning.

"Yes," he agreed, "for years now, God's been using the rocks and mountains to cry out to the world. TV and radio antennas are placed on top of mountains. He's been using all of nature to get out His message. And now He's using you to get it out through the rocks of outer space. Those satellites. Pretty impressive, right?"

"Yes," Danny answered, "pretty impressive." But something he learned later was equally impressive. Someone pointed out to him that the three angels of Revelation 14 are mentioned again in Revelation 18, which emphasizes their significance in last-day events. "Could it be," this person wondered aloud, "that the three angels John saw in his dream were three satellites circling the earth, spreading God's message at the speed of 186,000 miles per second?" Danny thought about that when he first saw what a satellite looked like—a box with a winglike structure sticking out on each side. Flying through the air, Danny could see how satellites might indeed look like angels to the apostle John. Interesting, isn't it? Especially when you consider that three strategically located satellites could blanket the world! Revelation 10 talks about a fourth angel helping the three.

Three Angels Broadcasting Network had been broadcasting the three angels' messages on two satellites since October of 1996. This allowed 3ABN to reach a major portion of the world's people, but not all. In the fall of 1999, 3ABN began beaming its signal to a third satellite that covered most of the rest of the world—Asia, India, China, Japan, Indonesia, and the Philippines—allowing 3ABN to come very close to fulfilling the commission God gave it "to reach the world." In 2000, 3ABN had three satellites covering the world and a fourth being used as a distribution satellite. Since that time, 3ABN has begun broadcasting on even more satellites to make sure people everywhere get a strong, clear signal. Praise the Lord!

It's the message of the three angels that will warn the people of the world to prepare for last-day events. And it is this message that promises them that they will overcome if they trust in God. This is the message that will make the difference between life or death, peace or turmoil. Every day Danny and the dedicated staff at 3ABN feel it is an incredible honor and privilege to be called by God to proclaim this lifesaving message!

4
Broadcasting Begins
and Expands

"I the Lord have spoken it: it shall come to pass, and I will do it;
I will not go back, neither will I spare, neither will I repent;
according to thy ways, and according to thy doings,
shall they judge thee, saith the Lord God"
—Ezekiel 24:14.

Gonzalo Santos answers God's call to 3ABN

As the construction progressed on the original 3ABN uplink production studio and office building, a new need developed. The outside shell of the building was finished, but now the workers needed an electrician who understood three-phase power and how to wire a satellite uplink transmitter. One day, as Danny walked toward home, he was praying for an electrician. As he neared his back door, he heard the telephone ringing.

"Hello, is this Danny Shelton?" asked the voice on the other end of the line. "I'm Gonzalo Santos. I heard that you need an electrician. I want to know if I can help you with this job. Have you found someone?"

Gonzalo lived in Chicago and offered to drive down on weekends. "You must not know where we're located," Danny interrupted. "We're three hundred miles south of Chicago!"

"I know," Gonzalo replied. "I've driven through southern Illinois before."

"But I can't pay you," Danny told him. "We don't have money to hire an electrician."

"I don't expect pay."

"But you don't know what is involved. This job is quite complicated. My brother is an electrician, and he won't even touch this project."

"I'd like to see if I can help," Gonzalo persisted.

"But we need a commercial electrician; one who knows how to build an uplink station for a satellite."

"Yes, I know," was the response. "I've put up two stations before. I've been a Seventh-day Adventist for about five years now, and I'm preparing to go to the mission field."

Danny couldn't believe that he had just tried to discourage the very man who was God's immediate answer to the prayer he had just been praying! Thankfully, Gonzalo was not easily discouraged.

Week after week, every Friday after work, Gonzalo drove the three hundred miles to the 3ABN site and spent Sabbath. Often he brought along a friend. Together, they would work late Saturday night, all day Sunday, and late into Sunday night before heading back home, where their regular jobs awaited Monday morning.

The Gonzalo Santos family

"Can't we give you something for all the work you are doing?" Danny would ask. He knew Gonzalo had a wife and children. He made sure Gonzalo knew he didn't intend for him to work for nothing. "Please let us pay you something," Danny would plead. But Gonzalo wouldn't take any money.

"I'm not working for you," he would respond. "I'm working for the Lord. If I were working for you, then you could pay me."

As a new Christian, Gonzalo had an amazing amount of zeal—just exactly what God needed to move this work forward so that 3ABN could start broadcasting as soon as possible. When Danny realized the broad scope of Gonzalo's expertise, he asked if Gonzalo would be willing to join the 3ABN ministry full time. He didn't agree at first. But after Gonzalo got the building wired and the satellite was broadcasting, he finally said "Yes" to repeated pleas. Gonzalo moved his family to 3ABN and became the station's operations manager. How blessed the ministry was to have him!

Without Gonzalo, 3ABN wouldn't have been able to start broadcasting when it did. Most new television satellite networks plan for at least five years, and maybe as many as eight years, from beginning construction until they are ready to broadcast. But in November 1986, just two years and one week from the time God called Danny to this ministry, 3ABN started broadcasting a few hours a week. Six months later, on April 1, 1987, it began broadcasting eighteen hours a day. And a few months later, 3ABN's signal was being transmitted seven days a week, twenty-four hours a day!

People ask how such a feat was accomplished. Danny's answer is that the group never lost sight of their objective. Their goal was not to get a building built, although that was important. It was not to generate programming, although that was important, too. The goal was to begin broadcasting just as soon as possible, and they went for the goal, just like Danny's father had taught him to do on the basketball court!

Danny recalls, "My father came to watch one of my basketball games. Our team was really struggling, so we'd call time out to plan a new defense. But no matter what we did, we just couldn't stop the other team. So we'd call time out again, huddle together, and try something else. But we were still getting beat, so again we'd call time out. Finally, my dad got off the bleachers and came over to where we were huddling. 'Boys,' he said, 'what's happening?'

"We explained that we couldn't figure out a defense strategy that would stop the opposing team, so we kept calling time out, hoping we could come up with a winning game plan.

"Now you have to understand that my father had never played basketball when he was a kid. He really didn't know much about the game. So I was surprised when he said, 'Boys, you've already got a game plan. See those two hoops?' he asked, pointing to the basketball hoops. 'The object of the game is to get the ball in the hoop. Don't worry about what the other team is doing, just get the ball and put it in the hoop. That's how you win the game.'

"We decided to follow Dad's advice. We stopped concentrating on what the other team was doing. Instead, we went out, got the ball, and began shooting—and we won."

Danny has thought about his father's wisdom many times when he has been considering a game plan for the 3ABN ministry—"Just put the ball in the hoop."

In the beginning, it would have been easy for those involved in the ministry to get sidetracked by thinking they had to have everything lined up before they began broadcasting. They could have said, "We've got to have studios, an office building, a certain number of television programs in the can, or enough money in the bank to pay the transponder bill for six months." Instead, Danny has maintained the vision of his father. He can still hear his dad's words ringing in his ears, "Just get the ball in the hoop."

Purchasing the satellite dish

One of the first requirements to begin broadcasting was to get the satellite dish purchased, built, and installed. The problem was that a transmitter system and dish cost $350,000, and the group had only a $10,000 donation for this project. How would it be possible to move forward?

Danny called Scientific Atlanta to order the giant thirty-two-foot uplink dish and was transferred to the finance department. The company was used to working with large commercial television stations that had plenty of financial backing and excellent credit ratings. 3ABN had neither. Sue, the head of the finance department, explained that the standard practice required a deposit of $70,000 to get the planning and production started. In addition, the company normally required evidence of funds to complete the project. Approximately $160,000 was to be paid upon delivery of the system, and the balance of $120,000 would be expected when installation was completed.

Sue asked how 3ABN planned to pay for the satellite dish. "We have $10,000 cash," Danny told her. "We can send that immediately. God will provide the rest."

"Can you get a letter of credit for the amount you need?" she asked. When Danny replied that 3ABN's policy was not to borrow money, Sue pointed out that if it couldn't borrow and had no line of credit, she couldn't do anything.

A few days later, the district sales representative for Scientific Atlanta called Danny. He had visited the station site before and was impressed with what 3ABN was doing. He suggested that

Danny call Sue back and tell her more about 3ABN's ministry.

Danny did just that. He shared with Sue that 3ABN was a faith ministry and how God had provided in the past. He didn't ask her to make an exception to the company's financing policy, but he knew

that unless something happened, 3ABN would have to wait a long time to get the equipment needed to begin broadcasting.

Finally Sue asked, "How do you intend to pay for this system?"

Again, Danny told her the truth—that 3ABN had only $10,000 at the moment—and nothing except a conviction that God would provide the needed funds.

The first satellite dish being constructed

Then the most amazing thing happened. Sue replied, "I'm a Christian, too, and I think we can make an exception this time." She agreed that the company would begin working on the project for a deposit of $10,000! But she was nervous about it. Each time a payment was coming due, she would call Danny to make sure he would have the money. Many times it came just in the nick of time.

Broadcasting begins

On November 23, 1986, just two years and one week after God called Danny to the 3ABN television ministry, broadcasting began from a tiny transmitter shack beside the partially completed 3ABN uplink production studio and office building.

Danny will never forget the excitement of that first night on the air. His mom, stepdad, and other family members were there, plus church members and 3ABN workers. They were all huddled together outside the transmitter building, a room about twelve by twenty feet, which at the time housed master control for the network.

Clarence Larson, the engineer who had first told Danny about the possibility that there was an interference-free uplink site in the

The first master control and the transmitter building from which the first signal was sent

Thompsonville area, was by now spending much of his time at 3ABN. He had brought in a router, a switcher, a couple of monitors, and a three-quarter-inch videotape deck. The group set the equipment on crates and cardboard boxes because they didn't have the finances to properly install the equipment in racks. They loaded tapes in the tape machine to send the signal directly to the satellite. Danny, Linda, and a few others crowded inside. The rest looked through the door or stood outside as they began the countdown to 8:00 P.M. Clarence was busy getting everything technically ready. They were going on the air with the *It Is Written* telecast with George Vandeman! Finally, the big moment came with cheers and tears of excitement! Clarence threw the switch, and 3ABN has been broadcasting the three angels' messages ever since!

If someone was watching 3ABN during those first few hours, most likely it was because they just happened to come across the new signal while surfing channels. To find out if anyone was actually watching, Clarence developed a page to flash on the screen with a free book offer and the 3ABN phone number. As soon as Clarence put up the number, the phone rang. It startled the little group. Danny tried to answer the phone, but the noise inside the transmitter room was so loud he had to take the phone outside in the dark to hear the caller. Calls continued to come in! Danny answered the phone as if this were a major network that had computerized equipment in lovely office buildings, instead of having to stand outside shivering in the cold. He asked callers where they were calling from: "I'm calling from Colorado." "I'm in Alaska."

Tears filled the workers' eyes. Their dream was coming true. People were responding, and free literature was being sent out. Their goal of "reaching the world" was beginning to happen!

At first, 3ABN broadcasted just two hours a night, two nights a week—on Mondays and Thursdays. Since 3ABN had no production studio of its own, it broadcast sermon tapes produced by other Adventist ministries such as *It Is Written,* with George Vandeman, Faith for Today's *Westbrook Hospital* series, with Harold Fagal, *Amazing Facts,* with Joe Crews, *The Quiet Hour,* with LaVerne Tucker, and programs by various evangelists or pastors. After 3ABN's first broadcast, the group went to Nashville and made a little promotional tape that they superimposed over whatever program was airing. It gave the telephone number and informed viewers that they were watching 3ABN.

The early years of 3ABN

The next challenge was to begin production. When the building for the uplink production studio was completed, Joe Crews, director of *Amazing Facts,* offered 3ABN some television equipment in exchange for air time. Because of this gift, there was never a need for the equipment Pastor Hal had donated, which by this time was somewhat outdated. However, the ministry still needed state-of-the-art, high-quality cameras. At this time, RCA had a few discontinued cameras, worth over a hundred thousand dollars each, that were available for only thirty-three thousand dollars apiece. In faith, 3ABN asked for three. The RCA representative, after visiting 3ABN, was so impressed with God's leading in bringing about the miraculous sequence of events that got the network started that he confessed that his visit to the ministry was a "spiritual high" in his life. When the deadline came, 3ABN had enough money for only one camera. But when the representative from RCA heard this, he responded, "From what I've seen and heard, I'm certain the ninety-nine thousand dollars will come in. I believe the 'Man up there' wants you to have these cameras." He delivered one camera to 3ABN and reserved the other two for the ministry, without interest, until the money became available!

When 3ABN started broadcasting, it didn't have any employees. Some of the early volunteers later became employees. By the time Clarence flipped the switch to send the first 3ABN signal to the satellite, he was already putting in hundreds of hours of volunteer time. Whenever he was needed, day or night, he would come out to help. As he saw Danny and his family and friends moving forward, Clarence finally felt impressed to join them, even though it meant giving up his secure eight-hour-a-day job at another station for long hours at 3ABN with little pay. (See Clarence Larson's story in chapter 20.)

Just as God brought Clarence to 3ABN, He brought other dedicated workers who were willing to learn and willing to work long hours. Tommy Shelton's son, Ricky, Danny's nephew, was just a teenager, but he helped, as did Lanny Allen. Cindy Barwald, who had a little television experience, joined that fledgling group and became the first television director. At about the same time, John Filkins came aboard and worked audio. In the early days, the employees (and volunteers) carried many responsibilities, learned various jobs, and did whatever was necessary to keep the station operating on a minimal budget. (And it's still that way!)

In the fall of 1986, Art and Pat Humphrey heard about 3ABN. At the time, Art was employed in corporate television and had worked previously in public and commercial television. Art and Pat were impressed to visit 3ABN, but wanting to be certain the Lord was leading, they decided to make it a matter of earnest prayer. On the third day of Pat's three-day fast, their little five-year-old daughter told her parents about a dream she had. "An angel came into my room," she told them, "and said that you're supposed to go to 3ABN. Jesus is coming soon, and you are to help with this ministry." Art immediately quit his job with a private corporation in Huntsville, Alabama. The couple put their unfinished dream house on the market, and two weeks later they moved to Illinois. The Humphreys were valuable help during the next year before moving on to the Review and Herald Publishing Association in Hagerstown, Maryland, where Pat became assistant editor of *Message* magazine and Art worked in the media department.

While at 3ABN, Art trained a number of workers in studio production and control-room operations. Many were young people without family responsibilities or debts. Instead, they had youthful enthusiasm and were willing to work hard for little—and to learn. They quickly picked up how to use computers and electronic equipment. Some stayed on to become valuable employees at 3ABN.

Between 1991 and 1995, with Tommy Shelton as production manager, the staff made tremendous strides in professionalization. During this time, Douglas Garcia joined the fledgling network. He stayed for twelve years, making a significant contribution with his talents and experience in production, editing, lighting, graphic design, and the choice of music—much of which is still on the air. Bobby Davis followed Moses Primo from the Boston station in 1993 and was the only one of the production team at the time with commercial television experience. He is currently making a valuable contribution as producer of *3ABN Today* and editor of *3ABN World* magazine. Rodney Laney, a cameraman during the growing years, is now a director; John Dinzey, who was assigned to camera shading, is now the director of the pastoral-ministry team; and Tammy Larson has moved beyond makeup artist to become a first-rate camera person, illustrator of children's activity books, and vocal recording artist. And none of it would have gone on air without George Bozarth, who has rotated over master control's 24/7 shifts since the early years.

Commenting on these early years, Linda said later, "As we began to grow, the employees became more conscious of making quality productions. They watched other television shows and picked up new ideas for lighting and camera angles. They studied the sets, the backgrounds, and the graphics—things most viewers wouldn't even notice. They stayed up late trying to reproduce what they had seen. Their desire was to achieve high-quality programming even though we lacked the resources and budgets of larger television networks. It was inevitable that the quality of our programs increased due to the drive and energy of our dedicated workers."

With Gonzalo Santos as operations manager, Clarence as engineer, and 3ABN beaming its signal to RCA's Satcom IV satellite twenty-four hours a day, the next task was to figure out how best to get the signal into homes. The naysayers first said, "You'll never get the signal up." Then, when 3ABN did, they said, "You'll never get it down." In 1986, approximately two million homeowners in North America, as well as many motels, hospitals, and churches, had satellite dishes. Those were the days of big dishes! In addition, there was a potential cable audience of fifteen million, but to get that audience, 3ABN had to be aired on those cable systems.

The next five years were a flurry of activity, applying for downlink television stations, installing dishes, and making contracts with cable companies to carry 3ABN. Then, in 1991, with the Iron Curtain of communism falling, 3ABN answered the call to enter Romania—requiring Gonzalo Santos and his family to move there to establish a television station and production studio. The following year Russia opened up. The timing is significant. God was removing manmade barriers so that the gospel message could reach the masses just at the time that 3ABN was ready for the task. Imagine—less than eight years after God called Danny to a worldwide television ministry, 3ABN was ready to go global!

Moses Primo joins 3ABN

Moses Primo

It was July 1992. The 3ABN signal was being beamed up 22,300 miles at the speed of light to satellite S1, transponder #7, with a footprint encompassing North and Central America and reaching a potential audience of five to seven million people with home satellite dishes. Downlink TV stations were being established, with approximately a dozen operating stations and new construction permits being applied for and granted. And 3ABN's cable outlets alone had the potential of reaching over a million people!

Now at exactly the right time, God called upon the scene His servant Moses, a man whom He ordained to lead this ministry technically through the next phase—that of stretching to reach the world. Meet Moses Primo.

Moses' journey to 3ABN wasn't a forty-year trek in the wilderness, but it was interesting, nevertheless. It allowed Moses to get some of the best training the world could provide as he worked in major television networks in both Brazil and the United States. But let me start back at the beginning.

Moses was born into an Adventist family in Brazil. After obtaining a degree in engineering, he interned at Globo Network (the largest uplink television network in South America). His four-year sojourn there was fascinating. He was actually fired four days after he began because he wouldn't work on Sabbath!

In Brazil, as it is in many countries, sometimes the only way (or the easiest way) to get things done is to have the right connections. In this case, Moses' sister happened to work for a physician who knew one of the corporate officers of Globo Network. This officer had the power to reinstate Moses in his job. Armed with this information and the employee badge that had not yet been taken away from him, Moses went to see the officer. "My sister works for your friend . . ."

"And what do you need?" the officer asked.

Moses told his story. He made it clear he would volunteer to save lives if the place were burning. But he would not actually "work" on Sabbath under any circumstances. Impressed, the officer went to a direct-line phone, called the man who had fired Moses, and simply said, "Hire Moses Primo." And it was done.

Four years later, when Moses decided to come to the United States to learn English, he didn't want to leave the company without obtaining the money that had been taken out of his check for retirement. But the only way that was possible was to be fired. If a worker left voluntarily, he left his money with the company! Moses' immediate supervisor—the same man who fired him in the beginning—would not fire him now! So Moses went back upstairs. "Remember me?" Moses asked the officer. "Yes, has anyone been giving you problems?"

"No," Moses said, "but now I need to be fired." He explained why. The officer shook his head, went to the same phone, called Moses' supervisor and simply said, "Fire Moses Primo." And it was done!

God knew exactly where He would be needing Moses some day. And the devil must have figured out God's plan and tried to take him out! There was a terrible automobile accident. Moses' head was so badly crushed that one of his eyes fell out of its socket, and the non-Christian doctors gave him no hope. His mother and sister transported him to an Adventist hospital. Although the hospital didn't have the expertise to put Moses back together again, personnel found outside physicians who could, and prayer did the rest.

The second phase of Moses' "wandering" was to be on the campus of Atlantic Union College, a Seventh-day Adventist school in South Lancaster, Massachusetts. Here Moses learned English. In Worcester, Massachusetts, he took a second degree in engineering. After working at Globo Network in a job that put him at the top of his profession, his "wilderness" experience was working in the college bindery to pay his living expenses and tuition.

From the wilderness, God took Moses to a television station in Worcester, Massachusetts for seven years; then took him to the top once again. Moses became chief engineer for the first station owned and operated by the Fox Television Network in Boston, where Moses had a 1.5 million dollar annual operating budget. Plus, Fox paid for Moses to get his master's degree!

Around 1984 (just as 3ABN was starting), God put a burden for ministry in Moses' heart. Moses recalls, "I was thinking I would do something for the Lord, but I wanted to do something that would also benefit me. I bought some equipment and started Primo Media, a video production company. I bought a van and outfitted it with remote equipment so that I could shoot on location. The business had potential, but regardless of how much I invested, it didn't grow."

In 1994, 3ABN was planning to produce a historical program on Ellen G. White to be shot on location in New England. Rick Odle went to host the program, and the person funding the project hired Moses to produce it. When Danny saw the finished product, he asked, "Who did this?"

Rick told him it was a fellow in Massachusetts who had his own company.

"Too bad he isn't an engineer," Danny commented.

Rick started to laugh. "He's the chief engineer for Fox!"

Danny asked Gonzalo to contact him!

Moses responded, "I'm very flattered you like the tape, but I have a full-time job, and I'm not looking to move." He promptly forgot about the call. Gonzalo didn't.

He called again. "I'm getting ready to go to Romania for a year. We have no one else to work with Clarence."

But when Moses heard the salary 3ABN was offering, he responded, "I couldn't possibly afford to work there."

Gonzalo went to Romania for a couple months. When he returned, he called Moses for the third time. "Just come visit," he pleaded. Out of curiosity Moses took off a few days to visit 3ABN. He had no intention in the world of accepting a job.

The first day Clarence Larson showed him around. Moses was impressed with what 3ABN had accomplished, but he was not impressed to join the ministry. That night, Moses stayed in the apartment in the uplink center right next to master control. The phone wouldn't stop ringing. He overheard the master control operator praying with people. That night, Moses had a "burning bush" experience as the Holy Spirit really worked with him about taking the 3ABN job.

The next morning, being a practical person, Moses listed the pros and cons. Even though the list of cons was much larger, he was impressed to accept the job. He went back to Boston to talk to his family. He told his wife, "I really feel the Holy Spirit has called me, but it doesn't make sense. If we go, we will have financial difficulties!" He was counting on her to veto the call. Instead, her response was, "If the Holy Spirit is calling you, who am I to go against that decision?"

So Moses joined 3ABN, and the Lord planted in his heart the same goal He gave to Danny—to reach the world. Has it been easy? Moses recalls, "One night seven years later, I was having a difficult time. I felt like walking away. The challenges were too much. I felt I had failed the Lord by not being smart enough to solve all the problems. When I told Danny I was going to quit, he reminded me that I hadn't come to 3ABN for myself—or for Danny; I came because God called me. He said, 'I'm going to ignore this whole conversation. You can no more quit than I can.' Danny and I never spoke of it again. And God was good and gave me a second chance to recommit myself to His plan for my life. Now every day I pray that God will give me the wisdom to accomplish the things that need to be done in order to take the gospel to every nation, kindred, tongue, and people."

God has answered that prayer, for He has used Moses to put together the satellite system that has allowed 3ABN to reach the world.

In September 1996, 3ABN began broadcasting twenty-four hours a day throughout Europe and North Africa on an international satellite—Intelsat K. This amazing digital system was capable of broadcasting in many different languages simultaneously. This system was in place when 3ABN and the North American Division of the Seventh-day Adventist Church joined together to broadcast NET '96, the second live evangelistic series with Mark Finley. 3ABN brought

One of the satellite dishes that beams 3ABN's message around the world

translators from eight different countries and aired the entire series. Churches and homeowners with large dishes could watch the evangelistic meetings live. After the success of that event, there was no longer a question about the value of live-media evangelism. Now church leaders and members urged 3ABN to find ways that the signal could go around the world in various languages. Moses started researching the digital compression system that would make it possible for a signal to be heard in various languages and then started negotiating with satellite companies.

In 1998, 3ABN went on Dominion Sky Angel's direct-to-home system, making it possible for hundreds of thousands of small-dish subscribers to watch 3ABN.

On June 28, 2000, the dream of going worldwide was technically fulfilled. On that date, 3ABN began broadcasting around the world by sending its signal from Illinois to a satellite (GE-4 which became AMC-4) that covers North and Central America and Hawaii. At the same time, the signal went to the PanAmSat (PAS- 9) satellite that covers North, Central and South America as well as Europe. In Rome, Italy, the signal was downlinked and sent to Hotbird, the most watched satellite in Europe. In Jerusalem, the signal was downlinked again and sent to the Thaicom 3 satellite, which covers Asia, Africa, India, and Australia. And over the United States, Dominion Sky Angel (on an Echostar satellite) made it possible for viewers to receive

3ABN on an eighteen-inch dish. It's interesting to note that 3ABN has sold more Dominion Sky Angel dishes than the company itself!

In 2004, cable companies across the United States were able to receive 3ABN television on the Intelsat 907 satellite through the OlympuSAT Faith and Families package. During that year, New Zealand and Australia began receiving 3ABN's signal on a one-meter dish from Globecast's Optus B3 satellite, the most watched satellite in those countries. TrendTV direct broadcast service also began carrying the 3ABN television channel in a subscription package to Western Africa, beginning with Nigeria.

With these eight satellites, 3ABN's signal can now be received on every inhabited continent of the world. And the incredible thing is that it takes only eight seconds for the signal to go from West Frankfort, Illinois, all the way to Australia!

In addition, 3ABN is continuing to work on the challenge of broadcasting in the different major languages of the world. Today, the 3ABN Latino television network broadcasts 24-hour programming in Spanish and Portuguese and has experienced such rapid growth that it now can be seen on cable in all but one of the Spanish-speaking countries in the world! It's illegal for Cuba to carry programming from the United States. In addition, 3ABN studios have been, and are being established in Russia, Brazil, Uganda, Philippines, Portugal, Puerto Rico, and France. Many of the 3ABN programs in English are being translated so that individuals can hear the broadcasts in their native tongue. And for those people who don't have access to satellite equipment or local stations, all of the 3ABN television and radio networks can be seen and heard free of charge on the Internet worldwide.

In 2000, Moses, working with a high-power "KU band" satellite company, designed a small thirty-six-inch satellite dish system for homes, churches, and other institutions to receive 3ABN English and Latino television, 3ABN radio and radio 74 from France. Later, other Seventh-day Adventist media ministries signed on to the same system, which now carries The Hope Channel in English and Spanish (Adventist TV Network), Loma Linda Broadcasting Network, and LifeTalk Radio Network. The installation kit contains the dish, all the equipment, and the video instructions needed for installation. And the best news is that this kit is available from 3ABN (or any of the above ministries) at a very low cost, with no monthly or annual fees! Now everyone, almost anywhere in the world, can receive 3ABN programming in his or her own home, even without a downlink station, cable, or Internet access. Praise the Lord!

As 3ABN begins celebrating twenty years of miracles, Moses was asked how he feels about his success in getting the signal around the world. He commented, "As I take time to look back, I can see the Lord's hand in my entire life preparing me for the work that I'm doing here at 3ABN. When I was working at Fox, I considered it unbelievable that I, a foreigner, could hold such a lofty position. There had to be some reason for me to be there, working with the very latest and best technology in the field of television. Now I realize that it would be very difficult for me to have done what has been accomplished at 3ABN if it were not for the experience God allowed me to have at Globo and Fox. God had a plan for my life, and knowing that He has this personal interest in me has enhanced my connection with Him."

In 2005 (as we go to press), Moses Primo is serving as 3ABN's director of operations and engineering.

* * * * *

The story of 3ABN going to Romania, Russia, Europe, Africa, India, and the Pacific Rim countries is a fascinating story that continues in Section III, "3ABN Stretches to Reach the World." But before we go there, it's time for a personal touch—a look at the Shelton family heritage and Danny's unique philosophy of life.

Section II
A Personal Touch

"Unless the Lord builds the house,
They labor in vain who build it. . . .
Behold, children are a heritage from the Lord,
The fruit of the womb is His reward"
—Psalm 127:1, 3, NKJV.

The miracles are awe-inspiring. Miracles of buildings being built. Miracles of millions of dollars' worth of equipment being ordered with nothing in the bank but faith—and God never missing a payment. And miracles of signals beaming up to satellites circling the earth. But behind the scenes, other miracles are happening in the hearts of people who are willing to do whatever God asks them to do; people who defy reason and step out of the boat and "walk on water," knowing that it is only God's almighty power that holds them up. Why is it that some have "mountain-moving" faith and others don't?

What makes someone like Danny Shelton willing to withstand criticism and go forward with no assurance that money will follow—other than God's promise to meet the needs of His ministry? As you read the story of Danny's growing-up years, you'll discover significant factors that affected him and shaped his values. Plus, you'll discover the life experiences that gave him a passion for helping people who are hurting—for mending broken people.

I think you will agree that twenty years ago, Danny would have been selected as the *least* likely person to be the administrative leader and inspirational on-camera representative of a worldwide satellite television ministry. But isn't God good? He knew what Danny would be doing some day. God chose the family who raised Danny; God allowed heartache to hit; and God brought Danny to the place where he was humble enough to be trusted with His mighty work. It is true . . .

"You saw Danny before he was born.
Every day of his life was recorded in your book.
Every moment was laid out before a single day had passed"
(Psalm 139:16, personal paraphrase).

Come with me through these next few chapters as we peek into the past and meet Danny's family, catching a glimpse of his winning personality and fun-loving character as he has traveled the world for the Lord and has led this ministry from its humble beginnings in a cornfield in West Frankfort, Illinois, to a thriving worldwide ministry.

5
The Shelton Family Heritage

"Teach your children to choose the right path,
and when they are older,
they will remain upon it"
—Proverbs 22:6, New Living Translation.

An apple never falls far from the family tree. So to understand why Danny feels so strongly about certain things, why he has such a strong simple faith, and why he is so committed to the lifesaving message of the Seventh-day Adventist Church, it is important to understand his heritage.

The miracle of Grandpa Shelton

Danny's grandparents were poor country people who had very little education. Danny's father, Tommy, was the fifth child of fourteen children born to William and Netty Filkins Shelton. William, Danny's grandpa, couldn't read or write, and he often came home drunk. Life was hard in Arkansas, so when his grandpa learned about the money that could be made in the coal mines, he moved his family to southern Illinois. At the time, Tommy was just six years old. In the town of Orient, Tommy became the first in the Shelton family to graduate from eighth grade. That was quite an accomplishment!

Grandpa andGrandma Shelton

In addition to working the mines, Grandpa Shelton was a farmer who worked his children from sunup to sundown. Most of them missed so much school, they just dropped out. One day, a truant officer came by the farm and announced that all the kids had to be in school.

"What?" Grandpa Shelton yelled. "What do *you* have to say about *my* kids?" Then he hollered up to the house. "Quick, Ma, bring me my gun. I gotta shoot this guy." And Danny says he probably would have, if the man hadn't taken off!

Grandpa Shelton had a pretty mean temper when drinking and was known for his shooting sprees. When they started, his kids would run for the nearest cover—sometimes bumping into each other as they dove under the neighbor's porch. Some of the kids left home early, but Danny's dad stayed on the farm until he was twenty-two years old. He probably felt an obligation to try to make a living for his younger brothers and sisters.

Grandpa Shelton thought work was a cure for just about everything. Danny knew firsthand about how hard Grandpa worked his kids and grandkids, because during the summers, Danny sometimes helped him on his farm. The grandkids grumbled about being worked like slaves, but they knew their grandpa loved them, and they loved him. Even though Danny worked hard, he and his cousins had lots of fun at Grandpa's place, and they loved to listen to his stories. Grandpa used to say, "One boy is a boy; two is half a boy; and three is no boy at all." Obviously, the more grandchildren—the less work done!

As Danny recalls his heritage, he starts with Grandpa Shelton because his life illustrates what God's love can do to mellow a man Through the influence of the families of two of his sons (Uncle Olen and Tommy, Danny's father), Grandpa Shelton became a Seventh-day Adventist Christian. During the last few years of his life, he enjoyed nothing more than having Danny read the Bible to him!

Although at times testy, opinionated, and—before his conversion—intoxicated, Grandpa Shelton was known by everyone as an honest man. For example, when selling produce, he would always put the worst vegetables or fruits on the top so there were no surprises underneath. The thing that had the greatest impact on Danny's life was his grandpa's honesty. And Danny determined to be like him in that regard. Grandpa Shelton died at the age of seventy-seven, when Danny was just sixteen.

Danny's parents: Tommy and Goldie Shelton

In contrast to Grandpa Shelton's testy, opinionated personality,

Danny's father, Tommy, was a kind, principled man who never drank or smoked. He enjoyed a good time and had a great sense of humor. Music was his life. He enjoyed nothing better than playing guitar and singing lead in country bands. Danny's mom, Goldie, was a waitress at Manis Cafe in West Frankfort where she and Tommy met. Tommy was good-looking, and Goldie was cute. But when Tommy heard Goldie's beautiful singing voice, and she heard him harmonizing with her, they were immediately attracted to each other. A few months later, they married.

Goldie was from a family who enjoyed making country music together. She was one of Joel and Mamie Rice's five children, born and raised on the Rice homestead about three miles from where 3ABN is now located. Goldie's father was a coal miner by trade but loved playing the banjo. Her mother played the violin, one sister played the banjo, two brothers played guitar, while Goldie played the mandolin. Her favorite instrument, however, was the piano. Goldie felt that a piano was like a meal—absolutely essential to life. The first piece of furniture Danny's folks got after they were married was a piano.

Tommy and Goldie helped form a country music group called the Melody Kings, which became extremely popular in the 1940s, both on the

The Melody Kings (Tommy is second on the left)

nightclub circuit and on the radio. They made a couple hundred dollars each weekend from their music, which kept food on the table. They also had a radio program for five years which featured country music and talk.

Events that changed the lives of Danny's parents

Neither Tommy nor Goldie were practicing Christians at the time of their marriage. Tommy's brother, Olen, and his wife, Mildred, had become Adventists; they gave Goldie Bible studies for two years. But her Methodist background kept her from accepting

Tommy, Goldie, and children

the Bible truth of the Sabbath and the state of the dead.

Then suddenly in 1949, before Danny was born, Goldie came down with polio. Her arms and legs started withering before her eyes. None of her family could imagine what was happening. Dr. Galula made a house call and broke the terrible news to Tommy that his wife had polio of the worst kind. "We will have to send her to Barnes Hospital in St. Louis," Goldie heard the doctor tell her husband and their three young children—Tommy, Kenny, and Ronny.

Danny's father called his brother, Olen, who was the only active Christian in the family at that time, and Olen brought along the Seventh-day Adventist pastor. They anointed Goldie with oil. She then rolled off the bed into a praying position and pleaded with the Lord, "If You heal me, I'll never sing in another tavern. I will give my life to You and raise my children in the church." Within minutes, they watched a miracle occur in front of their eyes as color returned to Goldie's cheeks and all of her functions were restored. Thirty minutes later, it was as though nothing had ever happened. There was no sign of polio!

What rejoicing there was! Olen and the pastor had prayed for Goldie, and now she didn't even need to go to the hospital. The Lord had healed her!

"How do you explain this?" Danny's dad inquired of the doctor. "What do you make of it?"

The doctor replied, "There must be a higher power than us doctors because there is no doubt in my mind that your wife had polio."

As a result of this miracle of healing, Danny's mother gave her heart to the Lord and never again set foot in a tavern to sing with the Melody Kings. Two years later, Danny came along, and eight years after that, Tammy was born.

When Goldie made her decision to never again sing in the taverns, she urged her husband to do the same. Performing, however, was the only thing he knew how to do, and he had a family to support.

It took Danny's dad another three years before he gave his heart to the Lord and quit playing in the clubs. But this decision wasn't without a struggle. At the time, the Sheltons were living in an upstairs apartment. One time, Tommy had a Friday night engagement. Goldie pled with him not to go, but Tommy said he had made a commitment and needed to keep it. As he went out the door, however, he fell down the stairs and broke his ankle. Tommy later bought a septic tank truck, which blew up on him on a Sabbath when he felt he had to work. It seemed that every time Tommy disregarded the Sabbath, something happened. So he finally said, "Enough is enough!" He gave his heart to the Lord and accepted the seventh day as the Sabbath and obeyed God's fourth commandment: "Remember the Sabbath day, to keep it holy. Six days you shall labor and do all your work, but the seventh day is the Sabbath of the Lord your God. In it you shall do no work" (Exodus 20:8-10, NKJV).

One of the characteristics Danny admired most about his dad was his consistency. Once he made a decision to serve the Lord, he never wavered. Many times the family didn't know how they would get their next meal. His friends in the music world would beg him, "Tommy, we'll give you a hundred dollars for just one night. Or, we have this big gig in Carbondale. You could earn lots of money!" But Tommy would always say, "No, boys, I can't."

"Doesn't the Bible say you are to take care of your family?" his friends would counter.

"Well," Tommy would reply, "I won't go to the clubs to do so. God will provide."

Tommy never *sent* his kids to church. He *took* them with him! He held up the standards and expected the rest of the family to do the same. The rule was, "If you get up on Sabbath morning, you go to church." Even the neighbors knew that sickness was the only reason a Shelton stayed home from church.

Before having children, Goldie had often prayed, "Lord, give me some children to use in Your work." Her prayers have certainly been answered. Because music was the love of her life, Goldie hoped she would get a quartet, and at times the kids have all sung together.

One of Goldie's earliest memories of Danny is of him bringing home literature from church. After lunch, he would say, "Mom, I'm going to give out literature." Then he would go down the street singing, "I've got a mansion just over the hilltop," as he passed out Christian pamphlets.

When Goldie first became an Adventist, Bertha Armstrong, the lady who lived across the street, would have nothing to do with her. Bertha thought the Sheltons had joined a cult. But that didn't stop Goldie from doing nice things for Bertha. Later, Bertha's husband became disabled, so one of the Shelton boys would mow her lawn. This broke down some prejudice. But apparently, Danny felt he should try to convert Mrs. Armstrong; he would give her literature. This made quite an impression on her. At one time, Bertha said to Goldie, "Honey, I want to tell you something. God has got something big in store for that boy of yours. He will be given jobs of responsibility. Whatever the Lord wants, Danny's willing. Yes, that boy is gonna do something big." Bertha later became one of Goldie's best friends, saying, "I'd like to be the kind of friend you have been to me."

Living on the edge of poverty

It was extremely tough for Danny's father to find a decent job that didn't require him to work on Sabbath. It was a real sacrifice for this dedicated man to go from knowing the glory of a performing musical artist to being a trash collector and a honey dipper—that's what they called someone who operated a septic tank trunk.

To earn a little extra money, Tommy would take his children out on the highways to pick up glass for recycling. The kids would always break the bottles as they threw them into the truck to make room for more glass. Three-year-old Danny was trying his best to help when a sliver of broken glass wedged in his right eye and blinded him. He didn't complain until the next morning. His folks took him to Carbondale, where a surgeon cut out the shard of glass, but the scar permanently blinded Danny in that eye. In 1979, after another accident with a splinter of wood in the same eye, Danny had to have a cornea transplant. In 1990, surgery was once again required as the cornea seemed to be retracting. The transplant makes his eye look normal. The accident happened so early that Danny can't remember what it's like to see with two eyes.

The Shelton family collected anything that could be recycled—junk cars, scrap metal, and even old furniture. Sometimes Danny's folks and Uncle Olen would take the family north to Indiana, where they became migrant workers, living with the Amish people and picking tomatoes and other crops. Some years, the kids would be six weeks late getting back to school because they were picking produce.

One summer, Danny's family and Uncle Olen's family lived in a barn with cardboard partitions they put up to divide their space from other families. Another year, the Sheltons lived in an old two-story farmhouse with a big front porch but no running water. Family members would start picking at six in the morning and sweat through those hot, humid days of summer. Each evening they would come back to their migrant home around six-thirty. They took turns bathing in an old washtub, and then they would sit around and sing until they were exhausted and fell asleep.

One of Danny's fondest memories of his family's migrant farm years was when both their family and Uncle Olen's family would line up and start picking their way down a row at the same speed. When they did this, it was easy to tell if someone was slacking off and getting behind! While picking, someone would start singing, "Somewhere beyond the blue, there's a mansion for me." Danny never remembers learning harmony. Music just happened! Music bonded the Sheltons and made them *family*. Music dulled the pain of sunburn, heat, and fatigue. It made life worth living. The capstone of contentment was on Sabbaths when the family would sit under the giant shade trees worshiping and singing hour after hour.

The Shelton family was poor, but they never went hungry. Danny's folks taught him how to work hard and do the best with what he had or do without. Danny recalls how embarrassing it was to wear a coat to school and hear another kid say, "That's my old coat that my mom gave away!" Goldie used house paint to turn Danny's black tennis shoes white, like those of the rest of the team for the team photo. There was no money for a second pair. But Danny learned to cope. At lunch break when all his school friends would go out to eat, Danny didn't want anyone to know that he didn't have enough money to buy lunch. So he would make some excuse and head down to the five-and-dime store and buy peanuts.

Danny's folks were so poor that they weren't able to give Danny a wedding present when he got married. His dad just shook his hand and said, "I wish you the best, son."

The Shelton family members had more than their share of health problems, which contributed to their financial problems. It might even have seemed that they worked the Lord overtime. Their mother's brush with paralyzing polio and God's miraculous healing were just the beginning. Danny's father was only thirty-six years old when he had a heart attack and became disabled. Then he was diagnosed with kidney cancer. But the family prayed, and what rejoicing there was when he, too, was miraculously healed of cancer. Danny's father died, however, at fifty-one of heart failure.

The family had no income during the time Tommy was disabled. Because he had never paid into Social Security, there were no Social Security payments either. Goldie worked at a dress factory, waited tables at a local restaurant, mopped floors, cleaned, and painted houses. Danny and his brothers hauled coal for the neighbors, mowed lawns, raked leaves, and did odd jobs to keep busy. Even at thirteen years of age, Kenny worked as a janitor after school, while Ronny, at twelve, learned auto mechanics from Elmer Filkins by working Sundays and every day after school. In the summer, Danny and Kenny learned the carpenter trade from Uncle Vernon Johns.

Tommy, who was the oldest child, had begun playing the piano weekends for a gospel quartet, contributing a portion of what he made to the family. At sixteen, Tommy quit school to play full time for a traveling Church of God evangelist.

While Tommy's passion was playing the piano, the rest of the boys were into sports and building things with their hands. One day when Kenny was fifteen, Ronny, thirteen, and Danny, eleven, they got the idea that they should build a little music room onto their house for their dad. Imagine Kenny and Danny constructing the walls and roof at that young age, while Ronny did all the wiring! That was the Shelton brothers' introduction to the building trade! What a pleasure it was for the boys to see their dad sitting in the room they had constructed, strumming on his guitar, and playing tapes for hours at a time. And what a sense of satisfaction to know that they had built it themselves! Their second project was to build an upstairs bedroom.

Work and play

Danny's father, just like Grandpa Shelton, believed that idleness was the devil's workshop. Dad Shelton raised his kids to work. If the children seemed to have any free time, Dad would find a job for them to do. When they would beg to visit their friends, Dad would say, "You must not have enough to do," and he would come up with more jobs for them. But it was good training. "Hard work never hurt anyone!" was an oft-repeated phrase in the Shelton household. The boys didn't always get to go to their friends' to play, but Dad always let them invite their friends to their house so that he would know where his boys were.

Dad made sure the boys weren't "all work and no play" by allowing them to enjoy sports as time allowed. The Sheltons' backyard had a basketball goal and a pole-vaulting and high-jumping set-up, as well as a seven-foot-high aluminum bar attached between two trees for a "parallel bar" from which to swing and do flips.

Kenny, Ronny, and Danny in softball uniforms

Kenny, Ronny, and Danny loved sports. They played softball all their lives starting with Little League. Even after high school, when both Kenny and Danny were in construction work, they continued playing fast-pitch softball in the city leagues during summer. But Danny also has a passion for basketball that has carried through the years. During construction of the large production studios in Thompsonville, as well as in Russia, Danny would bring in a basketball hoop and challenge workers to a game of one-on-one during breaks. Even in his fifties, Danny still plays basketball every Tuesday night. His uncle Bud Shelton is still playing in his seventies!

The Sheltons may have lived on the edge of poverty, but the Lord blessed them. As Danny has said many times, there are more important things than money. One of those things is discipline. And another is love!

Memories about discipline

If any of his kids would get into a dispute with someone, Dad Shelton assumed his kids were wrong and would take the other side. He would say, "Don't think you'll get special treatment just because you're ours." And if his kids got in trouble at school and got a whipping, Dad automatically sided with the teacher. When the kids got home, Dad gave them another whipping! Back then, no one questioned a teacher's judgment or disciplinary actions.

Goldie was quick to grab a little switch to correct her children's willful ways, but their dad would talk to them first. He set rules and expected his kids to live by them. "The day you don't want to live by these rules," he would say, "you can take care of yourself." He'd explain, "I'm not hard on you because it makes me feel better, but because it's best for you. Right now, you don't have sense enough to make good decisions. That's why God called me to be the parent and you the child. When you get older, you will come back to thank me that I'm doing what is best for you now."

Tommy Shelton never disciplined his children based on feelings. He disciplined by principle. When he saw his kids were in danger of doing something wrong, he would warn them, make sure they understood, and then say, "We'll never have this talk again!" The kids knew if they made the same mistake again, they'd get a whipping! There was no reasoning; no arguing. Once their dad made the conditions clear, he never budged! Dad Shelton believed that slapping kids made them mean. But he also believed that God provided padding in a special place for a special purpose, and he made use of it when necessary.

One time Danny asked his dad if he could sit next to his cousin Dennis in church. Dad said, "OK, but if you get to cutting up, there will be no warning. After sundown, you'll get it!" Danny knew very well what he meant and tried hard to sit quietly for a while, but the temptation was too great. Just as Dennis and Danny started to giggle, Dad caught Danny's eye, and Danny knew he was in trouble. After church, he asked his mom if he could go over to Aunt Mildred and Uncle Olen's and play with Dennis for the afternoon, thinking that maybe by evening his dad would forget.

As the afternoon wore on, Danny began to worry that this wasn't enough time for Dad to forget the whipping he had promised, so Danny begged to stay overnight. Again, approval was given, and it was Sunday afternoon before his folks came to pick him up. Before going home, they all spent some time together playing with the kids, sitting in the lawn chairs, singing and laughing. It appeared that Dad had forgotten the promised punishment. But as they were getting out of the car at home, Dad suddenly turned to Danny and said, "Oh, by the way, son, don't forget to come and see me before you go to bed. You have a good whipping coming!"

"My job," his father would say, "is to make a good person out of you. That's what God expects of me." Remembering this experience, Danny commented, "My father was the most consistent person I ever met. I knew I could always trust him."

Danny's parents were so consistent in doing what they believed that it affected him for the rest of his life. He was taught to never give up, to fight the odds, and to trust completely in God! His folks instilled within him the life commandment that you do what's right no matter what! God will take care of you. Danny learned never to compromise his principles for the sake of others or because of the pressures being put upon him.

Danny's dad was always jovial even though he had great health problems, and people can't be around Danny long without realizing that a whole lot of his dad's happy spirit rubbed off on him. Danny never doubted that his dad loved him. And because their home was so full of love, the Shelton kids felt secure and didn't realize that they were among the poorest people around.

Think less of self and more of others

Danny often says his dad was one of the wisest men he ever met. And as Danny gets older, he realizes how important this training was for the work he is doing today. For example, when Danny was a kid playing baseball and people were bragging about his talents, his dad would say something like, "So what if you can throw a ball harder or farther than anyone else in town? Does that put food on the table? Does it help someone?"

Dad Shelton never wanted his kids thinking they were better than others or that others were better than they were! Danny remembers the excitement the first time he pitched a no-hitter. "Well, that's good, Son," his dad said. "But there are a whole lot of people in this world who are better." He didn't mean to put his kids down. He just didn't want them putting themselves above others. Regardless of what positions people held or how much they were worshiped as heroes, Dad would always say, "They still put their pants on one leg at a time just like everybody else." Danny also remembers his dad saying, "You could be president, and it wouldn't matter. Everyone is just as important as the other. We are all the same. What they can do, you can do!" He would say, "Just because you don't have money or an education, that's no excuse. God gave you a brain. Use it!"

Time after time, Danny's father emphasized that no one was better than anyone else in this world. That point sunk deep into Danny's head until today, it's second nature for him to look at everyone the same. When it comes to soul winning, he doesn't make comparisons. "Just because one evangelist has thousands of baptisms, that doesn't make him any different from the person who wins one soul. Everyone is just as important as the other. We are all the same. We can do whatever God wants. There is nothing on this earth that we can do that others wouldn't be able to do just the same or better! The important thing is, if God asks us to do it, then we'd better do it to the very best of our ability." So in many respects, Danny's father's philosophy became his own!

Danny establishes his own family

During Danny's senior year of high school, he was invited to join a musical group, and that's where he met Mary Kay. Everyone called her Kay. She was older than he and had two daughters, Lisa and Rhonda. Kay had the most beautiful singing voice Danny had ever heard, and he fell in love. He had toyed with the thought of going to college, but his dad didn't see much sense in it. In fact, when Danny mentioned to his dad that he had been invited to freshman orientation at Southern Illinois University, his dad laughed and said, "College? You know, son, that's what I like about you. You're always joking." He squeezed Danny's

Shelton Trio, Tommy, Danny, and Kay—with Ronny playing bass

shoulder—his way of saying how much he loved Danny—and the subject was dropped. Danny graduated from high school in June 1969 and, shortly after, began working as a carpenter. He and Kay got married the next May— a week before Danny's nineteenth birthday. From the beginning, music was the passion of their lives. When their daughter was born, they named her Melody, dedicating her to God and praying that she would continue the family tradition of sharing Christ through music. Her name was prophetic.

When Melody was small, Danny and Kay, along with Danny's brothers, Tommy and Kenny, bought a diesel bus and traveled weekends for three years singing gospel music. Sometimes Danny's mom, Goldie, sang with them. Later, when Melody was nine years old, the Shelton family, Danny, Kay, Lisa, Rhonda, and Melody, began singing together.

Then on June 30, 1982, at one o'clock in the afternoon, everything changed. The family had just come back from a seven-thousand-mile concert tour through Michigan, Wisconsin, and northern Illinois. They had left their little poodle with someone in town. Kay took Melody to pick up the dog, saying she would be right back. Just minutes after she pulled out of the drive, Danny heard a terrible crash and the blaring of a horn that had stuck. An in-

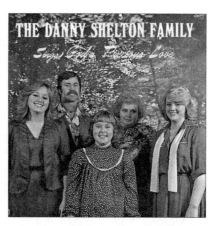

Kay, Danny, Rhoda, Lisa, and Melody

ner sense told him it was Kay. Within minutes, someone raced to Danny's door. "Your wife and Melody have been in an accident!"

"Are they OK?" he asked, panic registering in his voice.

"Melody's got a broken arm and lots of bruises. We can't find your wife."

"You can't find my wife?"

"She's not in the van."

Danny raced to the scene of the accident. What he saw made him shudder. A teenager who had just gotten his driver's license was going too fast and missed the stop sign, hitting the van Kay was driving. It spun out of control, throwing Kay face down into a ditch, killing her instantly. The van then came crashing down almost on top of her. Danny rushed over to the mangled van, reached under the bumper, and touched her. Immediately, he knew Kay was dead. Stunned, Danny then went to check on Melody; she was frightened and crying in pain. People had begun to gather at the accident scene. Since there was nothing he could do for Kay, he mumbled, "My little girl needs me" and went with Melody to the hospital.

While they were waiting for medical attention, Danny heard Melody praying for her mother. He knew Kay was dead, but he couldn't bring himself to tell his daughter. As the doctor finished putting the cast on Melody's arm and the nurse was washing her, Danny knew he had to say something. "Mommy didn't do so well," he began.

"Where is she?"

"I don't know how to tell you, but just think of the worst thing you can think of."

"When will Mama be here? Is she going to come and see me?"

Finally Danny said, "Honey, your mama didn't make it."

"What do you mean?"

"Honey, I heard you praying for Mama, but she's dead."

"Mama's dead?"

"Yes," he said simply.

"Oh," Melody responded staring off into space.

When they started to leave the hospital, she asked, "When are we going to see Mama?" And Danny had to go through everything once again. Melody just couldn't accept the fact that her mother was dead—and Danny couldn't either!

Melody and her dad talked all night. He didn't want Melody to blame God. Instead, he wanted her to see her mother's death in the light of the great controversy between good and evil. He wanted her to see what the true character of God really was like. Danny read a few Bible texts that he thought might encourage Melody. He read the counsel of 1 Peter 5:7, "Casting all your care upon him; for he careth for you." Then he turned to John 10:10, about how the devil, the thief, was trying to steal, kill, and destroy, but Jesus says, "I am come that they might have life, and that they might have it more abundantly."

Toward morning, Danny said, "Honey, we have to get someone to sing at your mama's funeral."

"Daddy," she said, "I want to sing. I think Mama would want me to sing."

The next day, Danny took Melody to the church and recorded her singing two songs to be used for the service. "Listening to that brave little girl sing was one of the most touching experiences of my life," he says. "I knew who had been number one in Melody's life, and I was second! Melody had not lost just her mother, she had also lost her best friend."

The next week, Danny's family was scheduled to give a concert in Berrien Springs, Michigan. When people heard about the accident, they said they could cancel, but Melody said, "We can do this, Daddy. You tell them we'll do it." So Danny, Lisa[1] and Melody went.

As Danny watched Melody's determination to continue the work of spreading the gospel through music, he decided that, for his little girl's sake, he would give it his all. He never went back to construction work full time. Instead, during the week, he took people to Nashville to produce records, while on the weekends he and Melody dedicated themselves to spreading the gospel and ministering to others through music. He literally buried himself in his work so that he wouldn't feel the pain of loss and loneliness.

The Shelton family and 3ABN

Two and a half years after Kay's death, God gave Danny the vision for 3ABN. Ten days later, Danny and Linda got married.

Because family has always meant so much to Danny, his first thought when God called him to this ministry was to include everyone who wanted to be involved. When the ministry began, all the Shelton brothers rolled up their sleeves and helped. Kenny and Ronny had construction skills, so one might expect to see them on the construction site. But even Tommy, who was never into construction, found himself hanging sheetrock!

Throughout the years, various family members have volunteered and worked for 3ABN, depending on the needs of the ministry and their interests and skills. In 2004, twenty years after 3ABN began, Ronny was back wiring the worship center and taking assignments to serve as 3ABN's representative to foreign countries. In June 2004, he was sent as 3ABN's representative to Russia, where he held revival meetings. Throughout the years, Tommy has helped with music. He often travels to 3ABN rallies, where viewers have grown to love his skill at the piano. In 2004, Tommy's role at 3ABN was expanded to include serving as production manager for 3ABN television. For the last few years, Tammy, Danny's younger sister, has been 3ABN's donation coordinator. She is responsible for the thrift shop, where donated items are sold for the benefit of the 3ABN ministry—and she sings.

On 3ABN's nineteenth-anniversary broadcast, Tommy commented, "One of the greatest things in my life has been watching my family grow up as a part of 3ABN. My three children have all worked here and performed here. For a year, my family traveled across country in a thirty-year-old renovated Greyhound bus representing 3ABN. The miracles that the Lord has worked on behalf of 3ABN have had an incredible impact on my children. When things seem impossible, the kids remind me, 'The Lord will provide. He always has.' It's been a wonderful experience."

Danny has grown up in a close family where music was their passion and miracles were their heritage! Nothing, except God and principle, means more to Danny than his family.

Danny and the grandkids

Now that Danny is a grandpa, he admits that Melody's four precious children—his grandchildren—are the light of his life! Indeed, they are his greatest joy. Hayley Kay is a grown-up ten years old. When she was about four, her "papa" (Danny) asked, "Hayley, what do you want to do when you grow up?"

"I want to be a boss at 3ABN."

"How can you be the boss when Papa is the boss? We both can't be the boss."

"Yes, we can both be bosses!"

"What will I do?" Danny asked.

"Well, when I get hungry, you can get me something to eat!" Hayley suggested.

Her "papa" says, "She's got the business head and already knows how to get her papa to work for her!"

Jesse Adam is nine and all boy. He loves the Lord, music, and anything that is dangerous. He has had his share of stitches. And he, too, is planning to work at 3ABN just like his papa!

Justin Lee is only six, but he is the musician in the family. He loves to play instruments, such as the piano, and has a good time singing on *Tiny Tots* and *Kids Time*.

Noah Aaron is five and is a principal "character" on *Tiny Tots*. He loves his TV "work." He can be on the set one day and the next morning eagerly ask his mom, "Are we going to work again today?" After a shoot, he'll often give his critique, "I think we're going to have to edit that" or "That's a take!" He's outspoken and has never met a stranger.

The Shelton heritage continues on!

Danny, Melody, and grandkids

---

1 Since Rhonda and Lisa were over eighteen years of age when their mother died, they soon moved on to establish their own lives.

6

The Gift That
Keeps Giving

"Freely ye have received, freely give"
—Matthew 10:8.

The giving principle

God's principles for abundant living don't make sense in a world based on selfishness and fear. Fear about whether or not you'll have enough money to make it to the end of the month. Fear that someone is going to take advantage of you. Fear that if you don't look out for yourself (or your ministry), who will?

But God's principles make good sense if your basis of living is Christ-centered love. Fear inhibits creative living; love demands it. Love means serving others—not yourself. Love means taking God at His word and acting on it!

Do you want to have your life filled with blessings? Of course! Then you must follow God's life principle found in Acts 20:35, "It is more blessed to give than to receive." Most of us would much rather be on the receiving end than the giving end. We love Christmas and birthdays, not so much because of what we can give away, but because of the expectation of what we might get. But if we really took God at His word, there would be a whole lot more giving in this world, because there isn't one of us who wouldn't enjoy a few more blessings!

Another life principle is found in Luke 6:38: "Give and it shall be given unto you." This principle doesn't make too much sense in our self-centered, fear-based world. Rationally, if you give something away, it's gone. You work to get; you invest to get; you sell to get!

But for most people, it doesn't make much sense to *give to get!* Yet that is exactly what God tells us to do.

In God's world of love, giving is the stimulus that makes supply so abundant that there is always plenty to go around. Stop the flow, dam up the source of giving, let one person in the chain get selfish and begin hoarding—and everyone down the line suffers.

These principles have become a way of life for Danny. If something is given to you and you don't need it, God expects you to pass it on to someone who does. You are to be a channel of blessing. This is Danny's personal philosophy of life, as well as his corporate philosophy for 3ABN. Some items that are given to 3ABN can be sold and the proceeds put into the ministry. But sometimes it takes time to sell such things. Rather than horde these items, waiting for potential buyers and letting depreciation eat up their value, why not allow that gift to bless others? The question is: Who makes the decision—Danny or God—when it comes to determining whom to bless?

For most of us, the following story is hard to believe, but it's a great illustration of what happens when you unselfishly share a gift that God has given to you with someone in need. The gift just keeps on giving. This story also illustrates, however, what happens when you're impressed to give, and for some personal reason you don't!

The gift that started the giving

Years before 3ABN, Danny was a weekday carpenter and a weekend gospel singer giving concerts with his family. He was just barely making ends meet as it was, and then catastrophe hit. He fell and broke his wrist. He had no insurance. Now, unable to do any carpentry for four months, his only source of income would be record sales or offerings at concerts.

Danny had a number of concerts scheduled in Michigan and Indiana, but the problem was that he didn't have a vehicle or enough money to get his family there. So he told the Lord about it and wondered how He was going to solve this one. What happened next still amazes him!

Shortly after Danny gave his problem to the Lord, Aaron Wilburn, a nationally known songwriter and friend from Nashville, asked him to come to the Marion Civic Center to attend a gospel song-writing seminar Aaron was giving. For almost two hours, Danny sat there listening. Then he began asking himself, *What am*

I doing here? Just then, he recognized Dean Stevenson, a gospel disk jockey who did radio every afternoon. Dean traded guitars and knew just about everything about everybody in the music business. The thought hit Danny that since it was wintertime, Dean might know where he could get an inexpensive motor home. Danny began to tell Dean about needing a motor home for his family to take to Michigan. As they were talking, a fellow walked up to Danny with a pleasant smile on his face. "I overheard you say you need a motor home," he said.

"I sure do," Danny replied, somewhat startled.

"You *really* do?"

"Yes, I do."

"Well," he said, "I'm Dale Smith from Dale, Indiana, about two and a half hours from here. You don't know me, but I've heard your family sing on the radio. I didn't mean to eavesdrop, but I have a motor home."

"You do?" Danny exclaimed, and he began to tell Dale how he needed to get his family to Michigan for some concerts.

"I'll let you use it for your trip, if you come over to my home in Indiana and pick it up."

Dale Smith

"Really?" Danny couldn't believe what he was hearing. He didn't even know this guy, and yet he was going to let him use his motor home for nothing!

Overjoyed, Danny came home and was telling Kay about what had just happened. Then suddenly he realized they didn't have even enough money to go over to Indiana and pick up the gift that was being given to them! They had hit rock bottom. The only place to go was to the Lord, so they told Him all about it.

The night before Danny was to go to Indiana to get the motor home, Dale called to tell him that his parents, who lived in Johnston City, were coming to visit him so they could stop by, pick up Danny, and bring him to Dale's house to get the motor home. Danny had only ten dollars, and he doubted if that would be enough for gas to get the motor home back to West Frankfort, but he decided to go anyway.

When Danny saw the motor home, he couldn't believe it. It was beautiful, insured, had new license plates, a full tank of propane, and a new set of dishes and towels inside.

"How do you like it?" Dale asked with a big smile on his face.

"I'm overwhelmed!" Danny exclaimed.

"Well," Dale said, "the Lord impressed me to do this. Go ahead, get in, and start it up." To Danny's surprise, it even had a full tank of gas!

As he began to drive away, he opened the window and asked, "We're going to need this for about a week, is that OK? And where do you want me to leave it when we return? Do you want it back here?"

Dale replied, "Danny, take the motor home; I'll call you if I need it. But there's just one thing—if anything goes wrong with the engine, I'll take care of it! I'll take care of the insurance, too."

Danny couldn't believe this was happening. Later, he found out that Dale was an unemployed coal miner at the time he gave Danny his motor home. He had no income! Yet this man knew that the Lord had spoken, and he did exactly what the Lord told him to do!

When Danny got back home, he and Kay rejoiced. God had just given him "the desire of his heart," but they still didn't have any money for the trip. "Let's pack just as though we're going," Danny said. "The Lord has brought us this far by providing a motor home. Surely He'll provide the gas." While they were talking about it, a man from their church drove into the driveway. He looked at the motor home and listened to Danny's story. "That's great," he said, "I'm really happy for you." And then he asked, "Do you have enough money to get to Michigan?"

"Not really," Danny replied.

"Well," he said, "that's why the Lord sent me over here! I heard you had the motor home, but I knew you probably didn't have any money since you haven't been able to work, so the Lord impressed me to give you enough to get there."

Once more the Lord provided. Danny and Kay used that motor home for the next two or three months, putting over seven thousand miles on it traveling from place to place giving concerts. The money they received through offerings and selling tapes at the concerts was enough to put them back on their feet. Then came the tragic accident in which Kay was killed. Danny didn't need the motor home anymore and returned it.

It had "DARMODY" written on it

Years went by, and Danny started the 3ABN ministry. Around 1992, he bought a previously owned motor home for 3ABN, thinking the ministry could use it as a remote truck for taping on location. But it never quite worked out.

Not long after, a well-known Adventist gospel singer, Steve Darmody, came to do some recording at 3ABN. He had recently stepped out on faith, resigned from his secure pastoral position so that he would be able to travel on the weekends, and had begun a full-time gospel-singing ministry. As Danny and Steve chatted, Steve mentioned that he had gotten a van and was just beginning to take his family along with him as he traveled to weekend appointments. Steve then made the comment, "But it sure would be nice to have a motor home!"

Suddenly, the 3ABN motor home that wasn't being used flashed into Danny's mind. He saw "DARMODY" written across the side of it in huge letters. Danny showed the motor home to Steve. "Think you could use this?" Danny asked. It was twenty-eight feet long with a lovely mauve interior.

"Wow!" Steve said as he looked at it. "But we could never afford anything like this."

"Well," Danny said, "I'll tell you what we'll do. You take the motor home and use it."

"What would it cost me?" Steve asked.

"Use it as long as you need it. There's just one condition. If anything major goes wrong with the engine, 3ABN will pay for it. We'll also take care of the insurance."

Tears came to Steve's eyes. "You mean, I can just take it?"

Steve and his family used the motor home for a couple of years until his kids got older and needed to be home for school and other activities. Steve then gave Danny a call. "We want to downsize," he explained. Danny sent him the title for the motor home, and Steve traded it in on a comfortable van that would better suit his ministry needs.

The gift goes around again and again

Here is where the story gets interesting! No sooner had Danny given the motor home away than he got a call from Dr. Raymond Moore, who has done so much in the field of homeschooling. "I have this nice motor home that's worth over thirty thousand dollars," Dr. Moore explained, "but Dorothy and I don't need it anymore. If you want it, I'll give it to you." When Danny saw the picture of the motor home, he couldn't believe it. It was nicer than the one he had given away!

A family group who often sings on 3ABN came to do some taping at the studio. They were a lovely Christian family, with both mom and dad and their four children serving the Lord in a full-time singing ministry. When they came into the 3ABN studio, Danny asked them how they were doing, and they told him that their van had broken down and they needed to replace it, but didn't have the money. As he talked to them, Danny thought about the motor home that the Moores had just donated to 3ABN, and the Lord impressed him to give it to them. Danny showed the family a picture of the motor home. "Could you use this?" he asked. "Someone has donated it to us, but we haven't picked it up yet. We'll give you a plane ticket if you'll go out to Washington and get it. You can use it as long as you need it. Just one thing. If anything major goes wrong with the engine, 3ABN will pay for it." The family put almost sixty thousand miles on it ministering to people in churches across the nation and sharing the 3ABN story with them.

Then came the time when they no longer needed the motor home and gave it back to 3ABN. Danny had the engine repaired. Then shortly afterward, he attended some ASI meetings in Chicago. There he met a singing group of about seven people from Wisconsin. "When are you going to do this full time?" he asked.

"We don't have anything to travel in," they replied, "and we're not going into debt."

"You need to come down to 3ABN," he said. "We have a motor home for you, if you want it." And so the circle of giving went around one more time.

"LESLIE LEMKE" was written on the Ford van

Just about this same time, the 3ABN ministry acquired a 1993 Ford van with a raised top. It was the nicest van Danny had ever driven. It had a TV and VCR and all the trimmings. And it was just the perfect size for the 3ABN ministry to transport guests to and from the airport.

About the middle of 1994, 3ABN brought Leslie Lemke to the studio to perform. Leslie is a blind, severely retarded man who can barely talk and get around, but he has an incredible gift of being able to reproduce on the piano up to twenty minutes of classical music by just hearing it once! He was raised by May Lemke, and when she died, her daughter, Mary Parkers, had taken over his care. Mary brought him to 3ABN. They were driving a 1974 Dodge van with no air conditioning in one-hundred-degree weather—and the van had engine trouble! Danny called his brother Ronny, who is a mechanic, to see if he knew of a good used motor they could buy for their van so they could get to their next concert. After making the call, Danny walked outside and there was that beautiful Ford van. In his mind, on the side of that van was written in big letters, "LESLIE LEMKE."

No! Danny thought. *I can't give this van away. We need it!*

Just give it! he heard. So Danny said to Mary, "What would you think about having a van like this?"

She looked inside. "Wow," she said. "We could travel to our appointments in comfort and the TV/VCR would entertain Leslie for hours."

"Well," Danny said, not believing that he was doing this, "The Lord's impressed me that 3ABN should give it to you. Use it. It's a gift from God."

Danny went several months without a transport vehicle, but he was at peace because he knew he had done what God had asked him to do. One day, he decided, "I'm going to take our old minivan down to the Ford dealership in Marion and see if they have any new vans." Danny didn't have any money, so he was just planning to look. But there on the lot was a perfect vehicle: a green 1996 van.

"I'll take your old minivan in on a trade for this one, if you can come up with $15,700," the dealer offered.

"No," Danny shook his head, knowing he didn't have the money.

"You want to make an offer?" the dealer persisted.

Almost in jest, Danny said, "I'll give you $15,000, but to tell you the truth, I don't have the money."

"Well," the dealer said, "we can finance it for you."

"No," Danny said, "I was just looking."

When Danny got home, the telephone answering machine was blinking. The message said, "You don't know me, but I know you. This afternoon the Lord has impressed me that you need $15,000, and I wanted you to know that God has just granted your need." The next day the money came via overnight express!

So with $15,000 in his pocket, Danny went back to the dealer. But when he got there, the dealer wouldn't take less than $15,200. "God provides for every need of our ministry," Danny told him. "He doesn't provide for every need except $200." He had started to leave when the dealer called him back. "It's yours for $15,000."

The gift that almost wasn't given

Danny had used that beautiful van for a year when Reggie and LaChanda Dupard came to 3ABN. Reggie, a former football player for the Washington Redskins, had given up his promising football career when he had become a Seventh-day Adventist Christian. For the last few years, he and his wife had been working full time in the ministry they had founded for troubled kids—Maranatha Youth Ministry.

Danny drove them into Benton for supper. As they were driving, Danny overheard LaChanda make a quiet comment from the back seat, "Wouldn't it be wonderful if we had a van like this for the kids we work with!" She had no idea Danny heard what she had said.

Danny didn't even want to think about this one. But all the way back from Benton he was impressed with the message, *Give these people this van. Give these people this van.*

But, Lord, he argued, *They're dressed so well, I'm sure they've got a lot more money than 3ABN does. After all, Reggie was a pro football player! No way am I going to give them this van.* So Danny didn't offer it.

Two days later, a friend who had given generously to 3ABN came to visit. Two years before, this person had told Danny about a Suburban he had just bought for himself, adding, "Maybe I'll give you one, too!"

Danny hadn't thought much about it, but now when the two men were alone for a few minutes, the friend brought it up again, "When you were at my place a couple of years ago, I was going to give you a Suburban, wasn't I? But since that time I donated some money to 3ABN, so I won't be giving the Suburban!"

God had provided a nice van for the ministry, but it was nothing like a Suburban! Danny went home that night so deeply troubled he could hardly sleep. "Wouldn't it have been a beautiful story," he lamented, "if I had given away the van and two days later God provided a Suburban!" But the problem was, he hadn't given away the van as God had impressed him to do!

Then the Lord spoke to him. *All this time you thought you were doing My will, but you were really doing your own will. You were giving to people whom you thought were in need. But when I asked you to give the van to someone you didn't think needed it, you turned Me down. The Suburban was much more expensive, and it could have been yours! I don't want you to obey Me just when it feels right. I want you to obey Me all the time, even when it doesn't feel right.*

Danny was shaken. He deeply regretted the mistake he had made and repented. But his feelings of guilt wouldn't go away. At the International ASI Convention a few weeks later, Danny saw Reggie and LaChanda Dupard again. "I need to talk to you," he said. "You know that van you liked so much? Well, I owe you an apology. When you visited 3ABN, God told me to give you that van, but I was too stubborn. I made a terrible mistake. I want you to know that if you will come back to 3ABN, the van is yours."

The van is now being used to bring youth to Christ. The Dupards have also unselfishly volunteered their time and funds to travel to 3ABN and help develop valuable programming for youth. A few months after giving the van to the Dupards, Danny's friend who had thought of giving 3ABN a Suburban called to say that he was, in fact, giving the ministry a beautiful Suburban. A number of years later, he donated another one.

When Danny first told this story, he said, "I have no idea how this chapter in my life will end, but I do know that God has always provided for *all* our needs at 3ABN. And it amazes me how this happens. From across the world, God impresses thousands and thousands of His people every month to live by His principles of abundant living found in Acts 20:35, 'It is more blessed to give than to receive,' and Luke 6:38, 'Give, and it will be given to you.' I have learned that, indeed, it's more blessed to give than to receive—and if we give, we'll get. The result is that whether it's ten dollars or ten thousand dollars, these people keep the floodgates of God's resources open. Every month *there is always enough*. I remember how I felt in 1999 when I learned 3ABN's monthly transponder bill was approximately a quarter of a million dollars. *That's a quarter of a million dollars every month!* Can you imagine? The thought boggled my mind!"

Now, five years later, the monthly needs at 3ABN total almost a million and a half dollars. In addition, 3ABN has just upgraded its master-control equipment to digital format at a cost of more than two million dollars, and it is finishing a 48,000-square-foot worship center, where camp meetings and special evangelistic events can be taped in a facility that seats thirteen hundred individuals. The ministry will need another couple of million dollars just to equip that building!

Danny says, "Each month I thank the Lord for those who listen to Him and give as He directs. They must be getting a tremendous blessing. God is using them as a channel through which His resources can flow. And from personal experience, I want to encourage them, 'Don't stop the flow!' Keep listening to the prompting of the Holy Spirit. If we all live by God's principles of loving, cheerful giving, there would always be more than enough for everybody."

Danny ends the story by saying, "Although it was a number of months before the Suburban came our way, every day that I waited, I was reminded of the lesson I learned about my own willfulness. I resolved anew never again to make the mistake of not doing what God asks me to do just because it doesn't seem right to me! I want to always be a living example that, indeed, it is more blessed to give than to receive."

As Luke puts it, "Give, and it shall be given unto you: good measure, pressed down, shaken together, and running over. . . . For with the same measure that you use, it will be measured back to you" (Luke 6:38, NKJV). Or as *The Living Bible* paraphrases it: "For if you give, you will get! Your gift will return to you in full and overflowing measure, pressed down, shaken together to make room for more, and running over. Whatever measure you use to give—large or small—will be used to measure what is given back to you."

Six singing sisters and another van

And so Danny has continued to listen to God, and the blessings have continued to flow. In 2002, the Cadet family came to 3ABN from Utah so that their six little daughters could sing for *Kids Time*. Just before they were ready to leave Utah, the family almost canceled because they were afraid their old minivan, with 258,000 miles on the odometer, would not make it all the way across the country. They stood in a circle around their vehicle, prayed, set out in faith, and limped into West Frankfort with the transmission leaking fluid.

The girls worked long hours taping twenty songs, with dress changes in between. They did such a great job, even the littlest one! That very day, something else was happening outside the studio. Larry Welch came to Danny and said, "I've found this great van for almost nothing, and I'm thinking 3ABN should buy it." But Danny didn't think 3ABN needed a van.

Early the next morning, with their family packed like sardines in their old van, the Cadets were ready to begin their long journey home. Danny drove up just as they were leaving and stopped to thank them for coming. "I hear you girls did an awesome job!" As he complimented them, he noticed that their van had seen better days. As he turned to leave, he remembered the beautiful van Larry had found the day before. Once again God seemed to be saying, "Danny, give it away! Give it to the Cadet family." As the Cadets drove off toward West Frankfort, Danny hurried inside the office to call Larry. "Get that van over to 3ABN right now." Then he rushed to his truck, stepped on the gas, and rushed toward West Frankfort to try to catch up with the Cadet family. All the way into town, Danny frantically looked one way then the other, trying to spot their minivan. Nothing. He feared they might have already gotten on the freeway, and he had no idea which way they might have gone. Then, just before the freeway, in front of the auto parts store, he saw the Cadets' minivan. They had stopped to get more transmission fluid. Danny pulled into the parking lot beside them. "Excuse me!" he called to Eddy Cadet. "I really need to talk to you. Could you follow me back to 3ABN?"

They did. When Eddy got out of the van, Danny said, "Could I talk with you for a minute?" Danny led him out of hearing distance of the family and over to the new van. "The Lord has really impressed me to give this van to your family."

"What do you mean?"

"I believe the Lord wants you to have this van," Danny repeated.

Eddy was overwhelmed when he realized Danny was serious, and tears formed in his eyes. They went inside and did all the paperwork, signing the van over to the Cadets. Finally, Danny handed Eddy the keys. Eddy, still in shock, went out to tell his family.

The last thing Danny saw was that precious family of six little girls holding hands around their new van, praying. This time, it was a prayer of thanksgiving!

From personal experience, Danny's advice is, "Don't let selfishness, fear, or your own perception of another's need rob you of the blessings God has in store for you if you will just give as God impresses you to give—regardless of how irrational it may seem."

By the way, in the last few months 3ABN has been given two more motor homes and an extended full-size van. All three vehicles are being used full time in God's work by people or groups who are sharing their musical talents and testimonies throughout North America as unofficial ambassadors for 3ABN. Plus, they are providing valuable programming for 3ABN. The channel of blessing appears to be alive and well!

The rest of the story

But that's not the end of the story. To complete it, we must go back to the beginning. Do you remember Dale Smith? He's the man whom God impressed to give Danny the motor home when his family so desperately needed it. It was Dale that gave the original gift that has kept on giving for twenty years now.

Well, Dale eventually moved from Indiana to Johnston City (near West Frankfort) to be close to his parents. He worked as a heavy-equipment operator in the coal mines in Indiana and Wyoming and at times drove a truck locally to support his family of three children. But at heart, Dale was a singing evangelist.

Not long ago, Dale and Danny were reminiscing. Dale said, "I remember one time when my family was leaving on a trip to a Kenneth Copeland meeting, and you emptied out your pockets and gave me eighty-two dollars and some change! And one time you gave me a recording machine. Do you remember?" Danny nodded. "That was about a year before 3ABN started. And now, look at what God has given to you. Not only a worldwide satellite television network, but a state-of-the-art recording studio!"

Now let's pick up the story twenty years after it first began: In 2003, Dale once again felt God was impressing him to reconnect with Danny in a special way. At the same time, he was planning to go back to Wyoming to work and hold revival meetings for three months. His family would need a home away from home in Wyoming. He had a slide-out camper that would fit in the bed of his truck, but how much more convenient it would be to have a trailer that he could pull behind his truck and put in a trailer park at their destination.

Dale and his wife began dreaming, praying, and looking. At the local trailer sales lot, they found a perfect trailer. They loved the way it was laid out. But, alas, the price was far beyond their means. The only thing Dale could afford was the free brochure that had the floor plan in it. So he took that home and continued praying.

Why did Danny keep coming to his mind in the middle of the night while he was praying? And why did God keep impressing him about Seventh-day Adventist churches? One day Dale was looking up different churches on the Internet, and "Seventh-day Adventist" seemed to be highlighted. Could it be that someday he would be preaching in Adventist churches? He decided to call Danny and tell him about his upcoming trip to Wyoming and the impressions he was having. "I have meetings lined up in Assembly of God churches in Wyoming, but I'm having impressions about the Seventh-day Adventist Church. I haven't even been inside an Adventist church, Danny. Give me some information. What should I do?"

Danny changed the subject, "What are you going to stay in while you're in Wyoming? Could you use a trailer?" Dale could hardly believe what he was hearing. "When can you come over and take a look?"

Dale immediately drove to 3ABN, and Danny took him to see a twenty-six-foot trailer parked behind the administration building. Danny tried to open the door so Dale could look inside, but it was locked. "I'll go get the key," Danny said.

"No, that's all right," Dale replied as he peered in through the window in the door. "I already know what it looks like." It was the exact trailer, with the same floor plan, that Dale's family had selected—only better. This one was four feet longer, and the bathroom was bigger!

Danny said, "It's yours for as long as you need it," a phrase that sounded vaguely familiar to Dale!

Dale's family took the trailer to Wyoming. "We had no idea where to park it," he says, "so we asked the Lord as we drove into town to lead us to the right location. The first person we saw directed us to a place. Before dark we were set up, and I was ready to go to work the next day. We lived in that trailer all summer, as I worked during the week and ministered on the weekends. Then we brought it back to 3ABN for someone else to experience the blessing. God was certainly in that."

What's next? Dale says he doesn't know. "On February 2, 1975, I gave my heart to God, and I'll do whatever He tells me to do. Right now, I believe I'm hearing Him call me again. God seems to be impressing me to keep talking with Danny. I'm open to wherever God leads."

In December 2003, Dale began working at 3ABN as a cameraman. A few weeks later, he said, "Since my decision to work for 3ABN, incredible things have been happening in my life." And he can no longer say he's never been in an Adventist church!

God wants to do incredible things for you, too. Why not do as God asks you? Give unselfishly as God prompts you to give, and you will experience for yourself how God blesses those who bless others. A God-inspired love gift always keeps giving!

7

Flying for the Lord

"Therefore by Him let us continually offer the sacrifice of praise to God,
that is, the fruit of our lips, giving thanks to His name.
But do not forget to do good and to share,
for with such sacrifices God is well pleased"
—Hebrews 13:15, 16, NKJV.

When Danny accepted the call to ministry, he never counted all the costs. He instinctively knew that financial sacrifice would be required, and he was right. For the first couple of years of the ministry, Danny chose—for the viability of the ministry—not to receive a salary. There simply wasn't enough money for that luxury. Many times Danny and Linda wondered how they were going to put food on the table and pay the bills, but they never went hungry. God provided for their needs. Even after donations increased to the extent that they could be paid something for their work, it was always a conservative amount.

But a cost that Danny and Linda didn't consider was the sacrifice of their personal time. Leading out in this ministry was not an eight-to-five job. It was a twenty-four-hour-a-day responsibility from which they could never walk away. They no longer had a private life. Wherever they went, there was the possibility that they would be recognized. Since they traveled as ambassadors for the Lord and 3ABN, their first and foremost thought was for others, "How can we be witnesses for Christ? To whom can we minister? Is there a brokenhearted soul God wants us to encourage?"

That's why some of the most interesting contacts Danny has made for the Lord have been on airplanes. I've selected three such encounters, and I think you'll enjoy hearing about these in Danny's words.

It happened in July 1990 (as told by Danny)

It had been a long week. It was Friday, and I was tired. Linda and I were flying to Boston. It's always stressful to me having to drive into St. Louis, deal with the traffic, wrestle with our luggage, get checked in, and get to the right gate to catch a flight. We were in row 20, near the back of a half-empty plane. The flight attendants were getting ready to close the door. "Praise the Lord," I said. "We are going to be able to each get three seats of our own, and I'll be able to stretch out and sleep."

"But," said Linda, "I think we should pray that if the Lord wants us to witness to anyone that He will have them sit by us."

That's impossible, I thought. *There are so many empty seats on this plane. Someone would have to be crazy to sit down next to us when they could have a whole row to themselves.*

"Honey," I said, "I'm really tired. What I really want to do is stretch out and sleep."

"Well, I still think we should pray that if God wants us to minister to someone, that person will sit beside us." So we held hands and prayed.

Right before the door closed, a flight attendant got on the intercom. "Sit anywhere you like, but please sit down quickly. Another TWA flight has been canceled, and we will be boarding more passengers. This is going to be a full flight!"

I reluctantly scooted over into the middle seat to leave the aisle seat for someone. People started boarding the plane—good-looking people in business suits. Then I saw him—all 312 pounds of him! He was standing up front with bleached-blond kinky hair, chains around his neck, huge rings on his fingers, and scars all over his face. He was the biggest, meanest looking man I had ever seen. "Linda," I said, "see that hulk coming down the aisle? I just bet he's going to take the seat next to me!"

I began offering the empty seat to some of the slimmer, well-dressed people who were coming down the aisle, but they either sat down before they got to our row or passed me up! "Everyone likes aisle seats! What's wrong with us?" I said to Linda.

Sure enough, you guessed it, this huge man bent over the seat next to me, lifted the arm rest because he couldn't possibly have fit between them, and plopped himself down next to me taking nearly half of my seat. I scooted over closer to Linda, but we were still packed in like sardines!

I whispered to Linda, "I wonder if he's going to split the cost of my seat!"

"Honey," Linda reprimanded me, "we asked God for someone to witness to when it seemed highly unlikely anyone would sit next to us. Now God has answered our prayer. I think you should talk to him."

By this time the man was buried in a newspaper.

"Hi. How are you doing?" I made a feeble attempt at a conversation. In response, I got a major sigh like air being let out of a balloon.

I waited a little bit and tried again, only to have him put his finger on the place he was reading, look my way, and sigh again as if to say, "Would you leave me alone!"

Finally, I turned to Linda. "This guy is definitely not receptive."

"Do you think it's a coincidence," she reminded me, "that this man is beside us? Please try again."

I gathered my courage and asked, "Is Boston your home?"

"No!" came his booming reply, and he turned back to his paper. He was obviously not going to get into a conversation with me.

"Don't give up on him," Linda chided.

"Do you want to trade seats with me so you can talk to him?" I asked her.

"If we hadn't prayed a special prayer, then I would say to give up. But I know God has sent him to you."

"I bet he's a professional wrestler," I thought looking at his bulk and his scars.

When they brought us chicken sandwiches for lunch, I turned to him once more trying to be friendly, "My wife and I are vegetarians. Would you like our sandwiches?"

"Why would I want to eat three sandwiches?" he scowled at me.

"I just know that we aren't going to eat them," I said meekly.

"Well, I don't want them either. I have my own." And once again he turned away.

"Linda, that's it. This isn't going to work."

"Let's have another prayer," she suggested. So we whispered a prayer. I'll admit, my faith was not very strong at that moment. Linda prayed. "Lord, we know You allowed the other plane to break down for a reason. Give Dan the wisdom to penetrate this man's heart."

Halfway through the flight, someone came by and asked the giant next to me for his autograph. I knew then that I was probably right about his profession.

"What kind of work do you do?" I asked.

Once more, he sighed that gigantic sigh, turned to me, and said, "I don't work. I just fly around for the fun of it. My father's rich." His speech was heavily punctuated with words I wouldn't want to repeat!

"That's interesting," I replied. "My Father's rich, too."

He locked in on me then. "What did you say?"

"My Father's rich, and I fly around a lot, too."

He slammed his paper down at that point. Then he turned toward me as best he could since we were crammed into our seats, raised his bushy eyebrows, and said, "Oh, really! Who is your father?"

"Look out this window," I said.

"I am looking out the window."

"My Father owns everything you see down there."

"Where are we?" he asked.

"It wouldn't matter," I continued. "My earthly father is dead. But my heavenly Father owns everything, and I'm an heir to His kingdom!"

"That's really interesting," he said. "I have never heard that before."

"We haven't gotten along very well," I said apologetically and started to introduce myself.

"I know who you are," he said. "I've seen your face on TV before. And I didn't want to be preached to today. That's why I've been so rude."

"What kind of work do you do?" I tried again.

"I'm a professional wrestler in the WWF (World Wrestling Federation)." When he told me his name, I recognized it. He had been a professional wrestler for almost twenty years—and a very successful one! He was known in wrestling circles around the world.

I then told him a little more about our ministry. He commented, "This is really interesting. Last week, I was going to Alaska and sat next to a Seventh-day Adventist minister. Today, I'm sitting by two more Adventists."

He then went on to explain, "The reason I'm so upset is that I usually sit in first class. I don't like people bothering me since I'm a celebrity. Second, I sit in first class because I'm too big for this seat—as both of us know. I weigh 312 pounds. This was the only seat I could find. So here I am, sitting in the back of the plane, with two Christian evangelists. That's why I'm not in a good mood!"

"To be real honest with you," I said, "Linda and I are to blame for you being back here in this seat."

"What?" he exclaimed. "Does your Father own the airlines, too?"

"In a sense, He controls everything," I admitted.

"How is He responsible for me sitting here?"

I then told him about our prayer that God would have someone sit next to us who would be receptive to accepting Jesus as their Lord and Savior. I told him how I wanted to rest and how right after we prayed that prayer, the announcement was made that passengers from another flight would be boarding our plane. "But to tell you the truth," I admitted, "I didn't feel like sharing my seat with someone as big as you!"

We laughed.

I continued, "That chain of events led me to be bolder than I perhaps should have been. So, if you have a need for Christ, today is the day."

"I really do," he admitted. "I've been mad at God for a long time. When I was four years old, my father died. They told me he is still in purgatory because we didn't have enough money to get him out. After that, I secretly rejected a God who would take my dad away from his family and punish him like that."

After just a short explanation of what the Bible says about the state of the dead, his face lit up and he said, "That really makes sense!" This man who seemed so bristly on the outside turned out to be very sensitive and open to spiritual things on the inside. He finally said, "I guess it's about time I got rid of all this bitterness."

"Would you like to ask Jesus to come into your heart?" I asked.

He nodded. Linda and I held his hands and prayed with him. I have no idea what the people around us must have thought to see that big tough guy with tears in his eyes.

Linda then asked him if he would like to have a book. She pulled out *The Great Controversy*. "That looks like an awfully big book," he said. "I don't know if I'll get through all that or not." Linda then told him about some of the historical facts he would find in the book. He said, "I'll take it and read it."

"You need to remember me in prayer," he said. "This is a tough life. What I would like to do someday is come to 3ABN and give my testimony. Even in my business, I don't do drugs. I'd like to talk about it on your station. Here's my home phone number," he said as he began writing on the back of a picture of himself in his wrestling suit. "Any time you're in north Dallas, please come by and visit me."

We got off the plane. He hooked up with another professional wrestler with whom he traveled. "These are friends of mine," he said as he introduced us. The other wrestler didn't say a word!

Someone started pointing a video camera our way. Obviously, they were wrestling fans. "We are in your video," I said. "Linda, let's get out of the way."

"No sir, you stay in the video with me," he said as he looped his massive arms over our shoulders and smiled at the camera. People immediately gathered around. "Who is it?" I heard someone in the crowd ask. "It's Danny and Linda Shelton from 3ABN television," the person taking the video replied.

This startled the wrestler. "I'm sorry," he said. "We'll get out of *your* video."

"No, you stay right here," we said.

I've thought about our wrestler friend a number of times and once called his number. A woman answered and said he was late for an appointment, but that she'd ask him if he could talk. "There's a Danny Shelton on the phone, do you want to take it?"

"I'll take it," he said.

"Do you remember me?" I asked.

"Sure, I do. I've been watching you on TV and reading your book." I knew he was rushing out to an appointment, so we spoke for only a few minutes. At the end of our conversation he said, "I really appreciate you calling. Keep me in your prayers." And we've done that.

Isn't it interesting how God engineers situations to bring into your life just the person He wants you to meet? I wonder how many times He does that, and we're oblivious to the opportunity because we're more focused on meeting our own needs rather than on meeting the needs of someone else.

It happened in August 1992 (as told by Danny)

About six of our 3ABN staff were returning with Linda, Theresa Boote (see chapter 16), and me from the International ASI Convention in Palm Springs. I went up to the airline counter at the gate to try to arrange seating so that we could all be together. I was especially looking forward to visiting with Theresa on the long flight across country and learning about all the contacts she had made.

But after three days at ASI hearing all the wonderful testimonies about sharing Christ, Theresa asked, "Why would we all want to sit together? I think we ought to try to witness. Let's split up and ask God to bring us the people He wants us to witness to and have them sit beside us."

We prayed and with anticipation began to wonder whom God would seat next to us. Linda and I were in the row just behind the bulkhead seats. The plane was almost full, and still the aisle seat next to ours was empty. Just before the doors closed, a well-built man with long hair came down the aisle. He was wearing gold necklaces, large diamond rings on his fingers, and a black leather jacket. I immediately said to Linda, "He's in a rock band."

"How do you know?" she questioned.

"Just look at him. It's obvious."

There were only two seats left in our section—the one next to me and one in the front row. He sat in front of us. Then a woman stepped out of the restroom, came down the aisle, and tapped the fellow on the shoulder. "This is my seat, sir."

He apologized and said his seat was the one behind, but thinking this one was empty, he sat in it because of the extra leg room. As he buckled himself in the seat next to me, I thought, *This is going to be interesting!*

"Hi. How are you doing?" I broke the silence.

"Fine."

"That's good," I nodded.

Since we had just prayed, "Lord, send us someone receptive to You," I decided I had better get on with the business of talking to him.

"What kind of work are you in?" I asked, knowing without a doubt he was part of a rock band.

"I'm with the Colts."

"Oh," I said, "is that a rock band?"

"No," he said, smiling, "I'm with the Indianapolis Colts. That's a football team."

Now, I really felt stupid. If he had said "Indianapolis Colts" I might have caught on, but I was obviously blinded by my own perception of the man.

"What position do you play?" I asked.

"I'm a receiver. I normally fly first class, but this is the best seat I could get on this flight. I'm just starting to work for the Colts. I'm on my way to Indiana to pick out a house to rent until we can buy a place."

He asked me what I did, and we started talking. I told him all about 3ABN and the miracles God was working for this ministry. He said he was raised a Baptist, but something happened, and he blamed God. Eventually, he quit going to church and got into football.

I commented, "God puts us where He wants us. I believe He's given you good hands and fast legs not just to catch a football, but to give you credibility with people, especially young people. Young people need good role models. Just think about all the lives that could be changed for the good, if you were still serving the Lord."

"I've thought about that so many times," he replied with a sad look on his face. "I'm not really happy with my life right now, even though I'm making good money. I was much happier as a nine-year-old in the Baptist church. My life seemed more fulfilled then."

"If you would like," I offered, "Linda and I will pray with you. We have all sinned and come short of the glory of God, but we are saved by grace. All we have to do is repent, and God will do the rest."

"I would really like that," he said. So we held hands, and I prayed. There were tears in his eyes when we finished.

During the three-and-a-half hours we had been talking, I hadn't really paid any attention to the people around us. The person in the middle seat in front of me had reclined his seat so all I could see was his ear, but I hadn't thought anything about it. We landed, and the person in that seat got up, turned to us as we began to gather our things, and said, "You know, this is the most interesting flight I've ever been on. I'm a professor of theology at a university. I have been one of those who don't subscribe to modern-day miracles. I have believed that miracles ended when Christ died on the cross. After listening to your entire story, I've been thinking about 3ABN. Maybe we do serve a God who is working miracles today!"

Wow! I thought. *We prayed for one receptive person to sit beside us, and the Lord gave us two!*

It happened in June 1999 (as told by Danny)

It took sixteen hours for us to travel from our home in Thompsonville, Illinois, to Medford, Oregon—a trip that should have taken eight hours. Our flight was late getting out of St. Louis, so by the time we got to Denver, our flight to San Francisco had left without us. United Airlines rebooked us for a later flight, but that meant we missed our San Francisco connection to Medford, which was the last flight of the day. We had to speak the next day in Medford for the eleven o'clock church service and for an afternoon meeting. We were scheduled for an evening meeting in Grants Pass. We couldn't wait until the next day for a flight to Medford. So, in San Francisco the airline routed us through Portland with twenty-five minutes to make a connecting flight back to Medford.

By the time the flight to Portland closed the door and taxied out to the runway, Linda and I were laughing about our misfortunes. But that was only the beginning. The captain announced that there were six flights on the tarmac in front of us, so we'd be there for a short delay. Every minute that ticked by meant one less minute to get to our connecting flight to Medford. Then, when we were number one to go, for some reason they decided to close the northbound runway. We waited again. When they reopened the runway, they said they had a number of international flights that needed to go first. We ended up sitting on the tarmac for another twenty minutes! Obviously, we weren't going to make our connection to Medford, which meant another three-and-a-half hour wait in Portland for the next flight.

Everything seemed to be going wrong. We began to joke between the two of us about our situation. I tried to make a phone call from our seat, only to discover the phone was broken, and I had to borrow the one from another row. To make matters worse, we were in the next to the last row of the plane, so by the time one of the attendants who was handing out snacks got to me, she said, "I'm sorry, sir, but we've run out of snacks." That was too much. Both Linda and I were laughing hysterically by this time.

Finally, Linda said, "Honey, I'm so glad I married you. You are the greatest entertainment anyone could have. I'm in stitches. I don't need a TV. I don't need a radio. I don't need computer games. As long as I'm with you, you're the only entertainment I need."

"Well, I'm glad I'm good for something," I replied, laughing.

I had noticed the guy sitting across from us when we first got on the plane but had no idea he was watching us and listening to our laughter, until he asked, "Are you trying to get to Medford, too?"

We shared a little of our story. Then he said, "I have my own story." He told us that he started from Ventura, California, for the Los Angeles airport two and a half hours before flight time, but he got caught in traffic. Even though he arrived at the airport before his flight left, he had to return a rental car. Then because he was too late to get his luggage checked, he carried it to the gate, only to discover that because it was oversized they didn't have room for it in the cabin of the plane. It had to be checked on the next flight—and he would have to go with it. So he, too, had missed his connection and had ended up on this flight.

He was wanting to get to Medford so that he and his wife could go rafting the next day. He explained they both traveled a lot and really cherished their time together. "This traveling, with its delays, is really bad news!"

"I know," I said. "I travel a lot, too. I was in Switzerland two weeks ago, now Oregon, and next week I'm leaving for New Guinea."

"What is your work?" he asked.

"I work at a Christian television network."

"What network?"

"3ABN."

"3ABN?" he commented in surprise. My in-laws watch 3ABN day and night, and so did my parents. "What are your names?"

"Danny and Linda—"

"Shelton, isn't it? I've seen you on TV. Whenever we visit my in-laws they have it on all the time. I think they are wanting to convert me, or they're hoping something will rub off!"

He then began to tell us his story. "I was raised in the Adventist Church, but I never saw a happy Christian. My home was a very sober, legalistic one. My father had an addiction. He felt he wouldn't go to heaven unless he overcame it. To counteract the habit, he would pass out books and preach to people on the street. He'd try to kick his habit for a while, but he would always slip back. His overwhelming guilt made him feel crazy. Eventually, he had to be committed to a mental institution. There was no laughter, happiness, love, or joy in my home. That's why I'm so surprised to meet Christians like you folks who are so happy. It's amazing you can even laugh over all the bad things that have happened to you on this trip."

"I think being a Christian is the most exciting, happy thing that can happen to a person," I commented.

The man continued, "My wife and I don't go to church anymore—even though we believe the doctrines. Instead, we have our own ministry of feeding over a hundred people every week. This is so much better than being in a legalistic church."

"That's great to feed people, but you could do that, be happy, and still attend church."

The idea of being a Seventh-day Adventist Christian and being happy was so difficult for him to put together that he asked, "I know you are the president and vice president of 3ABN, but are you Seventh-day Adventists?"

We assured him that we were. Then he commented, "Well, you're my kind of people!"

When we got to Portland, we had a three-and-a-half-hour layover. We talked the whole time. At one point he phoned his in-laws. When he came back, he exclaimed, "I'm the envy of the family now. They can't believe that I'm on the plane with Danny and Linda Shelton and have all this time to talk and fellowship. A bad trip has turned out to be a blessing. They are really envious of me."

Before we landed in Medford, I said, "I know you're planning to go rafting tomorrow, but if you get a chance to come to church, we'd love to see you and your wife." He said they might be able to come to the Saturday night service but made no promises. That's why I was shocked to see them in church the next morning. They came again to the Saturday evening meeting where I made an appeal. That night he and his wife took their stand for the Lord. They said these meetings were just for them. And it all started with two Christians on the plane laughing because of the bad things that were happening to them!

Someday I'm going to ask my guardian angel how many angels it took to engineer that meeting. It must have taken dozens to snarl up the traffic, to delay planes, and to have airlines book us for flights with impossible connections. Being a Christian is the most exciting, happy way of life there could possibly be!

8

Danny Shelton
Off-Camera—and On

"A relaxed attitude lengthens a man's life; jealousy rots it away. . . .
Wisdom is enshrined in the hearts of men of common sense"
—Proverbs 14:30, 33, TLB.

If you could follow Danny Shelton around for a day, you would find a dedicated, hardworking, fun-loving, Christ-centered man who has the unique ability to make everyone he meets feel special. He carries on his shoulders the responsibility for a worldwide ministry with an annual budget in the multimillions, but you'd never know it by the way he treats people. Danny never makes you feel that he's rushed, although you know he has zillions of things to do—phone calls to return, letters to answer, papers to sign, people to interview, and problems to solve. Nor does he dress to impress. If you drop by 3ABN for a visit, Danny will be the guy running around in his boots and 3ABN baseball cap. He doesn't act like a celebrity. There's not a pretentious bone in his body. Danny is simply that gospel-singing, hometown country boy from the coal-mining region of Illinois, grown a little older and a little wiser over the years.

Danny has a passion for people. His thoughts constantly are centered on what others need to make their lives a little better and how to help them find a closer relationship with the Creator of the universe. He sees potential in people. He offers opportunities—not based on résumés and degrees—but on Holy Spirit-inspired impressions. And people grow under such circumstances. They find talents they didn't know they had. They begin doing things for the 3ABN ministry that they would have never imagined they could do.

Danny loves to talk. He is never at a loss for words—as you may have noticed watching him on television—and he always has a great story to tell. But you may not have realized that under that fairly serious television persona is a crazy character who delights in joking with his friends, playfully teasing, pulling pranks, and making people laugh. He's the happiest, most optimistic Christian you'll ever meet. He's just plain fun to be around.

That's why most people have no idea that Danny lives with what Christians might term a "thorn in the flesh"! For decades, he has suffered incredible back pain. Sometimes it's difficult for him to walk, and sometimes sitting for long periods of time is almost more than he can bear. Like the apostle Paul, Danny has prayed to have it removed. Physicians and specialists have examined, prescribed, and manipulated. Sometimes it helps; sometimes it doesn't. But the pain has never been fully removed. Yet Danny understands that God knows what is best for him.

God never removed Paul's "thorn in the flesh" so that he would not be "exalted above measure by the abundance of the revelations." Paul's response was to proclaim, "Concerning this thing I pleaded with the Lord three times that it might depart from me. And He said to me, 'My grace is sufficient for you, for My strength is made perfect in weakness.' Therefore most gladly I will rather boast in my infirmities, that the power of Christ may rest upon me" (2 Corinthians 12:8, 9, NKJV). Other servants of God, such as Martin Luther and Ellen White, had chronic health problems that helped them maintain an attitude not only of humility but also of total dependence upon God. So without complaining, Danny lives with pain, knowing that God's strength is made perfect in weakness.

Danny may not have academically-earned degrees,[1] but God has gifted him with wisdom. He isn't intimidated even by courts of law. In fact, he seems to enjoy whatever comes his way, which can sometimes unnerve people who are control freaks or who have an agenda. Because his confidence comes from the Lord, he doesn't have to play games with people. While others may wilt with criticism or worry about winning strategies, he has the assurance that God is in control, so he rolls with the punches and always comes out standing on his feet.

Who else but Danny would *enjoy* being a witness in court and have so much fun answering the opposing lawyer's questions that at the end of the hearing the judge actually *gave* him the witness seat? Yes, it's for real.

Danny goes to court

If you've ever been cross-examined in a court of law, you know that most opposing attorneys try to get what they want through subtle (or not so subtle) intimidation. Witnesses, therefore, usually dread being interrogated. Danny wasn't really looking forward to it, but he had nothing to hide and was happy to talk about 3ABN. He was confident that the ministry, a nonprofit 501(c)3 religious organization, should not be assessed property taxes for buildings used for ministry. So Danny got to the courtroom early and was sitting in the witness seat before anyone else arrived.

But when it was Linda's turn, she was so scared that Danny didn't think she was going to be able to speak. He felt for her. He wanted to lighten things up and make her feel more relaxed. And he knew what usually worked. So as soon as she was sworn in, Danny said, "Hey, Linda," and began to sing, *"I'm happy in the Lord anyway . . ."*

The opposing attorney objected. Danny ignored her. "Linda, harmonize with me," he said. And together they sang, *"And it really doesn't matter what comes my way today, I'm gonna wear a smile and hold my head up high and say, I'm happy in the Lord anyway."*

When they finished singing, the judge had a smile on her face, "Thank you very much for that," she said. Later, Danny learned that he could have been thrown out of court for his actions, but the judge understood what Linda was going through. Graciously, the judge allowed him to lighten up the oppressive courtroom atmosphere for Linda's sake.

At the end of the hearings, the judge said, "There's just one more item of business . . ." and that's when she gave Danny the witness seat, saying, "I have never seen anyone enjoy being a witness so much. So, I think you deserve to take the seat home."

"You mean, it's mine?" Danny questioned.

"Yes," she said, "you can take it home now, if you want."

The above example wasn't exactly a typical day in Danny's life! But regardless of what happens, you'll never hear him complaining. You'll not read any more in this book about the legal harassments or power plays Danny has endured from entities wanting to take advantage of 3ABN. Nor will you find in these pages an account of the friendly fire 3ABN has taken from individuals who had their own ideas about how things should be run and weren't above criticizing, threatening, and delivering ultimatums. The fact is, Danny gets his orders from the Lord, and when he is convicted of a certain principle or plan of action, all the elephants in Thailand can't move him. He simply does what He feels God wants him to do, and God blesses.

Almost everyone who has gotten to know Danny has a story to tell about him—something crazy he's done or some unusual act of kindness. These stories give an inside view into the private life of the public person you've grown to love and admire over the years. And Danny's not above telling a few stories on himself. So sit back, relax, and enjoy getting to know Danny Shelton off-camera—and then laugh at some of his on-camera bloopers.

Giving away lawnmowers!

One summer day in 2001, as Danny was driving past a certain house, he had a strong impression to go home, get his new twenty-four-horsepower riding lawnmower that he'd purchased less than a year earlier for three thousand dollars, and give it to this neighbor! It didn't make any sense. They had merely a passing acquaintance, but Danny knew the man already had a riding mower; he'd seen him on it recently. What would the man think? Besides, Danny needed the mower himself. What would Linda think if he gave it away?

When he arrived home the impression became stronger. *Go get your mower and take it to your neighbor.* Danny doesn't hear voices, but he has grown accustomed to doing what God impresses him to do, even if it seems rather strange. So he went to the barn, cranked up the mower, and drove it down the driveway. Suddenly, he was impressed that he should clean up the mower before giving it away. *Wait a minute,* Danny thought, grinning, *it's bad enough giving it away. But, Lord, do I have to clean it up first?*

So Danny gave it a good washing until it looked like new, dried it, and started down the road to his neighbor's house, feeling a little foolish. He had never socialized with this man before . . . and now, to come calling on a lawnmower? It did seem rather strange!

The neighbor and his wife were outside washing their car when Danny drove up. "What can I do for you?" he asked. Danny blurted out, "I've been impressed to give you my lawnmower."

The man looked startled and replied, "You must be kidding!"

Danny went on to explain that he wasn't the type of guy who goes around hearing things, but the impression that he should give this man his lawnmower was very strong.

What happened next was totally unexpected. Tears welled up in his neighbor's eyes as he shook his head in disbelief and said, "You can't mean this!"

The man's wife spoke up, "You have no way of knowing that in the last few months my husband has quit drinking, and we have really tried to turn our lives around since we've been watching 3ABN. But since we've tried to become Christians, several bad things have happened to us. So much so that we wondered if we had done the right thing. We agreed that if we could just be given a sign, it would help us continue cleaning up our lives. Then just this morning, the engine on our lawnmower blew up. It seemed almost like the last straw, because we didn't have the money to fix it. I began to question whether or not the Lord really did love us."

The man added, "You couldn't have known about this, since it just happened a little while ago. You will never know what this means to us." Danny glanced toward the open barn door, which he couldn't see from the road, and saw that the lawnmower had been taken apart where the man was trying to repair it.

Danny hadn't known that these people were watching 3ABN. But it would have made no difference. Once again, God proved that He knows what He's doing—even if it doesn't seem rational to us at the time.

Danny delivers God's message

Not long after 3ABN began broadcasting, Danny received a call from a man who had been watching the programs. He identified himself as a deacon in a church in San Diego. He wanted to pay for Danny and his family to come there to hold meetings. As they made arrangements, Danny had the impression that he should tell the man that God cared for him and would help him stop smoking. But it didn't make sense to tell a deacon in the church something like that, so he didn't say anything.

All night, Danny wrestled with the thought that he should have said something. The next morning, Danny called the secretary of the church and asked her if she knew the man who had called him. "Yes," she replied, "he's a deacon, and we have been close friends since he joined the church a few years ago."

Danny hesitated. He really didn't want to ask about the smoking. Surely a deacon wouldn't have a smoking problem. Finally, Danny blurted out, "Do you know if he smokes?"

There was silence on the other end of the line. After a few seconds, the secretary asked, "Why do you want to know?"

Danny explained that the Lord had strongly impressed him to tell the man that God cared for him and would help him stop smoking. He didn't want to say anything, however, if the man didn't smoke.

Again there was a pause. Finally, the secretary replied, "Yes, he has had a very difficult time giving up his smoking habit, but hardly anyone knows. I think you should tell him what God has impressed you to say."

Danny called the deacon and gave him the message. The man was surprised. They prayed together. And from that time on, the deacon was never again tempted by tobacco.

Cutting up in NYC

Ruben Carr, Jr., tells of his encounters with Danny in 2002 and 2003:

When I first met Danny, I was intimidated. After having watched him so much on TV, seeing him in person was a shock. I felt about Danny as many people feel about pro football stars. Never in my life would I have ever believed that I would have the opportunity to spend some time with a television personality I admired so much. After all, I came from a poor, dysfunctional background. Most celebrities wouldn't give a person like me the time of day. Yet, I found an instant friend in Danny. Every time we are together our time is filled with jokes and so much laughter our stomachs hurt!

One time, as we were driving the streets of New York City, Danny asked John Lomacang and me to teach him how to be black in Brooklyn. We told Danny to cross his arms, look serious, and say, "What you lookin' at? You want a piece of me?" Danny practiced again and again until he could do it without laughing. That night, he went up on stage at the rally in front of all those black folks in the church where John Lomacang had grown up. He said, "Ruben and John have been teaching me how to be black in Brooklyn." He crossed his arms and said, "What you lookin' at? You want a piece of me?" and the crowd roared in laughter.

Another time John and I were showing Danny and Darrell Marshall, who is also white and from West Frankfort, around New York City. Danny and Darrell began acting like the Beverly Hillbillies in a big city. "Look at that highway. I bet there are two hundred cars a day that goes on that highway!" one said.

"Naa," the other replied, "not dat many."

"Look at that Empire State Building, it must be a hundred feet high, you think?"

"Naa, it ain't dat high."

"Hey, over there's the Statue of Liberty. You reckon dat's the real one?"

"Naa, the real one's in North Carolina."

When we came to a toll station. I started to pay. Darrell stopped me. "No, we'll pay," and he shoved six dollars my way. "Now," he said to me, "you guys go out to some fancy restaurant for a big steak dinner." (As if six dollars would pay for more than a couple Big Macs!) We howled with laughter!

During that visit to New York City, Danny was up on the stage surrounded by black church leaders. Darrell Marshall turned to me and said, "This is the best seat in the house. Man, look at Danny up there with all those black people. He looks like a hundred-watt light bulb!" I nearly cracked up!

Basketball stories

Danny loves basketball. Tuesday night is basketball night at the Thompsonville Christian School gym. It would have to be something pretty big to make Danny miss it!

Steve Darmody, gospel singer and Danny's good friend, is head and shoulders taller than Danny. He's been trying for years to beat Danny on the court. Steve might have a chance if Danny would ever get close to the hoop, but he delights in frustrating his opponents by making three-point shots from quite a distance. And Danny enjoys rubbing it in by pointing out that he beats Steve in spite of his height.

One time, Steve brought his twelve-year-old daughter, Jaclyn, to 3ABN to do some recording. Danny challenged Steve and Jaclyn to a game of HORSE*. Guess who won? Jaclyn did! Danny had met his match!

One day, Danny challenged a professional basketball player to a game of HORSE. He had come to do an interview at 3ABN. The guy probably looked at Danny's five-feet, eight-inch frame and thought, *No sweat!* But Danny beat him. I wonder how this professional player explained to his colleagues that he got beat by a short, fifty-year-old grandpa playing basketball in cowboy boots?

Grandma's homemade buns!

Tammy Larson tells about a time she was behind one of the cameras taping a cooking show. The guests began to reminisce about what they remembered from their childhoods about cooking. Someone asked Danny, "What do you remember best about your grandma?" Without hesitation, Danny replied, "I remember Grandma's big old buns." Tammy burst out laughing. Danny then realized what he had said. He looked over at Tammy behind the camera and said, "Your thinking's in the wrong place!" and the show went on!

Oh, nuts!

Danny was playing around with his little three-year-old grandson, Noah, getting ready for a live program with him. Danny said to Noah, "Say, 'Oh, nuts!' " And when Noah did, Danny would give him a kiss. They played the game again and again. Then it was time for the broadcast. The countdown was made. Thousands were tuning in to this broadcast from around the world. The problem was, Noah didn't know the difference between goofing around before the program—and the real thing. So, as the cameras began to roll, Noah piped up, "Oh, nuts!" Danny reached down and kissed him as if nothing unusual were happening. A few seconds later, Noah said again, "Oh, nuts!" Once more a kiss! By this time the camera crew was in stitches, but trying not to laugh out loud. Noah did this about

---

*HORSE is a game where if one makes a basket, the other has to make one from the same place or he gets a letter from the word HORSE. The first person to get all five letters loses.

three more times before Danny was able to get him onto something more appropriate for the program. It should be good footage to play at Noah's sixteenth birthday!

Be careful what you ask!

It happened on one of the early interviews. Richard Bland from United Prison Ministries had brought some ex-convicts who had been converted by watching 3ABN. They were to be interviewed on a live program. A woman by the name of Bertha, probably in her fifties, was sitting on the end of the couch. Danny established that she was from Alabama. Then he said, "I can tell by your beautiful smile that you probably only did one thing bad in your entire life."

"No, sir," she responded, "that's not right. I did many things."

"How long were you in prison?"

"Twenty-three years, sir."

"Well, what could you have ever done to end up in prison for twenty-three years?"

"I killed my preacher!"

Her answer caught Danny off guard, and surprise registered on his face as he replied, "Well, I want to make it clear that I'm not a preacher!"

"That's OK," she said, trying to help him gain his composure, "I don't kill preachers anymore!"

Wasp survivor

During a live program in 1989, a wasp started to buzz around Danny. Tension gripped the control-room staff, but they couldn't do anything but gasp when the wasp landed on his shoulder and began a slow walk toward his neck. Danny kept talking as if nothing had happened. He usually leans forward when he talks, then leans back when others speak. When the wasp disappeared from view, the control-room staff could just imagine what was going to happen next. Danny would lean back, crush the wasp, and get stung.

But nothing happened. As soon as the program was over, everyone came unglued. "Where'd the wasp go?" they wanted to know.

"It was walking around my ear and inside my shirt the whole time," Danny explained.

Belly crawling for the Lord's work

Danny has learned to be pretty comfortable on camera and not to become distracted by what may be going on around him, especially during live broadcasts. Then came the day when something needed to be fixed in front of the set, just below the view of the cameras. The only way to get to the problem without being seen on camera was to belly crawl across the floor. At first Danny kept a straight face as one of the staff began crawling. But as the crawling continued across the set, Danny lost it, started laughing, and had to explain to the audience what was happening.

Danny's bodyguard

In 2003, Danny took his cousin Donnie to the Adventist-Laymen's Services and Industries (ASI) International Convention. Since Donnie would be representing 3ABN on a number of assignments, Danny was introducing him to various people. Donnie happened to be dressed in a black shirt, had a shaved head, and wore sunglasses, so he looked quite impressive. At one point, someone overheard Danny jokingly say, "This is my bodyguard. I take him everywhere I go." The next thing he knew, word had spread throughout the convention that his life had been threatened and that he had to have a bodyguard with him at all times! If you happened to be one of those who heard the rumor, you now know that the only person wanting to do away with Danny is the devil . . . and it's prayer that Danny needs, not a bodyguard!

Vice presidential pardon?

In 1988, Danny attended the National Religious Broadcaster's convention (NRB) in Washington, D.C., where his good friend and fellow musician Wintley Phipps was scheduled to sing. It was the same general assembly in which Vice President George Bush was to make an appearance. Danny had a little time to kill, so he asked directions back to where Wintley was waiting.

He was given fairly complicated directions, involving taking an elevator to another level. As Danny came out of the elevator, he found himself face to face with the vice president of the United States! Both were shocked to see the other! Within seconds, six Secret Servicemen pounced on Danny, spread-eagled him against the wall, and searched him for weapons. Danny tried to explain that he was a friend of Wintley Phipps and had been given directions that brought him down on the elevator. He tried to make it clear he had no idea the vice president was there. The Secret Service agents didn't seem inclined to believe him.

Just then Danny saw Wintley and yelled, "Wintley, tell them I'm your friend and was coming to see you."

Because Wintley enjoys joking around, Danny was afraid he might say, "I don't know the guy!" But thankfully, Wintley realized the seriousness of the situation and explained who Danny was. Reluctantly, the Secret Service let him go.

When complete honesty didn't pay

Danny has made numerous mission trips to India, Bangladesh, and Hong Kong—to mention just a few countries. But it was Cuba that was almost Danny's undoing! Flying from the United States, American citizens must have special permission to visit Cuba; it takes a ream of paperwork. However, entering Cuba by flying from Cancun, Mexico, is legal and relatively easy. So the tour leader had taken the group into Cuba via Mexico. The key is to not mention when you re-enter the United States that you have been on what U.S. officials consider to be forbidden soil. This announcement was made to the tour group. Unfortunately, Danny didn't hear it. So when he headed through U.S. Customs and the official asked, "What countries have you visited?" Danny mentioned a few—including Cuba. The customs official looked surprised and asked him to go to another line. The next customs official started interrogating Danny, "So, you went to Cuba? What did you do there? Can I have your paperwork?"

"Paperwork? What kind of paperwork?"

"Paperwork that gives you permission to go to Cuba."

"I didn't know I needed permission."

"Do you have a passport?"

"Yes."

"Well, if you look inside, you'll see that you're not allowed to go into Cuba without special permission."

Danny replied, "Sir, I have car insurance, but I've never read all the small print in the policy. And it never occurred to me to read everything in my passport."

"What did you buy in Cuba? Cigars?"

"No, just four little T-shirts for my grandchildren."

"No cigars?"

"No, I don't smoke."

"What about for your friends? Did you buy any for them?"

"No, I love my friends more than that. I don't want to kill them!"

Finally, the customs official said, "Well, I'm going to let you go this time, but your name is being put on a list. If you ever do this again, we will prosecute you to the full extent of the law."

Danny was relieved when they finally let him go. Later, he laughed as he recalled the incident. "Next time, I think I better listen more—and talk less!"

Danny's airport angel

Danny, Bob Ellis, and Gonzalo Santos were on their way to Romania. Their flight from St. Louis was late getting into Chicago. On arrival, Danny was running down the concourse looking for flight information. He had no idea where the departing gate was for their flight. Suddenly, a big black man, with a couple of front teeth missing, asked, "Do you know where you're going?"

"Tarom Airlines!" shouted Danny.

"I know exactly where that is. Follow me." The man picked up one of their suitcases and began running. A few seconds later he took another suitcase to balance his load and led them right to the gate. He wore no uniform that would indicate he was an airport employee, and when Danny offered to pay him, he declined. "I'm just happy to help you," he said.

On their return from Romania, the flight into Chicago was late again, which meant that their connection was going to be very close. The group had a number of suitcases to take through customs before rechecking them on the domestic flight to St. Louis. Danny grabbed two or three suitcases, leaving Bob and Gonzalo to bring the rest. He planned to run ahead and try to hold the airplane for them.

But when Danny got to customs, the official gave him a hard time. "Are those your bags? Open them!" Rarely did this happen. When Danny finally got through customs, the TWA rechecking service had closed, so he had to carry his luggage to the gate—and it was nearly flight time.

"Can I help you?" a big black man asked. "Where are you going?"

"Gate G3!" Danny yelled.

"I know where that is, and I think I can get you there on time." He picked up a suitcase and started guiding Danny through the busy terminal. It wasn't until the man smiled as he turned to leave that Danny noticed his missing front teeth.

Quickly Danny learned that Bob was already on the plane, but Gonzalo was not there yet. "Sir," said the flight attendant, "you need to get on the plane. We're shutting the door."

"Please wait just a minute," Danny urged. "One of our party is missing. He should be here any second."

"Sir, it's FAA regulations. . ."

Just then a man came running around the corner, and the attendant was satisfied that the missing person had arrived. But the man ran past the gate. "That isn't your guy?" asked the surprised flight attendant.

"No," Danny admitted.

Just as the attendant made it clear that she could delay the flight no longer, Danny saw Gonzalo. "There's my guy!" he shouted. This was just enough of a delay to keep the attendant holding the door open.

It wasn't until Danny and Gonzalo were safely on board that Danny realized that the black man who had directed them to the right gate on their flight to Romania was the same person who had helped them find their gate on their way home. Danny says that when he gets to heaven he knows what his guardian angel is going to look like. He's going to be a large black man with a couple of front teeth missing!

---

[1] On May 11, 1997, Danny and Linda were granted honorary Bachelor of Arts degrees in Communications from Union College in Lincoln, Nebraska.

Section III
3ABN Stretches to Reach the World

" 'Go therefore and make disciples of all the nations,
baptizing them in the name of the Father and of the Son
and of the Holy Spirit,
teaching them to observe all things
that I have commanded you;
and lo, I am with you always, even to the end of the age' "
—Matthew 28:19, 20, NKJV.

In 1987, the 3ABN signal was being beamed up 22,300 miles at the speed of light to a satellite blanketing the United States (and beyond) with twenty-four-hour-a-day programming. The first phase of the task that had started with Danny's call in 1984 was accomplished—the North American uplink phase.

The second phase, the North American downlink phase, took place during the next five years. The small, hardworking, dedicated team of 3ABN workers pushed themselves to establish downlink sites in North America by building television stations and a network of cable carriers. In addition, a large variety of English language programs were produced at 3ABN. But the mission to reach the world was just beginning.

In 1991, 3ABN began the third phase: reaching the world. Politics, especially the fall of communism, played a major role in what happened next at 3ABN. Romania's dictator, Nicolae Ceausescu, was ousted. Board member May Chung, chomping at the bit to reach the world, nudged 3ABN to establish a television station in that war-torn country.

Then in 1992, as Russia opened up, 3ABN stepped in to build a television production studio and the largest Protestant evangelism center in the former Soviet Union. The detailed story of 3ABN in Romania and Russia is in chapter 9.

In 1996, Europe came online as 3ABN broadcast Mark Finley's Net '96 evangelistic crusade in eight languages. Results were impressive. For example, in war-torn Croatia, twenty-six churches had 312 baptisms, and in "post-Christian" Germany, there were 303 baptisms from 145 downlinks. Since then, more dishes have been installed, many countries are now receiving 3ABN through cable, and television and radio stations are being established. In 2003, 3ABN was added to cable in Denmark and Iceland and began airing on full-power radio stations in Iceland. 3ABN-France is now a reality where a new remote-production truck has been built. And there are plans to build a studio in that country that will produce French-language programs that will meet the needs of the Muslim population, as well as those in French-speaking Africa.

As time on earth moved into the new millennium, 3ABN began broadcasting to Asia and the Pacific Rim countries. You'll read the detailed stories of 3ABN-Philippines and 3ABN-Papua New Guinea in chapter 10.

But, Thailand has a story too. In 2003, Owen Troy reported that in Pattaya, Thailand, 3ABN was on a cable company reaching a potential audience of seventy thousand nationals and also a number of luxury hotels with guests from around the world. Other cable systems have also come on board.

3ABN has now formed a new corporation called 3ABN-Thailand, with the goal of opening a translation and production center. At first, they will be translating two hours of 3ABN programming each day into the Thai language and hope to soon be producing local programming. There is also the possibility in the future that 3ABN will be available via cable in many more locations.

3ABN's outreach has exploded in recent years.

In 2003, 3ABN became available via cable to the U.S. Virgin Islands of St. Croix, St. Johns, St. Thomas, and Water Island. 3ABN can also be heard on radio on a number of these islands.

As 3ABN Latino began broadcasting in 2003, downlink stations and television production studios began in a number of countries. Within a few months of 3ABN Latino's debut, every Spanish- and Portuguese-speaking country except Paraguay, Uruguay, and Cuba had already established cable connections. In 2004, Paraguay and Uruguay had 3ABN on cable.

And then there is India, where, in 2001, 3ABN was added to the cable lineup in the city of Ongole, with a potential viewing audience of one million. It happened when Danny approached the cable company after a fifty-village evangelism blitz in which 3ABN, Maranatha, Global Missions, Seventh-day Adventist layman Bob Paulsen, and the Garwin McNeilus family combined their efforts. The result was fifteen thousand baptisms!

Then in 2004, a major contract was signed with Siti Cable company. This contract means 3ABN is now available in the forty-five largest metropolitan areas in India, reaching a potential viewing audience of one-quarter billion people! That's a lot of people! This contract, alone, tripled 3ABN's potential world-viewing audience. No wonder God impressed Danny that the 3ABN theme for 2004 should be "You haven't seen anything yet!"

In March 2004, Australia and New Zealand suddenly became wide open to the gospel as the people "down under" were able to get a clear signal as 3ABN added its feed to their Optus B3 satellite. It is estimated that eight hundred thousand viewers already have these free-to-air satellite dishes, and the praise reports are pouring in to 3ABN!

And what about Africa? In 2000, 3ABN International sent Owen Troy to Africa to share the possibilities of downlinking 3ABN. In many countries, the process began of incorporating and applying for licenses to establish 3ABN television stations. Other countries have made cable arrangements, and the work is going forward!

In 2004, 3ABN-Nigeria signed a contract with Trent TV, the second largest small-dish direct-to-home service, making 3ABN available to over eight hundred thousand homes in western Nigeria. In the next year, 3ABN-Nigeria will be expanding to southern and eastern Nigeria, reaching an additional one million homes! And some 3ABN programming is being aired on national television in Africa—

especially during late-night hours—because 3ABN was willing to pay for the equipment, making it possible for these stations to get the 3ABN signal without cost. They have found that a large percentage of those who are desperate for answers watch TV late at night.

In addition, Mugonero Adventist Hospital in Rwanda now has a dish, so patients and staff can benefit from 3ABN. The hospital is planning to establish a television studio to produce programming in French and is applying for a license for a low-power station that will make 3ABN available to every home in the community with a television set.

Throughout Africa, dishes are now being installed not only at private homes but at churches and pastors' homes. In the absence of rebroadcasting capability, people who have access to a satellite dish are copying 3ABN programs and sharing them with others. Many are opening their homes for their friends and neighbors to come and watch. The interest and momentum are building.

We can't talk about Africa without mentioning the work of Enoch Mogusu, who lives in Kenya but is busy installing dishes throughout Africa. He also trains metal workers how to construct satellite dishes from local materials. It's amazing. After two days of instruction, his students are able to build their own dishes and get excellent signal quality!

Enoch tells an interesting story about installing two dishes on the metal roof of a woman's house about 140 kilometers from his home. He had arrived at about four in the afternoon and needed to finish the task quickly because rain was threatening. The angle of the roof made the installation seem impossible, yet because of the tall trees surrounding the property, there was nowhere else to put the dish. After praying, the gardener brought a tall ladder and placed it so that it leaned against the roof at the same angle, making it possible to climb to the top. Enoch had only an hour to complete the task because the gardener would be leaving with the ladder.

Enoch reports: "As I nailed the last cable saddle in place, the rain started, and it was time for the gardener to leave. I went into the house just as the homeowner's daughter came home. She lived in a cottage behind the main house. The daughter asked if she would be able to receive the signal in her house. Since her system got its signal from the main house, I said it was possible and went with her to adjust her television so that she could tune in to the 3ABN channel. As I worked, the daughter began telling me about some of her problems. I listened and suggested we pray for guidance from the Lord.

"The next morning around eight o'clock, the telephone rang, and the daughter thanked me for installing 3ABN. She was extremely happy with the content. Then she dropped the bombshell. She informed me that prior to talking to me, she had decided that suicide was the only way out of her problems. She was planning to kill herself that night before her husband returned home. But after watching 3ABN, she changed her mind. Six weeks later, she again phoned me and told me how 3ABN had changed her life and that of her family. She and her husband had reconciled their differences, and she was now expecting their second child."

The third phase of 3ABN's mission—reaching every country and language group with the gospel message—will end only when Jesus comes in the clouds of heaven. This is the exciting phase in which 3ABN finds itself today! As we go to press, letters and emails have come to 3ABN from the far corners of the world. A sample of the countries heard from includes Afghanistan, Australia, Bahrain, Botswana, China, Cyprus, England, France, Holland, India, Indonesia, Iran, Iraq, Israel, Italy, Kenya, Kuwait, Nepal, Portugal, Qatar, Saudi Arabia, Scotland, South Africa, Switzerland, Turkey, United Arab Emirates, and Zambia. A number of letters from Iraq say that since the country is in turmoil, all there is to do is to sit at home and watch TV. 3ABN has become their "church."

Although I have sketched a quick overview of the worldwide work of 3ABN, two fascinating stories need to be told in detail because there are just too many miracles associated with them! The first is the saga of 3ABN's work in the postcommunist countries of Romania and Russia, and the second is the tale of 3ABN in the Philippines and Papua New Guinea. As you read, you'll shake your head in wonder about how it all happened. And if you're anything like me, you'll want to shout "Praise the Lord!"

9
Reaching Romania
and Russia

"And a vision appeared to Paul in the night.
A man of Macedonia stood and pleaded with him, saying,
'Come over to Macedonia and help us.'
Now after he had seen the vision,
immediately we sought to go to Macedonia,
concluding that the Lord had called us to preach the gospel to them"
—Acts 16:9, NKJV.

The apostle Paul had plenty to do in Asia Minor where he was preaching, but when the call came to reach people who had never had an opportunity to hear about Christ—people from the country of Macedonia—he immediately made preparations and went!

The call from Romania and Russia in the early 1990s could be considered a modern-day Macedonian call, since for decades these countries had been denied the freedom to hear the gospel message. Have you ever wondered where the ancient country of Macedonia was? It was north of Greece. Interesting, isn't it, that Romania and Russia are also north of Greece! Borders have changed over the centuries, but a section of Romania today is considered to have been a part of the ancient country of Macedonia!

As communism fell in Romania, the call came to 3ABN, "Come over to Romania and help us!" A year later, as the Soviet Union collapsed, another call came: "Come over to Russia and help us!"

Reaching Romania

It has always been 3ABN's policy to move forward in faith as God opens doors—until those doors close. That's pretty much the story of 3ABN in Romania. The call came in 1991; it appeared the doors opened, and 3ABN moved forward to establish a presence in a country that had been denied religious freedom for decades. Over four hundred large dishes were installed on Adventist churches throughout the country so that the people could downlink 3ABN programs that would help them grow spiritually and bring them vital lifestyle information.

It soon became evident, however, that to really reach the people, programming had to be developed in the Romanian language. To do that, a television studio was needed. And plans were made for a television station to be established. Space was made available in an Adventist building in Bucharest. 3ABN viewers gave over $250,000 to send equipment to Romania. In August 1992, 3ABN sent Gonzalo Santos and his family to Romania to supervise and train eight local workers to set up the necessary equipment and obtain the appropriate permits needed for a local television station from Romanian government officials.

The problem was timing. 3ABN was in Romania before Romanian law allowed for the nongovernmental ownership of television stations. It was thought the laws would soon be changed, but weeks went by with nothing happening. Eventually, licenses were issued with four construction permits, but some of the church leaders still weren't ready to move forward. So, in spite of the prayers, the hard work, and the generous donations of many, the doors that at first seemed open began to close. In 1993, a decision was made to move 3ABN's television equipment to Russia, where there was an immediate need for producing programs for Russian television.

Romania had already been active in developing important radio programming; this continued, and although 3ABN initiated the television work in Romania, God called others to produce programs for Romanian television stations. 3ABN's role has been to provide Romanian translation for all the important evangelistic crusades that have been broadcast on 3ABN. Jozsef Palhegyi, who was one of the first 3ABN employees in Bucharest, even moved his family to the 3ABN worldwide headquarters in Illinois to provide this important service.

Seventy-five thousand people attended the Net 96 meetings in Romania at 419 downlink centers throughout the country. They heard evangelist Mark Finley in their own language, broadcasting live on 3ABN, resulting in many baptisms.

None of this would have been possible without the pioneering work of 3ABN in Romania. In a way, it could be said that 3ABN's presence in Romania paved the way for 3ABN-Russia.

Reaching Russia

In June 1991, Russia held its first democratic election. In August came the coup of '91 when President Boris Yeltsin, standing in front of the White House in Moscow, faced down the communist tanks, banned the Communist Party from Russia, and confiscated its property.

Late in the fall of that year, just a month or so before December 25, 1991, when Mikhail Gorbachev resigned as president of the Soviet Union and it ceased to exist, John Carter, speaker/director of *The Carter Report* television ministry, came to 3ABN for a Thursday night *3ABN Presents* program. Just before the start of the live broadcast, John enthusiastically told Danny about what had been happening in his ministry during the last few months.

"The Lord has put a passion on my heart to take the gospel message to the Russian people who have for so long been denied Bible truth," he said. "Last April, when I gave an evangelistic series in Moscow's Palace of Culture, Pastor Peter Kulakov, a church leader in Russia, talked to me about booking the Palace of Congresses at the Kremlin for another series in 1992. I was excited about the opportunity, and before leaving the country, I put down a deposit on the hall. Can you imagine holding an evangelistic crusade and preaching Christ in the Kremlin!"

He continued, "Months ago, I contacted General Conference officials, who said they would make arrangements with the local church leaders to get the rest of the deposit paid. They have assured me that this is a wonderful idea. And I'd like 3ABN to accompany us and tape the entire series. The problem is, we don't yet have the funds needed to hold this crusade."

Danny was immediately caught up in John's enthusiasm. "An evangelistic crusade in the Kremlin? That's tremendous!" Danny exclaimed. "When our listeners hear about this, I think they will want to help." During the last half of the live program, John and Danny talked about John's dream to preach in the Kremlin. Immediately, calls came in pledging the amount needed—and more!

A few weeks later, John was awakened at 6:30 A.M. by a phone call telling him the shocking news that the church administration had decided that it would be best if someone else held the meetings in the Kremlin.

"What?" John questioned. "That was my dream!" He was told the church wanted another television evangelist to hold the first series of meetings in the Kremlin.

"But," replied John still in shock, "we have already raised the money."

"You can go to another city," they suggested. "For example, there's the town of Gorky, now called Nizhny Novgorod. It's 250 miles northeast of Moscow on the Volga River. During the communist years, Westerners were not allowed to visit this strategic industrial area where the MIG fighter jets and nuclear submarines were built. Since the people there have never heard about Christianity, probably not very many will come to the meetings. But it is the third largest city in Russia with a population of three million, if you count the surrounding area."

Understandably, John was disappointed. But if you believe God is ultimately in control, disappointments like this become divine opportunities for God to use you in ways and places that you may have never chosen yourself. God had an incredible work for evangelist John Carter and 3ABN to do in Nizhny Novgorod. Only God knew how receptive the people would be. And God already had leaders in high places that could open doors of opportunity to 3ABN that would be almost impossible to open in any other location in Russia. God had *big* things in mind, far bigger than John or Danny had ever dreamed! Far bigger than the Kremlin!

In January 1992, John Carter visited Nizhny Novgorod to make arrangements for the meetings. In May, he went back, accompanied by 3ABN's camera crew, to hold the evangelistic crusade. No one was quite prepared for what they experienced the first night of the meetings.

The Carter Report had rented the Palace of Sports, which seated six thousand people. A few weeks before the meetings started, television advertising had begun. The archbishop of the Russian Orthodox Church in the area was livid when he heard about the meetings. He went on the air telling people not to attend. But his warning backfired. Since communism had just fallen, the people considered themselves free to make their own choices. No longer would they let someone, not even the archbishop, tell them what to do. In fact, his threats and condemnations aroused their curiosity, and the people flocked to the meetings by the thousands.

That first night when Danny, Linda, and a local American journalist, Bob Ellis, approached the Palace of Sports, there were only a dozen cars parked in the lot, yet ten thousand or more people were milling around outside the building. Danny wondered why the security guards hadn't opened the doors so the people could go in and be seated. What the 3ABN group didn't understand was that there were already seven thousand people inside the building! It was impossible for any more people to get in! The parking lot was empty because in 1992 only a few people in Russia owned a car.

John held three meetings that first night, each lasting an hour and a half. He spoke to more than twenty thousand people, and still a thousand or more waited outside the building badgering security to let them in. Finally, a security guard on the inside yelled at the crowd, "Go home. There will be no more meetings tonight. Come back tomorrow night." An old fellow in his seventies began beating on the window, yelling back at the security guard, "We've been waiting for seventy-three years to hear about God. Let us in. We demand you let us in. We can't wait any longer." Some people began to ram the back door. Soon all the doors were broken. Security guards came with dogs. Soldiers were sent to control the crowd.

After thirty nights of meetings, six thousand people accepted Christ. On the final Sabbath, a baptism was planned in the cold Volga River. People were bussed and trucked to the site, and even though twenty-seven pastors baptized people as quickly as they could, the baptism took four hours. A total of 2,532 people were baptized.

John conducted another six-week series in Nizhny Novgorod in 1993, followed by another one in 1994. As a result, more than five thousand converts were added to the Seventh-day Adventist Church in this city in just three years—a city where it was predicted that very few people would attend evangelistic meetings!

The miracle of money for the 3ABN Russian Evangelism Center

After that first series of meetings, Danny recognized that the church in Nizhny Novgorod had a problem—they had built it too small! How would the little group provide church services for more than 2,500 new converts when the current building seated only 250 people?

Danny asked the church officials to meet with him in a Russian hotel the morning he was scheduled to fly home. He went down to the lobby about twenty minutes early. An older man—maybe in his seventies—came up to him carrying a tape recorder. "Hi, my name is Manny Trefz from California. You don't know me, but I've watched you on 3ABN. Please tell me about 3ABN so that I can record it and share it with my friends."

"I'm sorry," Danny apologized. "I have a meeting coming up in a few minutes. Are you with the Carter campaign?" (*The Carter Report* team had brought fifty lay people from the United States and Australia to help with the meetings.)

"Yes," the man replied. "I just felt compelled to come. I thought I could hand out Bibles or usher, but so far I haven't felt I was needed that much." Tears welled up in his eyes.

Danny talked to him for fifteen or twenty minutes until the Russian church leaders arrived. As Manny turned to leave, Danny was impressed to ask him to join their meeting.

Danny immediately got to the point as he sat down with the Russian church leaders. "You have baptized 2,532 people. Your church holds 250. What are you going to do with all these people?"

"This is a good problem," the leaders agreed, "but we have no money to build another church. We have fifty-six million people in our territory to reach, and our evangelism budget is the equivalent of six thousand U.S. dollars a year. We spent three thousand of that to buy a bus to transport the people. That doesn't leave much for a church!"

"How much would it cost to purchase a large abandoned building—one that could be renovated into a church that would seat a couple thousand or more people?" Danny asked. He had noticed that there were a number of such buildings in the city.

"Maybe a hundred thousand dollars. But we could never raise that much money."

When the church leaders mentioned a hundred thousand dollars, Danny remembered the thousands of dollars viewers had pledged when they heard about the series of meetings in the Kremlin. He was certain God could impress the people once again. All he had to do was go back and let 3ABN viewers know the need. He mentioned that possibility to the Russian leaders. They looked astonished at the very thought.

At the end of the meeting, Manny, who had been quietly listening, spoke up, "I think I know why God brought me to Russia," he said thoughtfully.

"Why is that?" Danny wanted to know.

"I'll give the hundred thousand dollars needed for the building."

Danny couldn't believe it. Had he heard correctly? After he confirmed with Manny that he, indeed, was willing to commit the entire amount needed to purchase a building, Danny turned to the Russian church leaders and said, "We don't have to go back to the United States to raise the money. This man," he pointed to Manny, "will give a hundred thousand dollars."

It was a heartwarming experience. Everyone was in tears. What had seemed like a chance meeting had been ordained of God. What if Danny hadn't stopped to talk with Manny? What if he hadn't invited him to sit in on the meeting? What a blessing would have been missed!

The Russian leaders began to search for a building. In August, Danny went back to Russia to look at a possible facility. The building the leaders had selected was a huge structure on eight acres; it had been planned as a Palace of Culture for the workers of a nearby metal factory. The original plans had called for a movie theater, a gym, and facilities for various social and educational activities. Construction had begun fifteen or twenty years earlier, but the metal factory never got enough money to finish it. The bottom floor was dirt, and trees had grown up inside; the roof and walls were unfinished. You could look right through them. But Danny envisioned not only auditoriums where church services could be held, but space for a medical clinic, health-food store, community services, activities for youth, and, most importantly, a television studio where 3ABN-Russia could produce programs in the language of the people! The building was purchased for a hundred thousand dollars.

Governor Boris Nemtsov and Julia Outkina

To understand the significant part God wanted Dr. Julia Outkina to play in His plans for Russia, we must go back to that first series of meetings that John Carter held in Nizhny Novgorod. At the end of the six weeks of meetings, John Carter told Danny, "Governor Boris Nemtsov has summoned us to a meeting with the archbishop of the Russian Orthodox Church at the governor's mansion. There has been a complaint over the large number of people who have been baptized."

After asking God for wisdom, John Carter, Bob Ellis, Danny, and a cameraman went to the meeting. The governor began, "The Orthodox Church is upset because you are holding meetings and baptizing Orthodox members who have already been baptized when they were young. Don't forget, you are a minority. Russia is an Orthodox country. The Orthodox Church was persecuted during the years of communism, and we need to protect our historical and cultural roots."

John Carter rose to the occasion with holy boldness and replied, "Governor Nemtsov, you pride yourself in being democratic, and your territory is the first in Russia to privatize business, which is a good thing. But do you know what a real democratic government means? It means that you undertake to protect the rights of minorities. You have a responsibility to ensure that Seventh-day Adventists, as well as other religious groups, have the right to hold religious meetings. You must make sure that each person has the right to worship without fear of reprisal from the government or the Orthodox Church. No one should be persecuted because they chose to attend the meetings."

The governor asked, "What can you give the people that they don't already have, Mr. Carter?"

"Sir, I'm glad you asked. Since I have been here, I have received six thousand letters from people who have been attending the meetings. Here is one that I received last night, written in beautiful English by a local citizen. I believe it can provide an answer for you."

He then read the following letter:

"*Pastor Carter,*

After attending the meetings for several weeks, I now feel as though I have been brought out of darkness to marvelous light. I know there is a God. I have learned to love Him in a personal way and know that He loves me. This is life-changing for me. Thank you for coming."

The governor was not too impressed. "So . . ."

Pastor Carter continued, "Maybe I should read the name of the person who wrote this letter. It's signed by Julia Outkina."

The governor gasped. "Are you sure it is Julia Outkina?"

"Do you know her?"

"Yes, she's my sister!"

After that, the governor's entire attitude changed. He looked at the archbishop, then at John Carter. "People," he said, "we have to learn to live together. We want a democratic society here. We want to help ensure that the people have equal rights."

Then he addressed the two opposing parties: "Mr. Carter. Archbishop. Stand up, shake hands, and hug each other while the newspapers take pictures. If you can't work together, our big enemy, communism, may come back. And none of us wants that." He then turned to John Carter and said, "We will uphold your rights."

Governor Boris Nemtsov kept his promise, and he proved to be very supportive of the work of 3ABN! The governor had already opened the door to private ownership, long before most other areas of the former Soviet Union had done so. As a result, he brought Western and foreign money into his city. Twelve other unfinished buildings in Nizhny Novgorod, like the one purchased for the Adventist Church and 3ABN facility, were privatized that year. However, the 3ABN facility turned out to be the only one that succeeded and is still going strong. All the rest couldn't get through the rigorous red tape that was required. Danny commented, "Governor Nemtsov proved to be a great friend and a very caring person."

Through the influence of Julia, his sister, Governor Nemtsov learned much about God's law and was very favorably impressed by the positive influence of the Seventh-day Adventist Church on Russian society with its health and family messages, programs against drugs and alcohol, prison ministries, and teaching people high morals and practical ethics. In 1998, Governor Nemtsov rose in the political ranks and moved to Moscow to become the first deputy prime minister of Russia under President Boris Yeltsin.

Julia Outkina, with a Ph.D. in linguistics and a specialty in English, has made a profound contribution to 3ABN-Russia. In fact, without Julia and her supportive family, it is very likely that the following story might never have happened.

Julia came to the meetings in 1992 just to hear English spoken. Prior to that time, she hadn't had a chance to meet any Americans or practice speaking the English language because Nizhny Novgorod was closed to Westerners. The Americans who came for the Carter campaign were among the first Americans to go to that city after the communist ban was lifted.

After attending the meetings for a few weeks, Julia began to feel a new spirit moving within her, and she was overwhelmed with the presence of God in her heart. After she accepted Jesus Christ and was baptized, and after the work began on the abandoned building that was to become the 3ABN Evangelism Center, Danny told her, "I'd like to hire you as a translator. How much are you paid as a professor of English?"

"I make fifteen dollars a month," she responded.

"I'll pay you twenty-five," was Danny's quick reply.

"Oh, no," she countered, "fifteen dollars is a good salary. I don't want to make more working for the Lord than what I would be paid working for the government."

And so from the very beginning of the work in Nizhny Novgorod, Julia was there, translating, and then organizing, directing, and dreaming of the day when 3ABN could start producing television programs in the

Julia Outkina, whose involvement has been so crucial to 3ABN's work in Russia

newly built Russian studio. 3ABN-Russia would not be what it is today without Julia Outkina as the director.

Russian television production starts

3ABN-Russia began producing Russian television programs in 1992. There was no studio and no professionally trained staff. All Julia and her team had was a dream and a small high-8 video camera. With that little camera they taped interviews, sermons, children's stories, and musical selections. They taped wherever they could, in churches or apartments. They sometimes took three different takes at different camera angles, so in the final editing it would look like they had three cameras, instead of just one! Then Julia gathered up the tapes and headed to 3ABN's headquarters in West Frankfort, Illinois, where the segments were edited. None of the United States production staff understood Russian, and yet they seemed to instinctively know when it was time to roll in a segment or when to change camera shots as Julia was taping her intros and hosting the programs. Once the cameras started taping, they almost never stopped until the shoot was completed. In addition, the editing went amazingly well.

Armed with finished programs, Julia headed back to Russia to find television stations on which they could air. One small station in Nizhny Novgorod finally agreed to air her thirty-minute program each week for six weeks. A free offer of a Bible was made at the end of each program. After the first program aired, 3ABN-Russia received over a thousand letters requesting free Bibles. The station was stunned at this response. Not even the big local stations got that kind of viewer response from their most popular programs! Soon they were asking for more programs, until they were airing Adventist programming for a total of three prime-time hours each week. Eight years later, the smallest television station in Nizhny Novgorod had become the largest! God blessed!

Alexei and Anna Ronzhin and Alexei Budnikov were among the first Russian workers—and they are still actively involved with 3ABN-Russia. Alexei Ronzhin became an excellent editor; Alexei Budnikov worked magic with the camera; and Anna helped in administrative areas. Over the years, 3ABN has brought a number of Russian workers to the United States to be trained. Most of the Russian 3ABN workers were baptized as the direct result of the John Carter meetings or the presence of 3ABN in their country.

In April 1996, five years after building began, the television studio in the 3ABN Russian Evangelism Center was completed. Now, instead of taking the tapes to the United States for editing, the staff began producing their own programs. In 2004, there were thirty-seven full-time employees, taping more than twenty different series of programs on theology, family, health, children's programs, youth, poetry, and nature. The programs air free of charge on 186 television stations and two satellite channels in the former Soviet Union, reaching a potential audience of 54.5 million people! One hundred thousand adult Bibles and eighteen thousand children's Bibles were given away in the first years. Two of Danny's books, *The Forgotten Commandment* (on the Sabbath) and *Does God Love Sinners Forever?* (on the state of the dead and hell), have been translated, and five thousand copies have been given away. In addition, untold thousands of Bible-study courses have been sent out. In the middle of the Bible-study course, the people are offered a free book, *Steps to Christ,* and at the end, a Bible. Much of this literature is printed in four-color at the 3ABN-Russia facility.

Currently, 3ABN-Russia syndicates its programs, marketing them with a short promotional tape to the various television stations. Julia says with a satisfied smile on her face, "We are competitive! But I'm convinced, it's not our skills or our hosts that make our programs so popular; it is the hunger of the Russian people to know God and His Word."

3ABN pays the salaries of the Russian employees and provides equipment. The staff of 3ABN-Russia, then, works with the Russian church leaders and lay members to produce the programs. The flagship program in Russian, *Face to Face,* is hosted by Julia. She interviews people who have meaningful testimonies or who can offer helpful information on lifestyle topics. As a result of this ministry, the number of baptisms continues to increase.

Valeri Nikitiouk, president of the Volga-Vyatka Conference of the Seventh-day Adventist Church (the local conference in which Nizhny Novgorod is located), reports that in the year 2000, since the 3ABN Russian Evangelism Center had been built, the conference has expanded from twelve local Seventh-day Adventist churches to fifty-seven, and the membership has grown from two thousand to well over seven thousand.

In 2000, the Russian-produced television programs began to be broadcast two hours each week on RenTV, a satellite station in Moscow. Moscow has a potential viewing audience of about 11.5 million people! A number of local television stations even downlink the 3ABN-Russia programs and rebroadcast them. The 3ABN-Russia programs are the only regular Christian programming that is produced in Russia for the Russian people by Russians in the Russian language and available for Russians. God is stretching the reach of the good news to multiple millions of souls through these programs.

Building the 3ABN Russian Evangelism Center

Now we must backtrack once again to pick up the story of the building of the 3ABN Russian Evangelism Center. After 3ABN purchased the abandoned building, journalist Bob Ellis returned to Russia with Danny, excited to see the magnificent structure that Danny had described to him. Bob's reaction when he saw the building is worth quoting:

I was appalled, utterly devastated by the broken-down condition of the structure. Yes, structure. I wouldn't dignify it with the aesthetic description "building." It was horrible! Knowing Danny's keen sense of humor, I even allowed mo-

The new 3ABN Russian Evanglism Center is the largest Protestant center in the entire former Soviet Union.

mentarily for the possibility that this was an extravagant practical joke on me, that we would back the car out and drive to the real location. But no, this was indeed the "magnificent" grounds and building that he had been so excited about back in America. . . .

The building was big, for sure, but all ground floors were dirt and mud inside the building. There were wooden planks to walk on to avoid most of the quagmire, but where there were no such hastily devised walkways you were left to your own devices to negotiate the interior layout. Such as it was, the building seemed endless, three floors high with cavernous areas in its bowels. The sky was visible from virtually every unfinished room in the structure. I wanted to just plop down (in the mud) and weep. I was certainly in no mood to patronize Danny. When I frankly expressed my disappointment and trepidation about the daunting technical problems of construction, not to mention the monumental cost of working in a foreign city where equipment and material were rationed only to government agencies and projects, he was not offended in the least. That is because he had worked out all of these problems and details and patiently explained it all to me.

As he looked around him, at his "magnificent structure," he said simply, "God will provide. . . ."

Today it can arguably be described as one of the most magnificent privately owned buildings in all of Russia that is dedicated to improving the quality of the lives of Russian citizens. It is teeming with people who, through the center today, become educated in many skills, as well as learning good health habits. Healthful cooking and eliminating alcohol and drug abuse is taught. . . . Young people can find sports and other healthy activities at the center and in the process many of these people find God, too (*A Channel of Blessing,* pp. 208-210).

The 3ABN Russian Evangelism Center is the largest Protestant center in the entire former Soviet Union. This building houses a television, radio, and music production center with an adjoining office complex, two large auditoriums for church services, offices for the local Seventh-day Adventist Conference, and guest facilities. The Russian people truly see this center not only as a demonstration of the love of their brothers and sisters in America but as a demonstration of the love and favor of God!

To really understand the miracle that it took to transform this "structure" into a "building," let's turn again to Bob Ellis's firsthand account of the renovation process:

Through the incredible indomitable spirit of those that believed in the project from the start and who were willing to lend backbreaking labor, an inspiring transformation has taken place. This all happened in a city of shortages where such basic items as light bulbs and toilet paper were unavailable, and the tools of construction and basic building materials were as rare as hens' teeth. If the workers wanted ten tons of sand from point A to point B, they formed a human bucket brigade. The elderly men and women who worked side by side with younger workers most often peopled these lines. Even to get materials to the upper floors this ancient "human chain" method had to be used. One story especially accentuates the lack of available working tools and building materials. On one occasion Danny said he needed some brooms. A couple of workers started off toward the woods. They scoffed at the idea of simply "buying" brooms even though money was available. There were no such sweeping devices to be found in stores in the city, and the workers, as they always did, were going to make their own (pp. 211, 212).

Danny recounts another typical experience early in the construction process when eight people with hammers and chisels were trying to "drill" some holes through the seven-inch concrete roof. These holes were needed every two feet for about eighty feet. At the rate they were "drilling," it would have taken forever! Danny asked them why they didn't buy a drill. The answer was, "It's too expensive!"

When Danny suggested that he would give them the money to go to a lumberyard and buy one, as we would in the United States, they looked surprised. Lumberyards were unheard of in their country. They did know, however, where they could find a drill. But again, they stated that the price would be prohibitive.

"How much?" Danny questioned.

"Maybe as much as ten or fifteen dollars," they replied.

Danny immediately gave a man fifteen dollars and the "drill hunter" took off across the field to the road to hitch a ride. After a few hours, he returned. He had found an electric drill at another construction site for ten dollars and gave Danny the change. There was no tracing the purchase and no receipt!

In the early 1990s, very few people in Russia had transportation, so a lot of time was wasted going for supplies. Danny decided the project needed a full-time person just to provide transportation. He flagged down a car he thought was a taxi. The man seemed pleasant and spoke a little English, so Danny asked, "Do you work for a cab company?" When Danny learned that he owned his own car, Danny offered him a job six days a week, nine hours a day, to provide transportation for the project at thirty dollars a week, plus the cost of fuel at seven cents a gallon. The man said he would think about it. Danny gave him a phone number where he could call back if he was interested. To Danny's surprise, he called back. "I have talked to my wife, and I will agree to do it."

When Danny returned to Russia the next time, he asked what happened to the driver. Danny was told: "The man you hired was an aeronautical engineer and was the head man in the MIG jet factory. He was a genius and had spent three years in the sixties in Cuba setting up Fidel Castro's defense system. The money you offered him was so much more than he made at his job in the factory that he took a leave of absence to work for us for a while. He's now back working at his old job."

It didn't take Danny long to realize that strong, savvy leadership was needed on the construction site. So he asked his cousin's husband, John Kantor, one of the best professional construction men he knew, if he would consider going to Russia for a "few months" to oversee this project. John tackled the challenge with enthusiasm and ended up spending three years there. In the process, he learned the Russian language so he could better communicate with, and gain the respect of, the hundreds of Russian workers—both paid and volunteer—that it took to turn a deserted structure into one of the most magnificent buildings in Russia.

The 3ABN Russian Evangelism Center was formally dedicated on February 28, 1998, and at the grand opening ceremony, the Lord performed a beautiful miracle. Julia's mother, a retired physician and who at the time lived with Julia's brother, Boris, was not as sympathetic about the center as was Julia. It had taken six years of hard work before the evangelism center was finished. Julia's mother, then in her seventies, was not a Christian, and she had been unhappy over the large amount of time and energy Julia had been dedicating to the Lord's work. However, since Julia had begged her to come to the dedication, she agreed to attend for her daughter's sake.

At the conclusion of the morning meeting, Julia approached Danny and asked him to pray for her mother because she was stooped over with back spasms and was asking Julia to take her home. Julia's mother did not believe in the power of prayer nor did she want to get involved in any such thing, but she finally agreed for Danny, Julia, and David Everett to pray for her. At the conclusion of the prayer, Julia gasped, "Mother, it's a miracle! You're standing straight!" But her mother only grunted and shook her head, not wanting to admit that a miracle had taken place. Everyone was amazed when they saw that the posture of this woman had completely changed!

Although Julia's mother had been making preparations to leave the dedication services because of her pain, she stayed the rest of the afternoon for the remaining meetings—without complaint. Months later, she was still experiencing the result of the prayers that were offered for her at the dedication service.

This was just the first of many miracles that would result because God chose to bring 3ABN to Nizhny Novgorod, Russia.

3ABN-Russia now has a Web site, <www.3angels.ru>, in both Russian and English,[1] which has been averaging about thirty hits a day. The site has also received many requests for literature.

The 3ABN Russian Evangelism Center has indeed become a light on a hill that cannot be hid. As Bob Ellis put it, "Against impossible working conditions and against all odds, they built it. Overcoming savage weather, they built it. Staving off a hostile political environment, they built it. Comprising over 100,000 square feet, they built it. God bless them, they built it. On subsequent visits to Russia I have stood in awe, witnessing and embracing the glory that so richly belongs to them. And to Him" (*A Channel of Blessing*, p. 212).

Not only is the 3ABN Russian Evangelism Center a beautiful building to look at—inside and out—but more importantly, it is home to a dynamic ministry sharing the love of Jesus and building beautiful people with beautiful Christlike characters in a country that a few years before knew only darkness and oppression.

Because of the 3ABN Russian Evangelism Center, the glory of God and His three angels' messages shines in many places in the former Soviet Union. But 3ABN is looking forward to expansion. In all these years with all their programs, 3ABN-Russia hasn't had a network of its own. Plans are being made that in the near future— perhaps a year or so—there will be a new 3ABN Euro-Asia network opened alongside of the 3ABN English and 3ABN Latino networks, which will have time slots for different languages. 3ABN-Russia will have its block of one to two hours a day with Russian language programs. Julia says, "We are ready for it. We are now developing very creative and dynamic programs so that this part of the earth can be illuminated with the glory of God and more Russian people can learn the truth, believe it, and be saved for eternity."

---

[1] The upper right corner of the homepage has a button with "ENG" on it. Click this button to read the Web site in English.

10

To Asia and the Pacific Rim

"All the kings of the earth shall praise You, O Lord,
When they hear the words of Your mouth.
Yes, they shall sing of the ways of the Lord,
For great is the glory of the Lord"
—Psalm 138:4, 5, NKJV.

The story I'm about to tell you may sound like it comes right out of the Old Testament. But instead of Daniel advising the kings of Babylonia and Media-Persia, we have Bien Tejano, a Seventh-day Adventist pastor who became a Philippine ambassador, advising a succession of presidents of the Philippines. And instead of Joseph, whom God prophesied would someday be in a position that his brothers would bow down to him, we have Silas Atopare, who became the head of state in Papua New Guinea. These men were chosen by God to be in the right place at the right time to do His will!

What does all this have to do with 3ABN? Well, that's an incredible story! The amazing part is that it all started around the time God called Danny to the 3ABN ministry in 1984. In fact, on the very same day that God gave Danny the vision of starting a worldwide television ministry, God gave a bush pastor in the highland jungles of Papua New Guinea a prophecy about one of the lead players of our drama, His Excellency, Sir Silas Atopare. But I'm getting ahead of the story. First, let me tell you about how God brought 3ABN to the Philippines.

3ABN in the Philippines
The story starts in the 1980s when May Chung, a 3ABN board member, knew Bien Tejano as a pastor and health director in the Philippines. He was known for his role in helping to feed the hungry

and ministering to those in trouble. Plus, he was recognized as a gifted organizer. He became the trusted advisor of Fidel Ramos when he was a governor. Bien continued in this role when Ramos became the president of the Philippines in 1992. When Joseph Estrada was elected president on May 11, 1998, he also benefitted from Bien's counsel and appointed him to be the Philippine ambassador to Papua New Guinea, Kiribati, the Solomon Islands, and the Fiji Islands.

Bien Tejano was a man with a dream. Ever since he had first heard about 3ABN from May Chung, he dreamed of the day when a Christian television station in the Philippines would reach its citizens with the full gospel message, and he finally spoke to May Chung on the telephone about the possibilities. May has always had a deep desire to reach Asia and the Pacific Rim countries with the gospel, and she commented at the time, "It was a thrilling moment to realize Ambassador Tejano wanted a television station in the Philippines. *At last,* I thought, *we are going to reach Asia!"*

Ambassador Tejano's next step was to visit 3ABN's headquarters and consult with Moses Primo to determine the best way to proceed. The ambassador taped several programs with May Chung and shared his enthusiasm for the project.

After visiting 3ABN, Ambassador Tejano returned to the Philippines and started the tedious task of filing forms, gathering background information on 3ABN, and making plans to apply for a television license. For three years he tried in vain to obtain a channel. He was told that all the available channels were already assigned and that there were forty-two hundred applications in line for a full-power commercial channel—if one became available.

Being a man of perseverance, Ambassador Tejano found a friend who had a television application that had been pending for more than five years. His friend had all but given up because of all the red tape. The friend told him that if the channel were approved, he would let 3ABN use it for a monthly fee. Now, it was up to God to work out a way to get the approval of the communication department of the government and a construction permit from the city.

What an opportunity! This channel would allow 3ABN to reach over twenty million people in the metro-Manila area. Almost everyone in Manila has access to local UHF television channels; only 15 percent have cable. When Danny visited the Philippines, he reported seeing many areas in Manila where about fifty lines were hooked up illegally to power lines, enabling even the street people living in cardboard boxes and metal shanties to watch television. It was interesting to see these makeshift living quarters—with rabbit ear antennas poking out the top!

It's no wonder the government had received forty-two hundred applications for a television channel, including some from large networks offering millions of dollars for a permit. At this time, only one channel was left for broadcasting full time in Manila, so a television construction permit offered incredible opportunities for reaching an immense number of people.

Once again, our twentieth-century Daniel (Ambassador Bien Tejano) enters the scene. The ambassador felt strongly that the people of the Philippines would be best served with the health, family, and inspirational messages broadcast on 3ABN, but the possibility of 3ABN cutting through the red tape seemed hopeless. He called Danny to discuss the situation.

"Do you really believe the people of the Philippines would benefit far more from 3ABN than from any of the other stations?" Danny asked.

"Yes, of course," the ambassador replied.

"Then ask President Estrada to give 3ABN the station."

Ambassador Tejano hesitated, "I'm not sure I can do that." He seemed overwhelmed with even the thought of going in before the president to ask such a favor.

"Ambassador, I believe God has put you in this position to do this very thing. The people of the Philippines need everything that 3ABN offers."

"But . . ."

"Ambassador, what's the worst thing the president could do to you if you asked him to give 3ABN the channel? Will he shoot you? Put you in prison? Slap your wife around?"

"No."

"Well, it seems to me that the worst thing he could do is say, 'No,' so why not try?"

The ambassador couldn't refute Danny's logic, so he prayed that God would prepare the way. He made an appointment with the president, Joseph Estrada, to request that 3ABN be given the permit for this television channel.

As Ambassador Tejano handed President Estrada the application that was pending, the president asked, "Are you aware of how expensive this station will be to build?"

"Yes," was his reply.

"Can you afford to finance this?"

Again his answer was, "Yes, I think so, Your Excellency. We have a worldwide church and have brothers and sisters all over the world. When we have a project like this, they all come and help carry the load."

Again, President Estrada questioned him, "Do you know that there are many applicants for this permit?"

"Yes," the ambassador replied, "but you should know that this will be the only television station that will continually broadcast about Jesus Christ." Then he began to describe the health, family, gardening, cooking, and music programs carried on 3ABN.

The president picked up his pen and wrote something in the margin of the application that was on his desk, then signed his name. He handed it to the ambassador, who read the note addressed to the minister of communication. It said, "Please release all the necessary permits to 3ABN, immediately."

Now began the devil's major battle to keep 3ABN from reaching the Filipino people. As 3ABN's former marketing director, Gene Warfel, put it, "Getting a full-power station on the air has been like a hard climb up a tall mountain. Facing obstacles that often seemed too great, a small group of Christians clung to the vision of using television to reach the masses, and continued to pray for God's blessing and guidance while they filled their days and nights with hard work to make this station a reality." They had just eighteen months to get the station operating! The clock was ticking!

First, the local authorities wanted to charge an incredible amount of money for 3ABN to obtain a construction permit to build the television station. God provided an inexpensive, but successful, detour around this seemingly insurmountable barrier. Here's what happened.

Land was purchased for the station, a building permit was obtained from the city, and construction was beginning. Someone calling himself an "inspector" came from the local village and said the land was inside the village boundaries. He explained that before 3ABN could continue building the station, a construction permit had to be obtained from the village. The village wanted ten thousand dollars a month, but after negotiating, the "inspector" said he would take five thousand dollars a month. Moses felt this was very unreasonable, so he halted construction. The next day, when Moses went back to the construction site, a neighbor who had an FM tower next to 3ABN's land asked why construction had stopped. Moses explained.

The neighbor said, "Your land is right between the two villages. Why don't you talk to the chief of the village on the other side of you?"

Moses met with the man, who said he would be happy to give 3ABN a permit. "Besides," the chief explained, "the other village does not have the right to give you a permit because they do not have a certification number with the city hall. They were just trying to take advantage of you."

Next, three-phase power was needed. 3ABN was told that it would take three months to have this power hooked up. Another station, located just three hundred feet from the 3ABN station, had to pay a lot of money to entice the electric company to come in one month. But God intervened, and the technicians were on the site, installing the electricity, in just three days—without any bribes!

The next challenge was to get the television equipment through customs. A dispute arose with the Filipino authorities over the import duty to be paid for the equipment. It was first decided that the equipment was for a commercial station, so the duty would be 150 percent of its value. It was then lowered to 100 percent. But that was still outrageous because this was not a commercial station! Moses Primo explained to the customs official that the Manila station, although worth a million dollars, was owned by a nonprofit organization, and therefore, it qualified for nonprofit tax breaks. The official responded, "I wish I could just tell you there will be no tax, but it's election time, and if I do that, I won't get re-elected."

Moses pleaded, "Isn't there some legal way to get the tax lowered?"

The official said, "Yes, there is." He then had Moses fill out the papers in such a way that the equipment was released with only a 7 percent tax.

The next challenge was to find monthly support for the transponder fee for the satellite that would reach this part of the world. May Chung put her money where her heart was, and with others matching her gift, the goal was met and arrangements were made to start uplinking to the Thaicom 3 satellite.

The devil's last stand had to do with a barrage of engineering problems. The technicians experienced major difficulties in downlinking 3ABN's signal from the satellite to the station transmitter on Antipolo Mountain—the same location used by the other local television stations. This location offered a huge transmission range with no signal obstructions. On previous occasions, 3ABN technicians had been able to receive the satellite signal from Antipolo. But when they completed the station, the satellite signal was jammed illegally from somewhere in Manila. They tried tracking the source, but the task proved too difficult. Moses contacted several experts in satellite technology, but none of them could filter out the interference. 3ABN appealed to the broadcast officials in the Philippines, but to no avail. Moses traveled from Illinois to Manila on several occasions to try different methods of acquiring the signal, but every route came to a deadend.

It was puzzling, as the weeks turned into months with no answer in sight. Everyone involved with the project pleaded with the Lord to show them the way. Once again, as always, God was right on time! Moses finally traveled to Manila in December 2001 with a new plan of action. God had impressed him to set up an additional satellite dish on the other side of the mountain, effectively blocking out the interference from Manila. The technicians worked through the night in pouring rain to get the signal to the transmitter. The solution came at the last minute, just a few hours before they were scheduled to fly back to Illinois.

Manila Station

Today, a full-power, sixty-thousand-watt transmitter blankets the city of Manila twenty-four hours a day with the good news of salvation via 3ABN television programming on channel 45. To make this a reality, Moses traveled the twenty-two hours each way from West Frankfort, Illinois, to the Philippines more than ten times! When the station was finally up and operating, Moses commented, "The Lord showed me one more time that He can overcome any obstacle. It is not always easy and not always fast, but as we trust in Him, He delivers us. In my twenty-seven-year career, this was the largest project that I have ever been involved with in terms of physical needs and challenges. But I would do it all over again! To see the Filipino people, and to know that they have the choice of eternal life and to know that we had a small part in bringing that option to them is very fulfilling."

Shortly after 3ABN was on the air in Manila, Ambassador Bien Tejano was walking through a first-class American hotel in Manila when he heard a blind man playing the piano and singing "I Want to Spend My Life Mending Broken People." The ambassador asked the man, "Where did you learn that song?" The man explained, "I heard it on a new channel in Manila. It's called 3ABN." Isn't the far-ranging influence of 3ABN amazing? This man, Andrew Habagat, is now a baptized Seventh-day Adventist Christian evangelist. At his first crusade, 75 souls were baptized. Then, using just his Braille Bible, he presented what he had learned to his mother and father, his two sisters, their husbands, and his brother. All are now baptized Seventh-day Adventist Christians. Andrew says it was the song that Danny so often sings—*Mending Broken People*—that sealed his conversion and commitment to serve the Lord.

May Chung says, "The completion of the Manila station is one of the most satisfying things I can recall. It's one of the greatest moves forward toward our goal of reaching the world that we could have ever prayed for."

Today, 3ABN is reaching far more people in the Philippines than just those twenty-plus million in the Manila area that are tuning in to channel 45. Because 3ABN is on satellite, it can be downlinked by both individuals and cable companies. Even before channel 45 was operational, news was filtering into the 3ABN headquarters that various cable companies were carrying 3ABN programming even without an official contract! The excellent programs that are found on 3ABN are meeting needs, and others are recognizing their value and rebroadcasting them. Here is just one such experience taken from a letter to 3ABN:

I think it will do your heart good to hear the news that on February 27, 2003, 3ABN started airing in the city of Iloilo, in the central Philippines. My son had heard that in Mindanao 3ABN had been broadcasting already four months previously. He kept asking me, "Ma, why don't we have that here?" To make a long story short, he learned that there are three satellite dishes in Cebu and went there to arrange to pick up the equipment necessary to start the telecasts here in Western Visayan Islands—all at his own expense! My son knows the manager of Sun Cable, so he asked regarding the possibility of airing the programs. We solicited from the lay people and raised the funds. That's how the telecast began! Ambassador Bien Tejano agreed to come launch 3ABN on cable channel 47, so a motorcade of sixty-plus cars was organized and courtesy calls to the governor and city mayor, as well as a press conference, were arranged. 3ABN is bringing stature to the Seventh-day Adventist Church in the Philippines. My prayer is that God will continue to give us the means to support this project so it can be sustained and many may be brought to the feet of Jesus. God bless!

Danny with the president of the Philippines, Gloria Macapagal Arroyo, and her husband

In February 2004, Danny and Linda Shelton were invited guests of Her Excellency, Gloria Macapagal Arroyo, the current president of the Republic of the Philippines, and her husband. They attended breakfast at the palace, where President Arroyo stated that 3ABN has changed the people of the Philippines for the better. Then the president addressed the crowd of over five thousand inside and two thousand outside that attended the inauguration of channel 45, 3ABN's full-power television station in metro-Manila, held at the Philippine International Convention Center. She began her address with, "Happy Sabbath evening to all of you!" Then she continued, "This is the beginning of what will surely be another of your valuable and significant contributions to Philippine culture. Through your programs on health, education, community service, science and technology, family counseling, and Christian ministry, you offer Filipinos what we need most—a healthy mind in a healthy body, anchored on faith in God."

President Arroyo then told about a personal connection her family had with a Seventh-day Adventist hospital. When her brother was fourteen, he apparently was sleepwalking and fell from a second story window in the middle of the night. At dawn, a household helper woke up and saw him on the landing of the stairs, his mouth frothing, his eyes open and unseeing. The family was sure he had suffered brain damage. They rushed him to the emergency room at Iligan Sanitarium, where he had brain surgery. He is now a very successful businessman with no damage to his brain. She commented, "And so my family knows what it is like to be grateful to the Seventh-day Adventist Church for a sound mind in a sound body, a healthy body anchored on faith in God. With God's guidance and with your help, with the beautiful things that you will be spreading with 3ABN, we will win this battle for change!"

In addition to the address of the president and that of Ambassador Bien Tejano, hundreds of Filipinos gave testimonies that their lives have changed after they watched 3ABN; they have accepted the Lord as their Savior and been baptized. Praise God!

Danny shared with Her Excellency that God puts presidents into office for a purpose, and giving every person in the Philippines access to the gospel and to the positive lifestyle messages on 3ABN is certainly one of the reasons she has been given this position.

She agreed!

3ABN in Papua New Guinea

To tell the complete Papua New Guinea story, we must go back a few years to May 1998. In the middle of the night Danny was awakened by the ringing of the phone.

Danny and Linda Shelton meet with Sir Silas Atopare, Governor-General of Papua New Guinea, his wife, and Ambassador Bien Tejano (far left).

"Hello," he answered sleepily.

"Hello, is this Danny Shelton?" the voice asked in a broken accent. "Yes."

"I'm from Papua New Guinea, and I'd like to talk with you."

"It's kind of late," commented Danny. By this time Danny was wondering who the caller was and how he had gotten his unlisted telephone number.

"I'm Bien Tejano from the Philippines, and I'm sorry it's late. I am the Philippine ambassador to Papua New Guinea, and right now I'm with the head of state—the governor general—of Papua New Guinea, His Excellency, Sir Silas Atopare."

Danny was too shocked to make a comment.

"Ahhh, Mr. Shelton, I'm sorry to call you at a bad time. Would it be better if I called you back?"

By this time Danny was wide awake. "No, sir, this is a good time!" Ambassador Tejano then handed the phone to Sir Silas Atopare.

"I would like you to come to Papua New Guinea and build a television station to reach the whole nation of 4.5 million inhabitants."

"Does that mean you are inviting 3ABN to build stations through-out Papua New Guinea?"

"Yes."

To make sure he wasn't dreaming, Danny asked, "Could you put that in writing?"

By the time Danny got to the office the next morning, there was a fax requesting him to come to Papua New Guinea to make arrangements for a 3ABN station in a country that had been known through the years for its exciting missionary stories among primitive, jungle, head-hunting tribes.

Within a few weeks, Danny, Moses Primo, and May Chung were sitting in the office of Sir Silas Atopare, the governor general of Papua New Guinea. They noted a large picture of Queen Elizabeth of Great Britain behind his desk. Above the queen was a picture of Jesus with His nail-scarred hands.

"How do you like my pictures?" His Excellency asked. Then he explained, "Jesus is the head of this state. I'm not. Queen Elizabeth is not." Then he told this incredible story:

When I was nine years old, I went swimming in the river. A current took me downstream. I thought I was going to drown. Out of the sky came a large hand that picked me up and put me on shore. By then I was unconscious, but the people on the shore saw the hand and later explained to me, "God of heaven must have saved you."

Not long after this, Seventh-day Adventists came to our village and built a school. Even though I was from a Catholic family, I attended grade school and academy. Eventually, I became an Adventist.

In my early twenties, I became ill with hepatitis. I got worse and worse. Word spread, "He's going to die." We prayed. I'm not sure what happened, but almost overnight I got better. By the next day when the doctor came to see me, he asked, "What kind of religion do you have?" He knew we had been praying.

"I'm a Seventh-day Adventist."

"Well, whoever the God of the Seventh-day Adventists is, He is very powerful."

I ran for parliament, since I felt this was one way I could spread the knowledge of Christ. I was a member for five years.

I had dreams and aspirations to climb my way up in politics. Then on November 15, 1984 [the same day that God had given Danny the dream to build 3ABN], I lost the election. I was so distraught. I knew God wanted me to be in parliament. I went to an old Seventh-day Adventist jungle pastor and asked him, "Would you pray for me, and tell me what I have done wrong." As the man began to pray, I saw him go into a trance. He was in vision for a while, and when he came out of it, he said, "Oh Lord, God, great God of heaven," and then continued to tell me that God had showed him that although I had been faithful in some areas of my life, there were smaller areas where I had failed. "Therefore you are going to have to wait thirteen years from today. There will be an election on November 15, 1997, when you will become, if faithful, the governor general of Papua New Guinea." He said, "Get a book and write down what I'm telling you so you will not forget."

I did this. During those years I worked for the government, but nothing in the higher ranks where I desired to serve. After thirteen years, I wanted to run for governor general, which is the equivalent to the president of a country, but the parliament actually chooses the person to fill this position.

On November 15, 1997, I waited. When the parliament was down to six names—and I was among them—I told a few of my friends that the parliament was going to choose me.

"How do you know?" they questioned.

"The Lord told this to a jungle pastor in 1984," I explained.

But at 10 A.M., they announced they were down to five names. Mine had been eliminated. My friends doubted the prophecy. My reply was, "It's not 3 P.M. yet."

At 3 P.M., they announced that Silas Atopare had been elected to the highest office in the country. They explained that they had put my name back in the running. When I heard the decision, I began to cry. I saw that my task as governor general was to be faithful in honoring God. So when I moved into the presidential suite, I went before parliament and explained. "Your governor general will not work on Sabbath. He needs to be fed. I need to go to church Friday evening and Saturday and do God's business." I chose to never fail God again, for I felt God had something special for me to do.

Then the governor general explained once again about the pictures. "For the last hundred years in this office, the pope's picture has hung above the picture of the queen, and beside the pope was a picture of Mary. When I came here, I said, 'The pope is not the head of state, nor is Mary. Jesus is the Head of State.' So I ordered their pictures taken down and put Christ's picture in their place. I determined to be faithful to God."

After Silas Atopare's selection as head of state, he sent someone into the jungle to the highland village to find the jungle pastor whose prophecy had been fulfilled. "I requested that they bring him to me. I told the pastor, 'I never forgot that you prayed for me and what you said. I want to honor the God of heaven this day. I need your wisdom and counsel. I want you to be a full-time prayer warrior for me and this government. I want you to live on the grounds and come into the parliament. I need the counsel of the Lord on important decisions. And I believe God speaks through you.' "

When Danny, Moses, and May heard this story, they felt they were witnessing something straight out of the Old Testament. God was alive and working in the twentieth century in the same way He worked thousands of years ago! Amazing!

In 1997, when Silas Atopare became governor general, 3ABN was ready to stretch to reach new parts of the world. The technology was at last in place to reach all of Papua New Guinea, as well as the Philippines, via an Asian satellite. This would not have been possible in the previous thirteen years. Obviously, God knew what role He wanted Silas Atopare to play in spreading the gospel in Papua New Guinea. So when everything else was in place, when the stage was set, God put him in the highest leadership position in the country so that His plans could be carried out.

Papua New Guinea was—and still is—an unsettled country. It had only three channels available: One was a government channel; one was a foreign television station from Australia; and the last one would be for 3ABN or another Christian network. Now began the politics to determine who would receive that third channel.

When it was advertised that a new channel was opening in Papua New Guinea, a well-known Christian with a television healing ministry came to Papua New Guinea and went back home announcing that the channel would be awarded to his ministry. Danny had heard this news just days before coming to visit the governor general. He decided he should call him before making the trip. Danny was told the channel was still open and that he should make the trip.

When Danny, Moses, and May arrived in Papua New Guinea, His Excellency explained, "The prime minister invited the faith healer here. The man came and talked about the channel, but he went back to America and never applied for it. If 3ABN wants to apply, you will have the first opportunity. If you take care of this matter before you go home, the last national channel will be awarded to 3ABN."

Danny then recalled the headlines of the newspaper that he had read during their trip from Sidney, Australia, to Papua New Guinea. "Prime Minister of New Guinea resigns." Interesting isn't it, that at this moment, when the 3ABN delegation arrived to apply for the television channel, that the whole government seemed to be in favor of 3ABN. The opposition—if there had been any—had been removed from office just hours before the 3ABN group had arrived. Three days later, a new prime minister was announced, one who shared the same faith as His Excellency. Once again God's timing was perfect!

The governor general explained, "I will send my head man, the secretary, to meet with PANGTEL [the communications regulatory agency of Papua New Guinea] and with you." When it was questioned if a man of such a high rank should be sent, the governor general said, "I sent him when the Australian television network was seeking approval, and I will send him with you."

In the meeting with PANGTEL, Danny, Moses, and May learned that there were twenty provinces in Papua New Guinea—and few roads. The only way to get to certain places is by helicopter. However, the government had already built eleven towers throughout the country, which made it possible to reach the entire nation through repeater stations. They told Danny that 3ABN could use what was already in place. There was plenty of room on the towers for 3ABN's antennas. The gift of "tower space" would save hundreds of thousands of dollars. God seemed to be opening some incredible doors.

The next day was Sabbath. Danny, Moses, and May—along with His Excellency—were escorted in official flag-bearing cars led by a motorcade of police from one location where Danny gave the sermon and then to another where he spoke in an afternoon meeting.

The following day, Sunday, Danny had to fly back to Illinois. Moses was left behind to meet with the IPA (Investment Promotion Authority) on Monday, which was the office which would determine whether 3ABN, as a foreign corporation, could do business in the country. Moses was hesitant. "I'm the technical guy. I'm not the best communicator. I wish you would stay and make the presentation," he pleaded with Danny.

"You will say the right things," Danny assured him.

As it turned out, most of the people Moses met with on Monday had already heard Danny speak during the church services. They assured Moses that they would help 3ABN set up as a foreign business. Danny learned later that at the time there were over 300,000 Seventh-day Adventists in the country, and out of the 109 members of parliament, twenty six were Adventists. It was amazing to find such strong Christian leadership in that nation.

The date on the Papua New Guinea newspaper was December 4, 2000. The headlines read: "New Guinea Welcomes 3ABN!" One article stated, "It is a new day for New Guinea. We believe 3ABN's programming will change the nation for the better."

In December 2003, Danny and Moses traveled to Papua New Guinea to participate in a ceremony in which a television license to broadcast to the entire country was presented to 3ABN. Governor General Sir Silas Atopare, several members of parliament, and members of PANGTEL, as well as other VIPs and media representation, were in attendance.

There are 4.5 million people in Papua New Guinea, and over eight hundred dialects are spoken there. But English is the main language. Therefore, millions of people will have an opportunity to hear the gospel, in a language they can understand, from this full-power station located in Port Moresby and four repeater stations in major cities that will bring the signal to almost the entire country.

Thinking back over the incredible miracles that took place to bring 3ABN to what some may term "the end of the earth," Danny commented, "Wouldn't it be awesome if the fall of the latter rain[1] would start in the country of Papua New Guinea, a country that, just fifty years before 3ABN's presence there, was known as a country of head hunters—the country that is often referred to as the last uncivilized country of the world? Once the people catch the revival spirit, what a testimony to the rest of the world! What an awesome privilege for 3ABN to have a part in finishing the work in the Pacific Rim."

---

[1] The outpouring of the Holy Spirit that has been predicted will happen before the second coming of Jesus. See James 5:7.

11

The 3ABN Ripple Effect

"The Lord has done great things for us, Whereof we are glad. . . .
He who continually goes forth . . . bearing seed for sowing,
Shall doubtless come again with rejoicing,
Bringing his sheaves with him."
—Psalm 126:3, 6, NKJV.

3ABN has become the hub of a wheel with spokes reaching out to the world just as the dream given Hal Steenson had predicted over twenty years ago.[1] But it is not only the television and radio signals that do the work of worldwide evangelism. It's the dozens and dozens of other ministries that would not be alive and thriving if it had not been for 3ABN promoting them and encouraging donors to support them. I call this the 3ABN ripple effect. Let me give you a few examples:

Dr. Billy Burks

Evangelism Partners International
(P.O. Box 1401, Hendersonville, TN 37077)

Dr. Billy Burks has worked as a professional musician (accordion and vibraharp), a dentist, owner of a commercial recording studio in Nashville, and one of the founders of Evangelism Partners International (EPI). Ten years ago, Billy would never have dreamed he would be heading an evangelism ministry in Russia that was responsible for winning over eight thousand souls to the Lord in just four years! Here's the rest of the story in Billy's own words:

Danny and I have been friends since the early 1980s, when he used my recording studio for a number of projects. In 1988, I brought a guitarist friend, Wayne Parham, to 3ABN, and Danny, Tommy, Wayne, and I taped a musical program. That was the beginning of the small part I've played in helping to contribute music for 3ABN programming.

Around 1997, Danny and Robert Folkenberg, then president of the General Conference of Seventh-day Adventists, were on the Thursday night *3ABN Presents Live* program. The subject was evangelism, particularly concerning the 10/40 window from Spain through Asia to the Pacific Ocean where much of the world's population live and where resources are few. Elder Folkenberg wanted two thousand people to pledge two thousand dollars annually. Each pledge would support a minister and his family for two years to raise a new Adventist congregation and church.

The idea rolled around in my head. *If others could do this, why couldn't I? What if I started a supporting ministry to fund evangelists around the world?* I recruited six more families, each contributing a thousand dollars, which together with myself made a total of seven thousand dollars. Lawyer Herald Follett helped us establish an account at both the General Conference and the Euro-Asia Division of Seventh-day Adventists. Thus, a new ministry was born—Evangelism Partners International (EPI). Today, 100 percent of EPI funds gathered sponsor evangelistic campaigns.

When Herald mentioned that he needed to raise money for a large crusade in Russia, EPI gave him a check to cover it. The evangelist was a young twenty-two-year-old Russian, Vadim Boutov. In his first crusade, 579 souls came to Christ. That began a wonderful partnership for the Lord's work.

We have continued to support Pastor Vadim, as well as many other evangelists. At one time we had twelve different crusades going on at one time in twelve different cities. We sponsored a former Russian wrestler, turned Adventist, to travel to Siberia. His goal was to place 3ABN Russian programming on new television stations. We sponsored two older ministers to travel to prisons, which resulted in the conversion of a number of prisoners. EPI has also sponsored many ministers and their families to go out into remote areas and raise up new congregations and churches. In turn, these churches are active in soul winning that has resulted in two thousand more baptisms.

In 2003, Vadim, along with Frank Baylon, EPI's treasurer, and I appeared on 3ABN. Vadim mentioned that he wanted to build a school of evangelism in Russia. He can graduate one hundred trained workers per year. His students will be ministers, missionary pioneers, and laymen. A few days later, I received a call from a woman in Oregon asking if God had supplied the funds for building the school yet. When I said, "No," she immediately said that she wanted to have that privilege. A few days later a check for fifty thousand dollars arrived!

Evangelism Partners International exists today because of 3ABN. Not only did 3ABN programming spark the idea for EPI, but Danny is always willing to share with the world-wide audience what EPI is doing, and the Holy Spirit inspires people to give. We now have hundreds of partners, and the work is expanding. Our goal is a thousand souls for Christ every day of the year. With God's grace, it shouldn't be long until this goal is a reality.

People ask me how many trips I've made to Russia to administer this work. The answer is, "I've never been there." It would cost at least four thousand dollars for a trip. EPI can sponsor a major crusade for four thousand and win hundreds of souls for Christ! That's where I'm putting my money!

Donnie Shelton

Touching Hearts Ministries

(Email: touchingheartsministries@mchsi.com)

In 2002, Donnie Shelton, Danny's cousin, began to feel that God was calling him to preach full time. This was surprising, because Donnie had spent thirty years in the radiology field. He felt unworthy to preach because he was not trained in theology. But when he was asked to preach in his little church, he accepted. In November 2002, Donnie held a revival in Mt. Vernon, Illinois, and felt exhilarated. In

December, the Lord opened up a few more opportunities. Then Donnie began to pray, "Lord, broaden my borders." Within three months, nine different churches asked him to preach.

Donnie then got a little bolder and told the Lord, "If You want me in full-time ministry, You've got to put me there."

And the Lord answered, *If you don't make yourself available, I can't do that.*

Donnie immediately stepped out of his comfort zone and resigned from his job as director of radiology in Du Quoin, Illinois. That was the first week of October 2003. On October 10, Danny called and asked, "Do you want to go to Africa as a representative for 3ABN?"

"If I can preach," was Donnie's eager reply.

And preach he did. Enoch Mogusu, who builds satellite dishes and is actively involved in promoting 3ABN in Africa, emailed Owen Troy's daughter, Carmelita, who was helping her father with the work of 3ABN International. He said that the African people appreciated Donnie Shelton's messages. "When Donnie is on fire for the Lord, he preaches like an African, and he was well received."

Donnie made this comment about the trip, "I went to Africa to be a blessing to the people, and I got touched. The African people are starving for Jesus Christ. Here, people fall asleep in the pews. I was in a poverty-stricken area on Sabbath morning. It was pouring down rain, yet six hundred people packed that church, some of whom had walked for miles to attend. My life will never be the same."

When Donnie returned from Africa, Danny encouraged him and his wife, Brenda, to set up a nonprofit corporation. They called it Touching Hearts Ministries, and its goal is preaching Jesus, "Because," says Donnie, "when you make preaching Jesus your goal, doctrine and everything else falls into place. Then almost immediately, 3ABN sent me to India to work with Hal Steenson, now a Seventh-day Adventist layman, where I preached every other night to thousands of people. Just think, a few months ago I was taking X-rays, and now I'm preaching to thousands."

Donnie went on to say this about 3ABN: "If it weren't for God using 3ABN, I wouldn't have a ministry. Not only have I had an opportunity to be 3ABN's representative to Africa, but 3ABN has allowed me to share Jesus Christ on television. Viewers have been blessed and have called to invite me to preach in their churches or camp meetings. God, through 3ABN, has opened a door of opportunity for me to fulfill His calling. I've never been more excited about life. And the amazing thing is, the needs of our family have been supplied by God. We're not growing rich, by any means, but our basic needs have been met. Each month, the love gifts are just enough. As Danny so often says, 'Where God guides, He provides!' I believe that soon our ministry will have enough funding that Brenda can give up her day-care business and minister with me full time as we travel around the world reviving dying churches with the incredible love of God."

Cheri Peters

True Step Ministries

(Website: www.truestep.org)

Cheri Peters is one of the most vivacious, joyful, compelling Christians you'll ever meet. You'd never guess she used to be a homeless heroin addict. But Cheri is no longer living on the streets. She found Christ. He gave her the victory, and she's been giving Him the glory ever since.

Cheri says 3ABN "adopted" her when she was new in ministry and had nothing but her desire to help others discover the power of Christ to overcome addictions. She came to 3ABN to tape some segments on *Teen Pathways*, bringing with her some teens who had been on drugs—kids from homeless shelters, gangs, and domestic violence shelters. She had been working with them in her hometown of Boise, Idaho, and the teens had all made the initial step of accepting Christ in their recovery process. They gave powerful testimonies about what Christ was doing in their lives, and everyone at 3ABN was so encouraging to them. The people accepted them, brought food to them, and gave them love and affirmation. The kids left 3ABN believing that they could do something positive with their lives. Cheri also hosts *Crossroads*, a weekly program aired on 3ABN Radio.

Let me have Cheri tell the rest of the story in her own words:

When I first came to 3ABN, I had no job. I knew I felt called to bring Christ to drug addicts who were societal outcasts. But no one would hire me to do that. In desperation, I even asked 3ABN to hire me. I was considering returning to my nursing career when 3ABN did what no one else would do. Instead of hiring me, 3ABN encouraged me to continue in my own nonprofit organization, True Step Ministries. I had no confidence and felt very insecure. I wasn't a fund-raiser, so 3ABN supported True Step Ministries for the first three critical years until I was able to stand on my own. Because of 3ABN, I have been able to minister in every state in the United States and in many countries of the world.

In Bangkok, Thailand, my group of workers, with the Lord's power, not only set drug addicts free, but we also rescued children sold into prostitution. The mafia threatened to "gut us," and put a contract out on us. But God protected.[2] I took a team to Russia and worked with the 3ABN Russian Evangelism Center. We taught parents how to work with their heroin-addicted children in such a way as to not enable them. We handed addicted kids back to their parents—clean. One father was so grateful that he said, "I knew 3ABN was coming here to help drug addicts, but I never thought they would give me back my own son." One person who had been an alcoholic for thirty-five years not only determined to give up alcohol, but Christ miraculously took away his urge to drink. During our six-week stay, we tried to educate the Russian people about addictions in every way possible, from street ministry to speaking in almost every Seventh-day Adventist church in Nizhny Novgorod and the surrounding area.

Because of the *Teen Pathways* program on 3ABN, our ministry was invited to go to a youth retreat in the West Indies. While there, we even went into a prison in the midst of a riot in which inmates burned down 80 percent of the building! I told them, "I know 100 percent that God doesn't intend for you to live like this."

They countered, "You have no idea. . . ."

"Oh, yes I do," I said. "I was a heroin addict for ten years and lived on the street. Now I'm the president of a nonprofit organization, and I travel around the world helping others. God has a plan for you, just as He has a plan for me. You just have to trust Him." It's amazing how they listened when they realized where I had come from and how Christ had brought me victory. Perhaps for the first time they had hope!

True Steps Ministries is an official site for "RADAR" (Regional Alcohol Drug Awareness Resource Center). We work with drug enforcement and at-risk teens in places like elementary, junior high, and high schools, as well as juvenile halls and homeless shelters. We bring kids the latest drug and lifestyle-improvement information. When we go into a city for an intensive week of drug prevention and recovery, the final meeting is always held in a Seventh-day Adventist church. We give everyone we have worked with during the week a special invitation to that final meeting—a meeting to hear more about a God who loves you and will bring love and light into your darkest places. What miracles we have seen!

What's so amazing about all of this is that 3ABN had faith in a homeless girl when no one else did. They didn't look at credentials—only at my calling. Every day I praise the Lord for the opportunity that He gave me through the support and affirmation of my friends . . . my family at 3ABN.

Kenneth Cox

Kenneth Cox Ministries

(Website: www.kennethcoxministries.org)

Ken Cox became a full-time evangelist in 1970, long before 3ABN was in existence. Shortly after Danny had the calling to start 3ABN, he went to visit Ken in Keene, Texas. He shared the vision of 3ABN and asked Ken's opinion about starting a worldwide television ministry.

"It needs to be done," Ken encouraged him.

A couple of years later, Danny had a dream in which he saw Ken Cox on TV. He immediately told Ken that he was to be one of 3ABN's regular speakers. Danny never forgot that dream. Over the years, the Ken Cox evangelistic campaigns have become an important part of 3ABN's broadcasting schedule. And 3ABN has become a vital part of the reaping work done by the Ken Cox crusades.

Ken says that at almost every campaign someone tells him, "I'm here because I've been watching 3ABN." He has also had numerous people tell him that they watch 3ABN because, for a time, 3ABN was the only channel they were able to see. One interesting example was a prisoner who wrote admitting that he had secretly wired his TV to get more stations, but the only channel he could pick up was 3ABN. He watched the Ken Cox series, became convicted of Bible truth, and was baptized.

Ken adds: "There is no question in my mind that we would not be seeing as many people baptized if it weren't for 3ABN. But there's more. Because 3ABN gives our ministry such wide coverage, people respond with financial gifts. This helps us continue to give twelve to fourteen campaigns each year."

After thirty-four years of doing full-time evangelism on all five continents, Ken is not about to retire. The 2004 schedule took the Kenneth Cox team to Oregon, Texas, Bermuda, Ohio, Nova Scotia, New York, Oklahoma, Guam, and Pennsylvania, where Ken plans to find many more individuals ripe for the harvest because they have been taught and nurtured by 3ABN.

Hermon and Sonnie Harp

Herman and Sonnie Harp

(Website:www.hermanandsonnieharp.com)

Herman and Sonnie have an incredible music ministry that keeps them on the road much of the time. Their concerts are a blend of old favorites and Sonnie's original compositions that speak to the hearts of people today. Interspersed between songs are words of encouragement and inspiration that glorify Christ Jesus.

I caught up with Herman on his cell phone, because—you guessed it—he was traveling to another concert location. When I asked him what 3ABN had meant to his and Sonnie's ministry, he told me about their experience with the Albuquerque Heights Church in New Mexico, where they gave a Sabbath morning concert that was followed by a free vegetarian meal. 3ABN was on the local cable station there, so many people in town recognized Herman and

Sonnie's name when the concert was advertised. The phone lines were flooded with people calling for tickets. And because 3ABN viewers were acquainted with the cooking programs on 3ABN, they knew the meal would be special.

Herman concluded with this statement: "Without 3ABN it would be difficult to reach the community with advertisements alone. When people recognize the names of artists, they can feel confident that it's worth their time and effort to come out—and to invite their friends to attend. That's why we are finding that the attendance at our concerts has increased since 3ABN is now on many more stations and cable outlets.

Steve Wohlberg and family

Endtime Insights Radio and TV Ministry

(Website: www.endtimeinsights.com)

Steve Wohlberg, a Jewish Christian, was a pastor in Kansas when he was first invited to 3ABN to do a number of programs on the series *Give Me the Bible*. 3ABN recognized his interest and expertise on the subject of Israel in prophecy. The series was so popular that 3ABN aired it again and again, and the material became the core of Steve's book, *Exploding the Israel Deception*. When he became an evangelist for Amazing Facts Ministries, Steve continued to fly to 3ABN when he was invited to do live programs. One program pointed out the dangers of the Harry Potter books, and another dealt with the fallacies presented in the popular Left Behind series of books.

Steve then moved to Texas, where, in addition to serving as a pastor, he and his team started a television ministry and produced three television series that have aired on 3ABN. Steve currently pastors the Templeton Hills Seventh-day Adventist Church in California and serves as speaker/director of Endtime Insights Radio and TV Ministry—a ministry that has developed because of his passion to reach the world through media. Here's what Steve has to say about 3ABN's role in taking his ministry to the world: "God's call on my life to lift up the cross of Jesus Christ and to teach straight Bible truth has taken me from small handwritten flyers to books to radio and to television. On this journey, there is no other television network that has given our ministry more of an opportunity to reach the masses than has 3ABN. As a result of 3ABN's airing of *Israel in Prophecy, The Antichrist Chronicles,* and *Amazing Discoveries,* our God-appointed ministry has touched the world. We receive responses from places around the globe, from the United States to Saudi Arabia, from Europe to Australia. We praise God with heart and soul for 3ABN. His truth is marching on!"

Steve's new book, *End Time Delusions: The Rapture, the Antichrist, Israel, and the End of the World,* was published by Destiny Image and is available in Christian bookstores. And it will likely result in some vitally interesting television programs. Keep watching 3ABN!

Health Seminars Unlimited
(Website: www.hseminars.com)

Curtis and Paula Eakins

God calls people to ministry in many different ways. For Curtis and Paula Eakins, it all began after Curtis had been watching some cooking segments on 3ABN. *My wife can do that,* he thought. *She's been conducting cooking classes for more than twenty years!* He sent a short video clip of his wife's cooking demonstrations to 3ABN, and the Eakinses received an invitation to tape some programs for 3ABN's *Food for Thought* series.

That was in 1996. The taping went so well that the Eakinses were asked to stay to do a demonstration for the Thursday night *3ABN Presents Live* program. Before they left the studio, the viewer response had been so great that they were offered their own television series.

"We'll have to pray about it," they said. Cooking on television looks easy, until you have to prepare finished product dishes, as well as assemble all the ingredients for the demonstration. All week the Eakinses had found themselves up until three or four o'clock in the morning trying to keep ahead of the production schedule!

At the moment they were asked, Paula was so tired she couldn't imagine cooking one more dish! Besides, they had intended to just do a few programs and then return to their own careers: Paula as a teacher at Oakwood College in Huntsville, Alabama, and Curtis as a physician's assistant in the surgery department of the Huntsville Hospital.

Curtis and Paula prayed about the invitation, and the next morning they woke up excited about the possibilities. Within a few minutes they came up with thirty-two titles of programs they could do. That number has obviously expanded. They have taped 140 programs and have done five Thursday night *3ABN Presents Live* presentations in the last seven years!

Soon calls began coming in from all over the world for the Eakinses to do weekend health seminars and cooking schools. Curtis found himself away from his job so many four-day weekends that he was afraid of getting demerits. Three years after they began their work for 3ABN, Curtis said, "I'd better quit before they fire me!" But resigning from his stable job with benefits and prestige was a giant test of faith. After fasting and praying, the decision was made. On the very week Curtis decided to leave his job to go into full-time ministry with his wife, the employees in his department were given the largest raise they had ever received. People thought he was crazy to quit, but Curtis knew his decision was God's will—and that God would take care of them. And so He has!

When asked how 3ABN has affected their lives, Curtis commented:

> Wherever we go, people want our autographs! People don't realize we're just humble folk doing God's will. We redirect their praise to God and often paraphrase Philippians 2:13, "For it is God working in us to will and to do His good pleasure." And James 1:17, "Every good gift comes from above, coming down from the father of lights."
>
> We have our weekends booked six to nine months in advance. We've ministered all over the United States and in Canada, Bermuda, and the Cayman Islands. But when people contact us for health information or a cookbook, we want to be the entering wedge; therefore, we always send them the Amazing Facts Bible study on health. We track each Bible

study with an identification number. Some are filled in and returned to Amazing Facts; others we grade ourselves. When there is an interest in learning more, we send the person all twelve of the Amazing Facts Bible studies. In the past seven years, we have handed out thousands of tracts. And when someone graduates from the Bible course, we send them a certificate.

If it weren't for 3ABN, we wouldn't have this ministry. We praise God every day for the work He is doing to spread the full gospel message through the television and radio ministries of 3ABN. And what a blessing for us to be chosen by God to have a small part in this great work!

Doug Batchelor

Amazing Facts Ministries

(Website: www.amazingfacts.org)

Doug Batchelor, president of Amazing Facts Ministries, is known by many as the caveman, because he was living in a cave in the mountains around Palm Springs, California, at the time he found Christ and became a passionate Bible student and disciple.[3] 3ABN has had a significant impact on his ministry. Here's Doug's story:

In 1993, I was an evangelist in northern California, holding meetings in Redding, when I began hearing people talk about 3ABN and how touched they were by this television ministry on their local television channel. Since my wife, Karen, and I had videotaped the Redding meetings, I sent the tapes to 3ABN to see if it would be interested in airing them. The tapes sat on a shelf for many months before Danny pulled them out, watched one, and exclaimed, 'This bald guy is pretty good.' Even though the quality of the tapes was not the best, 3ABN began playing them—and I started getting invitations for speaking appointments.

About the time that I became the pastor of the Central Church in Sacramento, Joe Crews, the founder of Amazing Facts, watched one of my tapes. Although he was a rather serious fellow, my presentation made him laugh. "This man is making a difficult subject easy to digest," he commented. He felt impressed to ask me to work with him, training me to take the director's position. Before I could do this, however, Joe died unexpectedly, and I was asked to take his place! If it weren't for 3ABN, I doubt if I would be with Amazing Facts today!

I've appeared numerous times on the Thursday night *3ABN Presents Live* program, and the callers enjoy asking questions. In 1997, I did a live evangelistic series with 3ABN and then did the live Net 99 series from New York. Plus, Dwight Nelson and I did a series of meetings at Andrews University, which 3ABN has aired. Through the years, 3ABN has continued to play my tapes over and over again.

Currently, 3ABN broadcasts *The Everlasting Gospel,* the Sacramento Central Church service, and Central Church Sabbath School. In addition, Amazing Facts also has a program on 3ABN Radio. In the last ten years, Amazing Facts Ministries has grown from twenty employees to over seventy! And God has really blessed us financially, allowing us to operate the Amazing Facts College of Evangelism and Bible Study School. We employ Bible seminar speakers who hold meetings throughout the country. We have a radio, a television, and a print ministry that produces Bible studies, books, and pamphlets. I've also had the privilege of holding evangelistic meetings not only in the United States but in such far away places as Africa, Australia, India, Russia, and South America.

3ABN is changing lives. I meet these people everywhere I go. And I'm becoming more and more convinced that 3ABN is angel possessed! I hear too many "stuck dish" stories not to believe God's angels are enjoying allowing the remote battery to go dead so the person in a hospital bed can't change channels. Or the gear motor on the satellite dish to go out— and, you guessed it, 3ABN is the only channel that can be seen. God has a way of getting people's attention. And if they will just stop long enough to watch 3ABN, they are finding Christ and getting baptized. Praise God!

The Carter Report

(Website: www.cartereport.org)

John Carter

John Carter and his wife, Beverley, were born and raised in Australia. They have spent nearly forty years sharing the good news around the world, as well as caring for the needs of local congregations. Since 1991, the Carters have been involved in evangelizing millions in Russia and Ukraine. John conducted the first ever evangelistic series in Moscow when the flag of communism still flew over the Kremlin. Then came the historic 1992 Palace of Sport Nizhny Novgorod meetings that were filmed by 3ABN and supported by 3ABN viewers (see chapter 9).

It was during that series that a KGB general declared that John Carter was more like a scientist than a preacher because he gave facts that proved the Bible, rather than asking people to just "have faith." This general was so impressed with the meetings that he invited The Carter Report team to visit KGB headquarters to proclaim the truths he had heard at the Palace of Sport. Over a thousand KGB officers sat in awed silence as Pastor Carter declared, "You are not an animal, you are not a machine, you are a child of God." The general, after hearing an appeal to accept the great Creator, stood to his feet and invited his team of a thousand officers to respond. They did, many with tears running down their cheeks.

Another story that John tells about the Nizhny Novgorod crusade has to do with meeting Julia Outkina at her brother's home. She approached John and said, "When you preached on the Sabbath, I went out in rebellion and bought a piece of meat on the Sabbath. A bone from the meat stuck up under my fingernail. All week long my finger has said to me, "Remember the Sabbath day to keep it holy."

During the past few years, The Carter Report has conducted great campaigns in the Ukrainian cities of Kiev, Dnipropetrovsk, Kharkiv, and Odesa. On the opening night of the 1995 campaign in Kiev, thirty thousand people attended in two sessions, and over a hundred thousand had to be turned away. So many people came that the city proclaimed a state of national emergency and closed down the metro to stop the flood of people coming to the meetings. The result was the largest baptism in Europe in a thousand years–3,488 souls were baptized in the Dnieper River. These campaigns have been the largest gatherings of secular people attending religious meetings anywhere in the world.[4]

What role has 3ABN played in making all this possible? Here's what John has to say:

> The Carter Report has been airing on 3ABN since 1987– the year 3ABN began broadcasting. Through the years, Danny has come to the aid of The Carter Report on several occasions and has helped us raise money for evangelism in Russia when no one else would stand by us. It is hard to see how all we have been able to do could have been accomplished without the support of 3ABN. Danny Shelton and his team have stood with us, and money has come from faithful souls who viewed the programs on 3ABN.
>
> In addition to our crusades in Russia and Ukraine, I pastor one of the finest churches in Arcadia, California. When we had to raise one and a half million dollars for this facility, Danny invited me to do a Thursday night *3ABN Presents Live* program during which he asked the viewers to support us. In January 2003, Danny even came out to our church and did a live broadcast. During the church service, which was seen worldwide, Danny told the viewers, 'Folks, don't send money to 3ABN this month, send it to The Carter Report. They are doing a wonderful work of evangelism and are winning thousands of souls for Christ.' Our weekly church services are taped from this facility, as well as the Russian television advertising that is so successful in bringing individuals to our meetings in Russia.
>
> For years, The Carter Report and 3ABN have joined hands in the public preaching of the everlasting gospel. I have appreciated the friendship and support of Danny. Together we have been able to accomplish far more for the Lord than either one of our ministries could have done alone. I am confident that when the roll is called up yonder, a great multitude from the former Soviet Union will answer when their names are called.

David and Beverly Waid with one of the orphan children their ministry cares for

Bangladesh Children's Sponsorship Service—America

(Website: www.banglacss.org)

Years ago, David and Beverly Waid began sponsoring Christian schooling for orphan children in countries where poverty was rampant—Guatemala, India, and Bangladesh. After sponsoring a number of children in Bangladesh, David and Beverly wanted to send these children something special. They were told, however, that the only way to make sure the gifts would reach the children was to personally deliver them. In 1993, a friend urged David to travel with him to Bangladesh. It seemed impossible, but Beverly urged her husband to go. He was not prepared for the abject poverty that he found there. It was much worse than Guatemala or Mexico. One problem is the sheer numbers of people; imagine putting half the population of the United States in an area the size of Colorado!

Upon returning from Bangladesh, the Waids began Bangladesh Children's Sponsorship Service—America, a nonprofit organization. They leased their home and traveled around the country in a fifth-wheel camper to encourage individuals to sponsor these needy children. Their organization built a number of orphanages. One day in 1997, 3ABN invited the Waids to share with viewers what they were doing in Bangladesh.

One of those who happened to watch the program was Merilee McNeilus. She quickly told her husband, Garwin, and they put their resources to work. As of 2004, two hundred village churches and schools have been built. Two boarding schools have been completely renovated, another is being worked on, and plans are being made to build a receiving center for orphans where these little children can have a home until they are old enough to attend an orphanage school.

Global Mission heard about the Waids' work in Bangladesh and invited them to share their experiences on *Global Mission Frontline.* Viewers are now sponsoring entire schools. In 2004, three thousand dollars would pay all the expenses of operating a school of thirty children for a year—including one hot meal a day.

David admits that 3ABN has been the avenue that God has used to provide for the needs of God's abandoned children in Bangladesh. The Waids are incredibly thankful for 3ABN's willingness to help others be able to help others. David says, "Without 3ABN, Bangladesh Children's Sponsorship Service—America would not be helping the thirty-six hundred children that we are currently sponsoring, nor would we have been able to build the beautiful orphanages and schools that have been built through the donations from individuals who have responded to the needs presented over the 3ABN worldwide satellite network."

Gospel Outreach
(Website: www.goaim.org)

Frank Stanyer began Gospel Outreach in 1993 after visiting the Philippines and observing some two thousand students coming out of chapel at Philippine Union College. God impressed him with the thought, *What could these students do for evangelism if they were provided some support?* Frank immediately felt he should start a fund-raising organization that would give stipends to people wanting to do evangelism in their own countries. But just as quickly, he argued, *Lord, why me? With my background, I'm the wrong person.* Eight years went by. Then in 1992, he couldn't put it off any longer. He said, "The Lord bothered me every day with the thought that I should be empowering people to work in their own countries where the need was greatest. And Gospel Outreach was started.

Frank knew that others would be happy to help these people if they were aware of the need. And that's when he and his associates began the *Adventures in Missions* telecast seen regularly on 3ABN. And that's when 3ABN began supporting Gospel Outreach.

Frank Stanyer reports:

Today, mainly because of 3ABN and the "ripple effect," Gospel Outreach is supporting more than eleven thousand evangelists in forty different countries. Seventy local missions are spread across the 10/40 window in Asia and Africa, where the need is greatest. In Mali, for example, before Gospel Outreach support, the local conference budget allowed only for the mission president and one other worker.

Mission personnel were pleased with fifteen or twenty baptisms a year. We helped fund five evangelists, and that first year two hundred people were baptized.

We have four hundred evangelists in India. In the Calcutta area alone, with its forty million people, there were just two Seventh-day Adventist churches until we sent in ten evangelists and later sent twenty-five. There are now thirty Adventist churches in that city. Ron Watts, president of the Southern Asia Division of Seventh-day Adventists, projects there will be three hundred churches in Calcutta by the year 2015—as they are baptizing people by the thousands.

Without 3ABN we would still be limping along. When God's people hear about the needs, they are eager to help. We thank 3ABN for the opportunity to share the story of what God is doing to change people's lives in the countries of the world where the need is the greatest.

Mike Ryan

Global Mission

(Website: www.global-mission.org)

Global Mission was established in 1990 as a church planting venture in areas of the world where there was no Seventh-day Adventist presence. In 1993, the frontline workers who advanced the message of hope became known as Global Mission pioneers. These dedicated people leave their comfort zone and, with only a small stipend, move into an unentered area and donate their time for three to five years with the goal of establishing a church. They live among the people, caring for the sick, teaching health and agricultural skills, running literacy programs, holding evangelistic meetings, and giving Bible studies. These are not foreign missionaries. These pioneers have the same cultural background and language as do the people living in the area where they serve. Global Mission pioneers care for the whole person. And people are responding like never before. Here are just a few facts:

• In 1990, no Seventh-day Adventist church existed in Cambodia. Ten years later there were four churches, thirty-two companies, and nearly 3,200 members.

- After eighty-six years of mission work, the Adventist Church in Bangladesh (population: 126 million) had only 12,000 members. In just a few years with Global Mission pioneers and other dedicated ministries, that number almost doubled, to 23,100.
- During the early 1990s, members were added to the Seventh-day Adventist Church at the rate of 1,700 to 1,800 a day world-wide. During 1999 and 2000, new believers averaged 2,925 a day. Today, more than 3,000 new members are added each day, reminiscent of the Day of Pentecost, A.D. 31. That's more than one every twenty-eight seconds!
- According to the United Nations, there are 228 countries and areas in the world. The Adventist Church now has a presence in 209 countries—mostly because of the dedication of Global Mission workers.
- Global Mission has established study centers around the world to help find more effective ways of sharing the good news about Jesus among those believing in Buddhism, Hinduism, Judaism, Islam, and secularism.

Fascinating facts! But how does one tell the fourteen million members of the Seventh-day Adventist Church about the rapid expansion of God's work through the world? Here's where 3ABN enters the picture.

In the early 1990s, Mike Ryan co-hosted a Seventh-day Adventist news program on 3ABN with Shirley Burton. When Shirley retired, Mike continued the program, calling it *Global Mission Frontline,* with Gary Krause as producer. The program shared the exciting stories coming out of the vast activities of Global Mission. When I asked how 3ABN had affected Global Mission, Mike responded:

One of the greatest challenges of the Seventh-day Adventist Church, which has members in so many different countries, is to let members know what their church is doing worldwide. 3ABN is one of the most effective ways to reach such a diversified population. It has a network of television stations, cable outlets, and dishes, making it possible for people to learn of the advancement of God's work and feel that they are a part of a vast movement.

Almost all ministries operate on the donations they receive from dedicated people. Global Mission is the same. As 3ABN has increased the awareness of a worldwide population to the work of Global Mission, our donations have increased. In addition to our regular weekly program, Danny has interviewed us on *3ABN Presents* and has invited us many times to share with the 3ABN family of viewers on Thursday night *3ABN Presents Live* programs. He is always generous in encouraging listeners to support the work of Global Mission.

And just as 3ABN has had a ripple effect by blessing other ministries to such an extent that they can do their work more effectively, we have tried to do the same. We have interviewed the directors of a number of other mission-driven ministries so that our listeners can become acquainted with their activities and support them if they choose. For example, Maranatha Volunteers International, Gospel Outreach, Bangladesh Children's Sponsorship Service—America, Adventist Frontier Missions, Adventist World Radio, and Adventist Development and Relief Agency (ADRA).

We all have the same goal, to complete the gospel commission to go into all the world—for then shall the end come. We are very appreciative that 3ABN has given us time on its airwaves.

James Gilley

A statement by James Gilley

At the 2004 3ABN camp meeting, James Gilley, vice president for evangelism of the North American Division of the Seventh-day Adventist Church, made this statement:

I'm excited about the work that 3ABN is doing to help the Seventh-day Adventist Church in evangelism. If you look at the history of this church, it took a hundred years, from 1860 to 1960, to reach the first million members. In the next thirty years, we moved up to about six million members. That's about the time that 3ABN came on the scene and became a part of evangelism through satellite technology. Since that time, the membership of the Seventh-day

Adventist Church has more than doubled and now has approximately fourteen million members. I feel that 3ABN has made a major contribution to this growth.

Later, Jim added:

In 1975, I was impressed that God wanted me, through the Adventist Church, to start a television network that would broadcast Bible truth to the world. I began by purchasing a media company that was able to fund forty-three evangelistic crusades, but I wasn't able to get beyond that point. Nearly everyone I spoke to in church administration felt that the idea of a television satellite network was beyond our reach. During this time, a television station in the Los Angeles area came up for sale. I made a presentation to some media leaders about purchasing this station as the beginning of a worldwide network. They were not interested. They said, "It's impossible for us to produce more than an hour-and-a-half of programming a week. How could we ever produce enough for twenty-four hours a day even if we could afford to buy the station?"

That's why I've been so excited to see Danny step out in faith and do what others thought was impossible. Because of the inspiration and cooperation of 3ABN under Danny's leadership, there are now a number of full-time Seventh-day Adventist satellite networks worldwide. If Danny had not been willing to move forward and show what God can do, others may not have had the courage to try. To show the extent of 3ABN's ripple effect, in 2003, the Adventist Church's television network, Hope Channel, was officially launched with an announcement on 3ABN!

Lyle Albrecht

Lyle Albrecht

Lyle Albrecht is an evangelist for the North Pacific Union Conference of Seventh-day Adventists. You'll want to tune in to 3ABN's *Revelation Insight* program and see Lyle Albrecht in action, doing what he's done full time for thirty-two years— evangelism! Lyle's testimony of the effect

3ABN has had on his ministry is just one validation of Jim Gilley's statement about the major contribution that 3ABN has had on church growth. Here's what Lyle says:

> I have been associated with other Adventist media programs over the years and have always tried to follow up on the interests they have generated. I was even an evangelist for the Adventist Media Center for three years. I'm thankful for the programs produced, but all the other Adventist media combined do not come close to the interest generated by 3ABN. In fact, 3ABN has changed my ministry.
>
> About 50 percent of all those who now attend my meetings do so because they have been watching 3ABN. Therefore, I have become very selective in choosing the cities in which I will hold meetings. I will go only where 3ABN is available on cable or a local channel, because 3ABN is the sower and nurturer of the seeds of Bible truth. It's not just my program, but all the other evangelists who are helping to grow that seed. People who have been watching 3ABN are eager to attend my meetings. They know they are coming to hear more about what Seventh-day Adventists believe, so I no longer have to start in a neutral location for fear some will be prejudiced. Instead, I start in the local church. Renting large halls can be expensive, so I'm saving a lot of money! And since I've been on 3ABN, the number of people who are baptized at the end of the meetings has doubled.
>
> I have only five more years to work full time before I retire, and I want to get the maximum benefit out of that time. Just like farmers spend most of their time working in the fields that are most productive, that's what I'm doing. I am also actively encouraging church members who don't have 3ABN on cable or can't get it on a local channel to write and call their cable companies and request 3ABN be made a part of their offerings.
>
> I see the 3ABN ripple effect in my ministry. Someone is baptized, and they tell their family and friends about 3ABN. They begin listening, come to my meetings or a local church, and they are baptized. Then they tell their family and friends. The miracles of this expanding circle of influence could fill a

book. God has blessed 3ABN, and I feel privileged to be a part of this worldwide media ministry.

The Great Commission

It has been a difficult task to select only a few of the many ministries that 3ABN has affected over the years. Each has interesting and exciting testimonies of how God has allowed 3ABN to bless them so that they could bless others. There are the dedicated musicians who give of their time to provide 3ABN with fine Christian music and who, as a result, have experienced 3ABN's ripple effect in the growth of their musical ministries. There are the health professionals who share their knowledge over 3ABN, and in return, people have found their way to their lifestyle centers or seminars for more intensive medical information and service. There are the ministries who have shared their mission and testimonies on 3ABN, and people have caught the vision, supported the ministries, and their work has grown. And there are those who have shared their personal experiences, which have encouraged and blessed viewers and have either resulted in the establishment of a new ministry or the publishing of a book. The list could go on and on.

God's commission to His people is to go into the all the world. The task of reaching the billions of individuals who make up the world's population sounds enormous. But just as a shock wave on one coast travels thousands of miles through oceans and eventually washes up on a far distant shore, so can God's three angels' messages travel around the world if we will each choose to be a part of the ripple effect.

Don't let the blessings of 3ABN stop with you. Pass them on. Allow God to inspire you with a passionate mission of your own. Pray that God will give you a longing to save souls. Reach out and mend the brokenhearted people around you with a smile and a touch of Christ's love. Step out of your comfort zone and tell someone about Jesus. Or relieve their suffering—as Jesus did. When you do, you will find joy in the service of the Lord, and you'll become a vital part of 3ABN's ripple effect.

---

[1] Larry Welch had a similar dream.

[2] You can read more about Cheri's experiences in Thailand in her book, *God Is Crazy About You,* available from True Step Ministries or Pacific Press Publishing Association.

[3] Doug Batchelor's book, *The Richest Caveman,* is available from Amazing Facts.

[4] Other evangelists, such as Billy Graham, may have drawn bigger crowds of Christians, but not of the unchurched, which was the focus of the John Carter meetings.

Section IV
The 3ABN Mission Expands

"I have been given complete authority in heaven
and on earth.
Therefore, go and make disciples of all the nations,
baptizing them in the name of the Father
and the Son and the Holy Spirit.
Teach these new disciples to obey all the commands
I have given you.
And be sure of this: I am with you always,
even to the end of the age"
—Matthew 28:18-20, New Living Translation.

Although God called Danny to a television ministry that would blanket the world with His message, He didn't spell out the specifics. As the years went by, it became evident that even though beaming an English-language television signal twenty-four hours a day to satellites circling the earth might technically "reach the world," this alone was not enough to truly reach everybody in the world. What about different language groups? What if people didn't own a television set? What about the "international" language of beautiful music that is sometimes even more effective than the spoken word in calling a sinner to repentance and presenting the love of God? What about reaching to the ends of the world with printed material that can be passed from person to person and spread like the leaves of autumn? What was the best way to reach the cities?

To better fulfill the gospel commission, 3ABN has expanded into four new ministry fields—and is planning a fifth! 3ABN Latino, a 24/7 television channel broadcasting entirely in Spanish and Portuguese; 3ABN Radio, broadcasting around the world in English, 3ABN Music, now that the new sound center has been completed, and 3ABN Books. This fourth area of ministry, launched on July 1, 2004, has the mission to reach the world with printed material and to supplement 3ABN's television and radio ministries with follow-up products—books, pamphlets, manuals, and Bible lessons. *Mending Broken People* is the first publication from 3ABN Books. If you're enjoying this story of faith and miracles, you'll be happy to know that 3ABN will publish many more books in the years to come. God inspired Danny that the theme for the year 2004 was to be *"You haven't seen anything yet!"* 3ABN Books is just one area where that theme is being validated.

And what's the latest? Plans are being laid to begin a new television network, Urban Inspirational Television, that focuses on urban needs and interests around the world. It's a truly exciting prospect as 3ABN once more steps out in faith to better meet the needs of people who live in cities.

Because 3ABN Books is too new to have its own miracle story to tell and the urban network is still in the planning stages, what follows in this section are the stories of 3ABN Latino, 3ABN Radio, and 3ABN Music. You'll learn how God called them into being, about the people God enabled to lead and supply special needed skills, and what these ministries are doing today to better reach the world with the three angels' messages and biblical truth.

12
3ABN Latino

"Tell me the story of Jesus
Write on my heart every word
Tell me the story most precious,
Sweetest that ever was heard."
—*Fanny J. Crosby*
(But please, tell it in my own language!)

On August 24, 2003, at the stroke of midnight, Moses Primo, 3ABN's director of broadcasting and engineering was in master control. He flipped the switch, and 3ABN Latino television immediately began broadcasting the story of Jesus to more than 619 million potential viewers who speak either Spanish or Portuguese.

Within an hour and a half, Moses received an email from a viewer in a Portuguese church in California. The email message read: "The signal is great!" No one knew when broadcasting would begin on 3ABN Latino, but in anticipation, this viewer had purchased a dish, had it tuned to the satellite, and was waiting and watching!

"Within four weeks of going on the air, 3ABN Latino was added to cable systems or local stations in twenty-one countries—Argentina, Aruba, Belize, Bolivia, Brazil, Colombia, Costa Rica, Dominican Republic, Ecuador, Guatemala, Guyana, Honduras, Jamaica, Mexico, Nicaragua, Panama, Peru, El Salvador, Trinidad, the United States, and Venezuela, as well as Puerto Rico, a U.S. territory. That's every major Spanish-speaking country except three—Cuba, Paraguay, and Uruguay!" reported Sandra Juárez, director of 3ABN Latino.[1] "This is incredible! It took the English-language telecast years to achieve such widespread cable coverage. It is impossible to estimate the vast potential audience that 3ABN Latino will reach in the next few years. Cable companies in the United States are also extremely interested in 3ABN Latino's programming, since

The staff of 3ABN Latino (L to R): Sandra Juárez, Moses Primo,
John Dinzey, Jorge Pillco, and Hernando Cruz

the Hispanic population is now the largest minority in North
America."

How 3ABN Latino began

Almost as soon as 3ABN was on the air in English, the question
arose, "What is 3ABN going to do to reach population groups in their
own languages?" And because so many people speak Spanish and
Portuguese, these languages were the logical next step.

Almost from the beginning, God called bilingual, Spanish-
speaking and Portuguese-speaking workers to 3ABN. One of the
first was Gonzalo Santos, the electrician who came to 3ABN in 1985.
It was through Gonzalo's influence that 3ABN first began to broadcast an hour and a half of programs in Spanish each day shortly after the ministry began broadcasting in the fall of 1986. Moses Primo,
who joined 3ABN in 1992, was also very interested in reaching the
Latino people—especially those who speak Portuguese. These workers were influential in making sure some of 3ABN's air time was
devoted to the Latino people.

In November 1989, when John Dinzey first came to work for
3ABN, he was excited about the potential of reaching the Hispanic

audience through the hour and a half each day that was devoted to Spanish programming. Even though this was a very limited amount of time, it was better than nothing!

Then as 3ABN scheduled more programming for English-speaking listeners, the time slots that had previously gone to programming in Spanish were filled by programs in English. At first, programming in Spanish went down to five days a week. Next, to just Monday, Wednesday, and Friday.

Then came a phone call that informed 3ABN that channel 21 in Puerto Rico was for sale. This television station reached a potential audience of 1.5 million Latinos. The asking price of $300,000 was a lot of money in the early 1990s (it still is), but channel 21's signal was excellent, and 3ABN board members, such as May Chung, were eager for 3ABN to reach the world. They viewed this acquisition as a step in that direction and urged 3ABN to purchase the station. After much prayer and many telephone calls acquainting people with the opportunity of reaching a Spanish-speaking population group, $275,000 were pledged for the station. Just $25,000 more was needed—but every avenue for funds seemed to have been exhausted. Even the local Seventh-day Adventist conference in Puerto Rico had no money to give to this project. When pockets are empty, $25,000 might as well be a million dollars. Time was running out. The seller announced, "If you don't have the money here by 5 P.M. tomorrow, I'll sell the station to someone else."

When John Dinzey heard this, he called Abdiel Acosta, the president of the East Puerto Rico Conference of Seventh-day Adventists, presenting the urgent need for $25,000. "Our staff is just going into worship," President Acosta announced. "We'll make it a matter of prayer. This will be a wonderful way to reach the people of Puerto Rico with the gospel message. I believe God has a way to work this out."

At worship, the secretary of the conference, Pastor Carmelo Rivera, made the announcement, and the workers knelt and pled with the Lord for $25,000 by five o'clock that afternoon. That day a retired minister, Pastor Juan Rodriguez, just "happened" to be attending the worship service. He felt God tapping on his shoulder. After the devotional, he approached Pastor Rivera and said, "You can put me down for $15,000."

Pastor Rivera knew Pastor Rodriguez was not a man of means. "Are you sure?" he asked.

"Yes, I want this to happen," Pastor Rodriguez replied.

With only $10,000 more to go, excitement mounted. The conference leaders believed that God wouldn't have brought them this far without providing the means to go forward. They decided to call people they knew and ask for pledges. The people responded, and channel 21 was purchased. God's timetable was perfect!

Three years before this purchase, the people of Puerto Rico had developed a little television studio to produce a half-hour weekly Spanish-language program for a local channel. Danny saw this as evidence that the Lord had been preparing the conference to have a studio and programs to supply channel 21 with local programming. So with three years of thirty-minute programs, channel 21 already had a head start to begin broadcasting to the people of Puerto Rico in their own language. The Hispanic staff at 3ABN were encouraged by this purchase because having a television station would likely mean that more Spanish-language productions would be needed at 3ABN.

The ironic thing is that in 1992, just as there was a need for more programming in Spanish to feed to channel 21, 3ABN English cut back programming in Spanish by one more day, to only one and a half hours on Monday and Wednesday—again to make a slot available for more English-language programming. Many Spanish-speaking individuals were interested in purchasing a dish and a receiver, if they could receive more than three hours of programming in Spanish a week. But if 3ABN were to increase Spanish language broadcasts, it could cause English-speaking listeners to change channels when Spanish-language programming was aired—and they might not return to 3ABN.

The Spanish-speaking population is very media-oriented. It's not uncommon for Latinos to keep the radio on all day, listening to music, talk, and news. Plus, Latinos tend to watch more television than those in the English-speaking culture—almost four hours more a week. The Spanish-speaking workers at 3ABN began to talk in the hallways, "We need a Spanish 3ABN channel!" But it would take ten years before that would become a reality.

In 1994, the need became even more apparent. A television station on the other side of Puerto Rico was for sale for an unbelievably low price. It was owned by the brother of the person who had sold channel 21 to 3ABN. The brother considered selling his station to the Catholic Church, but when his mother found out, she said,

"Son, if you sell it to the Catholic Church, you are going to break my heart. Do me a favor; offer it to the Adventist Church. They will do something good with it." Although his mother is a member of a Pentecostal church, she has a great appreciation for the Seventh-day Adventist Church.

"OK," he responded, "I'll call the Adventists."

When the local Adventist conference received his call, it in turn called 3ABN for advice. It sounded like an incredible bargain. The 3ABN board voted "Yes," and the people responded with generous gifts. Now there were two full-time Spanish-language stations needing more programming in Spanish! The need for a 3ABN Spanish-language channel had just doubled!

This was also the time when Moses Primo joined 3ABN with a burden to reach the Portuguese-speaking populations of the world.

But it was after Net 95 and Net 96, when Mark Finley's live satellite evangelistic meetings were sent around the world with a Spanish-language feed, that people really began to call and write to 3ABN pleading for a Spanish-language channel. When Net 98 with Dwight Nelson and Net 99 with Doug Batchelor were broadcast around the world with a Spanish-language feed, the interest mounted.

In 1999, the North American Division, in cooperation with 3ABN, produced *La Red* (The Net), the first live Seventh-day Adventist satellite evangelistic series in the Spanish language. The speaker was the South American Division evangelist Alejandro Bullón, and the meetings were held in Orlando, Florida. Hundreds of Hispanic churches purchased dishes to watch this series in their own language. One man who was watching in San Juan, Puerto Rico, had no idea that his ex-wife was actually attending the meetings in Orlando. They just happened to talk that week, and she mentioned she was attending meetings conducted by a most powerful preacher. Suddenly, he realized he was watching the same series on 3ABN in San Juan—which was about a thousand miles away!

He said, "I believe our marriage failed because we didn't have Jesus Christ in our lives."

She agreed. He then said, "I would love to get back together and make Jesus the center of our home. Do you want to try again?"

"Yes, I would really like that," she responded.

So he flew to Orlando, and on the last day of the series they were baptized together and were remarried shortly afterward.

John Dinzey

In 1999, just as interest in Spanish-language programming was growing and there was increased need for more programs for the two stations in Puerto Rico, Spanish-language programming on 3ABN's English-language channel was reduced to just two hours a week! Meanwhile, John Dinzey, 3ABN's director of pastoral ministries, and Sandra Juárez, programming director, had a growing burden to reach the Hispanic people of the world with the everlasting gospel. The need for a Spanish-language channel was confirmed when they went to camp meetings and churches and heard people asking, "When is 3ABN going to have more Spanish programming?"

One night while Sandra was visiting her parents (who do not speak English), the need hit home. After watching a popular Spanish-language Saturday-night secular program, she turned to her father, "Dad, I

Sandra Juárez

know we enjoyed ourselves watching this program, but what did we learn from it?"

"Well, my dear," he responded, "we don't have options; we don't have anything else to watch!"

That incident had a great impact on Sandra. She saw clearly the great need to give people a better option, an option that would help them make decisions for eternal life through Jesus Christ.

The meeting with Danny

Then came the year 2000. Each year, the first working day is set aside as 3ABN's Day of Prayer. All the employees meet together for prayer for 3ABN. One of the last things Danny said to the staff on that particular day was, "If you have a burden to do something for the Lord, if you have something that the Lord is impressing you that 3ABN should be doing, come and talk to me about it. Together, we can seek the Lord's guidance."

John Dinzey was impressed to take Danny up on his offer and present to him the need for a Spanish-language channel. His first job was to gather the data. How many Spanish-speaking people were there in the world? In what countries were they located? While John was researching this, Derrell Mundall was researching the Hispanic cable market. John found that a couple of years earlier it had been estimated that by the year 2010 there would be 30 million Spanish-speaking people in the United States. But that number had already been reached in the year 2000—a decade earlier than expected. There were now commercials in Spanish for McDonalds, Coca Cola, and Pepsi. Major magazines, such as *The Reader's Digest,* were publishing Spanish-language editions. It took a number of months for Derrell and John to put their facts together. John then asked Derrell (who grew up in a Spanish-speaking country) and Sandra Juárez if they wanted to go with him to visit Danny and make the presentation for a Spanish-language channel. "Count us in!" they responded.

John asked Mollie, Danny's assistant, for an appointment. She promised to call John as soon as there was an appropriate time. Three weeks went by, and during this time John began to hear rumors that 3ABN's contributions for the year were down by almost a million dollars. When he heard this news, he shared it with Sandra because he thought Danny might not even entertain a proposal for something new at that point. John and Sandra began to pray more earnestly,

"Lord, prepare the way. May Your timing for this meeting be perfect."

Then the call came from Mollie; Danny could see them. John grabbed his folder and alerted Derrell and Sandra to meet him at Danny's office. In the lobby, before going in to see Danny, they paused for prayer. "Lord, we don't know if 3ABN is over the financial crisis, but we believe You have put this burden on our hearts. Please prepare the way."

They began the meeting by presenting the statistics about the vast Spanish-speaking and Portuguese-speaking population groups, including the number of Hispanic cable viewers.

"People like to hear the gospel in their own language," Danny agreed. "They will listen to a translation, but as we have learned from our work in Russia, there is a much better response when the programming is in their own language."

John nodded, "That was going to be my next point! That is exactly what we have heard from viewers of the translations of Net 95, Net 96, Net 98, and Net 99. Based on this, we believe that 3ABN needs a Spanish-language channel."

"Good," Danny responded enthusiastically. "Let's find out how much it's going to cost. If we can do it right away, let's do it!" He told the group to get Moses Primo involved to work out the technical aspects of the project. Then Danny gave the marching orders, "As soon as that's worked out, let's move forward!"

When the meeting ended, they knelt together before the Lord in Danny's office, praying that God would bless what they knew He wanted them to do. As they were leaving, Danny commented, "We all need to earnestly pray. We are still a million dollars behind in general operations, and this will be costing us at least another million."

John came out of the meeting shaking his head. "Danny caught the vision! This man still believes God can do anything. Most would have said, 'We'll move forward as soon as we have the budget deficiency taken care of.' Not Danny. Instead, he said, 'If the people want it and need it, let's give it to them. Let's just pray a little harder!'"

And so was born the idea for 3ABN Latino, broadcasting the three angels' messages in Spanish and Portuguese full time. Moses Primo got involved in the technical aspects of this new challenge, and the project was announced beginning in August 2001 with a live rally that was broadcast from San Juan, Puerto Rico. It was the first 3ABN-produced, on-location, live broadcast in the Spanish language.

How God provided programming

Putting a 24/7 network on the air requires 168 hours of programming a week. One of the challenges Sandra faced as program director was to obtain high-quality programs in Spanish and Portuguese that could be aired on the Latino channel. God knew that 3ABN Latino would become a reality, so He began impressing people from Spanish-speaking and Portuguese-speaking countries to produce programs. Praise the Lord! Sandra found enough programming to get started. Meanwhile, 3ABN began the process of building another studio so that there would be one available for the full-time production of programs in Spanish and Portuguese.

One of the first programs Sandra developed with a team of talented Spanish-speaking children and teens was *Amiguitos de Jesús*. This ongoing series features talented young people hosting segments on nature, music, Bible stories, and interviews with other kids. Sandra says, "We praise the Lord for the efforts of Mrs. Rocio Chávez, the producer, and the army of dedicated parents who harnessed the energy of more than thirty children to make these programs! Most of them traveled to 3ABN from Texas and Mexico. One even came from as far away as Argentina. Currently, 3ABN Latino is producing many new programs."

One of the most successful evangelistic tools the Latino community has found are the live "net" programs that 3ABN has helped broadcast annually since 1999—*La Red* 2000, 2001, 2002, 2003, and 2004.

At one of the *La Red* series, a church in New York City decided to put a large screen outside the church so passers-by could watch. One day as a man came out of the subway, he saw the big screen and was curious. He stood outside the church and watched the rest of the program. The next day he got off work early just so he could watch the program from the beginning. Three or four days later, as the man stood outside the church watching, the evangelist on the screen made an appeal. "Jesus is calling you. 'Come home, My child.' If you are in a church and would like to give your heart to Jesus and renew your relationship with Him, please come forward now. There is a pastor who would like to pray with you."

When the man heard Christ's invitation, "Come home, My child," he knew what he had to do. Immediately, he opened the door of the church, walked down the center aisle, got down on his knees, and with tears in his eyes gave his life to the Lord. Many years ago, when he had come to the United States, he got all wrapped up in making money. His lifestyle began to change as he pursued the mighty dollar. Eventually, he left his church. Now, years later, hearing the call, "Come home, My child," he knew Christ was speaking directly to him.

In May 2003, 3ABN cooperated with the Illinois Conference of Seventh-day Adventists to produce and broadcast *Felicidad Sin Limite (Happiness Without Limits)*, the first 3ABN-originated, live evangelistic series in Spanish. The meetings were held in Chicago. John Dinzey was able to attend during the final days of this series and was pleasantly surprised when he saw that an old friend, Manuel, was there. The last John had heard, Manuel's marriage had broken up, he had left the church, and he was living a worldly lifestyle—drinking, dancing, and partying. Now seven years later, he was in church. What happened to bring him back?

A girl he met in a dance hall had asked him to go to church with her. "I can't attend your church because it doesn't follow the Bible," he explained. He then gave her a Bible study on the importance of keeping the seventh-day Sabbath holy!

"If you know all these things," the girl replied in utter amazement, "why aren't you going to church?"

They started attending a Seventh-day Adventist church and, eventually, were married. Then Manuel shared with John the great news that his wife was being convicted during these meetings that what she was hearing was Bible truth and was being baptized on the last day of the series.

In 2003, a woman from Texas became convicted that her unchurched family in Venezuela needed 3ABN Latino. She traveled to that country and approached a local cable company and requested that they make 3ABN Latino available to their viewers. They did. Her family began watching, and today they are in the church!

Now, 3ABN Latino is reaching millions of people across the Americas and Europe with the gospel of Jesus Christ twenty-four hours a day. Church leadership and laity alike have expressed strong support and gratitude for this tremendous means of reaching into homes, lives, and hearts with a life-changing message.

---

1. In 2004 3ABN Latino began airing in Paraguay and Uruguay, leaving Cuba as the only Latino country where 3ABN Latino is not on cable. It is illegal for cable systems in Cuba to carry programming from the United States.

13
3ABN Radio

"Come and hear, all you who fear God,
And I will declare what He has done for my soul"
—Psalm 66:16, NKJV.

Radio reaches people TV never will

Radio is portable. People can take radio with them. They can listen while working at the office or at home, as they are driving, while jogging, when going to sleep, or when waking up. It's a wonderful way to reach busy people—people who don't have time to sit in front of the TV set. Television is an equally wonderful way to reach people; it's great for those sitting at home or in a hotel room. But it's different from radio. Radio has the potential of reaching people whom television would never reach. In areas where television requires cable or a satellite connection, radio can be easily accessible.

Plus, small churches and communities that could never afford to purchase and maintain a television station find that establishing a small radio station is affordable.

Radio reaches 75.2 percent of persons twelve years of age and older every day, and 95.3 percent every week. There are no seasonal slumps in radio listening. Adults in the United States spend more time with radio between 6 A.M. and 6 P.M. than they do with any other form of media. Radio is also the most interactive form of major media, allowing the audience to bond rapidly with the program, station, or network.

Because of all this and more, Linda Shelton felt called to radio.

3ABN Radio receives funding

3ABN had a free audio subcarrier that went to the satellite that could be used for radio—an unused resource that God had provided. Because Linda had worked extensively over the years with 3ABN's television programming, she felt a significant number of the programs could be used for radio with little or no editing.

She approached Danny about starting 3ABN Radio. Danny, at that moment, had many other responsibilites. He was already on overload. He could understand Linda's reasoning; it did make sense to go forword with radio, but he just didn't feel God wanted him to divert his energy in that direction. However, he said, "Linda, it's obvious that God has placed the burden for radio on your heart. I think you should start the radio network, and I'll support you." He also suggested she involve Moses Primo and apply to ASI Missions, Inc. for funding.

Before proceeding, prayer support was needed. Linda encouraged two groups—a local church group and the 3ABN staff that meets each morning for prayer—to start praying that God would give a clear direction concerning radio. Linda's personal prayer was, "Lord, if You really want this radio project to happen, make a miracle that is so distinct that there will be no doubt that this is really You." The groups prayed together for about six weeks. During this time, Linda developed a budget of what the start-up costs would be for radio. It came to $375,000. She submitted the proposal to ASI Missions Inc., and in less than two months, the ASI Missions board voted to give $250,000 for 3ABN Radio, and an individual ASI member was impressed to give the remaining amount!

Never before in its history had 3ABN received that kind of upfront money for a project. Radio was Linda's very first project. She asked for the entire amount needed, made one appeal, and it was funded. Danny shook his head. "Maybe donors just have a weakness for beautiful women pleading for money!" he joked.

But Linda made the real reason clear: "Time is shorter now than ever before. There is an urgency to get the message out using various media. God wants 3ABN to do bigger things than it has before. So God provided the money and is basically saying, 'I've done My part, now I'm waiting for you! What are you going to do with what I've given you?' "

Funding for radio was indeed an answer to prayer. God provided in such a significant way that there was no doubt radio was on His agenda for 3ABN.

Building radio studios

Radio meant new offices, new studios, new equipment, new personnel, and new challenges. Running a radio network is quite different from television broadcasting. And Linda knew nothing about it. But she plunged in, believing the Lord was in it. She recalls that time before 3ABN Radio began broadcasting:

> One day I was walking through the radio station when it was just a big pile of lumber and sawdust. Two others were with me. I was chattering to them about the wonders of reaching the world through radio and how terrific this new outreach was going to be. I was rather stunned when they both started to say things like, "It will be a miracle if this happens" and "Are you sure you know what you're getting into?" They brought up problems and obstacles that I had never even thought about. My eyes saw an exciting, thriving, effervescent, earth-shaking ministry, but those with me saw only the piles of lumber and sawdust and a mountain of headaches. I knew my optimistic "eyes" had to come from Jesus because I had not always looked through these kinds of glasses in the past.
>
> I'm convinced that when beginning a ministry, we desperately need eye salve! We need to see prosperity when there is an empty bank account. We need to see growth and movement when it seems like nothing is happening. We need to see light in the darkness . . . and in a nutshell, we need to look through the eyes of the Divine. Because without a vision, we perish! (from Bob Ellis, *A Channel of Blessing*, pp. 189, 190).

Amid the piles of lumber and sawdust and the mountains of headaches, Linda prayed, "Lord, whom should I ask to lead out in building a qualified team of professional radio people?" Over and over again, her mind went to one person—someone who knew nothing about radio. Finally, Linda did what God had been impressing her to do. She asked Theresa Boote to take the job as operations manager of 3ABN Radio. (You can read more of Theresa's story in chapter 16.)

Theresa steps out of her comfort zone to make radio a reality

Why Theresa? Danny and Linda had first met Theresa in 1987 when she and her family came to 3ABN to be baptized. Although she was a vivacious Christian, an enthusiastic person, a hard worker, and a strong woman of faith, she didn't have any background in radio. She admitted she never listened to radio. She didn't even like radio. It just seemed to her like background noise! Nevertheless, Linda continued to feel that Theresa had the organizational and leadership skills needed to pull a team of professionals together to make radio a reality.

Linda first talked to Theresa about radio—and the role she had in mind for Theresa to play—at an ASI meeting in 1998. Theresa responded in shock, "Oh, Linda! You know I would do anything to help you. But this is just not me." Three different times, Linda called Theresa at her

Theresa Boote

home in Canada and set up appointments to talk with her about the job. Each time, Theresa cancelled. She finally faxed Linda, "I just don't think I'm the person for the job." Then a few days later, Linda's assistant got a message from Theresa. She was on her way down to 3ABN!

After Theresa said "No" to the job offer, the strangest thing happened. She would go to bed in peace, quoting Proverbs 16:3 (NKJV), "Commit your works to the Lord, and your thoughts [plans] will be established." She trusted that God would solve the problem of who was to lead out in establishing 3ABN Radio. There was no reason to worry—because she was quite sure she wasn't the one. Then at about three in the morning, she would awaken with the agony of indecision. "Lord, I thought we settled this at eleven o'clock when I went to bed. And now it's back on my plate at three in the morning!" She would turn on the light and read Proverbs 16:9, "A man's heart plans his way, but the Lord directs his steps." Could it be that God wanted Theresa to do something different from what she wanted to do? Could it possibly be that He wanted her to help 3ABN establish a radio ministry? With these thoughts tumbling around in her mind, she suddenly decided to just get into her car and drive to 3ABN. She felt if she were actually there, perhaps she could see the situation more clearly. She had to settle this thing once and for all.

Her first day at 3ABN was torture. The more she thought about radio, the more terrified she became. "I don't even know what kilowatts or kilohertz are. I can't even figure out the phone system at 3ABN, how can I possibly figure out radio?" She was feeling so inadequate that she decided to give up and go home. On Thursday before leaving, she confided in a friend, "I feel like going home, but I don't want to feel guilty if I should be doing something I don't want to do."

And her friend wisely suggested, "I think you should listen to what your husband thinks you should do."

So she called her husband, Frank. Theresa expected him to say, "Come home!" Instead, he said, "You were called there to coordinate, not make technical decisions. Your job is to direct the team, and you are very good at that."

So Theresa reluctantly accepted the challenge and began to assemble a team of professionals. That was May 1999. During her first week on the job, she met Jay Christian, a veteran of radio who had driven from Walla Walla, Washington, for an interview. Theresa was instantly impressed that he was sent by the Lord. In August, he was on board to help make radio a reality.

From May to September, Theresa worked as a volunteer—waiting for a work permit to be issued that would allow her to receive a salary. Then the devil once again tried to stop the progress being made under Theresa's leadership. On September 10, Theresa was halted at the border and denied entrance into the United States.

She was told she needed a religious worker's visa even to cross the border! She could do nothing but return home. Thankfully, just a few weeks before, Jay Christian had come on board and was able to continue the work she had begun. Again, God foresaw what Satan would do and had already provided a way the work could continue.

A few months later, Theresa was back on the job—with her work visa in hand. An audio library was started. Pastor Samuel Thomas, Jr., and his wife, Karen, agreed to host a two-hour morning call-in talk show, and Jay tackled the challenge of producing a two-hour afternoon drive-time musical program.

Then on February 28, 2000, just nine months after Theresa first arrived, 3ABN Radio was on the air! Theresa recalls, "It was 11:55 P.M. Sunday evening, five minutes before the birthing of 3ABN's new baby. The radio staff gathered for prayer and listened to B. J. Thomas's rendition of 'Amazing Grace.' Then as the countdown clock zeroed to midnight, the on-air button was pushed and 3ABN Radio launched its 24/7 signal to satellite. A praise applause was rendered to the Lord, and a new sound reverberated on earth. It was programming that would shape the destiny of many for eternity. Praise the Lord!"

Theresa later confessed that during those first meetings with her staff, she felt she understood only about 5 percent of what was being discussed because she had no technical background. Before and after each meeting she would get on her knees and plead with the Lord to give her wisdom and to increase her understanding. "I've often wondered," Theresa commented, "why the likes of me was asked to do this job. The only answer is that we're living in end times, and God is calling all hands on deck. 3ABN Radio is not a result of committees; it exists as a result of prayer."

God's perfect timing

As it turned out, God's timing for radio was perfect. In March 2000, just a few days after 3ABN Radio went on the air, the FCC opened a filing window for low-power FM radio stations that would allow for small stations across the country to rebroadcast the 3ABN Radio signal. Incredible, isn't it?

Jay Christian explains what was happening in the radio industry at the time:

Some time before, Congress had passed laws allowing the deregulation of radio. This meant that owners of radio stations were no longer limited to fifteen stations. Big companies started buying smaller stations, until some networks controlled sometimes two hundred or more stations. The result was that there were too many commercial radio stations owned by big companies that offered the same programming across the country. Because of this, radio lost much of its local flavor. For example, a local radio station might be owned by a big broadcasting network in New York, so money and interest would flow from a small community to a big corporation hundreds or thousands of miles away. Small radio stations were no longer serving the community, so they had no voice.

To solve this problem, the FCC opened up a filing window to allow nonprofit organizations with a board of directors to apply for a low-power FM radio station (referred to as LPFM stations) under the stipulation that they would provide a certain amount of local programming. In other words, 3ABN, a satellite radio network, could not apply for one of these stations. However, a local church group could form a nonprofit corporation separate from the church and apply for a 100-watt station that would cover an approximate radius of ten miles. Most were required to generate eight hours of local programming a week, but they could broadcast 3ABN Radio the remainder of the time.

God's timing was miraculous. Just as 3ABN Radio began broadcasting and was ready to establish downlink stations, two such application windows opened up, each for a short time. If 3ABN Radio had started earlier, the only possibility for downlink would have been to purchase an already existing station, which could prove quite expensive for a local community. And the reality was, few were available. The good news is that since 2000, 3ABN has been able to purchase two of these already existing stations. Listeners can also get 3ABN Radio over the Internet. Or, if they purchase the dish system that 3ABN offers, they can enjoy radio programming in their own home via the audio track on their TV. But these downlink sources are limited to a few individuals. Most churches are interested in 3ABN reaching their entire community.

Establishing an LPFM station is the ideal answer for spreading the gospel locally.

If 3ABN Radio had started any later, these windows of opportunity would have already opened and closed without 3ABN being able to take advantage of them! God knew exactly what He was doing when He impressed Linda to start 3ABN Radio *and provided immediate funding*. His timing was perfect!

In March 2000, when the FCC opened the first window for applications for LPFM stations, God brought in over ninety applicants from every walk in life. Nikki Anderson, administrative assistant, has been involved with many of these applications and has had a chance to get to know the people behind them. Their experiences have deeply affected her life. She says, "Most of them called to say that they didn't know anything about radio, especially the technical aspects, but God had impressed them to get involved. I had no previous radio experience myself, but I kept encouraging them that this was possible. When some became discouraged, I kept reminding them of the struggles when 3ABN was first beginning. Through the process, I've made friends from one end of this country to the other. I love them like my own family. I have seen many miraculous accomplishments. It has increased my faith."

The people involved in the 3ABN Radio LPFM groups have almost turned this opportunity into a "grassroots movement" to spread the gospel to their friends, families, and communities. Elderly widows, healthcare workers, pastors, construction workers, and retired couples are typical of those involved with these stations. Some groups are fortunate enough to have engineering help available within their community, but very few have that resource. 3ABN, through the expertise of Jim Morris and radio engineer Mike Babb, is providing training and technical advice when needed. But mostly, they have relied heavily on the Holy Spirit to lead and direct.

God brings Jay Christian and his family to 3ABN

Jay Christian wasn't really interested in coming to 3ABN when he was first contacted in 1998. He and his wife, Annette, were comfortable in the Walla Walla, Washington, area. He had worked at KGTS, the Adventist radio station at Walla Walla College and was now the TV manager for Blue Mountain Television, an affiliate of

3ABN. A year later, Annette, who had a prestigious marketing position and job security working in a secular healthcare corporation, made the comment, "I'm so tired of working for the world. I think I'd like to find something to do for the Lord." Not long after that, Dee Hilderbrand phoned from 3ABN. "Linda just asked me to call and touch base with you. We are hoping you will reconsider and accept a position at 3ABN Radio."

"Funny you would say that," Jay commented. "Annette and I were just thinking maybe we should both be working for the Lord. Would there be any jobs available for my wife and daughter? He mentioned that Annette's expertise was in marketing and that Cari had done television editing and camera work. The family was not able to drive to 3ABN for interviews until May 1999, at which time they were all offered jobs. Everything fell into place for them to begin work at 3ABN in August.

When Jay arrived, the first task was to build offices and studios. When the project was almost completed, the staff realized that the current air conditioning system was inadequate for the new studios. Two air conditioning companies came to look at the problem and recommended various plans. However, both saw no solution short of tearing out walls and installing air ducts for a new system. The cost was prohibitive. Plus, the time it would take to tear down and rebuild what had just been completed would mean a delay in broadcasting. As the second air conditioning consultant walked out of the room, Theresa said to Jay, "We can't afford this. We have to go to the Lord." She prayed, or more precisely, she begged the Lord. "We have no idea how You are going to solve this problem, but what has been proposed is too time consuming, too expensive, and too destructive. We need Your direct intervention to help us solve the air-conditioning problem."

Just as Theresa said, "Amen," the air conditioning consultant returned. "I just had an idea," he said. "I don't know why I didn't think of it before. But in Europe, they are using smaller wall units that can air condition just the main room in the house. The compressor is outside, so it's very quiet inside. You could easily mount the unit on the wall with only a few holes for screws. Plus, it's a much less expensive solution—and it heats as well as cools."

Talk about an answer to prayer! Within a few weeks the units were installed. There was no destruction of what had previously been built. And it was surprisingly inexpensive. The system has worked great for the last five years!

How God shaped events to bring Jim Morris to 3ABN

In 2002, just as Theresa began to feel that she had pretty much accomplished what God had called her to do at 3ABN and that she should return to her family in Ontario, Canada, God was shaping circumstances in Jim Morris's life that would influence him to link his passion for radio with the growing 3ABN Radio network and become its general manager.

Jim's involvement in radio started when he was a freshman at Madison Academy, where he served as an announcer and DJ for a low-power AM station on the campus. This interest in radio extended into his college years at Southern Missionary College, where he served as DJ and audio engineer for WSMC, the college station.

Jim chose to earn a bachelor's degree in business administration and a master's in hospital and health administration. After graduating, Jim spent the next twenty-seven years working in healthcare administration. He never lost his love for radio, but other than becoming an amateur radio operator, Jim did not work again in radio until 1999. It was Jerry Jacobs who influenced Jim to accept the challenge of leasing and rebuilding WBLC, an old full-power AM radio station in Lenoir City, Tennessee, that was owned by Horne Radio Group. Jim met Jerry while he was recovering from open-heart surgery in the hospital where Jim had been the administrator.

WBLC had been built in 1966 and had been off the air for almost a year before Jim and Jerry began the process. It was a labor of love; both had full-time jobs and could do the radio work only after hours. They rebuilt the transmitter to original performance specifications, retuned the tower and antenna, and installed an automation system.

At one point, after working for three hours on the preamplifier, Jim gave up in frustration. He slapped the side of the transmitter and muttered, "God, we have tried every approach to fixing this transmitter, and nothing works. If You want us to continue to broadcast Your Word, You had better get busy and fix this transmitter."

He recalls, "At the time, Jerry and I were standing behind the transmitter with the door removed, looking at the transmitter's in-

The staff of 3ABN Radio. (L to R) Nikki Anderson, Jay Christian, Jim Morris,
Angela Lomacang, Joe Bivin, Martha Weber, and Michael Babb

terior. Ninety seconds later, the problem was fixed. We were just looking at the circuitry, and all of a sudden, the audio cleared, and we've had no trouble with it since. I believe that the heavenly "Electronics Creator" commanded His angelic associate to fix the problem while we were watching. We didn't see anything or feel anything, but the transmitter was fixed right before our eyes. I still get chills when I think about it." This was just one of many prayers that were sent heavenward as Jim and Jerry brought WBLC back to life as a 3ABN affiliate station for east Tennessee, and Jim became its general manager.

After a few years, the owners of WBLC decided to sell. Jim approached 3ABN with the possibility of buying the station, and WBLC became 3ABN's first full-power AM radio station.

About this same time 3ABN contacted Jim about helping with the radio ministry. Jim had been interested in 3ABN since 1988, when he moved to Knoxville, Tennessee, and purchased a dish to view 3ABN exclusively. At first, Jim worked as a volunteer because he was still employed full time in healthcare administration and working as general manager of WBLC. But God seemed to have other ideas. Circumstances changed on the healthcare work front, and in 2001, Jim was impressed to walk away from his comfort zone and help 3ABN Radio grow. In February 2002, Jim accepted the full-time position of marketing manager of 3ABN Radio, at considerably less pay than what he was offered in the healthcare field. In 2004, Jim became general manager.

The success of 3ABN Radio is a witness of God's power to enable dedicated, willing individuals to do an awesome work for Him. The amazing fact is that, of the original team that got 3ABN Radio up and running, only one member had any prior radio experience.

3ABN Radio is a marvelous way to saturate a community with the good news of Jesus Christ. One example is what the Borlands have done in Belize. After visiting friends in Texas and becoming acquainted with 3ABN Television, Wendell Borland and his wife, Addy, returned home to Belize and donated a satellite dish to their local cable company, which began airing 3ABN Television. They purchased more dishes and gave them to other cable companies until all the cable companies in Belize were offering 3ABN. But there were still pockets where television didn't reach. Here's where radio came in. In 1999, the Borlands built a 350-watt radio station that reaches a vast population. Quickly, twenty-three baptisms resulted directly from this radio ministry. The Borlands were then given a location for their radio transmitter on a tower at the highest point in Belize, which allowed the signal to be heard in other countries and islands of the Caribbean. Ten years after 3ABN was first introduced into the country in 1991, the Adventist Church had grown by eighteen thousand members!

In July 2003, 3ABN purchased WDQN, a full-power FM station that covers most of southern Illinois. It happened in an unusual way. Gonzalo Santos felt strongly that a radio presence was needed in the West Frankfort area where 3ABN headquarters is located. It might have been possible to blanket the area with a number of low-power FM stations, but it seemed more reasonable to obtain a full-power station, if one was for sale. Gonzalo began listening to stations in the area. One station in particular caught his interest—WDQN. It covered a wide area but did not have any national account support. Gonzalo knew that a radio station like this was expensive to operate, so he thought it might have financial challenges and be willing to sell. He called the station. "I'm Gonzalo Santos. I work at 3ABN, and I was wondering if you might be interested in selling your radio station."

Gonzalo learned that the good Methodist people running the station had previously thought about selling it and were interested in talking. After a long process of negotiation, the owners chose to sell the FM part of their station to 3ABN and retain the AM station (which was more local) for their own purposes. So 3ABN obtained WDQN at about half of the original asking price. Once more God was leading.

In addition to the two full-power radio stations owned by 3ABN—WBLC and WDQN—and the forty-three LPFM affiliate stations, there are nine full-power affiliate stations in the United States and four full-power stations on foreign soil: one in Belize, two in the Philippines, and one in San Miguel, El Salvador. Three cable companies and more than sixty Internet outlets carry 3ABN Radio full time. In the United States, nearly twenty LPFM affiliate station are in various stages of planning. Plus, 3ABN Radio has signed affiliate agreements with groups planning to build stations in Grand Cayman, St. Lucia, and St. Croix. There is also significant interest by non-Adventist stations to add 3ABN lifestyle programming to their lineup.

Nikki Anderson picks up the story

Is 3ABN Radio reaching people? Nikki Anderson reports:

We receive more and more calls, letters, faxes, and emails every week from new listeners who have just found 3ABN Radio in their area or on their travels and appreciate the programming. For example: A truck driver called to say he drives a gas delivery truck throughout southern Illinois. During the night he heard programs on WDQN with a message that he'd never heard before and called to order copies of two programs. Another caller said he was traveling through the area when he heard *Dimensions of Prophecy* on WDQN. Halfway through the program, he realized he was getting out of the reception area, so he pulled over on the shoulder of I-57 for half an hour to hear the whole program! He ordered a copy of the program, "The Antichrist," by Kenneth Cox.

God said He would come back for His children when every person of every language group of every nation had heard the gospel message. To His little group of twelve disciples praying in the upper room, it must have seemed like an impossible assignment—until they heard the rushing wind and saw the tongues of Holy Spirit "fire" sit on each of their heads, allowing them to speak to the crowd of people in the languages of those present. In one day, three thousand believed. When those believers left Jerusalem, they took the gospel back to their own people. Pentecost! What was impossible to man was possible with God!

Just as God is the God of languages, He is also the God of technology. Today, far more than three thousand hear the gospel via television and radio as it blankets the world 24/7. While television reaches millions each day, it's almost impossible to estimate how many more are reached by radio, because almost all population groups have access to radios!

Through television *and* radio there's the potential of hundreds of thousands being saved in a day's time. There is no doubt that 3ABN Radio was God's idea, His plan, and His miracle.

14
3ABN Music

"Make a joyful noise unto the Lord, all ye lands.
Serve the Lord with gladness: come before his presence with singing"
—Psalm 100:1, 2.

Danny's dream comes true

God gave Danny the dream to build a television station, but Danny's real lifelong heart's desire was to build a state-of-the-art recording studio. Danny began recording more than twenty years ago in Dr. Billy Burks's studio in Hendersonville, Tennessee. Billy had two professions; he was a dentist and a musician. Right beside his dental office he had built a high-quality recording studio. There, at Doc's Place, Danny met Bobby Bradley, a gifted sound engineer. As Bobby moved on to work at other studios, Danny followed, doing various projects with Bobby. But he still held on to his dream to someday build his own studio.

One of the many reasons why Danny wanted his own studio was because of the high cost of recording in rented facilities. It was not uncommon to pay as much as a thousand dollars a day to rent space, plus an additional two thousand a day for all the professionals needed to run the equipment. It was easy to spend fifteen thousand to thirty-five thousand dollars for one album, or CD as we call it today. The cost made it almost prohibitive for many talented artists in Christian ministry to record, including Danny!

In 1982, after Kay, his first wife, died, Danny built a small studio in his home. This became the seed that twenty years later would grow into one of the finest recording studios in the world, known today as the 3ABN Sound Center.

But it was not as if Danny didn't try to build a sound studio earlier. When the original 3ABN building (now the uplink center) was built, Danny designed the back part of the building to be a sound studio, but the television needs were far more critical, and the space originally planned for the recording studio was used for video.

When the new production center was built, Danny designed the building so that a sound studio would be a part of that complex. But with 3ABN's sudden growth in the mid-nineties, the need for office space again put his plans on hold.

Danny, however, never gave up his dream. As he puts it, "Nonstop television and radio broadcasting requires a lot of music! They need music for program background, opens, and credits. For nature videos; and for promotional spots; as well as musical accompaniment for singers and musicians who share their talents every day on both the English and Latino networks! I didn't like seeing all that money going to commercial studios, when 3ABN needed it. I knew we could save travel time and hundreds of thousands of dollars a year by providing this service."

In God's plan everything has its season. It wasn't until God's goal was in sight—a television signal that would reach the world—that He said, "Go for it," and the 3ABN Sound Center became a reality. It was almost as if God were testing Danny to see if he would be obedient to His calling. Then with the 3ABN signal blanketing the world, God allowed Danny to build what he really wanted in the first place!

One interesting note: Now that the sound center is complete, with numerous CDs coming out each year under the 3ABN Music label, one might think all this is an excellent source of additional income for 3ABN. But Danny's objective was never to make money. Instead, 3ABN Music is a ministry. As he puts it, "Many musicians and artists who support 3ABN and provide music for us are themselves struggling financially. The Lord has impressed me not to charge these folks for recording a CD. That's our way of taking what God has given us and channeling it to someone else. They can then go out and sell their CDs to support themselves in doing God's work. Hopefully, this will make it possible for them to come back and help 3ABN again in the future. Just a few of the artists blessed by the use of this facility are Vonda Beerman, Kelly Mowrer and Dona Klein, Mark Trammell, Maddy Couperus, the Cadet Sisters, Darrell Marshall, Kris and Larry Paxton, and Allison Durham Speer. The beauty of the 3ABN Sound

Center is *that God has paid for this million dollar-plus project as it was being built,* and we are simply passing on His blessing."

In addition to allowing the artists to use the facility, 3ABN staff have, themselves, made a number of CDs. These include Tammy Larson, Danny and Tommy Shelton, and Melody Shelton. Danny has recently completed his own solo album—the first one in twelve years. The sale of these CDs helps to support financially this part of 3ABN's ministry. The sound center has truly been a blessing.

Three people played a significant role in making the sound center a reality: Danny, with his dream; E. T. Everett, with her calling; and Bobby Bradley, with his expertise.

E. T. Everett

Years ago when Danny had a studio in his home, E. T. Everett and her husband, David, were in a gospel-singing quartet. The group wanted to make a recording for a competition, and a musician friend, who had played backup for Danny, told them about Danny's home studio. They contacted him, and when the recording was finished, they stayed in touch. Over the years, the Everetts watched 3ABN grow and were impressed by how God raised this ministry from a dream to a reality.

After 3ABN began broadcasting, E. T. and David had a musical group called New Beginning Ministries that taped a number of musical segments for 3ABN. When Danny's brother, Tommy, moved to Virginia, E. T. began playing the piano when needed for 3ABN programs. She and David also began traveling on weekends with Danny and Linda to 3ABN live rallies.

One day in 2000, Danny,

Bobby Bradley (left) and E.T. (middle) meet with other Sound Center staff members

Linda, Dave, and E. T. were in a hotel room talking, eating, and resting from the long flight to Oregon. E. T. remembers Danny sitting on the window seat when he suddenly said, "That's it! The Lord's telling me that it's time to build the recording studio." He looked at E. T. "If you will come on board, we will build it."

"What are you talking about?" questioned E. T.

"I've been trying to build a studio for years, but now God's impressing me that you're the one to do it."

"But, I don't know how to build a studio!"

With no commitment made, the Sheltons and Everetts ministered to the receptive Oregon audience on Friday evening and again on Sabbath. The meetings ended earlier than Danny had originally anticipated, so he arranged for them to take an earlier flight home. Because of this, the Everetts were able to attend their church Sunday evening.

The guest speaker looked out over the congregation and began to say various things that God impressed him to say to specific people. He looked at E. T. and said, "You have found favor with a man who reaches the world. God's telling me that you have many CDs coming out of you. All you have to do is say 'Yes.' "

E. T. was stunned. Danny, Linda, and Dave were the only ones who knew about the conversation that had taken place two nights earlier. E. T. took this as a sign that she was to call Danny and say "Yes!"

Danny drew up some building plans, and E. T. took on the role of foreman for the building project. She started researching music sound centers, visiting studios to learn all she could. She enlisted the help of an acoustical engineer and other experts in the field. In the process, she talked to Bobby Bradley, and he jumped on board. Joe Carrell, one of her fellow church members, offered to help. His first few months were spent assisting E. T. with decisions that had to be made about the structural part of the sound center. He got together with Bobby and started wiring the building. Bobby picked out the equipment. On New Year's Eve 2001, the new state-of-the-art 3ABN Sound Center was dedicated.

At last, Danny's dream was realized!

E. T. wears many "hats" as general manager at the sound center. Not only is she the administrator, but she writes, arranges, and produces music in the studio. She also schedules artists and musicians and oversees the "sound" ministry. E. T. says, "This ministry is not just about producing beautiful music for our Lord; it's about people. Already there have been many opportunities to witness and share Jesus at our sound center, and we know there will be many more!"

Bobby Bradley

Bobby was born into Nashville's music industry. His uncle, the late Owen Bradley, was something of a legend around Nashville. He was the popular big band leader of The Owen Bradley Orchestra. At the same time, he worked for WSM Radio on the morning show—along with some music greats such as Snooky Lanson and Eddy Arnold. He is credited as the creator of the "Nashville sound" and is in the Country Music Hall of Fame. Bobby started working for his uncle in 1971 at the original Bradley's Barn, which burned down on October 20, 1980. The following year Bobby worked at Doc's Place, where he met Danny when he brought Melody in to do a recording shortly after her mother's death. After that, Danny began bringing other people down to Doc's Place to record. And when Bobby moved to other studios, Danny followed.

When Danny was certain God had said "Go" on the sound center project, he knew the person he wanted to design the facility and oversee the engineering operations: Bobby Bradley. Actually, this was the third time he had asked Bobby to build a studio for him! First in the original building, then the new production center, and now. When Bobby actually saw the ground being broken for the sound center, he caught the vision and began designing a center that would use the latest technology.

In case your mental picture of a recording studio consists of a small soundproof room with a tape recorder in it, let me have Bobby take you on a verbal tour of this facility.

> We start out in the tracking room, where the musicians play. There are three smaller glassed-in rooms that are isolated but in view of the main room. These are for the vocalist, the piano, and the percussion. Each musician is connected by headphones, and the sound of each is recorded on a separate track on hard-disk drive machines. This allows the sound engineer to work on improving the sound of an individual instrument or voice without interfering with the sound track of other artists playing the same music.

The final phase of the recording process is when the hard drive is taken to the pro-tool room; we call it the tool shop. Here sounds are broken down on screen. Within this editing suite, each nuance of voice or music is evaluated and corrected. This is where we tune things if they're out of tune. We take pops or excess air sounds out of the vocalist's track, and if an instrument isn't quite on beat, we correct it. If the singer sings a better chorus one time than another, we cut out the bad and edit in the good! Then we take the hard drive back to the control room where I sit—I guess that's why Danny calls it "Bobby's room." We mix it, blend it together, and add effects such as chorusing, reverb, or delays. Then when it's all blended, it goes to digital audio tape, from which the CDs are mastered.

You might also be interested to know that the average insulated wall in the building is sixteen to twenty inches wide to accommodate the mandatory acoustics. There are also several layers of sheet rock and a layer of cloth on the walls, with air space between. Plus, additional insulation has been blown in over that. The floors are "floating," or individually set under each room so that no sound can escape under foot. Danny never does anything halfway! This facility ranks among the best in the world. And I'm honored to have had a part in designing it. Now I have the joy of using it!

Danny and I have been good friends for twenty years. We started out together with Melody's recording in October of 1982. It's interesting that exactly twenty years later, October 2002, we were recording another CD for Melody. We've come a long way from those record cutting days to CD digital technology!

Danny's comments

"For years I dreamed of having a studio that would not only make beautiful music but would also make beautiful people. This is exactly what God has given us. Not only is the finished product a superb piece of artistry when it leaves the 3ABN Sound Center—hopefully blessing each listener—but we pray that the warm, friendly atmosphere, plus the assurance of the highest quality professionalism and equipment, will bless the various artists as they come here to share their talents. What we're doing is not just music but a ministry to those who are ministering to others through their music."

15
Volunteers for Jesus— and 3ABN

"Trust in the Lord, and do good; so shalt thou dwell in the land,
and verily thou shalt be fed.
Delight thyself also in the Lord;
and he shall give thee the desires of thine heart.
Commit thy way unto the Lord; trust also in him;
and he shall bring it to pass."
—Psalm 37:3-5.

Where God guides, He provides. That's certainly been true with the finances needed to keep this ministry beaming Bible truth around the world. It's also true, however, with the people God has provided to fill important ministry needs—both paid employees and the growing staff of volunteers. Plus, there are those in different cities, countries, and continents all donating their time and talents to move forward the work of God through 3ABN. To truly get the flavor of 3ABN's worldwide ministry, come with me and let me introduce you to a few of these incredible people who have heard the call to come to 3ABN and have unselfishly accepted.

Brenda Walsh

Brenda Walsh: *Children's programming is no small project!*

When you watch 3ABN programming, it is tempting to think that, for the most part, the television programs are produced by organizations with the necessary talent, resources, and financial backing to create great quality productions—and then these organizations pay 3ABN for air time. That's true with some of the programming. However, an incredible number of programs are produced by 3ABN on a shoestring budget with a host of volunteers giving of their time and talents.

The largest volunteer production 3ABN has ever attempted has been for their smallest viewers. It's the children's programming directed by Brenda Walsh from Knoxville, Tennessee. And yes, you guessed it, she volunteers her time, energy, and gifted creativity to produce two major

Cinda and Linda with tiny tots

programs, *Kids Time* and *Kids Time Praise,* plus holiday productions and cooking segments with her sisters for the *3ABN Today* program.

How does she do it? It's a miracle, but it sure helps to have two talented sisters, Linda Johnson and Cinda Sanner. Cinda produces *Tiny Tots for Jesus,* and Linda hosts the program. And yes, they volunteer, too! The three women, known as the Micheff sisters, are multi-talented and totally dedicated to the ministry of 3ABN. They've even made two vocal CDs with the proceeds going to . . . you guessed it again . . . *Kids Time!*

But I'm getting ahead of the story. Let me have Brenda tell you in her own words, about her calling and her mission for children and about the hundreds of volunteers who work with her.

It all started when I was inspired by the stories Danny Shelton told about praying to be used of God and the incredible miracles that resulted. I lived in Boston, Massachusetts, at the time. I was an occupational health nurse in a large company. I also owned my own floral business, the largest supplier of air-dried roses in New England. My husband, Tim, was the vice president of a video conferencing company. God had been good to us. I should have felt totally fulfilled, but I didn't. I longed for the kind of relationship with God that would result in stories like Danny experienced. So I began to pray that God would use me in a very special way. Two weeks later, I was impressed to begin baking cookies. I had no idea why I was doing this. For twelve hours, I baked cookies! Not knowing what else to do with them, I put them in the freezer.

Several weeks later, I took them out of the freezer with no knowledge of why I was doing so. Realizing what I had done, and not knowing what to do with the now-thawed-out cookies, I was impressed that I should give them to a soup kitchen. When I arrived, they had no one to help prepare the meal, and they had forgotten the dessert. I was at the right place at the right time, with bags full of cookies for dessert! It couldn't have been just a coincidence. Suddenly, I felt alive! God had answered my prayer and really used me. It was amazing!

3ABN interviewed me, and a day after the "Cookie Lady" program aired the second time, I was going up an escalator in a department store when a man turned and looked at me. Shaking with excitement, he exclaimed, "It's a sign! You're Brenda Walsh, the cookie lady, right?" He told me that he'd just gotten out of jail the day before and had gone to his mom's house for a cooked meal where he happened to see the cookie story on television. He was so touched that he prayed, "God, give me a sign, and I'll give my heart to You, too." He hesitated and shook his head in disbelief. "Tell me, what are the chances that the very next day I'd be seeing the cookie lady in my own hometown!" He gave his heart to Christ right there. This incident opened my eyes to the incredible influence 3ABN was having on people's lives. I was thrilled to have a small part in it.

When 3ABN's vice president asked me to produce *Kids Time,* I was sure she was kidding. I started spouting excuses— "I'm a nurse, not a producer." "I already have two jobs." "I live in Boston."

The vice president was quiet for a few minutes. Then she turned to me and asked, "Brenda, tonight you were talking about how you wanted to be used by God. Did you just mean in your comfort zone, or did you mean however God wanted to use you?" Now I was quiet.

I prayed, "God if You want me to do this, give me ideas, because right now I don't have a clue about what to do." Almost immediately, God overwhelmed me with ideas. That night, I couldn't even sleep, my head was so full of possibilities! I claimed Philippians 4:13, "I can do all things through Christ which strengtheneth me." Immediately, I called 3ABN and accepted the job. I asked about the budget and recieved the reply "Well, this is a faith project. There isn't any budget." I was told this job was a volunteer position, but was assured that it wouldn't require more than two weeks a year. When I asked about money to design a new set, I was told there was no money for a new set. I did get permission to paint the old one and add new carpet, but that was all!

In order to produce *Kids Time,* I began flying back and forth every month between Boston and St. Louis, the closest major airport to 3ABN, paying my own way. That first month my phone bill was over nine hundred dollars! Not only was I volunteering my time, but it was costing me a lot of money! However, that didn't matter, because I could see that God was using me. The miracles were beginning to happen.

One of the greatest miracles occurred when I started painting the background of the seven-panel set for *Kids Time.* I asked for two weeks to do it. I was granted only three days because the set was in the middle of the production studio, and 3ABN could not produce anything while I painted! To give myself a fourth day, I started painting on Sunday, but I soon realized that doing the job myself was impossible within this narrow time frame.

I tried to think of people to help. Who would have my same style of painting? God kept putting into my mind Smitty, my old art teacher. But he was eighty years old and lived in San Jose, California! His schedule was usually full because of all the traveling he did, and it would cost a fortune to get talent like his. Impossible! But God kept saying *Smitty.*

In desperation, I gave him a call. Believe it or not, he was home! I explained that we had no budget. I was shocked that he was willing to volunteer. He left California immediately and was in St. Louis by eight-thirty the next morning. We painted a Bible scene on one side and a nature scene on the other, representing God's two books, the Bible and nature. For the next two and a half days, we worked frantically, sleeping only a few hours. And we completed the set. Talk about a miracle!

So *Kids Time* began. I soon realized, however, that it wasn't a two-week-a-year job. It was more like two weeks every month—and would soon be full time! As *Kids Time* began to take more and more of my time, and the expenses for my plane tickets mounted, my husband and I made a major decision. I would quit my two jobs in Boston. We would sacrifice the convenience of living close to our two grown daughters and a precious grandson who were in the Boston area, and move to Knoxville, Tennessee, which was centrally located enough for Tim to drive seven hours each Sunday afternoon to commute to his work in Washington, D.C., where he was now president of a company, and I could drive six hours in the opposite direction to 3ABN.

People ask me how I can do this. I couldn't without my husband's 100 percent support. He never complains. He just says, "Honey, praise the Lord that God answered your prayer and is using you." When I give sermons or speak at women's retreats, Tim is so proud of me. "Honey, look at all the people you are helping. God is using you in a powerful way."

Each time I leave home and take that six-hour trip, I'm flooded with ideas and enthusiasm. I can hardly contain the joy I feel! God was good to have allowed me to raise my children before He called me to this work, but if He would have called me sooner, I would have accepted. There is nothing more exciting and soul-fulfilling in this world than to be used by God.

One of the most amazing things about our children's programming is that everyone volunteers their time and pays their own expenses to come to 3ABN. Everyone you see on the programs, both adults and children, are volunteers. Then there are dozens who work behind the scenes. 3ABN now has three children's programs, and my sisters work with me. All I did for *Tiny Tots for Jesus* was name the program. They've done the rest. Cinda produces it, and Linda hosts it and writes all the programs. But that's not all they do. Linda is Story Time coordinator for *Kids Time*. She writes most of the scripts and acts in many. She recruits actors, arranges for guest housing, and listens to every detail of each story to make sure it is biblically correct.

Cinda works behind the scenes preparing food as her daughter, Catie, hosts the cooking segment for *Kids Time.* By the way, Catie's the author of a *Kids Time* cookbook, called *Cooking With Catie,* and all the proceeds go into children's programming.

As long as I'm talking about my family, my mom, Bernice Micheff, is volunteering full time, too. She heads up *Kids Club* and sends fifty-two Bible study lessons, six at a time, to each child who asks. She corrects them and sends the answer sheets back to more than a thousand kids who have enrolled. Our oldest "kid" is an eighty-year-old lady who gave her heart to Jesus late in life. She watches *Kids Time* to see what she missed as a child. She loves the Bible studies!

We now have well over a thousand kids from all over the world enrolled in Bible studies! One was a fifty-six-year-old lady who enrolled and gave her heart to Jesus because of the studies! She called me and was so excited because she "found Jesus!" She said that she had never owned a Bible. When she enrolled in Kids Club, she went out and bought her first Bible. She is now going to a Seventh-day Adventist church! Stories like these fuel my energy level!

I could go on and on about all the volunteers, for example, Dr. Buddy Houghtaling, who heads up the segment, *Music Time With Buddy.* He and all the children who sing with him give up their vacations two times a year to come from Michigan to southern Illinois to tape. Jim Snelling, who is Ranger Jim, ends up traveling all over the country to shoot his segments for 3ABN. Ben Roy heads up *Learning Time.* He not only organizes all the scientific experiments but brings a children's audience from Georgia with him every time he tapes. Then there's Mike Adkins, a professional songwriter and singer who is Farmer Mike. I can't even imagine what Mike would get paid if he were singing with children on a commercial program, and yet, he happily donates his time and talent for *Tiny Tots for Jesus.* Now Chuck Fulmore has taken over that role and become Grandpa Chuck—another incredibly talented musical artist.

Then there's my wonderful costume designer, Lucy Neuharth from Washington. She sews all year long just to get ready for taping, plus she flies out every time we're taping, bringing her sewing machine along for last minute adjustments on the hundreds of costumes she has designed and sewn. Her creations are so beautiful and professionally done that she could work in Hollywood and make a fortune! She personally donated several thousand dollars' worth of material and trim, not to mention her time spent sewing! Lucy has created a wardrobe department for *Kids Time* that is easily worth several thousands of dollars.

Finally, we couldn't have *Kids Time, Tiny Tots for Jesus,* or *Kids Time Praise* if it weren't for the dedicated parents willing to bring their children to 3ABN for taping sessions. The Cadet family from Utah and the Bond family from Montana are just two of many, many families.

3ABN is what it is today because of the thousands of volunteers who unselfishly give of their time, talent, and money to do the work God has called them to do, without thought of any reward other than the joy that comes from knowing they're being used by God.

Elora "Mom" Ford

Elora Ford *(lovingly known as "Mom" by the 3ABN family)*

One of the most vital volunteers at the 3ABN headquarters has been Mom Ford, who celebrated her seventy-eighth birthday in 2004. No one realized that the growing family of staff, volunteers, presenters, and performers needed someone to provide care, counsel, and a whole lot of love until God impressed Elora Ford to visit 3ABN in 1995. How thankful they are today that Mom Ford saw a need and, like Abraham, was willing to leave everything behind to come to a "strange" land. Here's how Mom Ford tells her story.

In the 1980s my husband was a physician in Napa Valley in northern California, and I helped him in his office. Word drifted out to us from southern Illinois about a young carpenter who believed God wanted him to start a satellite TV ministry. I felt that was a waste of money, and it seemed like a wild idea!

But after a few years, we bought a large satellite dish to find out what 3ABN was doing. I became excited about what I saw and taped programs so that I could listen to them again. We also got firsthand information from our son, who became a member of the 3ABN board of directors, about the many miracles God was working for this television ministry. So when my husband died in 1995, I decided to go out to Thompsonville and visit.

When I got there, I was impressed there was a real need for a guest home where people who were taping programs at 3ABN could stay without cost. I told Danny what I had in mind—a house close by, in a quiet spot, hopefully with a good place to walk and watch birds. Danny liked the idea but said there was nothing for sale in the area. However, someone suggested a property that joined the 3ABN property on the south. It wasn't for sale, but we went to look at it anyway. As soon as I saw the beautiful grounds, the lake, and a ranch-style home with a large walk-in basement, I knew this was it, so I made an offer. And somehow the Lord impressed the owner to sell it to me.

I then went back to California, sold my home, packed up my belongings, and moved "next door" to 3ABN to do volunteer work. Every day I've lived here, I've praised God for this roomy, convenient house, surrounded by acres of lawn and evergreen trees, looking out on a private pond for birds, located on a quiet road that I use for daily walks—a miracle beyond my imagination. And the hundreds of guests I've been privileged to have in my home have been like a taste of heaven.

Even though I retired in 1992, I go to work every day at 3ABN. I have many privileges in helping with opening mail, correspondence, phone calls, and tours. Daily, I look to the Lord for wisdom to speak His words. I pray for His grace to flow through the computer I use or the phone. I cry with those who are broken and sing with those who are blessed.

Often, phone calls bring unexpected questions. Some have questions about a Bible verse. Some want me to pray with them. One question that I often hear is, "What are the distinctive beliefs of Seventh-day Adventists?" I reply that I am happy to send printed material that will explain what we believe, but usually they say, "I want you to tell me," so here's what I say:

There are seven beliefs that are essential to Seventh-day Adventist doctrine—and each just happens to start with the letter *S*:

> **1. Salvation by faith in Christ** as a personal Savior from sin who was given to the human race by the Father because He so loved the world (John 3:16).
>
> **2. Soon second coming of Christ.** Christ is going to return in the clouds of heaven to get His bride, the church, composed of those in the graves who have trusted in His merits and the living ones who have been sealed in Him (2 Thessalonians 4:15-17).
>
> **3. Seventh-day Sabbath.** Remember the Creator God as you rest on the day in which He rested after creating the world in six days (see Exodus 20:8-11).
>
> **4. Sanctuary services.** These were given by God to describe events that take place in heaven: They illustrated Christ's ministry as a Mediator and His work of cleansing the sanctuary by blotting out sins, which prepares a people to stand in the judgment (Hebrews 9; Acts 3:19).
>
> **5. Spirit of prophecy,** which is the testimony of Jesus revealed during the last days to warn people of Satan's deceptions (Revelation 19:10).
>
> **6. State of the dead.** The dead are "asleep" in the grave until the resurrection; they have no thoughts or emotions. This is called the first death (Psalm 6:5).
>
> **7. Sin's final destruction.** Sin is to be eternally wiped out so that once again God will have a clean universe. The punishment of the lost (all who cling to sin) is eternal death—this is the second death (Revelation 20:14, 15).

Although Mom Ford was the first to respond to the need for guest housing at 3ABN, two other families came shortly after Mom Ford. Both built homes with free accommodations to serve 3ABN guests.

Charlie and Frances Clark came from Nebraska, and Bob and Bea Johnston had a farm in Kentucky. Both families have become an important part of the 3ABN family, and both graciously volunteer their time to do whatever is needed in addition to guest services. Charlie Clark, who has been "retired" for a number of years, still maintains two large ranches in Nebraska and Missouri with the help of his sons. But that doesn't stop him from volunteering long hours, helping to obtain needed equipment for building and farming and in his "spare" time maintaining 3ABN property.

In September 2004, Mom Ford moved to Chehalis, Washington, to be close to her son.

Donald and Grace Yost

Grace and Donald Yost: *Making 3ABN home*

In the pastoral department sits another vital volunteer, Grace Yost, busily answering letters of a spiritual nature. Her story is typical of hundreds of volunteers who have knocked on the door of 3ABN saying, "Here I am. Put me to work!"

Here's what Grace says brought her and her husband, Donald, to 3ABN:

We bought a satellite dish in 1996, began watching, and grew to love the 3ABN family. But we hadn't considered leaving Florida until Donald's sister from Tennessee made the comment, "When I retire, I'd like to go sit on 3ABN's doorstep and say, 'Here I am. Use me!' " That planted a seed in our minds.

Donald put his business up for sale. People seemed interested, but it didn't sell. In September 2001 at a 3ABN rally at Forest Lake Academy in Florida, as Danny was speaking, I felt impressed to go up to John Lomacang and ask if he could make arrangements for us to speak with Danny when he was finished. I wanted to tell him that we were impressed to ask the Lord to sell our business so we could give the funds to 3ABN. John immediately stopped me and said, "Did you hear what Danny just said?"

I replied, "No, I didn't because I was talking."

"He just said that he feels impressed that there is some-one here whom the Holy Spirit is impressing to sell a busi-ness and give the funds to 3ABN."

The timing of that comment impressed me. Later, when we talked to Danny about the possibility of moving to 3ABN to volunteer, he suggested we first make a trip to see if we'd like the area. In November, we drove to 3ABN to look around. I took one look and said, "No, Lord. Not here." But since we were visiting 3ABN anyway, we decided to look around for a possible home. We didn't find anything, even though the impression grew that 3ABN was where we were needed. We loved Florida, where we had a beautiful custom-built home with a Jacuzzi and a swimming pool, and where we had a wonderful family of church friends. But God had other plans for us.

In time our business sold, and we put our home up for sale. In February 2003, while we were volunteering at 3ABN, we got a call from someone who wanted to buy our house. We signed papers, packed, and moved to 3ABN a month later. We've worked in many positions, filling in wherever needed. We love it here. Believe it or not, because we are doing what God wants us to do, we don't miss anything we left behind!

Myrl and LaVerne Johnson

LaVerne and Myrl Johnson: *Coming and going for Jesus*

Another dedicated couple who volun-teer their time and talent in the 3ABN Call Center are LaVerne and Myrl Johnson. It's wonderful when God calls you to 3ABN full time, but even if He calls you for just a week or two at a time, you can contribute something special to His work. This dedicated couple, like hundreds of others, come as often as pos-sible and enjoy the spiritual high that ra-diates from the people and programs at 3ABN. They make a significant contribution to spreading the gos-pel to the world and then go back home as spiritually revived soul winners.

Here is their story as told by LaVerne:

We had been out of church for ten years. In 1995, both our mothers had strokes within about six months of each other, and we decided to take care of them in our home. They had been with us for four years when I met an old church friend at Wal-Mart. She asked, "Why don't you and Myrl come back to church?" I made an excuse that our mothers were living with us and required too much care. Then she suggested, "Why don't you get 3ABN?"

"What's that?" I asked.

She explained that it was Adventist television programming around the clock. That sounded good to me. I was raised Pentecostal, and my dad was an Assembly of God pastor, so my mom loved to listen to her "Sunday preachers." But that type of service got on my nerves, and I thought Adventist programming would be a welcome change. So we got a dish for our home right before Doug Batchelor's series, *The Millennium of Prophecy*.

My mom started listening, and we did too. In fact, Mother enjoyed it so much I got tapes of the series, and she watched them over and over again. Every morning she'd say, "Get my preacher tapes; I want to hear him." She accepted each point of doctrine. When we finally had to move her into a nursing home, she told the administrators there that she was a Seventh-day Adventist.

In 2001, soon after Myrl's mother had to be placed in the nursing home, 3ABN was advertising a media evangelism program. We decided to drive to 3ABN and attend. That next Sabbath a visiting pastor, Samuel Thomas, Sr., spoke on the prodigal son. When a call was made, we went forward and gave our hearts to the Lord.

That summer we attended the 3ABN camp meeting and stayed for three months to do volunteer work. 3ABN had given us so much; it was time to give something back.

We have tried to sell our house in Jefferson, Texas, and three times we've tried to buy a house close to 3ABN, but each time something has blocked the way. When the Lord slammed the door for the third time, we decided He must need us in Texas a little longer. When we went back home, a niece came to us crying tears of joy. "LaVerne, I've just given my heart to the Lord. I want to go to church with you." We spent four days studying with her from morning till night. On January 5, 2002, she was baptized. Then we started studying with her niece, Mary, who was baptized during the 2002 camp meeting at 3ABN. Mary and her husband were divorced, but one day he said, "I don't know what's wrong with Mary; she's so different. I want to go to church with you, too." He was baptized, and they were remarried! Another niece was also baptized, and my sister has now joined the church!

God knew our work in Texas was not yet complete, so we kept coming and going. We tried to sell our home one more time. Nothing. Our three sons are in the Jefferson area—maybe the Lord still needs our influence there.

Why do we keep coming back to 3ABN? We love the people here. We have a heart for ministry, but we're too old (or should I say that we don't feel called) to start our own ministry, so 3ABN fits us perfectly. There is so much to do in the call center, answering requests and mailing things out. We just want to have a small part in spreading the message. For us, this is the best place in the world to do it! Volunteers are absolutely essential to the success of this ministry.

Ruben Carr

Ruben Carr's passion for New York City

In case you're beginning to feel that the only way to be a 3ABN volunteer is to drive hundreds or thousands of miles to the 3ABN complex in West Frankfort, why not consider working for 3ABN right in your own hometown? That's what Ruben Carr, Jr. has done. The result is that it may now be easier for you to get 3ABN television on your local cable channel. When it comes to spreading the gospel, there is no such thing as being too poor, too uneducated, or too insignificant.

Here's Ruben's story in his own words. Enjoy!

I grew up in New York City without a dad. My mom suffered from the stress of being a single parent with not enough money to support my sisters and me. She became physically and verbally abusive toward me, gave me no love or attention, and took no interest in me. She said I looked too much like my dad. A wall built up between us, so at seventeen I left home to live on the streets. I had myopia and dyslexia. I couldn't read and couldn't get a job. I had no self-esteem.

While living on the streets, I met a young man who used to be an Adventist. He took me to some meetings, and I gave my life to Christ. I figured by joining a church with five hundred members that somebody would help me find a place to live. But they didn't know who I was or who my mom and dad were, so I continued to live on the streets. I washed my clothes in a slop sink in an old apartment and then dried them outside so I'd be as clean as possible when I attended church. At night I'd look up at the sky and pray, "Lord, give me a job, a home, a car . . . and give me New York City for You." I basically saw God as the only hope for the hopeless people in my hometown.

In February 1981, two years after I gave my heart to Christ, the suffering and mental stress of being homeless was so overwhelming that all I wanted to do was end it. But because of the Bible studies I had taken, I knew God was against me killing myself. So I began thinking, *If God puts me to sleep, then it's OK, and He will take me to heaven.* It was with this thought in mind that I left the shelter where I was staying and walked blindly for about ten miles in one of the biggest snowstorms of the season. I ended up in New Rochelle on Huguenot Street. I found a metal grate beside a tall building and noticed a little steam coming out. I was freezing cold. I fell asleep that Thursday night thinking about death.

Early the next morning, I was startled as a Mercedes-Benz pulled into the driveway next to the building. A nicely dressed man came over to me and said, "You're here kind of early." It was Andrew Bonnapart, the oldest son of the owner of a company that had its offices in the tall building. He presumed that

I had seen the ad in the paper for a job opening for a cable puller in his company, and wanting to be first in line for the job, I had fallen asleep waiting. He took me inside, sat me down, and gave me the application form to fill out. I explained that I had a problem reading and spelling, so he helped me fill it out. Then he said, "I don't know what it is about you, but something tells me that I should hire you. Get yourself some decent clothes and a haircut and come back Monday."

I couldn't believe what was happening to me. I knew it had to be God. I immediately went to my sister's house to ask her for money to get some clothes and a haircut. I told her I had just gotten hired at Eastern Telephonics. "Right, Ruben," she responded. "I don't have any money for you." I'm sure she thought I'd just waste it. "But there's a letter from the IRS. It looks like they finally caught up with you." I opened the envelope and found a check for $450! Apparently, because of my dyslexia, I had made a mistake when filling out some forms when I was in a special education work program, and the IRS was returning some money to me. The IRS must have traced my Social Security number to my sister's house.

I paid tithe, bought some clothes, got cleaned up, and reported for work on Monday. That was twenty years ago. I'm now the senior engineer for the company and know most of the police and firemen, the mayor, and many government officials of the city, because I'm the one they call when they need their phones fixed.

I've discovered that when you're in a deep pit of depression, it's no use looking out the window wishing someone will visit or call. The best thing you can do for yourself is to find someone in need and help them. That's why I'm volunteering my time, money, and energy to fulfill my passion to win New York City to the Lord. I've seen the plight of black families growing up in this big city without God in their lives. There is so much killing in the inner city. Some innocent kid is always being shot. Most have no fathers, and they have no one to look up to. I am trying to be a role model for younger kids, to give them hope and show them a better way.

In 1998, I decided the way to win New York City was via television. When I graduated as a certified producer from

Leman College, I started my own TV show on the public access station. But it was difficult to get pastors to come on the program. When I realized how few people we were reaching, I finally gave it up. Then the thought came to me to call 3ABN. If we could get 3ABN on cable, the whole city could be reached!

I printed flyers about 3ABN, and each Sabbath morning I'd go to five or six churches, taking a few minutes to explain the importance of getting signatures from people wanting 3ABN on cable and leaving some flyers. At first, churches were reluctant to participate. They really didn't know much about 3ABN. They thought I was just a dreamer. They still saw me as "that homeless guy." They thought that certainly nothing would come of what I was doing.

In 2002, 3ABN started working with me to plan a New York City rally. At first, when I told people about the rally, no one believed that Danny and Linda Shelton were really coming. Then I began to bring in cameras and lights for the taping. Suddenly, people realized they could be on television. Then everyone wanted to take part. The campaign was to get 3ABN on two cable systems in the city. The result was truly amazing.

3ABN broadcast its rally live from the historic Ephesus Church in downtown Harlem. Many people attended the meetings, finding out for the first time about 3ABN. Hundreds of Pathfinders marched in a thirteen-block parade down Malcolm X Boulevard to bring attention to city residents about 3ABN's health and family programming. At the last count, there were more than three million calls and requests for 3ABN to be on cable in New York City. This has resulted in Time Warner, one of the largest cable companies in the country, contacting 3ABN to sign a corporate agreement. This means that any Time Warner local cable company in the nation will have permission from corporate headquarters to air 3ABN, if members of their community request it. It's an incredible breakthrough. What's needed now is a host of volunteers in their own communities, doing the same thing I did to get the signatures required to impress the cable company that 3ABN programming would be valuable to its viewers.

I spend all my time and resources promoting 3ABN. And I am one of the happiest people in the world. Now everyone wants to be my friend. I get thirty to thirty-five email messages daily from people who have heard my story on 3ABN. The phone just keeps ringing. I'm fully alive today because I chose to get involved and volunteer for Jesus. I'd highly recommend it!

God is fulfilling my heart's desire. A large donation was given recently to purchase a mobile production truck, like 3ABN's, so we can do local New York City programming for 3ABN. Eventually, we hope to establish our own television downlink station. I'm looking forward to working full time spreading the gospel in New York City. It's my passion!

John and Rosemary Malkiewycz

John and Rosemary Malkiewycz (and Kermit): *Missionaries in Australia*

While some go from their homeland to be missionaries in foreign lands, John and Rosemary Malkiewycz were already missionaries in Nepal and Thailand when they felt the call to return to their homeland. No jobs awaited them. There was just a strong impression that God had a work for them to do in their native Australia. What has developed is a unique ministry that is spreading the word of 3ABN across the continent—and is winning souls for Christ. John and Rosemary are the official directors of Australian development for 3ABN. They have incorporated their ministry under the name 3ABN Australia, Inc. Because they do this on a volunteer basis, John has his own business, which he pursues when he and Rosemary are not traveling for 3ABN.

What does Kermit have to do with this ministry? Let me have Rosemary tell the story of what's happening "down under" and the important role that Kermit has in making all this possible. (By the way, you can contact 3ABN Australia via the Internet at <www.3abnaustralia.org.au>.)

John and I were both farm country kids born in Western Australia. My parents were Australian; John's parents were

Ukrainian immigrants who came after World War II. My family moved to Melbourne when I was thirteen. I returned twelve years later, married and with a new baby. After my second child was born, my marriage broke up. Later, John's marriage also ended, leaving him with two children. John and I had both become Adventists when we married Adventist spouses. When our spouses left us for other partners, they left God, as well. The heartache and rejection John and I suffered, however, resulted in us becoming even more dependent upon God.

Soon after I met John, he was called (with his children) to Phuket, Thailand, as a volunteer missionary. Eight months later, I followed with my two children. We were married in Bangkok. After six years back in Western Australia, we went to Nepal as missionaries, taking our boys with us. I loved being a missionary—and still do. The foreign mission field is in my blood. I love working for God twenty-four hours a day in challenging circumstances.

We heard about 3ABN while we were in Nepal. Garwin McNeilus had someone send us the coordinates to receive 3ABN's satellite signal, but because we were inexperienced in using satellite equipment, we weren't able to get it. We felt frustrated. We had all the necessary equipment but lacked the knowledge needed to find the satellite.

After being in Nepal for two years, we moved back to Bangkok—once again as volunteers. It was there at the hospital that we first saw 3ABN. It was available in all patient rooms and staff apartments. Everyone seemed blessed by watching. My family and I began watching, too, even though at first I thought it was too American for me! We especially liked Danny's inspiring stories about how God had provided for 3ABN's financial needs and the testimonies of other missionaries who were experiencing similar miracles of faith.

At the end of 2001, John wanted to return home to Australia. Something just kept nudging him in that direction. Finally, I agreed. We began praying for a mission, and the impression came that we should find ways to get 3ABN into Australia—something my son James had actually mentioned back in Bangkok. We believed the church members needed to be awakened and inspired. The only thing we could think of that would do the job was 3ABN. It would give our Australian people a world vision of the Adventist Church as the remnant church of God at work around the globe. It would inspire people to join in the work of preparing people to meet Jesus. And it would win souls!

Slowly, the method we should use became clear. If people didn't know how to install a dish and find the signal, they would never experience 3ABN. We had to make it easy for them. Plus, it had to be affordable. We found a company that would provide satellite equipment at a reasonable rate. After we installed the first dish at our home, it took John ten hours to find the signal. We prayed a lot, asking God to help us, for how would we be able to install the equipment for anyone else if we couldn't do it for ourselves? God did answer our prayers, and each installation became easier. We began to install the dishes and to train others to do the same. We prayed with every family we installed a dish for, and as people were blessed by what they were seeing, their testimonies led others to want a dish. Soon there were networks of individuals in different areas of Australia promoting 3ABN and installing dishes.

We became 3ABN's volunteer traveling evangelists in Australia. We attended churches and camp meetings, held rallies, visited isolated members, and did whatever the Lord impressed us to do to spread the word about 3ABN and its potential to spread the gospel.

And that's where Kermit comes in. Kermit is our green (like the frog), 1983 diesel Toyota 4 x 4 Land Cruiser that we purchased to pull our trailer home through the outback country of Australia. Kermit is as much a missionary as we are, because painted on all four sides of it is a message about 3ABN. On the door panels and spare tire cover is "3ABN Christian satellite TV and Radio available Australia-wide," along with our mobile phone number. On the insect reflector over the bonnet (hood) is "3ABN Australia." On our first installation trip around Australia, we were quite a sight. We had up to eleven large satellite dishes on top of Kermit. Plus, we were pulling a trailer with all the supplies needed to mount the dishes and the equipment necessary to get 3ABN's signal.

We started with one hundred systems, but now we have installed so many we've lost count.

Here's one story about 3ABN's influence. A pastor friend in Victoria told about visiting a Pakistani family who were Muslims. He and the evangelist from the South Pacific Division weren't getting very far with this family until they began to realize the family had been watching 3ABN and already knew many of our doctrines. They had purchased a dish to watch the Arab stations from Thaicom 3, and the bonus is that the Holy Spirit led them to 3ABN, and their lives were being changed. The pastor and evangelist left the house praising God, because they realized how He could use 3ABN to interest people in Bible studies when they would not have done this by themselves. The family will soon be well grounded in Bible truth, thanks to 3ABN. It makes me wonder: If this Muslim family is watching 3ABN without us going to their door first, how many others out there have been led in the same way by the Holy Spirit because they have a satellite system in their homes? It is also exciting for us to be installing more dishes for non-Adventists who enjoy having 3ABN programming in their homes.

In March 2004, a contract was signed with Globecast so that 3ABN is now on satellite Optus B3 covering New Zealand and Australia with a clear signal that can be received on a small dish. This makes our job much easier, because no license is needed.

As we travel, we are amazed at how God is leading us to certain people; we are experiencing "divine appointments" all over the country. It really does a lot to build our faith in God and His love as we see Him leading in our lives. We love what we're doing. God is stretching our skills and talents to the limit. I've even made a vocal CD to help support this work, and we are selling this as we travel. What better way to be fulfilling our missionary calling than volunteering to help God use 3ABN to reach the world with the undiluted three angels' messages!

Section V

Harvesting the Apples of His Eye

" 'He found him in a desert land
And in the wasteland,
a howling wilderness;
He encircled him,
He instructed him,
He kept him as the apple of His eye' "
—Deuteronomy 32:10, NKJV.

There has been no sweeter reward for the time and effort that 3ABN's dedicated staff, board members, volunteers, and donation partners have been privileged to give to the ministry than the reward of plucking the ripe red "apples" that God told Danny in a dream would be ready for harvest. The following stories—told by the individuals themselves—are just a sample of the thousands who have felt the presence of the Lord through the ministry of 3ABN and who have become new creatures because of it, vibrant in the love of Jesus and the security of salvation they have found when they discovered Bible truth. Each person saved for eternity is, indeed, the apple of God's eye.

16
The Theresa Boote Story

" 'However, when He, the Spirit of truth, has come,
He will guide you into all truth' "
—John 16:13, NKJV.

Theresa Boote

The following is the story of my journey to truth. I was one of the ripe red apples ready for harvest that was shown to Danny in vision.

I was born in 1945 to a very devout Roman Catholic family. I wanted to be a nun, but when I attended a retreat for those wishing to enter the convent, I discovered that this way of life was not for me. I wanted to communicate with God, but the continual rote prayers did nothing for me.

For a while, I still wanted to be a missionary for God. However, I found myself questioning whether He was real. From my earliest years, I had been indoctrinated with the belief that the Roman Catholic Church was the only true church founded on Peter the rock, so I went to the local priests for answers. They parroted general statements of belief and scolded me for my lack of faith, my many questions, and my unhappiness with their answers. I wanted so much to believe! Each time I reached out unsuccessfully for answers, I protected my disappointed and aching heart with another layer of bricks. Eventually, the tears stopped.

When I took a history course at the university and learned about the corruption in the Roman Catholic Church in the Middle Ages, it was the last straw. Like the baby being thrown out with the bath water, I threw God out with the church. I had concluded that God was a fictitious concept, concocted by some well-intentioned religious zealots who were trying to help dying people cope with the thought of having to be thrown into the earth. Religion was a nice cozy fable—a fairy tale—and I didn't buy it. I turned away, never wanting to hear about God and religion again.

For twenty-one years, I made jokes about God, ridiculed religious people, and crossed the street rather than meet someone who might talk to me about God. I was angry that the Bible was such a contradictory book. If there were a God, why couldn't He have come up with a nice neat biography that would answer all the questions, end the division among churches, and stop the heartaches of those who wanted so desperately to believe? I began to dislike people who claimed to be Christians. I decided that if this so-called God was anything like Christians, I didn't want to ultimately go where they thought they were going. I wanted to go where all my unbelieving friends might be going—and it wasn't heaven if there were such a place!

Finding God

In 1985, my husband, Frank, and I moved to Ottawa, where we enrolled our seven- and nine-year-old daughters in the Catholic school. We believed it was the best in the area, and it was only a couple blocks away. What I didn't expect was that Tracy, our oldest, would become convinced that the God she was hearing about in school was real. She begged me to take her to church. I explained to her that there was no God. I had gone down that path as a child and had been so bitterly disappointed, and I didn't want that to happen to her. Finally, I told her I would take her to church if she wanted to go, but that I would have nothing to do with it.

She replied, "Mom, I can't believe that you think there is no God. Look at your favorite tree outside. At the end of every branch there is a little seed. People plant the seeds, but only God can make them. And when you really get sick, all people can do is put on Band-Aids. Only God can heal. Mom, for a smart woman, you're not very smart!"

I stood alone in the kitchen stunned by what she had said. Tears ran down my cheeks. *Here comes God again, making me miserable,* I thought. But then the idea came to me, *What if I'm wrong about God? Now, I'm not just leading myself astray but my two daughters, as well!*

When my children were born, I was so amazed at the beauty of each new life that I had begun searching for God again. I had asked the priests, "How do you know there is a God? How do you know the Bible is true? What is truth?" I got the same old meaningless clichés. So once more, I had turned from God. But why, oh why, was this God-thing surfacing in my life again? I sighed, "Here comes the Judge!" I felt rage well up inside of me. I cried aloud, "God, where have You been? Why have You been so vague? Why haven't You made Yourself real? You knew from the beginning I wanted to serve You. Why didn't You let me find You?"

Ironically, just two weeks before this incident, God had arranged for me to receive my first Bible. As a realtor, I had visited a lady to convince her to list her house with me. She invited me in, and after a short conversation, she made the astonishing remark, "I'm impressed to give you a Bible, because I sense that God is moving in your life." As she handed me the Bible, she said, "When you begin to read, don't start at the beginning. Start with the book of John." I thought, *Dream on, lady!* Then she took a nice little bookmark and marked the place. In my mind I shouted, *I don't want your Bible, I want your house. What a rip off!* But on the outside I politely took the Bible. When I got home, I threw it in my junk drawer.

Now, I thought of that Bible. Was this why it was in my house? I decided to give God an ultimatum. "Look, because of my two children, I will put You to the test. This is my last time with You. I am asking, 'Are You real? And if so, what is truth? Where do I go to find it? Is there truth in the earth, or is it scattered a little here and there? Is it Catholic or non-Catholic?' I'm giving You until Christmas. Beginning this moment, I will sit down, and I'll read that Bible a little every day. I don't know how You will get truth to me because if You are real, You are a spirit, and I'm not. But if You are not real, this whole exercise is just hot air going no higher than the ceiling, and nothing will happen. So here goes."

I immediately went to my junk drawer and pulled out the Bible, sat down in my rocker, and began to read in total apathy. "In the beginning was the Word, and the Word was God . . ." As I read, my body temperature started to heat up. I became warm and then hot. Those words just jumped off the page. God's Spirit came upon me, and I knew God was real. I wept, "I'm so sorry I said all those things, God." I read a little more, until tears blurred the page. I repented for my rebellion and blasphemy of His name through the years. I was happy to know God was real. For the first time in my life, I had real communion with Him. The concept of the reality of a caring God was instantly seared in my heart. I was so happy and amazed at His revelation of Himself. Relieved, I promised Him that I would read all I could of His Book. I would respect the Bible and trust Him to lead me to the truth.

My search for truth

I went back to the Catholic Church—the only church I'd ever known. But instead of relying on the priests, I began flooding my soul with God's Word, listening to tapes of the Bible when I couldn't read. Tapes were sounding throughout my whole house as I did my housework. Every minute on the road was devoted to the Word of God on tape. When I woke up in the night, I read or listened to tapes until I drifted back to sleep. Intensively, I began to study different topics. I'd share what I learned with my husband. He was shocked at the sudden turnabout of my behavior and attitude, but, nevertheless, he began to attend church with me. Although he really never disbelieved, God was just not that important to him. Now we began to grow together.

At first, I was welcomed into the church. I was asked to join a Marian group, but I replied that I couldn't since I was convicted from the Bible that Jesus Christ is our only Intercessor. My fervor for the Bible and the questions I asked caused friction. I began a community service organization called Amor Dei (Love of God) that reached out to the community. I gave Bibles to the people I visited and had mini Bible studies with them. This boldness threatened the priest. He insisted that I cease from this outreach because I could be leading people astray. I wasn't a cleric and had no authority or qualifications for such a mission.

In 1987, I began studying the Bible with Manuel, another Roman Catholic who later became a Seventh-day Adventist pastor. One Tuesday night, Manuel, my husband, and I got down on our knees and pleaded, "Where do we go to find truth if it's not in the Catholic

Church?" I had been taught so strongly against attending Protestant churches that I felt a curse would be put on me if I were even to put my foot on the front step of one. But now I was willing to do anything to find truth.

That next Sunday, I was asked to step down from all my church offices including my music ministry. I knew that was an answer to our Tuesday night prayer. I felt ripped in two. I didn't know where to go next. "Please, God," I prayed, "lead me to truth. I don't want to go in and out of other churches for the rest of my life. The exits are too painful!"

For the next few months, we attended a Pentecostal church. The people were joyful and happy, but I missed the ritual of the Catholic Church and felt robbed by not having mass. No candles, no statues— just talk. Was this worship?

I kept reading and growing, both in my faith and in my trust in God. But every time I came forward to fill an announced need or church office, there was a check in my spirit. When I backed off, it would go away. So I never really got involved in this church.

By this time, I was so hungry for Bible truth that Frank and I decided to get a satellite dish so that we could be more fully fed by the Word of God through the many Bible-based ministries.

I loved all the variety. My faith was building, and I began to do in-depth studies on various topics. When I studied baptism, I realized that the sprinkling I had received was not the same as the baptism by immersion that was talked about in the Bible. We made arrangements for our whole family to be baptized the first week of November.

About this same time, coming home from church, our daughters asked us if we would take them to play mini-golf and ride go-carts. I said, "You know, the whole Sabbath day is reserved for the Lord, not just an hour. I think I should start a new study on how to keep the Sabbath. We'll go today, but tomorrow I'll begin a new study." Our whole family joined hands then, and we promised each other and God that if He would show us truth, we would walk in it.

Early the next Monday morning, I got up to begin my study on the Sabbath. To my great surprise, when I opened my front door to let light in, a book on the Sabbath fell onto my feet. Could this be happening? Where did it come from? Who put it on our doorstep?

Shocked, I picked it up and began to read. With each defense of the true seventh-day Sabbath, I tried to disprove it, but after checking every text, I was convicted of Bible truth. This was not what I wanted to find! Saturday was our busiest work day. How could I break the news to Frank about what I had discovered?

God uses 3ABN to answer our prayers

About midnight I went into the family room where Frank was experimenting with the position of the satellite dish. He was so excited. He had just picked up the sound on a new station that was coming from a satellite so close to the horizon that receiving the signal should have been impossible. He turned up the volume to permit me to hear the clear sound, and there, to my amazement, was the voice of Kenny Shelton reading the entire fourth commandment! Then Kenny went on to say something about the Catholic Church and the papacy that blew my vessel out of the water! How could he be so bold? Surely this would cause World War III if anyone were to hear it! Did he not value his life? To what off-the-wall group did he belong?

The next morning, my husband was able to get a clear picture, and we began to watch 3ABN. Not only did I hear strange doctrine, but I was bombarded by a message that made me feel guilty about the pork I was eating and the twelve to fourteen cups of coffee I was drinking each day!

3ABN was new on this particular satellite. So when Danny asked people to write in and tell him where they were picking up the signal and how strong it was, I decided to respond.

We kept listening to 3ABN to see who these strange people were. Finally, on October 22, I called Frank at work. "They're Seventh-day Adventists," I exclaimed. "Sounds like a cult to me."

"Well," said Frank, "let's see if there's a church in Ottawa. If so, maybe you can go there and get some brochures."

I found an address in the phone book and went over to the church. Unlike the Catholic Church, it was locked up tight. I found someone carrying flowers out the back door and asked if he could give me some literature. "No," he said, "but we're not a cult, if that's what you're thinking!" I then went over to the church school and got a book about Adventists. As I read it, I thought it was interesting that October 22, 1844 (the day of the Great Disappointment when Jesus didn't come), was a significant day for Adventists—and I was reading about it on October 22!

Every night, we would stay up until midnight to watch the Revelation seminar given by Kenny Shelton. We were very interested in the things we were learning, but one thing kept troubling me. The date of our baptism into the Pentecostal Church was approaching. I felt it only fair to let the pastor know if we were going to cancel. What should we do? Frank and I finally told our daughters that we were going into our family room to pray about whether or not we should be baptized into the Pentecostal Church. We were going to stay on our knees until we had an answer. I instructed Tracy, "Please, don't disturb us. If someone calls, take a message." When Tracy rolled her eyes at the thought of going to yet another church, I commented that just as she would be disappointed if I stopped five miles short of Disneyland, so God would be disappointed with us if we stopped short of our spiritual destination of finding truth.

We prayed, "Should we, or shouldn't we, be baptized into the Pentecostal Church?" Then we continued to pray, "Lord, what do You want us to do?" Finally, Frank said, "Theresa, I don't think this is going to work."

I mentioned that Jacob had wrestled with the Lord all night when he wanted an answer. Maybe we should do the same.

Frank responded, "Wouldn't it be better, since we're new at this, to talk to someone who could direct us and tell us what we should do? For example, if we could talk to someone like Danny Shelton."

Just then, the telephone rang. Tracy answered it, and a few minutes later she came into the room. "I tried to take a message," she explained, "but it's Danny Shelton from 3ABN, and he wants to talk to you about baptism."

Apparently, when Danny received my letter he was impressed to call me, but he had put it off. He had come back into the station that night to do some work and once again had a strong impression to call me. He found my letter and dialed—right at the exact time when we were pleading to God for answers!

We had a strong commitment in our hearts to follow truth, no matter what the cost, and we had verified and believed all our newfound teachings with the Bible. Because of this, Danny invited us to come to 3ABN to be baptized. Now, there was no doubt in our minds but that this telephone call from Danny was indeed an answer from the Lord. Certain that we had at last found the truth, we were baptized in West Frankfort on November 22, 1987—live on 3ABN. It was the happiest day in my life.

But our decision must have made Satan furious. Almost immediately, terrible things began to happen to our family—things so awful, so painful, so destructive that I can only weep as I recall the abuse. But in spite of it all, I never gave up my faith in God. So deeply had He convicted me of both His reality and goodness that I refused to let Satan destroy our family. I clung all the more tightly to my Savior and Redeemer, gripping His promises as my own ropes of hope.

Through the years of heartache, the Lord used 3ABN as an additional source of support and encouragement. It helped to anchor us in Christ and His Word. Within the first year of my baptism, Danny called and asked me to operate the 3ABN booth at an ASI meeting in California, sharing my testimony when possible. I said I would. But when I got as far as St. Louis, the story changed. Danny called his aunt's house where I was staying overnight and said, "By the way, we're sending a camera crew with you. Please interview some people and get us twelve stories we could broadcast on 3ABN."

I panicked. I got a grapefruit-sized lump in my throat. Throughout the night, I had nightmares of countless failed interviews. I was unable to sleep, and I begged to be released from this assignment. But in the end, it was the best thing that could have happened to me. I met the most fascinating people who were filled with the Spirit and dedicated to service. It gave me a much brighter look at God's remnant church. I continued to do this each year, and it took my mind off my own painful situation.

3ABN has become God's channel of blessing to me, providing beautiful opportunities for service that keep me dependent on God alone for my strength. The testimonies of others, plus the reinforcing of Bible teachings, keep me focused on Christ and His sure Word. Truly, God has given 3ABN a special spot in my heart.

God has continued to open doors for me at 3ABN. Most recently, a need arose for someone to coordinate the launching of 3ABN Radio (see chapter 13). Even though I didn't know anything about radio, I decided to accept the invitation. Didn't I believe, and often say, that it was not so much our ability but our availability that God honored? My husband was going to be working in the Arctic for awhile. Instead of staying home and feeling sorry for myself, I could make a meaningful contribution to the spreading of the gospel. Once again, God's timing was perfect.

Throughout eternity, I will forever praise God for 3ABN. By counteracting the counterfeit, it led me to the truth.

17
The Rick Odle Story

" 'And you shall know the truth,
and the truth shall make you free' "
—John 8:32, NKJV.

Rick Odle

I had been raised in the Assemblies of God Church, worked in its general conference office in Springfield, Missouri, and had completed seven and a half years of college and graduate theological training. I had pastored and done evangelistic work for almost thirteen years and was now pastoring an Assemblies of God church in West Frankfort, Illinois, where we had gone through two major building programs—finishing a gym and adding extra Sunday School rooms. Everything was going well. We had a full-time youth pastor, the church was growing and pretty much paid for, and the members were happy.

I had only one problem in life, a thorn in the flesh that I was sure the devil was using to buffet me: I had a Ford Pinto that was in constant need of repair. Little did I know that God would use that car to introduce me to Bible truth.

My dad once told me that you had to either know cars or know your mechanic. Well, I knew Ronny Shelton to be one of the finest mechanics in the country. And I had lots of experience on which to base this opinion because, with all the travel I did as a full-time pastor, I had that Pinto in his shop every couple of weeks. He would never let me go without giving me a piece of Seventh-day Adventist literature. He had this big box full of it. I threw the first eight or ten pamphlets away. Then my curiosity got the best of me.

It happened this way. I couldn't pick up my car one Friday afternoon before Ronny closed his shop, so I told him to just leave the keys inside the car with the bill, and I'd pick up the car Sunday night. I thought to myself, *That's one way to avoid the literature!* But wouldn't you know it, when I opened my car door, there was my bill and a pamphlet with the title *Let's Get Acquainted: Your Friends the Adventists.*

My curiosity was piqued. Although I belonged to the local ministerial association and was friends with most of the pastors in the area and knew what they believed, the Seventh-day Adventist pastor wasn't a member, so I really didn't know what Ronny and his fellow church members believed.

I read the pamphlet. *This sounds good,* I thought. *It makes sense!* So I wrote to the Adventist headquarters in Maryland for some Bible studies. I didn't let Ronny know, because I didn't want him to dump more literature on me. And besides, as a Pentecostal pastor, I was merely curious to see what the Adventists might have that would be useful to me in my work.

After I began Bible studies, I looked back over the sermons I was preaching and found there were some major areas that I hadn't addressed, such as hell, the millennium, and the Second Coming. *This is pathetic,* I thought. It was my wake-up call! But if someone would have asked me if I'd ever be a Seventh-day Adventist, I would have emphatically said, "Never!"

I spent eight and a half years ministering in West Frankfort before Jan, my wife, and I had a feeling that it was time to leave. We had done all the good we could. We liked starting churches, but once they got bigger and the bureaucracy took over, we moved on. And what better time to leave than when everything was going great? I gave my board a thirty-day notice, and we began praying. It would have been easy to phone another Assemblies of God church and let the people there know we were available, but this time we decided we would wait for God to give us a call.

The days ticked by while Jan kept saying that we would know something by the end of thirty days. On Friday, the thirtieth day, at about six in the evening, I responded to Jan's assurance that God would come through by saying, "Do you know what the Bible says about false prophets?" Not only was I questioning whether God would come through, but I also was wondering if I should continue taking the Adventist Bible studies or not. Jan reassured me. "The Lord is going to let you know."

About two and a half hours later, Ronny Shelton called. He had no idea Jan and I had resigned the pastorate of our church, and I had no idea that Danny had called him and said, "I have this impression we should hire Rick Odle to work master control. What do you think? Could you check him out?"

So Ronny called me and said, "Rick, I feel compelled to ask you a question. You can tell me 'No' and I'll go to bed and sleep like a baby. As you know, I'm a lay minister, and I occasionally preach in other churches when there's a need. Tomorrow, I'm going to Eldorado and Harrisburg to fill in for the pastor there. I want to know if you would like to ride along with me. I know Saturday is your busiest day because of sermon preparation, but I'd like you to come!"

"Ronny," I said, "I'd love to go with you. What time will you come by?"

"You would?" he exclaimed. I don't think Ronny expected that answer.

On the thirty-mile trip to the church, I told Ronny that Jan and I had resigned. "You're kidding! That's amazing!" he said again and again as I told my story. He then shared the real reason for his invitation. "For the last thirty days, Danny says he's been seeing your face when he prays and is impressed that he should ask you to work master control at 3ABN. But it doesn't make sense to him. First of all, you don't know anything about master control. Second, you're an educated Assembles of God minister. Third, you're making a good salary, and this job would pay minimum wage. Fourth, it's the midnight shift, and who in their right mind would want to work all night? And fifth, Danny doesn't know if he can trust you to give Bible answers to the late-night callers!"

Apparently, the idea that God had planted in Danny's mind thirty days before was so ridiculous to him that he put off doing anything about it until he felt compelled by God on the thirtieth day to have Ronny make a contact. What Danny didn't know was that I had been studying Adventist literature. I wasn't ready to become a Seventh-day Adventist yet, but I was open to Bible truth.

On Sunday, Danny called and offered me the job. Now, I had to make a decision. The strange part is that the idea of working all night at master control for minimum wage seemed ridiculous to me, too. I had thought a lot about what God probably wanted me to do, and this didn't fit into the vision I had for myself. But I prayed as I claimed Proverbs 3:5, 6, "Trust in the Lord with all thine heart, and lean not unto thine own understanding. In all thy ways acknowledge him, and he shall direct thy paths." Then I called Danny back. "I'll take it!"

As it turned out, master control was God's way of taking me to the desert so that He could teach me. 3ABN was a far better instructor than seminary school. During those early years at 3ABN, we had to constantly monitor the color, so I had to be attentive to what was airing. I'd get out my Greek Bible and study along with the various preachers. I thought, *How blessed I am to be getting paid for studying the Bible!* If I didn't understand something or wanted to go back and check on the references, I'd play the tape again when I got off work. On many occasions I even took "Joe Crews" home with me! (At the time he was the speaker for the *Amazing Facts* telecast.)

After studying intensely for three years, I was baptized into the Seventh-day Adventist Church in June 1990 by one of my favorite television preachers, Tony Mavrakos. I could have joined the church by profession of faith, but what I had learned had enhanced my spiritual life so much that I demanded to be baptized.

My wife respected my decision, but she hadn't had the advantage of the hours of study I had done while working at 3ABN, so it was another year and a half before she joined me.

I now see the graciousness of the Lord to allow me to go through this time of searching. I wouldn't take anything for that experience. I would have been happy staying with master control for the rest of my life, if that's what God wanted.

When Kenny left 3ABN, I began taking the pastoral calls and referring the doctrinal ones to Dane Griffin until after I was baptized. Slowly, I began speaking in churches and helping Larry Welch with the pastoral department at 3ABN. As Larry moved more into the building area, I took over more of the pastoral responsibilities. After a few years, the Illinois Conference of Seventh-day Adventists approached me to become the official pastor of the Thompsonville Seventh-day Adventist Church, in addition to my 3ABN responsibilities.

I've kept close contact with my Assemblies of God friends. Some have felt I was throwing away a good career. But when I share my testimony about what finding Bible truth has meant to me, they can't dispute my decision. I'm so excited to have learned about the seventh-day Sabbath—that the dead are dead until the resurrection and that God doesn't burn people forever. It's changed my perspective about the character of God and created in me a new love for my heavenly Father. Some of my former colleagues have seen me on 3ABN television and have wanted to know what happened. I've even had a number of occasions to correspond with Paul Crouch, who was once my homiletics teacher and is now directing Trinity Broadcasting Network, the Pentecostal satellite network. I have no idea where my witness will lead.

Why is 3ABN important to me? The Bible truths I learned from 3ABN have changed my life. I no longer have to ignore certain doctrines because they don't fit into my theology. I feel confident and assured that God's Word makes sense. Bible truth has set me free (see John 8:32). And I've thanked God many times for that old broken-down Ford Pinto and the literature that my faithful mechanic gave to me!

Note: Rick Odle, well-loved friend and pastor to so many in West Frankfort, was the director of the 3ABN pastoral department and pastor of the Thompsonville Seventh-day Adventist Church until 2000 when God called him to move on to another Seventh-day Adventist congregation to build, encourage, and enable another body of believers, as God has gifted him to do. His vibrant personality and keen mind made a significant contribution to the advancement of the work at 3ABN. Once more, God had raised up just the right person, at just the right time, for the job that needed to be done.

18
The Hal and Mollie Steenson Story

"The glory of this latter house shall be greater than of the former,
saith the Lord of hosts:
and in this place will I give peace, saith the Lord of hosts"
—Haggai 2:9.

Hal's story

I first met Danny Shelton in the early eighties when the church that my wife, Mollie, and I were pastoring was building a new church structure on Main Street in West Frankfort. A friend of ours introduced us because Danny and his brother were in construction. What really impressed me about Danny was his kind attitude in spite of persecution. A friend of ours arrogantly gave him a hard time, ridiculing him about his religion. Danny didn't retaliate. Instead, he was humble, considerate, and genuinely interested in what we were doing.

Hall and Mollie Steenson

Every day we had a prayer meeting at the building site. Danny would come by, and we'd pray for him, and he would comment that he needed it. Other times, I'd be walking through the building, and he'd say, "Brother Hal, come over here and sing a song with me." I couldn't sing—at least not like Danny—but when he was around, he was always a blessing to me.

His carpentry work was excellent. He built special tables for the church nursery with hearts on the seats of the chairs, and painted them red and white. We tended to bond over that project as we talked together.

I also admired his singing ability, and we would ask him to come and minister in song to our congregation. One time when he came to sing, instead of taking up an offering, I was impressed to give him a check for a certain amount. I thought it was a strange figure. But when I gave it to him, along with twenty dollars a friend had given me for him, Danny commented it was the exact amount he needed to pay a bill that he had been praying about. It was then that I realized God was speaking to both Danny and me, and we became spiritual brothers.

Our church was a fledgling one that was growing so rapidly that we outgrew our facilities and moved six times in two years. In one of those moves we needed to be out of our church six weeks before our new facility would be ready. Danny was instrumental in making arrangements for us to use the Seventh-day Adventist church during that time.

During this rapid time of growth, I had been impressed to start a television ministry. A gentleman in our church wanted to video the services and bought a little camera. Then I heard about a pastor in Missouri who had a television ministry on a local station. When he left his pastorate, the new pastor was against television, so the equipment was up for sale. We stepped out in faith and purchased it and continued to purchase equipment as needed. For what we were doing, it was excellent equipment. Even the West Frankfort newspaper took note and did a full-page article on our church and its television ministry.

Although I was impressed to have a television ministry outreach in our church, I wasn't impressed to start a station. When we first began our television ministry, Trinity Broadcasting Network (TBN) was being aired on the local cable system. When the cable company took TBN off the air, I started a mini campaign to get it back on, and in faith continued to produce programs. I began working with Paul Crouch, president of TBN, who told me that if I would form a board, TBN would purchase the station for us. But I declined the offer and said, "God has not called us to start a station. I will help you get back on the air." I did that, and we had programs ready when TBN was once again airing on a local television station. At the same time I was beginning to feel that many of the

Christian television personalities had lost their original vision. Their promotions sounded more like Six Flags Over Jesus than like the original gospel message.

I recall that I was sitting in the television room of our church on November 17, 1984, when Danny and his friend Ann Greer came by to talk to me about starting a television station. He told me that two days before he had had a dream about building a television station that would reach the world. Danny has said some pretty surprising things over the years, but I have never heard him boast about himself—only about what God could do. I immediately thought, *A worldwide television station?* and exclaimed, "Danny, it will cost you a million dollars just to get ready to go on the air!"

Then I asked him, "What would you do if you had this equipment?"

"What do you mean?" he asked.

"I'm not sure," I replied, "but let me pray about something." I called Mollie in and told her that Danny was starting a television ministry and would need equipment. She just smiled because she knew that I had been impressed earlier that God was going to have us give this equipment away.

After Danny left, I told her, "I feel God's telling me to give this equipment to Danny Shelton."

Mollie said, "OK, let's do it."

I talked to the assistant pastor, and he agreed. Mollie pulled the inventory list on the television equipment. Later, we gave Danny a letter of commitment from our board of trustees. Giving to others was something that God had allowed our church to do. We had helped other churches in the area get started by giving them chairs and other things, so our board wasn't surprised at the direction we felt God was leading with the television equipment.

I believe that more than anything else, it only takes a spark to get a fire going. I don't think Danny really needed our television equipment. All Danny needed at that time was a spark of faith to get the ministry started.

Sometime later, Clarence Larson, a good friend who worked at the local television station that was broadcasting TBN programming, came to me seeking advice on whether or not he should change positions and work for 3ABN. Clarence had helped me solve some technical electronic problems at our church, and he was also volunteering to help get 3ABN off the ground. I told him, "God is going to sky-rocket 3ABN. Go for it. You have an opportunity to touch the world through this ministry."

This prediction has come true. As people began to catch the vision, 3ABN began to grow. There is no doubt in my mind but that God has filled 3ABN with His grace.

My background

I'm an old Alabama country boy. I was working with my brother in Decatur, Alabama, as an auto mechanic when Mollie and I first met. Fifty-one days later we were married. After we had been married for about six years, the Holy Spirit drew both Mollie and me to a saving knowledge of our Lord, and I felt called to the ministry. We moved to Lakeland, Florida, where I studied for the ministry at a Pentecostal seminary. I lacked just six hours of having my degree when the Lord said, "Go!"

A friend of ours who lived in West Frankfort, Illinois, invited us to come and explore the possibility of starting a church. We visited and shared our vision with a few people. They didn't like the idea, however, of starting another church. So we got back in the car and started driving home to Florida. It was raining and gloomy, which was symbolic of our state of mind right then. As we were crossing the Ohio River, I looked over at Mollie. She was quietly crying. "What's wrong?" I asked. "What do you think we should do?"

"Well," she said, "my head says, 'No,' but my heart says, 'Go.' " That was March 1981. We moved to West Frankfort in June. Mollie and I started the church with twelve people in our basement. I tell people that the first week I ran off four people with my preaching, so the next service we had only eight in attendance.

However, God was blessing us, sometimes in spite of us, it seemed. Over the next several years, our church grew to be one of the larger ministries in the area with the largest Christian school and a television ministry, and from all appearances, I was a successful minister.

My fall

Then my life fell apart. I started drinking and doing crazy things that resulted in losing my church and my family. When Mollie and I divorced, I moved back to Alabama. But God never gave up on me, and He is now rebuilding my life. Mollie and I were remarried on January 30, 1998, this time by Danny Shelton.

3ABN has blessed us by being there for our family when others didn't understand us. One of the things I've learned is that pride is the only vice that is competitive. People who drink, drink together; there is no competition. But prideful people don't communicate. Through this time of trouble, I had no one in my church with whom to talk. But when I was hurting most, I was able to reach out to Danny, and we shared a lot.

Those years were a time of terrible trouble for me and my family. Satan did everything to destroy us, but God is restoring us. There is still a work for me to do. The most grace-filled people I've ever encountered have been the Seventh-day Adventist people associated with 3ABN. I have felt their love and mercy. Having to see each other every day isn't what makes a true relationship. It's the fact that when you do see each other, you are able to pick your relationship right back up again. That's how it's been for Danny and me.

What I've learned

Hosea says that my people perish for lack of knowledge. I rejected Bible knowledge, and God said, "If you do this, I will reject you." Here is what happened.

In 1988, God began to lead me into new truth about the Sabbath, but I was scared of the consequences. I didn't want to become a martyr. I started teaching and talking about the Sabbath, but not really clarifying it as the seventh-day Sabbath. It scared me. Danny gave me some materials on the Sabbath from 3ABN, and to make a long story short, I rejected it.

The price I had to pay for rejecting God's truth was that God had to move me out of the church I was pastoring and humble me. God had to get me to the point that I was teachable again. It's been a terrible down time for me. It's one thing to be on a horse in the middle of the stream, but it's another thing to be on the wrong horse. That's what I was doing when I fell.

I ran from the Sabbath message because it was going to alter too drastically what I was doing in "my" ministry as a Pentecostal pastor. God had given me much truth, but the truth about the Sabbath I exchanged for error. Had I been a lay person sitting in the pew when I first understood the Sabbath truth, I would have immediately turned to it. But as the pastor of a growing church, it was too much of a price to pay. What I didn't realize was the price I would have to pay by rejecting this truth. I don't believe my loving Father brought this trouble on me, but He allowed it in order to help me really understand myself.

I don't claim to be a scholar, but as I studied about the Sabbath rest of God, something really affected me. Through the Spirit, I experienced the rest of the Sabbath. When that happened, I knew the truth of the Sabbath. It's scriptural, but it's more. It's not just a day in the week. Not just a commandment. It is a revelation that becomes a way of life.

Since I came to the truth of the Sabbath rest, I feel uncomfortable in most churches because of the hype and show. I can't watch most Christian television. There are so many sitting in churches who know that Jesus Christ is Lord but have never made Him Lord of their lives because they have never experienced the truth of the Sabbath. It is a rest. It is the peace that passes all understanding. So, in obedience to the Word of God, I began to keep the Sabbath as defined by Scripture. I began reading books such as *The Great Controversy* and *27 Fundamental Beliefs of the Seventh-day Adventist Church*. At last, I made the decision that it was time to join the Seventh-day Adventist Church. So on Christmas Day, 1999, Mollie, our son, Jeremy, and I were baptized.

Now that Mollie and I have embraced the truth of the Sabbath, there is no turning back. How can people be so blind to the clarity of God's Word concerning this matter? Mollie has a saying, "Grandma taught it, and we bought it." How sad it is that many desire to go all the way with God but hold on to tradition instead of Bible truth! In twenty-eight years of ministry, I have never encountered such a mind-set as the one that is against God's fourth commandment. The enemy has blinded the eyes of so many good Christians. It takes a Damascus experience for many before the scales are removed from their eyes so that they can see the truth of the Sabbath (see Acts 9:17, 18). When the scales fall off, as they did when Ananias put his hands on Paul and restored Paul's sight—and he was filled with the Holy Spirit—then, and only then, are we able to understand Revelation 14:12, "Here is the patience of the saints: here are they that keep the commandments of God, and the faith of Jesus."

Why are so many willing to run with the herd at the expense of their salvation? The answer is so simple and yet so elusive: Excuses! Excuses! Excuses! They might sound good at first, but they will not stand up at the judgment seat of Christ. If it takes a Damascus-road experience to knock us off our high horse of error, then by all means, let's allow God to "knock"![1]

I believe God has a place for me to work. I'm called to minister. It has just taken a few years for God to get me turned around, but I'm coming out of my Gethsemane experience.

Mollie's story

It was devastating to watch the man I loved fall from the peak of success and be shunned by the very people we thought were our best friends. We had been a team. For fourteen years, we had copastored the church we had established. Our church was our family. It was our total existence. When Hal was no longer able to carry out pastoral duties because of his addictive illness, the church people rejected and shunned him instead of helping him when he was down. I realize now that they re-

Mollie Steenson

ally didn't know how to handle the situation and were receiving some bad counsel.

For three more months, I continued in administration at the church and school that we had built. During this time of trouble, Danny and Linda stood by us and were some of our best friends. One day Danny came to me and said, "The day will come when they won't want you at your church anymore."

I thought, *How can this be? We birthed this church. These are my best friends, and they know this ministry is my life. They will never not want me.*

Danny continued, "The day will come when you won't be able to stand it any longer. When that day comes, there will be a place for you at 3ABN."

As it turned out, Danny's words were prophetic. The church board of trustees, which had once been so supportive and was made up of my best friends, came to me one day to say, "We think it is in the best interest of the church members if they don't see you in church anymore." They asked me to leave. No one stood by us or offered to help us. So with dignity, I left and found that not only was Hal shunned, but our son and I were shunned as well.

When I walked away from my church, I left behind my identity, my job, my place of worship, my church family, and so many of those whom I had called my best friends. Except for the Lord, my whole support system just fell right out from under me. In a matter of a few months, Hal and I were separated and later divorced. Plus, Hal and I had just built a beautiful new home, which I had to sell. I am told that there are six major things that cause the most stress in a woman's life: (1) changing jobs, (2) changing churches, (3) moving, (4) divorce, (5) a major health issue (by the way, I had a major health issue right in the middle of everything else!), and (6) the death of a loved one. Thank God there wasn't a death of a loved one in my life or I would have been "six for six"! As I walked through these very difficult times, I was always acutely aware that God's grace was surrounding me and enabling me to continue in His love.

After the church elders told me that I would need to leave the church, I called Danny and told him that I was ready to take him up on his offer of employment at 3ABN. He told me that I could start any time.

I began work on September 5, 1995. I remember the day well. Danny had neglected to let anyone know that he had hired me, and he was out of town. When I "showed up," no one knew what to do with me. His secretary put me to work answering correspondence. Actually, Danny had hired me as Linda's assistant. The new production center was under construction, but we weren't in it yet, and the building we were in was totally maxed out. There were no extra desks, computers, or even chairs. My office for the first few weeks was a box of unanswered correspondence and the desk of whoever wasn't in at the time. I also helped in the mail room and anywhere else as needed. Our job descriptions at 3ABN are very flexible. There is so much that needs to be done, and we work with a limited staff. I have found through the years that 3ABN is very conservative and a very good steward of all finances entrusted to it and that part of that conservativeness is maximizing personnel. After about a year and a half, I became Danny's assistant and the office manager—a fairly responsible position. However, when the commodes get stopped up in the lobby, guess who gets called to plunge them! As I said, our job descriptions are very flexible!

My work at 3ABN gave me stability when everything else was falling apart. I can remember coming to work when I was devastated by personal circumstances. Then, as I tackled a full day of new challenges and saw the miracles happening, my faith in God was reinforced. It kept me mentally focused. I reestablished my identity in the Lord—where it should have been all along.

Danny and Linda have proved to be very good friends. They would hold my hand and pray with me while I cried many tears during this time of trouble. Gradually, I became more involved in the ministry. For several years now, I have enjoyed reading Scripture for the television broadcast *His Words Are Life.* Coming to work has been a haven for me. 3ABN's theme is "Mending Broken People," and I am one of the many who have been mended through this ministry.

Around Christmas of 1997, Hal got a longing to get his life right with the Lord. He had a real heart change—not something that was just skin deep—and I knew it was time for us to get back together.

I never lost hope, regardless of how bad things were. The Lord was faithful to me and has brought restoration. I feel I am now walking in more of the light of God's Word. I took it slow when studying the new truths presented by Seventh-day Adventists, because I had to know that God, not man, was bringing me into new truth. I'll admit it was hard to attend the Adventist church at first because it was so different from what I was accustomed to. I went through some dry times. However, now that our church has been blessed with Pastor John Lomacang and his wife, Angie, as well as his assistant, Pastor John Stanton, things are beginning to move forward.

Through it all, my hope has been in the Lord. I have found Him to be faithful when He said, "For I know the thoughts that I think toward you, says the Lord, thoughts of peace and not of evil, to give you a future and a hope" (Jeremiah 29:11, NKJV).

Note: In February 2004, Hal and Mollie joined the Merlin Fjarli family, who led a group of approximately thirty lay people in a fifty-village evangelistic series in the state of Andhra Pradesh, India. Hal coordinated one of five teams who held evangelistic meetings in villages within a seventy- to ninety-mile radius from Bobbili, where the McNeilus family and Maranatha have built a school for the blind. There are over six hundred thousand villages in India, and only a hundred thousand of them have a Christian influence in them. That means that there are still a half million villages to be reached with the gospel. Hal's team included his wife, Mollie; Donnie Shelton (Danny's cousin), who often represents 3ABN; and two others. Hal and Donnie took turns preaching. On the first night several hundred people attended. By the end of sixteen days, four thousand to five thousand people were attending the meetings. Each night as the speakers made altar calls, it was made clear that only the people who had never prayed, who had never given their hearts to Jesus, and who desired baptism were to come forward. Yet every night many hundreds came forward to make Jesus Christ their Lord, and many others came to the altar for prayer. The team reached out to the people and touched each one as they prayed for them.

There was a mighty harvest. According to Elder Ron Watts, president of the Southern Asia Division of the Seventh-day Adventist Church, it is anticipated that six thousand baptisms will result from these meetings. Pastor Hal commented, "I saw in India the fulfillment of one of Mollie and my favorite texts, Haggai 2:9, where God says that the latter house will be greater than the former. I saw more people accept Christ as a result of my ministering in India for sixteen days than I experienced in sixteen years of ministering previously." Hal then made this offer: "If your church is ready for revival, we are ready for ministry!"

---

[1] For more on the Sabbath, see Danny Shelton's booklet *The Forgotten Commandment* or the book, *The Antichrist Agenda,* by Danny Shelton and Shelley Quinn available from 3ABN. To order your copy—or to ask for prayer or personal guidance as you study what God's Word says about the Sabbath—call 3ABN at 618-627-4651. You can also find key texts to begin your study of the Sabbath in Appendix 2, under belief #19.

19
The Shelley Quinn Story

" 'And blessed is she who believed
that there would be a fulfillment
of what had been spoken to her by the Lord' "
—Luke 1:45, NASB.

In 1999, my husband, JD, and I thought we had found the end of the rainbow. CPAs throughout the nation, with whom we had worked for eighteen months, were urging us to present business development seminars to their clients. That "pot of gold" was coming into focus, and we embraced our new venture with enthusiasm. We had invested significant funds and months of intense preparation into our new company, Impact Profit Solutions, when the Lord interrupted our plans.

Shelley Quinn

Seeking God for the answer to a deeper walk with Him, I was prompted to spend an hour each day journaling my prayers. The Lord taught me to seek His face and to learn to listen for His "still, small voice." It wasn't long before I knew God was calling me into full-time ministry. My interest in the new business venture was fading fast, and JD recognized that. One day, as we were traveling, he asked, "If you could do anything in the world, what would you want to be doing?"

In a flurry of words, I tried to explain how the Lord was leading. But I didn't mention God had impressed me that the decision to abandon our business must be left to JD. In fact, I dodged the direct approach and suggested I might start in ministry on a part-time basis, then evolve into full time. Sensing I was holding something back, JD's approach to the subject was blunt. He said, "You know what God is asking, don't you?"

My answer was simply, "I know God is calling me to full-time ministry, and I believe His timing is now."

Without a moment's hesitation, JD replied, "Who am I to argue with God?" That wasn't what I expected. I thought the decision would be agonizing for him. But as we drove down the road, we made the commitment to drop our seminar business and step out in faith at God's direction.

I had already asked the Lord to give me a sign if this was His perfect will for our lives. He didn't waste any time. The next day, a Christian broadcasting network tracked us down and asked me to be a program guest. I took that as my "sign," and *Word Warrior Ministries* was born. One television appearance followed another, and the network offered to produce a weekly program series at no cost to me. Eager to share Bible teachings, I accepted, and taping began. But before the programs were completed, a painful dispute arose. Walking away from the opportunity to share the gospel on that network was a bitter disappointment. Were my days of full-time ministry to last only eight months?

God had taught me so much in those first months of ministry. He had led me in a study of the temple and the Old and New Covenants. After He proved to me from Scripture that the Ten Commandments were eternal, I became a joyful Sabbath celebrator. I had learned obedience was the pathway to God's blessings. I had so much to share. God opened the door for home-group Bible studies. Soon, I was making regular rounds to five surrounding towns.

God was showing me things from His Word that had been fenced in and hidden from my eyes before. He was teaching me to know the voice of the Holy Spirit. He impressed me that He would join me to "one who is running fast" after Him and that JD would work shoulder to shoulder with me. At first, I wasn't sure I wanted to be joined to another man's ministry, but I figured if it was God's plan, it was for my best interest.

In March 2001, God impressed me that He was going to open doors for me to television, radio, and publishing. When I ran downstairs to share this exciting news with JD, he said, "Honey, it seems to me that He already did that, and you walked away. How is anyone going to discover you in the little town of Coleman, Texas, with a population of only 5,100?"

My response was a paraphrase of Luke 1:38, "I am a handmaiden of the Lord. Let it be done to me according to His word!"

God began to accelerate His plan in September 2001. Returning from a speaking engagement, I had plopped into my recliner and reached for the television remote control. Flipping through the channels, I landed on 3ABN just as Kenneth Cox said, "I don't know what everyone's problem with obedience is; it's all by faith anyway." That sure sounded a lot like the teaching God had given me on obedience by grace. *He must not be an Adventist!* I thought. So I listened to the rest of his sermon.

The Coleman Seventh-day Adventist Church had purchased the only locally owned Christian television station. I was disappointed when we lost Trinity Broadcasting Network programming. And although I had been a Sabbath celebrator for nearly two years then, I still stubbornly refused to watch 3ABN. I knew Adventists ran the network, and I had heard strange things about their beliefs. But now I was hopeful that they broadcast pastors from other denominations. So I tuned in the next day and heard a Doug Batchelor presentation. *Hey, he must not be an Adventist either.* He was teaching the same things I was teaching—salvation by grace, righteousness by faith—these preachers were good!

Soon I caught Steve Wohlberg's *Antichrist Chronicles* program. Now this was like nothing I had ever heard before. I had been pleading with the Lord to teach me the truth about Revelation, because nothing I had heard made sense—there were too many contradictions with other Scriptures. I would listen to Steve's program and then go study for hours on end. After a week, I called his ministry and ordered all of his books. Soon, my personal study convinced me that he was presenting the truth.

When I recognized that all of 3ABN's programmers were Adventists and that everything they taught was what the Lord had been teaching me over those past two years, I faced a major decision. I drained my ministry account (only seven hundred dollars) and sent it to 3ABN with a letter that said, "Please pray for me. I feel the Lord may be leading me to join the Adventist Church." The 3ABN monthly newsletter carried an excerpt from my correspondence. My hometown Adventist pastor read it. He went through all the red tape that 3ABN has in place to protect the privacy of its donors. Proving he had pastoral credentials and arguing that I was praying about joining the church, he finally convinced 3ABN that at least he ought to contact me by phone.

When Pastor Graves called, I invited him over immediately. He seemed somewhat surprised on that first visit to learn I had an interdenominational ministry, but that I was teaching the same

Bible doctrines that Adventists believed. Accepting his invitation to church, I began attending regularly in December. People were advising me not to join the Adventist Church because it might ruin the interdenominational thrust of my ministry. Even a few Adventists chimed in on the same side. They reasoned I could attend the church, but if I wasn't an actual member, people of other denominations would more readily accept these Bible truths from me.

Arriving early for a midweek service, I circled the block a few times. It was still daylight, and my car would be conspicuous if it were the only one parked at the church. Coleman is a small town. I didn't want people to think I was "one of them." On my third trip around the block, the Lord said, "If you won't identify with My people, how can you identify with Me?" I parked right in front of the church! Still do!

I asked Pastor Graves if we could invite Steve Wohlberg to give us a seminar. When he called, Steve told him he was booked a year in advance. But God planned to use Steve's ministry to introduce me to Danny Shelton. So Steve had a cancellation, and we booked him in Coleman in February 2002. Months after I met Steve, I learned that he had told my pastor, "You've got to get this woman into the church." Pastor Graves had already heard from God on this matter. The Holy Spirit impressed him to stay out of it. *God* was planning to bring me into the church.

I was earnestly seeking God's will, so I prayed, "Lord, if You want me in this church, You are going to have to show me. I haven't heard the Adventists speak of the baptism of the Holy Spirit. I know they believe in the Spirit, but do they recognize His importance in their lives?" The next morning, June 1, 2002, as I was getting ready for Sabbath School, I was listening to 3ABN. Talking with Danny Shelton, Pastor Dennis Smith was explaining his book on the baptism of the Holy Spirit. "Hallelujah," I shouted, "I'm joining the church, Lord!"

June 8, 2002, I joined the Seventh-day Adventist Church. Within weeks, I was working with Steve Wohlberg's ministry. In August, Steve asked me to operate his booth at the ASI convention. Just down the aisle from us was the 3ABN booth. I met Danny and shared how the ministry of 3ABN had brought me into the church. Of course, he seized the opportunity to have Theresa Boote interview me right at the convention. I also met Brenda Walsh and agreed to tape several *Kids Time* Bible stories. It was wonderful to meet these dedicated Christians in person. Still, I didn't recognize that God was opening the door for television ministry for me.

In October 2002, Dee Hilderbrand called to ask what I was doing for New Year's Eve. The ministry had failed to schedule a guest speaker for a live program that evening. She explained that she didn't know how it happened; she usually booked a year in advance. Driving to the 3ABN campus for that event, I commented to JD, "Just think about it, Honey, before we were ever born, God knew and recorded in His heavenly record book that we would be here on this very night." Following a few moments of silence, JD responded, "That's a heavy thought!"

After the New Year's program concluded, 3ABN extended an invitation to me to come to work at the ministry! That was an exciting way to start out 2003. Since I was scheduled to tape *Kids Time* in February, we decided I would stay a couple of weeks and see where I might fit in at the ministry. Those weeks were tense for me. My heart felt I belonged at 3ABN, but I didn't feel God had called me to administrative work. Danny and I met before I left, and he said, "We all want you to work with us here. But, the Lord has given you a special message, Shelley. He has shown me that I can't interrupt His call on your life. Instead of working in administration, I believe you should become one of our programmers."

JD was rebaptized into the Adventist Church in March 2003. In April, I received the call from 3ABN to produce a program and to write a companion book to accompany it. The Lord enabled me to write the book in just seventeen days. We recorded twenty-four programs of *Exalting His Word* in August. The program currently airs on 3ABN television and radio. I have also been privileged to host the *3ABN Today* program on many occasions. Other programming is in development.

God is faithful! Just as He promised, He has joined me to one who is running fast after Him—3ABN! He has opened doors to television, radio, and publishing. He has ordered all of our steps. I say "our" because JD is actively involved in *Word Warrior Ministries* now.

How can anyone believe that a God who loved us enough to send His Son to die for us while we were still sinners would not do all things for us? He has given me all that I need, including personal advice and counsel. If you will just seek His face, He will open His heart to you and share His deepest secrets with you, just as He has done for JD and me. We are in ministry together for Him because of 3ABN.

Note: In January 2005 Shelly and J. D. moved to southern Illinois so they could work full time for 3ABN.

20
Touching Lives
Close to Home

"I thank my God upon every remembrance of you, . . .
being confident of this very thing,
that He who has begun a good work in you
will complete it until the day of Jesus Christ"
—Philippians 1:3, 6, NKJV.

One of the most rewarding aspects of his work, Danny says, is seeing how God is using 3ABN to change the lives of those who work at the ministry and others he meets personally. Not everyone on the payroll is a believer; not all come from the same religious persuasion; not all practice the healthy lifestyle that is promoted by 3ABN. But almost all who choose to work at the ministry change over time. The influence of the messages heard and the atmosphere of acceptance that one finds in Danny and the rest of the staff bear witness to a real God who is personally interested in each individual.

Dave Turner, a long-time employee, is just one example: He had walked away from God in his early years, picked up some addictive habits, and pretty much hit bottom. He finally prayed, "God, if You will make a way available for me to use my talents for You, I'll do it." Dave came to 3ABN as a volunteer and stayed. He speaks for many when he says, "Accepting God's grace has made such a difference in my life. I've been blessed to grow with the ministry. Here at 3ABN we don't always get to see the immediate results of our efforts, but we know that God's promise in Isaiah 55:11 is true: His Word will not return to Him void. What a reward, to spend eternity with Jesus and those this ministry has blessed!"

Since 3ABN is God's work, Danny tends to rely quite heavily on God to impress him about whom he should hire. One example is

Mike Wilson. Mike told me his story in 2003 after working in 3ABN's accounting office for four years.

Mike, his wife, Teresa, and their two children, Michelle and Daniel, loved their country home and had no intention of leaving Missouri. Then his stressful job terminated, and he had time to watch more television, including 3ABN. At the same time, the Wilsons prayed about what God wanted Mike to do next. That's when they began watching *Pentecost 2000,* by Stephen D. Lewis. They were so impressed by what

The Wilson family

they were seeing that they decided to take off one weekend and drive to 3ABN to attend the live weekend meetings. Friday morning, they were given a personal tour of the 3ABN facilities. They met a number of people whom they recognized from watching 3ABN over the last three years, but they had not yet seen Danny. As they were standing outside the accounting office, Danny walked through the door. He immediately went up to Mike, introduced himself, and learned that he was currently unemployed. Danny said, "That's all I need to hear. The Lord has impressed me that you should be here at 3ABN." Mike turned white as a sheet. He had prayed that if God wanted him to work at 3ABN, He would let him know. His faith, however, had been so weak that he hadn't even told his wife or brought a résumé with him!

The next day Mike and Teresa ran into Danny four or five times. Each time, Danny asked, "When are you going to come work for us?" Still not believing this was a call from the Lord, Mike and his wife prayed that Danny would once again approach them with a job offer on Saturday night. Danny did. They drove home Sunday, packed a carload of things, and Mike reported for work on Tuesday.

Through a series of miracles, Teresa started Earth's Harvest, a vegan restaurant in Thompsonville that has become a warm and pleasant lunch-time gathering place for the 3ABN workers and many others in the community. She is also helping to provide programming for the vegan cooking segments on 3ABN.

Because I heard so many stories like this from the employees at 3ABN, I asked Danny if he ever made any mistakes when hiring people. As he reflected back over the years he said, "The mistakes I've made have always been because I relied on my own reasoning rather than acting on the impressions that God gave me."

The following stories are only a sample of the hundreds that could be told by employees and others about the influence of 3ABN on their lives. For many, it's the story of how 3ABN helped to mend their broken lives by touching them with God's love. You, too, will be touched as they tell their stories in their own words.

Clarence Larson

Clarence Larson's Story

Money was the driving force in my life. I'd do almost anything to get more. Finally, after working as an engineer in various communications projects, I had reached a place in my career that I was comfortable, secure, and making good money. I had basically built the Christian television station in Marion where I worked, and I had no intention of ever leaving. Then Danny Shelton entered my life.

As soon as I mentioned to Danny about the possibility of building an uplink satellite station in the Thompsonville area, I felt foolish. I had thought God was nudging me to share this with Danny, but when he didn't even know what an uplink station was, I knew I had made a mistake. That was in the fall of 1984. But as time went on, I realized that God had, indeed, impressed me to give Danny this information. What's more, He had an important work for me to do in helping Danny fulfill the call that He had given him to build a television station that would reach the world.

As the concept for 3ABN began to take shape, Danny would come to me and ask my advice. If he was going to start a satellite uplink station, he was going to need a lot of advice because he had no idea what was required to start a station. I was willing to give him advice and volunteer to help him, but I wouldn't work for him, even though he asked me repeatedly to do so.

Most people, when you turn them down, take you at your word and leave you alone. Not Danny. He kept coming back. There was no way I was ever going to work for him. He didn't have any money for wages, and I knew how much the project he had in mind was going to cost. I could just see him getting to a certain point and the whole thing folding. Projects like this commonly fail because there aren't enough resources. I felt it was just a question of time before the whole thing nose-dived and failed. If this happened, not only would the donor's money be lost, but where would I be?

We started having meetings to determine what needed to be done. Danny continued to ask, "When are you going to come and work for us?" The more I became involved, the more I realized how much I was needed, and the thought came to me that maybe God wanted me to quit my job and help out this fledgling organization.

I finally went to Pastor Hal Steenson. "Hal, I'm in a situation about whether or not I should work for 3ABN. How do I resolve it?"

"Put out a fleece. If it's met, you can rest assured that you should do it."

So I put out a fleece. I set up conditions that I knew were impossible to meet, because I really didn't want to risk taking a job that offered little or no financial rewards. My fleece had to do with the FCC giving us a satellite transmitter construction permit in a very short period of time. I knew how fast the FCC worked and how much time it usually took to get all the required permits. I knew I was home free and could keep my good-paying job. You can imagine my surprise when the fleece was fulfilled!

I went back to Hal. "I really don't want to do this project. I have it made where I am. It would be stupid to leave this job. This man doesn't have any money!"

"Well," said Pastor Hal, "put up the second fleece."

This time I made sure the conditions would be absolutely impossible to fulfill. Danny never had any money before he needed it. So I said to myself, *If Danny gets a sizable sum, say, three thousand dollars, up front in order to pay my wages, I'll take the job.* There was no way that was going to happen. However, in a short period of time, that fleece, too, was fulfilled!

I went back to Pastor Hal. "Everything has come to pass, what should I do?"

Hal said, "Two times the Lord has asked you to do this. Are you going to do it or not?"

So I went to work for Danny, expecting 3ABN to be a total failure. What I hadn't bargained on was Danny's faith—and God's faithfulness in supplying every need.

We began moving forward with the goal of being on the air in as short a time as possible. This meant that we needed equipment—expensive equipment. I knew the vendors, and they were used to working with big, financially sound companies. I knew they would never send us anything if we couldn't pay for it. Danny said to have them send it COD. He assured me that if God felt the equipment was needed, He would have the money in place by the time the equipment arrived. If not, we would assume we had made a mistake and send it back.

I began ordering. Time after time God had the exact amount of money in place at the exact time it was needed. Nothing was ever sent back.

I began to realize that this was not Danny's project, but the Lord's. He was doing something special here. My doubts made me question, "How long can this ministry walk on water and keep its eyes where they need to be so that it doesn't sink?" As the project got bigger and bigger and bigger, I worried that it would be like a balloon. How much could you blow into the balloon before it would pop? I also realized that some of the people in the Adventist denomination weren't supportive of 3ABN. This brought questions into my mind. But Danny never wavered.

Seeing his faith in action and how the Lord provided brought healing to me at a very painful time in my life. When I came to work at 3ABN, I was irritated with the Lord and wanted nothing to do with religion. Slowly I began to realize that money wasn't everything. I began to put more value on the peace and joy that I found at 3ABN than I did on financial security. After a dozen years of working for 3ABN, I was not the same person!

When I first worked for Danny, I thought the Seventh-day Adventist denomination was a cult. (That's what most people in this area thought.) But since 3ABN has been active, the perception has changed in this community. If you listen to 3ABN programming, it doesn't take long to realize the truth of the messages that are being broadcast. As time went on, and I was exposed to more doctrine, I started changing. Tammy, my future wife, came into my life, and I went to church with her. Rick Odle, a former Pentecostal pastor working at 3ABN, ministered to me. The more I got involved with

Seventh-day Adventists, the more comfortable I became, until I realized it was time for me to join the church. I saw the positive fruit of this ministry, and I wanted to be a part of a group of Christians that were making a difference in people's lives.

During all my years at 3ABN, solving many problems, meeting almost impossible deadlines, and working harder than I had ever worked in my life, perhaps the most challenging event was when lightning struck the transmitter and took 3ABN off the air for seven days. It happened five years to the day from when 3ABN began broadcasting. I think the devil didn't like 3ABN's programming![1]

We had no other engineers at the time, so the full responsibility of determining what parts were damaged and getting them replaced was entirely up to me. I literally began working twenty-four-hour days to try to repair the damage. The only sleep I got was in the back seat of the car on the way to St. Louis to test the various parts of the equipment.

Looking back, I'm convinced I did the right thing in walking away from security and financial gain to work for 3ABN. What a privilege it has been to make a major contribution to God's work. In the process, look what I gained—valuable technical experience and the satisfaction of doing something I'd never done before. With Tammy, my beautiful and talented wife, I've enjoyed a new healthy lifestyle, peace and joy, and a whole lot more faith, thanks to Danny!

Tammy Larson's Story

I grew up on a ranch in the sand hills of Nebraska. We raised crops and cattle. I had finished commercial-art school, and I wanted to do something with my artistic talents. Yet I couldn't find a job in New Jersey where I was living at the time. My mom called and said, "Tammy, you need to watch 3ABN!" I had never heard of it before.

When I moved back home to help my dad, I did everything farmhands do, including driving big tractors. But I was not fulfilled.

Tammy Larson

One day I collapsed on the floor and cried out to God, "There's got to be something better. I want to change my life. I want to work for You."

Then Danny Shelton came to speak at our little church group and stayed with my folks. Those were the early days when 3ABN was just getting started and Danny was still going around to small churches. I was shy, but I was so impressed with the work 3ABN was doing to spread the gospel that I mustered up my courage and asked if I could work for him. He said for me to pray about it and call him back. When I did, he hired me. I started work on July 7, 1989.

Although I didn't have any camera skills, my art training gave me an eye for composition, so that's where I started. To this day, I still love camera work, especially operating the big jib camera with its long boom that allows all types of fancy shots! I was also asked to do makeup on the guest performers. It helped me overcome my shyness. I have enjoyed learning about all aspects of television. It has become my whole life.

Linda saw other talents in me. First, she asked me to help her with the newsletters. Then she said, "Why don't you draw some kids' coloring books?" I was able to work these projects into my schedule during breaks between television production. I've now finished my eighth book.

I have always loved to sing in groups, but never solo. I began singing with some of the people at 3ABN, and my confidence gradually grew. Before I knew it, Linda had scheduled me for some solos, and I was singing in front of the camera! When the sound center was completed, Danny encouraged me to make a CD. He felt 3ABN's viewers had been blessed with the simplicity of my music, and he wanted to make it possible for them to have this music in their homes. Never in my wildest imagination could I have thought I would ever do something like this!

3ABN has blessed me immensely. It is touching lives twenty-four hours a day. How honored I am to have a small part in producing these programs. What I'm doing is a continual witness; even while I'm at home, my camera work is blessing someone. When I'm shooting on location, I'm surprised how many people come by to thank us camera people for the work we are doing for the Lord.

I come from a loving family. My folks, Charles and Frances Clark, not only farmed but took care of foster kids and adopted some. After retirement, my folks periodically visited 3ABN, and Mom noticed there was a need for guest housing for the musicians and speakers who came to 3ABN. My father finally gave in to my mom's pleading and built a small home with guest rooms to provide a service for 3ABN. Now, I even have a sister and her family living nearby.

But the greatest thing 3ABN gave me was my husband, Clarence. Yes, I married that kind, lovable, generous, and intelligent engineer whom God called to help Danny from the very beginning in order to make the vision for 3ABN a reality.

Ronnie Hogue's story

I was nineteen and in the middle of a card game when I was first saved. A voice in my head said, *If you don't stop what you're doing and live for Me, you are going to die.* Then a tingly feeling started up my toes. I let it get midway up my body when I realized I couldn't procrastinate any longer. I pushed myself away from the table and quickly stepped outside. The voice had been so loud I thought everyone had heard it. Outside, the voice repeated, *I want you to live for Me.* Then came the oddest part

Ronnie and Becky Hogue

of the message. *But don't run to a church. I will show you where to go.*

I waited a year and a half for more instruction, but nothing came. When I was introduced to Pentecostalism, I took matters into my own hands and joined the church. During the next forty-three years, even though I did everything I was supposed to do as a Pentecostal Christian, I was never completely comfortable with this form of worship. But I was afraid I'd lose friends if I questioned the doctrines. The easiest thing for me to do was just be quiet and hope I was where God wanted me.

Becky and I moved to Marion, Illinois, in 1982 and lived there ten years. There was a Seventh-day Adventist church about five miles outside of town. Five or six times I remember driving by that church on Saturday and thinking, *Look at those fools thinking they have to go to church on Saturday.* Then the thought came to me, *Yes! and you should, too.* But I dismissed the thought as irrational.

In 1992, Becky and I moved to West Frankfort. When flipping though the television dial, we discovered channel 17 broadcasting 3ABN. I hated that channel because of what it did to me. All the doctrine was taught directly from the Word, but it didn't jive with what

I had been taught for over forty years. I didn't even want to entertain the thought that I might have been misled all those years. Occasionally, I requested literature from 3ABN, but most of the time I
ended up throwing it in the trash.

One thing that really puzzled me, however, was Danny Shelton. I
didn't think he was for real. He was just too good a Christian, happily
quoting Scripture. It had to be an act. So I determined to check him
out if I ever had an opportunity. I felt if I could just touch him, I'd be
able to determine what kind of a person he really was. A couple of
days went by. I was heading out to the lake to go fishing when Danny
Shelton passed me in his truck. I immediately made a U-turn and
followed him. He went to the boat dock and started to unload a boat.
I started to walk toward him.

"Can I help you?" he asked.

I said, "No," and kept walking toward him.

"Do you need something?" he asked.

"No," I said, and continued toward him. About two feet from him,
I stopped, put out my hand and said, "I want to meet you and see if
you are real." We shook hands, and I said, "I'll see you," and left. I
had my answer. He was real. It made me kind of upset that he could
be so good!

Later when we met again, I asked Danny if he remembered me.
"How on earth could I ever forget you!" he replied. My strange behavior walking toward him was disconcerting!

When I learned about Rick Odle being from the same doctrinal
background I was and that he lived only four blocks away from me, I
decided to write him. I asked every question I could think of. I was
determined to catch some error. Becky didn't think he would take time
to answer. But Rick faithfully wrote back an eleven-page handwritten letter, answering every one of my questions with Bible references.

Now, I really was curious. Just what kind of people were these
Seventh-day Adventists? So Becky and I decided to attend their
Wednesday night meeting. That first Wednesday night we just sat
in the parking lot and watched everyone go into the church. Some
went into the sanctuary and others into a back room. We thought
that was weird. But we couldn't get the courage to go in ourselves. A
week later, we went back and started to walk into the door of the
sanctuary. A man stopped us and said, "You want the Seventh-day
Adventists. They're down the hall." We had no idea the Baptists held

their Wednesday night meetings in the Adventist church sanctuary! I'd never seen the man before. How did he know we were looking for the Adventists?

As I listened to what was said at prayer meeting that night, the little voice from when I was nineteen came back to me and said, *This is where I want you.* We began attending church. The preaching was so simple and down to earth. I knew this was it. What I was hearing was the Bible truth I had been looking for all my life. Becky wasn't so sure, however. "Don't try to turn me into one of them," she warned. But as it turned out, she was baptized before me!

Becky Hogue's story

I had a hard time understanding doctrinal issues until the Bible study that first night in the Seventh-day Adventist Church. As I continued to attend, Bible truth now seemed to make sense. I really got into it. I even began asking questions in the group, something I would never have done before. What I was learning was so easy to understand, especially about keeping the seventh-day Sabbath holy. I always knew Sunday was the first day of the week and wondered why Christians worshiped on that day when the Bible said to keep the seventh. I wanted to begin attending church, but I was a department manager of a large store and had trouble getting Saturdays off.

The more I studied, however, and the more I became convicted of the importance of following the fourth commandment, the more I believed God would work something out. We prayed and prayed. But my employer kept insisting I had to work Saturdays. Then it happened. I hurt my arm at work and could no longer use my wrist. The doctor said I had no choice but to change employment. I then talked to 3ABN about working for the ministry and began volunteering to see if I liked the work. The day after I left my old job, I started working at 3ABN. It has been the best thing that ever happened to me. These people have become our family. The 3ABN church family means everything to us. If we have a problem, they are always there to help.

Although I don't work at 3ABN right now, Ronnie and I live in Mrs. Summers' old house and take care of the property surrounding the original uplink building. We will always be thankful for 3ABN, for God used it to show us Bible truth. We already knew God, but not in the way we needed to know Him. 3ABN has made our lives complete. Ron calls 3ABN the Ellis Island of the religious world. At 3ABN, we meet people of all colors, from all walks of life. Our lives are enriched, and each day we feel blessed to be a part of God's work to spread Bible truth to the world.

Dee Hilderbrand's story

Dee Hilderbrand

In 1991, my husband, David, and I moved from California to Rogue River, Oregon. We bought twenty acres in a remote area with no TV reception. Immediately, David bought a big dish, and we found 3ABN. It happened at a pivotal point in our lives. David had grown up Adventist, but both of us had been doing our own thing since finishing high school. When we felt a need for spiritual renewal, we visited a number of churches, including the Seventh-day Adventist church. Before I knew it, I was taking Bible studies. 3ABN became our mentor and guide. We joined the church, attended Wednesday night and Sabbath services, and watched 3ABN in between.

When David was diagnosed with cancer, we were spiritually grounded because of 3ABN. We also received valuable health information we needed at that time. 3ABN was David's constant companion during his last few months. It gave him a connection to God's peace and comfort.

David passed away in March 1996, and I recommitted my life to the Lord. When I heard Danny and Linda were coming to Medford and Grants Pass, Oregon, the weekend of July 25, I cut my vacation short so that I could meet them.

I shared with Linda the impact that 3ABN had on our lives. I also mentioned a mix-up with a letter I had sent. Linda thanked me for sharing and mentioned how understaffed they were. Then she said, "Why don't you come to work for us? We need good help. Come out and visit us."

I felt this was the Lord's leading, so we set a date for me to look over 3ABN. I found a great deal on a flight, and my boss surprised me by telling me I had three more vacation days coming. I arrived at 3ABN, felt at home, and accepted 3ABN's job offer. This meant making a major change in my life—something grief counselors say you shouldn't do so soon after losing a spouse. In an amazingly short time, I sold everything but our property—which took two years to sell—and I moved to West Frankfort!

God knew what I needed. The job of production coordinator was challenging. I didn't have time for pity parties. Instead, 3ABN inspired me to do things I had never done before. I felt myself growing spiritually and healing emotionally. I became committed to 3ABN and felt fulfilled. I gave my all, and 3ABN gave me friends, information, and a sense of incredible value because I was working for the Lord.

John Leaman's story

I'm an audio engineer at 3ABN, and I'm thankful that I have an opportunity to be a vessel to mend broken people. It gives me a reason for living. Being here makes me aware of the fact that God put me on this earth to do something worthwhile. Not only do our programs go out to the world to heal hurting people, but it seems to me that many of the people whom God draws to 3ABN are broken on some level. We come here and find others who have come before us whose stories of healing give us

John Leaman

hope. We watch program after program of people who give their testimonies about what God has done for them. And we begin to think, *If God can do that for them, He can do it for us!*

All my life I've had trouble connecting with people, including my own family. My mom was an alcoholic, as was her father. Because I saw what alcohol did to my mom before she gave it up, I determined that I would never drink.

When I was sixteen, my brother brought home a couple of six packs of beer. "We'll each drink three tonight and then the rest tomorrow," he announced, excited with the novelty of it. Although I was reluctant, he convinced me to do it with him. He drank all three cans and was ready to save the rest as planned. No big deal. It had little effect on him. Not me. I drank one beer, and it was like finding God. Something happened in my brain—a feeling of euphoria. I felt connected. The lost feeling was gone. "This is what I've been searching for all my life," I told my brother. "I'm not stopping now. I'm going to drink until there's no more."

It was an easy step to other drugs—marijuana, cocaine, you name it. But my drug of choice was alcohol. By the time I graduated from high school, I was an alcoholic. I traveled the world as a sound engineer for some of the biggest names in the entertainment world—Kenny Rogers, Sadé, Elton John, Sting, Madonna, Bon Jovi. Being a part of the rock culture didn't help my addiction, but it didn't cause it either. Some of my coworkers who knew I had a drinking problem pleaded with me to get help. For nine years, I was able to drink and work. Each time I was warned, I drank less. I went to rehabilitation, but I ended up drinking again. Finally, my habit was interfering with my job to such an extent that my employer had to let me go. I had been on my way to the top of my profession. Now I had nothing.

It wasn't that I couldn't quit drinking. I quit more than thirty times, once for two years! But each time I tried to quit by myself, I eventually failed. I went to all types of recovery programs. The minute they were over, I'd find myself right back where I was before—only worse. During this time, I went in and out of jobs, each time sinking lower into despair. I lived to drink, and many times God saved me from myself.

There are two ways to die from alcohol. The first is to drink so much that your body shuts down. The second is to withdraw alcohol too quickly from a body that depends on it to function. They say that quitting drugs can cause severe withdrawal symptoms, but you won't die. Whereas, with alcohol, withdrawal can cause your body to go into seizures, and it can be life-threatening. That's what happened to me.

I finally reached a point in my life that I lived on alcohol until it ran out. I hadn't eaten in three weeks and was so sick I couldn't walk. My parents said, "John, you've got to change your life or you're going to die." Just a few weeks before, I had ruptured my stomach with strong dry heaves and had such severe withdrawal seizures that I ended up in the emergency room. Now I was in danger of the same thing, but I wouldn't allow my parents to take me to the hospital. Having a tube shoved down my throat and my stomach pumped was something I didn't want repeated. So Dad and Mom left, saying that if I didn't want help, they weren't going to stay there and watch me die. That night the shakes became so violent that I couldn't walk.

My knees gave way. I crawled to the bathroom. I scooted down the steps on my behind, for fear I'd fall. At last, I managed to call the ambulance.

After rehabilitation, I decided I was going to get involved with my father's church. He had become a Seventh-day Adventist. I went to church, read inspirational books, was baptized, and from the outside looked pretty good, but I was secretly drinking. For the first time in my life, however, I met a group of people who really loved me and held on to me, in spite of my addiction. I experienced God's love through these people. They even came to check on me in my apartment, in case I drank too much. They didn't want me to die. That impressed me. I finally managed to stay sober for about six months.

At about this same time, my father got a satellite dish so that he could watch 3ABN. Along with it came a 3ABN newsletter that mentioned a need for an audio engineer. He kept this newsletter for about six months. Finally one day, since I'd been sober for a while, he said, "John, I heard about a job opening for an audio engineer at a Christian TV station."

My passion was audio engineering. I wanted my life to have a purpose. I applied to 3ABN, and even though the person hiring me knew my past, we both thought it was behind me. So I came to work. After a few months, not having made close friends, finding television audio to be rather boring and having no support group of recovering alcoholics to hold me accountable, I went back to drinking. The first time it happened, everyone thought I had the flu. The second time, I spent four days in the hospital and then went to a twenty-eight-day recovery program.

The amazing thing is that as soon as Danny learned what had happened to me, he chose to work with me rather than fire me. He could have sent a pastor over to pray for me or a counselor to talk some sense into me, but he didn't. Instead, he sent over a long-time employee who was a recovered alcoholic who had found help from a twelve-step group. It was exactly what I needed. Through this program, I at last connected with God's power. I admitted I couldn't do it myself and surrendered my will to Him. I've been off alcohol for almost six years. I'm now an alcoholic *who has recovered from a seemingly hopeless state of mind and body.* God has removed my physical obsession for alcohol, and I have a wonderful support group who remind me that on my own, I'm powerless!

I'm convinced that, in spite of my addiction, God had a plan for my life. Knowing that He would someday need me at 3ABN, He allowed me to get the best on-the-job audio training in the world. And then, He brought me to a place where I could find complete healing in Him, can work in the profession I love, and can help others who have addictions.

Halima Martin's story

Halima Martin

My father was a member of The Nation of Islam, which explains the origin behind my name. Halima was the caretaker of the Nation's god, Allah. Even though my father encouraged me to believe the way he did, he never forced it upon me. My mother wasn't a member of my father's social group, so after his death, my mother encouraged me to make my own choices. In my search for truth, I studied the beliefs of Catholicism, Jehovah's Witnesses, Mormons, and others. I wasn't sure which way to go. But I was hungry for the Lord!

It wasn't until I went away to college at Southern Illinois University in Carbondale that my life became turmoil. My understanding of love turned into violence, my career choice in news broadcasting became unfulfilling, and my happiness became depression. But through it all, I held on to my passion for writing. I cried out to the Lord, "If You know the plans for my life, tell me what You want me to do!" At that moment, it became clear. I was to use the gift of writing for His glory, whether it was writing sitcoms, plays, movies, or books. It was so exciting to me to have felt God's calling! Now, before I open my eyes each morning, I'm full of joy because God has given me a purpose.

Upon graduation in May 2002, I had big plans to go to Los Angeles and pursue a career in the entertainment industry. I wanted to introduce broken people to the Lord in a way that had never been done before. I was so excited that the Lord was leading me that I wasn't aware that I, myself, needed healing and spiritual nurturing. My discipleship leader was praying that I would stay in this area a little longer. I was a new Christian, and there was so much more God needed to show me before I would be strong enough to work in a secular environment.

Thankfully, God answered my discipleship leader's prayer. After I spent weeks exhausting every possibility of job placement in big cities and far away places, my professor told me about 3ABN, just an hour down the road. When I interviewed, I fell in love with the place. I began to pray that the Lord would bless me with this job, not just because it was a Christian network, but because of the Christian atmosphere in the workplace. I had never experienced employees worshiping together in the morning and having a glass bowl full of employees' names that you could draw from and pray for. I was *amazed!* After being interviewed by Danny Shelton, it was confirmed. This job was for me!

While my friends moved on to Los Angeles to do menial jobs for well-known companies, I was given the opportunity to work in all areas of production—graphics, makeup, video, and camera operation. I now know that God had a better plan for me than I did. Not only have I been given the opportunity to learn everything technically here at 3ABN, but, more importantly, the Lord ministers to me continually in my work. From morning worship to typing Bible texts into graphics, I'm finding that God supplies exactly what I need, at exactly the right time, as I'm continuing to grow in my walk with Him.

Although I'm not a Seventh-day Adventist, working at 3ABN has forced me to search the Bible for myself and to test everything I hear with the Word. I'm learning things I didn't even know were in the Bible. I'm growing spiritually. And I'm happier than I have ever been in my life. It feels so good to know I'm where God wants me to be at this season of my life.

Cari Christian's story

In the early 1980s when I was still in grade school, I would lie in bed at night and try to imagine what was the most important and powerful job in the world. I decided that it must be working in television, because TV seemed to have more influence on people than even politics. As I lay there in the dark, I imagined the perfect television station, a big one that helped people by broadcasting only good Christian programs. At the time, I was unaware of any Christian broadcasters, much less

Cari Christian

one that understood about the Sabbath. Besides, big stations were in big cities. My dream place would have to be in the country because, even as a child, I knew that cities weren't for me.

My journey to 3ABN started one night many years later when I was talking to the Lord about what I should do with my life. The thought came to me, *You should be at 3ABN.* I really didn't want to move from my home in Milton-Freewater, Oregon. I definitely wanted to make sure I wasn't just imagining things, so I told the Lord that I wouldn't pursue the matter any further. If He wanted me at 3ABN, someone would just have to call and ask me for a résumé. I thought I was safe. No one at 3ABN even knew I existed. How could anyone call me?

Living in the Walla Walla Valley offered me just about everything I wanted. I was director of admissions and assisted with marketing for a local nursing home and retirement center. I enjoyed meeting the people with whom it put me in contact. I was respected in the community. My real joy was hosting and participating in the production of local programs for Blue Mountain Television, an affiliate of 3ABN. It also kept me in touch with my chosen field, since I had earned a bachelor's degree in communication arts.

As a result of my association with Blue Mountain Television, I met Dee Hilderbrand. She is the one whom God used to let 3ABN know that I existed. When I met her, I had forgotten what I told the Lord. I was too busy making my own plans.

I was shocked, one day, when I answered the phone and heard a familiar, smooth voice. "Hello, this is Douglas Garcia. Would you send us a résumé?" This request came on the heels of a major job offer that would promote me to the corporate level of the company for which I worked. The job promised avenues to use my creativity in addition to a nice salary, but it would mean I would be moving to a major city. But a deal is a deal. I had told God that if 3ABN called and asked for a résumé, I would be willing to go. So I mailed my résumé and secretly hoped that it was all God wanted from me.

The day my résumé arrived at 3ABN, I had a life-threatening grand mal seizure. By the time my parents found me on the kitchen floor, I had already turned blue. My mom and dad managed to clear my airway and kept me safe until the paramedics arrived. We didn't know what was happening! I had no history of epilepsy. Since no cause could be found, I was sent home. Later that night, I had another seizure that was just as severe. When the doctor heard about it over the scanner, he immediately gathered the emergency room staff and began praying for me. He didn't think I would live through this one. I am alive today only by the grace of God. After days of observation and numerous tests, medical personnel could suggest only stress as a cause.

Most people suffering seizures have only a few hours of confusion until their thinking and behavior return to normal. This was not so with me. I was confused and acted like a little girl for weeks. I prayed and asked the Lord to restore me. I wanted to be mentally sharp again. The very next morning, Roger Blood, a massage practitioner, called and said that he had been impressed that there was something he could do to help me. He offered me treatments at no cost. After the first two hours, I was back to normal and had regained my sense of smell.

But my health problems weren't over. For the next six months, sickness hit. I had always been healthy. Now, I caught everything that came along. My parents, Jay and Annette Christian, and I were asked to come to 3ABN for interviews. I got well enough to take the trip but was sick all the way home and for some time afterward. My aunt made an interesting observation: "It almost seems as if Satan has attacked Cari."

Then, as soon as I made my decision to work for 3ABN, I was better. No more illness or seizures!

I'm glad I came to 3ABN. I've seen firsthand the positive difference 3ABN has made in people's lives, including my own. I've been challenged to adapt as emergencies arise. After being here for two weeks, I was asked to take over the programming department so that Sandra Juárez could go on maternity leave. I've filled many roles in production from video and graphics to makeup, even working on the truck crew!

Since my main job is editing, I watch sermons over and over again, and the messages have affected my life. I'll admit, I probably wouldn't have watched these programs if it weren't my job! It's made me stronger to be supportive to people in need. I've also been blessed by meeting the presenters in real life. I see them year after year behind the scenes, so I know that what is seen on the TV screen is real!

Perhaps the biggest impact on my life has been the stories about the power of intercessory prayer. I've started my own prayer ministry.

It's fun to see how people's lives are affected—people I don't even know—because of my prayers. For example, one day in Dillard's, two sisters were arguing about everything as they tried on clothing in the fitting room next to mine. After I whispered a short prayer for them, I noticed a sudden change in their behavior. The fighting stopped, and they became sweet, loving sisters! My prayer may not have been lifesaving, but it did make a difference. My prayers are also changing people in my neighborhood. One neighbor gave his heart to Jesus before he died. His wife continues to live for the Lord and currently works at 3ABN. Another neighbor had a son who left a questionable lifestyle after I began praying for him. Our God is an incredible God and will do incredible things, if we have faith to ask and believe.

I know without a doubt the dream I had as a ten-year-old has been fulfilled. Where else, except at 3ABN, could one find a Christian, Sabbath-keeping, worldwide television station, located in the country!

Vandal family baptism

Paul Vandal's story

Elaine and I were living well. We had a nice car and a lovely home in Massachusetts with a big mortgage. As our family grew, so did the expenses. In 1992 my auto mechanic's shop began to fail. At the same time, I got sick and had operation after operation. We ended up losing the business and our house. We moved into a federal housing project when Elaine was nine months pregnant. I had lived there as a child. What a disappointment to have to raise my own four children in this environment from which I thought I had escaped! Things seemed hopeless!

My health continued to decline until my physician laid the cards on the table. "There's nothing more I can do for you, Paul. The only hope you have is to drastically modify your diet."

Just a few months before, I had been impressed to take my income tax refund and buy a Sky Angel satellite dish so that our family could watch decent programming instead of the trash on regular TV. Elaine had been surfing channels and had begun watching 3ABN because of the programs on health. When I told her the doctor's recommendation, she said, "I've been watching this station that has healthy cooking demonstrations on it. What do you think about cutting out meat?" I was eating prime rib twice a week, seafood, butter, cheese, and other rich foods. We even caught our son eating sugar straight out of the little packets you get in restaurants. The kids were hyperactive and were driving Elaine crazy. From what she had learned on 3ABN, Elaine felt their rich diet was contributing to their behavior problems. She continued, "In fact, let's go vegan!"

I thought, *What are we going to eat?* But God had been preparing Elaine for this moment. She already had dozens of tasty vegan recipes that she had gotten by watching cooking programs on 3ABN. So when we went vegan, we ate great tasting food and had no difficulty with the change. Within two weeks, we saw a tremendous difference in my health, and I was able to drop some medications. When I still had some health problems, we went organic, and I was able to stop the other medications.

The information we got from 3ABN literally saved my life. We were so thankful that we became avid listeners to the rest of 3ABN's programming. This introduced us to Bible truths I had never heard before. I was angry that my church and family had deceived me into believing tradition instead of truth. I was a fifth-generation Catholic and had been raised by nuns in Catholic schools. When I was taught the Ten Commandments, I asked my mom why we didn't worship on the Sabbath day. Instead of telling me that the Catholic Church had changed the day of worship to Sunday, I got a tirade on how terrible Protestants were.

We did our share of channel surfing, searching out other Christian stations, but were always drawn back to 3ABN to watch speakers such as Kenneth Cox and John Lomacang. We began attending the local Seventh-day Adventist church, where we felt loved and welcome. But because of the high cost of living in Massachusetts, we were getting nowhere financially.

Then a radical idea began to form in my mind. What if we moved to the 3ABN area, where we could be mentored spiritually by Pastor John Lomacang in person! It looked like a good place to bring up children and a cost of living we could afford. Elaine began to dream with me. The more we considered it, the more exciting the dream became. We could become Adventists. We could give our children what we had wanted so badly as children—the security of knowing truth and being nurtured by a loving God. Before we knew it, the dream began to unfold even more quickly than we had anticipated.

In August 2003, we packed for a two-week trip to scout out the Thompsonville area. Before we knew it, our kids were enrolled in 3ABN's school and were loving it. Two months later, we left our children with friends and went back to Massachusetts to pack up our belongings, not knowing how we were going to pay for the U-Haul trailer needed to get our things to Thompsonville. But God had it all taken care of. When we got back to Thompsonville, there was a check from Social Security for 2,500 dollars waiting for us. There had been an error made two years earlier on money due us, and Social Security had sent us a check at the very moment we needed it most! We had just enough!

We don't know what the future holds, but we are eagerly looking forward to what God has planned for us. Through 3ABN, He has shown us truth in both physical and spiritual health. It feels so good to be living life within the security of Bible truth instead of ignorance. Seventh-day Adventists are good people. We love them. I never imagined that I would experience the contented feeling of fullness that I now have. Thank You, Jesus!

John and Angela Lomacang

John and Angela Lomacang's story

Sometimes, God's call to ministry is a direct one. God says, "Go!" Other times, God calls you step by step toward the goal He has for your life. The story of how Angela and I came to 3ABN is a fascinating step-by-step call.

I was born and raised in New York City, had a heart's desire to live outside the rush and noise that becomes so familiar to city dwellers. After Angie and I were married, the call came for me to pastor in northern California, a step away from the big city, and we spent eighteen years there. We loved our church in Fairfield. It was growing, dynamic, and full of Holy Spirit energy.

We had become close friends to John and Rochelle Stanton, church members at Fairfield, and the four of us dreamed of going into ministry together. John Stanton was a business executive with all the pressures that come along with a six-figure salary. Rochelle was driving seventy miles a day to her teaching job. We talked about the four of us buying a big bus and going on the road doing evangelism. We talked and planned and prayed, but nothing seemed quite right.

Then without any warning, Angie and I were asked to move to St. Louis, Missouri, to begin a media ministry in one of the large churches there. Should we go? It was a giant step from the rolling hills of our northern California town to the big city of St. Louis with all its big-city challenges. When the call came, Angie and I put the Lord to the test. I was so stressed out to think about leaving California that my heart began to do strange things, and I was put on a twenty-four-hour heart monitor to determine what was wrong. The answer came, "There is nothing wrong with your heart; it's stress!" One of my elders assured me that if God wanted us in the Midwest, He would make it clear. It was Sabbath morning, and I needed to tell the church if we were leaving or not. I pulled out Oswald Chambers's devotional, *My Utmost for His Highest,* turned to February 2, and read, "Woe unto you if you put your foot in any other direction once the call of God has gripped you." That was it. Our hearts were settled. God wanted us to move.

In June 2002, we arrived in St. Louis excited about the challenge of establishing a media ministry that would be fully operational in three years. Almost immediately, however, things began to fall apart. My plans for how to build this ministry were not accepted because of the cost. I was shocked! But the administration did approve my request to hire an associate. I knew exactly whom I wanted to work with, and the call was extended to John and Rochelle Stanton to join us in St. Louis.

The cold reality came during the first week of January 2003, just seven months after we had moved. I was told, "It's just not going to work. The funds that have been budgeted are just not enough to build a media ministry." I was heartsick.

I had no idea that for months Danny Shelton had me on his mind. He felt that God wanted 3ABN to take the old museum building that had never been used and convert it into a major 3ABN worship center. The enlarged building would be used for taping church services and large evangelistic meetings. Just the right person was needed to pastor this growing church and to reach out to the community. Danny was impressed that I was that person. He knew, however, that I had just moved to St. Louis and that there was no way I would consider moving again so quickly. After months of struggling over my name, his coworkers at 3ABN urged, "Danny, you can't keep wrestling with indecision. You've got to call John and find out if he will come."

Danny called the second week of January 2003, just days after my dream for St. Louis was crushed. If Danny had called the month before or even a week before, I would have turned him down without a second thought. But at the moment he called, I was ready. And when Danny said, "By the way, you'll need an associate," John and Rochelle were also ready.

When our names were brought up to the Thompsonville church board, God had already brought Dick and Ellie Hutchinson to 3ABN to speak on our behalf.

"I can't think of a better ministerial team," Dick said when the board was discussing whether or not to extend the call to us.

"How do you know?" he was asked.

"Because I was the head elder and church treasurer for seven years when the Lomacangs and Stantons were at Fairfield."

The timing was perfect. Our entire ministry team packed up and moved to the country, the place of our heart's desire, where we can hear the sounds of nature and enjoy God's open spaces. I immediately found myself helping with 3ABN presentations and music. Angie's talents were desperately needed in radio, and she picked up all the technical stuff in a very short time.

Without warning, the little Thompsonville Christian School had so many students that there was an immediate need for another teacher. "God has provided," Danny told the school board. "Rochelle Stanton is here." What a satisfying experience that has been for her.

It can never be said that God makes a mistake. At the time, St. Louis may have seemed like a mistake. But looking back, I see God's perfect plan in motion. If I had not been in St. Louis for those few short months, just two hours away from 3ABN, I would not have been available to help 3ABN with music or an interview when someone was sick or a guest didn't show. This allowed Danny and me to become good friends. Without St. Louis, John Stanton would not have been in the ministry and ready to move to 3ABN as my associate. Without St. Louis, I would not have been primed for media ministry. God brought us here, step by step; it was His plan.

God knows the talents He has created in each person. He knew what John and Rochelle and Angie and I could do—even though some of those talents may have lain dormant for years. 3ABN has been a

John and Rochelle Stanton

stretching experience for all of us. What joy to know God is using all our God-given gifts here at 3ABN to help reach the world with His last day message!

---

[1] The devil is still not happy with 3ABN programming. On Monday, July 12, 2004, at 11:26 A.M., 3ABN's main satellite dish and transmitter were hit by lightning, destroying everything in its path: connectors, routers, the production switcher system, amplifiers, several control panels, the remote control for the satellite dish, computers, and the telephone system. Moses and his team at 3ABN were able to get the signal back up in less than an hour, but the estimated cost of damages was over twenty thousand dollars, and it was many weeks before all repairs and replacements were completed.

A couple days later, lightning struck again. This time it hit the transmission tower on 3ABN's Manila station. Electricity came down the transmission pipe and melted over a hundred feet of copper insulation. The station was off the air for a couple of weeks as replacement parts were shipped from the United States. Again, the cost of damages was approximately twenty thousand dollars.

That's not all. In the same week, the antenna for 3ABN's television channel 14 in Minneapolis, Minnesota, was hit by lightning, causing major damage and shutting down transmission for more than a week.

Lightning strikes to antennas and dishes are rare. Each has adequate lightning protection and very efficient grounding systems. And yet, 3ABN suffered three lightning strikes within a four-day period! Obviously, the great controversy between good and evil is intensifying.

And now for the rest of the story. On September 8, 2004, a couple visited from Arkansas. They met Danny in the hallway as they toured the production center and gave him a check for fifty thousand dollars. "God impressed me to give this to you. It should take care of the lightning damage." The devil is using every means possible to get 3ABN off the air, but God will not let the devil win. Please join 3ABN's prayer warriors as they daily pray a hedge of protection around 3ABN's broadcasting stations.

21

A Community Looks On

" 'But you shall receive power when the Holy Spirit has come upon you;
and you shall be witnesses to Me in Jerusalem,
and in all Judea and Samaria, and to the end of the earth' "
—Acts 1:8, NKJV.

West Frankfort, Illinois, is a small town (population 8,500) in Franklin County, pretty close to the middle of the lower forty-eight states. Interstate 57, a major artery that cuts through Illinois from Chicago to the southernmost tip of Illinois, borders the town. In the last few years, with hundreds of thousands of vehicles passing daily, Kmart and Kroger have moved in, making the little town seem not quite so small.

Most people in West Frankfort either still work in the coal mines or their parents, grandparents, or some relative once did. They have grown up playing on the beautiful rolling hills, farming the grassy fields, and fishing the shimmering lakes that dot the countryside, and they have felt comfortable there. This is home! Some have gone away for a while—to school, for adventure, or for the money that can be had in the businesses and industries of the big cities—but have returned to settle next to family and old high-school acquaintances. And most, over the last twenty years, have watched with wonder at what's happening seven miles east of town toward Thompsonville— the growing complex known as Three Angels Broadcasting Network.

At first it was just some project the Shelton brothers were doing, a Christian television station featuring programming consistent with Seventh-day Adventist beliefs. Most didn't pay much attention. They couldn't see anything unusual, unless they got off the main road and meandered through the countryside and saw the big satellite dishes next to the original 3ABN uplink site on the back two acres of Fonda Summers's land. And in the early years, they could watch 3ABN programming only if they had a big, expensive, satellite dish, which few had.

Then in 1991, people began to notice a large new studio and office complex being built on Highway 149, then a school, staff homes, a call center, a sound center, a medical clinic, and finally a large brick worship center that can seat thirteen hundred individuals. That's *big* for West Frankfort.

Now everyone within a hundred-mile radius can satisfy their curiosity about 3ABN by tuning into local programming, either over the local UHF television channel 15, through Mediacom cable, or by turning their FM radio dial to 95.9. Or they can access both the radio and television signal via the Internet. Better yet, they are welcome to just stop by and see what's going on firsthand. There's almost always a volunteer who will show people around. 3ABN is no longer a secret. It has employed hundreds of local residents over the years. In addition, it has attracted new residents to the area whose special skills are needed at 3ABN.

Change is not always easy for a community, and there is no doubt that 3ABN is an agent of change! So the questions arise: What does the community think about 3ABN? How has 3ABN affected individual citizens? What is 3ABN's influence on the community?

Perhaps these questions can best be answered in the stories of individuals who live in the West Frankfort area, people who have known the Sheltons for much of their lives and have found themselves influenced by Danny's friendship and the mission of 3ABN. For the most part, I'll let them tell their own stories.

Bob Ellis, journalist and mayor of West Frankfort

Bob Ellis has been one of the most influential citizens in West Frankfort since he and Kay moved to the area in 1967. He's a retired, award-winning journalist with more than thirty years of newspaper experience. He still writes a column, "The Hawk's Nest," for the weekly West Frankfort and Franklin County newspaper,

Bob Ellis

Review. *Bob first became interested in 3ABN when his newspaper,* The Daily American, *assigned him to cover its growth. Bob is currently serving his much loved community as mayor, but his relationship with 3ABN began in the early 1990s with a phone call from Danny. Here is Bob's story in his own words.*

Danny and I played sports together when we were kids, and then I lost track of him. I went into journalism, and he went into gospel singing. After a couple of years, I heard he had started a growing Christian television satellite station. I said, "It can't be; my Danny Shelton is a poor boy like me."

The next thing I knew, I got a call from Danny. "Bob, how are you?" his optimistic voice rang out. At the moment, I really wasn't feeling that good, but what he said next knocked the socks off me! "How would you like to go to Romania with 3ABN?" Nothing could have shocked me more. Danny then explained he was going to try to set up a television station in Romania and wanted me to come along. I told him honestly, "Danny, if I go to cover this for my newspaper, I will be objective. I won't put a positive slant on things just because I know you." That was no problem for Danny, so I went.

At the time, I knew nothing of 3ABN, had never watched the programming, and didn't know anything about Seventh-day Adventists because they aren't one of the dominant religious groups in our area.

I went to Romania with all my prejudices of Christian television intact. I was appalled at what I had read about Jim and Tammy Bakker and Jimmy Swaggart and their constant begging for money. I supposed 3ABN was similar. *They want ink,* I thought, trying to figure out why Danny wanted me to accompany him. It was not long, however, before my preconceived notions started to vanish. I began to realize that Danny didn't care if I wrote anything or not. He just felt it was important that I have this experience.

The first trip to Bucharest, Romania, was right after the revolution that took Communist Party General Secretary and President Nicolae Ceausescu out of power. The country was in disarray. Buildings were pockmarked from machine gunfire. There was a terrible drain on energy. Half the town was cut off from electricity. They even turned the airport runway lights on and off to conserve energy. The hotel was a horrible, cold place. An outside telephone call took six or seven hours to go through.

When we arrived, we were body searched by military police with automatic weapons. Finally, sometime after midnight, we cleared customs and were greeted by a friendly, happy group of Seventh-day Adventist Christians who insisted we come to their little flat for a meal. We were tired, but they had made special preparations for us, and we could not disappoint them. They offered us little pieces of potatoes, carrots, and other vegetables. I was touched when I learned that they shared with us all the food they had. Suddenly, all bets were off.

Eight months later, we took our second trip to Bucharest and found the country making progress toward normality. I was moved by the plight of the Romanian people, by the cruelty they had suffered, and by how little they had. But once more, I was impressed by the people's genuine hospitality to us and their gratefulness to Danny and 3ABN for the television equipment that he had brought for them.

Even though I classified myself as an unbeliever at the time, I was affected by the unbelievable things that happened as a result of prayer! Each morning, we would ask the Lord to guide us. One day Danny, Gonzalo, Adrian, and I got together to pray before going to the American embassy. I asked, "Danny, would you mind if I said a little prayer?" I'm sure Danny was somewhat surprised at my request. We knelt and I said, "Thank You, Lord, for delivering us safely. Help our labors to be fruitful. Allow us to help these Romanian people. If we are walking in Your light, show us a sign in some way."

No one commented on my prayer. But a little later the driver who was taking us around was distraught because he had lost the keys to his car and the police wanted it moved from in front of the hotel. After we prayed over the lost keys, Danny calmly said, "I know where your keys are. Go down the street to the men's store and ask the clerk for the keys in her left pocket."

Danny and I, along with the driver, went down to the store, and sure enough, the clerk had his keys in her pocket. How did Danny know where the keys were? He didn't say. Finally, hours later, I was overcome with curiosity and asked him. Danny said that earlier that morning when we went for a walk, he had gone to a men's clothing store to look for an overcoat while I went over to a newsstand. Looking back, that was a rather strange place for Danny to go since the store was for tall men, which Danny is not! A clerk recognized that Danny was an American and came up to him asking if he had lost his keys. When he said, "No," she showed him a set of keys and asked him again. At that time few Romanians had cars, so she apparently presumed they belonged to an American tourist. Danny gestured that they weren't his keys. Once again, she tried to give them to him. When he wouldn't take them, he saw the clerk put them into her left pocket. He had forgotten the encounter until they prayed about the lost keys. Apparently, the driver had dropped them on the sidewalk, and someone picked them up and gave them to the clerk in the nearest store!

This was too much for me! I didn't know what to think. It was awesome! Impressive! I couldn't explain it. I don't believe in flying saucers. And I don't know if I would have believed that something like this could happen, unless I experienced it for myself. God had given us the sign I prayed for, and we knew we were walking in His light.

Romania was just the first of my travels with Danny. As 3ABN's influence began to touch other countries, we made trips to Honduras and five trips to Russia.

My first trip to Russia was in May 1992 for the 3ABN filming of John Carter's evangelistic meetings in the sports arena of Nizhny Novgorod. This was my first exposure to evangelism. The meetings made a great impression on me. Crowds swelled around the building. It held six thousand people, and the team was holding three meetings a day, yet people still had to be turned away. The first night, as we were going into the building, I got separated from Danny and Linda and chose to stay outside for a while. I couldn't believe what I saw. As the doors closed, leaving a large crowd outside, they began shouting to be let in. I walked around to the back of the building and saw someone had broken out a window leading into the basement of the sports arena. There was a line of fifteen to twenty well-dressed people stepping through the window in order to get into the meetings. I was moved to see the response of the people as Bibles were given away. They fought for them. "Wouldn't it be great," I reflected, "if the people lined up around the block in West Frankfort to get into churches and wanted a Bible so badly they were willing to fight for one!"

I was most impressed as I watched the multimillion dollar 3ABN Russian Evangelism Center being built by the funds donated by 3ABN viewers. To the poor people of Russia, the building of this structure was a miracle.

What I experienced began to have an effect on me. It wasn't just 3ABN. It was the satisfaction and hope the Christ-centered messages had on the people after all those years when Christianity was forbidden. It was also the Seventh-day Adventists I met when I was with Danny. They were literally everywhere. It amazed me that in spite of unpleasant circumstances, they were happy. I kept expecting to meet a bad egg, a grouchy, unhappy, complaining one. But I never did. I traveled with a number of 3ABN board members, including May Chung, Walt Thompson, and Owen Troy. These were accomplished individuals, but they never spoke of themselves. And they never complained, even though we endured long, uncomfortable train rides, and we were staying in miserable hotels in the middle of winter with no heat. I ended up sleeping in my clothes, hat, and gloves, and piling the blankets high.

When I first began taking trips with Danny, I was skeptical. *There has to be a flaw somewhere in these people,* I thought. Years later I'm still looking! Nothing like this has ever happened to me in all my years of journalism. It has changed my life. I had been drinking and had some bad luck before Danny's first invitation. But because of the people I met in Russia, Romania, and Honduras, and the influence of people like the 3ABN board members whom I have traveled with, I am a more tranquil, contented person.

You can't help but be changed when you are standing on the shore of the Volga River watching pastors baptizing more than twenty-five hundred individuals who have given their lives to Christ. My wife is so happy with the changes 3ABN has made in my life that she even got another television set for our home. Now we can have one TV tuned-in to 3ABN all the time. I think differently now; I eat better. I've given up bad habits, and I want to be an even better person.

But above all else, Danny has made the biggest impression on me. When he first invited me to Romania, I figured it was only a matter of time until I picked up a flaw in his character. It was impossible to play the charade of a good Christian very long. I figured I would travel with him and catch him off guard. I'd hear him swear or find something bad about him. But this guy is what he appears to be. He's an optimistic, kind, positive Christian. And a little of that faith is beginning to rub off on me.

Once in the JFK airport in New York City, after being influenced by Danny and the other representatives from 3ABN, I walked up to two disgruntled women in their seventies or eighties who were extremely angry at the airline. "What's the matter?" I asked. Something had happened to their reservations, and they weren't given tickets. "Relax," I told them. "Don't get mad at the airline, it's not good for your blood pressure." Finally one said, "That's true," and the ladies settled down. Ever since then, Danny has called me "Pastor Ellis."

To say the least, this whole thing with 3ABN is pretty overwhelming to me. That's why I felt compelled to tell the story of 3ABN through the eyes of a journalist. My book, *A Channel of Blessing,* was published in 2002. It's one thing for Christians to accept what's happening at 3ABN as a "God thing," but when you have an old agnostic like me begin to see God in a new and different light, that's another. Writing the book about 3ABN was a small gift that I could give back to Danny and the ministry that has done so much for me.

Danny has become my spiritual leader and mentor. I know he loves me, and I never thought that about any other person in the world. He's under a lot of pressure and has so much on his mind. We kid a lot. I try to make him laugh and enjoy the moment. We have a great relationship! Let me just give you one example.

Danny, through 3ABN, has served the community in significant ways—like helping to sponsor anti-drug campaigns and other important community services. When West Frankfort was having a fund-raising campaign for a community swimming pool and recreation center, Danny brought a check from 3ABN for five thousand dollars[1] into one of the monthly fund-raising committee meetings. Everyone was so appreciative of this generous donation. Danny left the room, but a few seconds later, he opened the door again and announced, "I'll tell you what I'll do. 3ABN will give another twenty-five hundred dollars to this project if Bob Ellis will sing the national anthem by himself at the next meeting."

I responded, "No way am I going to do that!"

"Oh yes, you will!" the committee members voiced in one accord. I was a writer, certainly not a singer. I was terrified. But news spread through town, and everyone was looking forward to my performance, to seeing me make a fool out of myself. When the time came, the room was packed. It didn't make it any easier when Danny set up a television camera to record this once in a lifetime event in the history of West Frankfort!

The announcement was made. Reluctantly, I stood and started singing a cappella in a shaky voice. After a few phrases, I began getting into it, and so did the crowd. They were enthralled. When I finally came to, ". . . the land of the free and the home of the brave," Danny joined in, as did some others. It turned out to be an incredible experience. Danny gave the promised donation. Then, as he started to leave the room, he called, "Oh, by the way, I would have given the donation, whether Bob sang or not!"

It was amazing what that event did for our town. Everyone was talking about it for weeks, and the donations for the project increased. You can see why Danny and his family are well respected in this area.

In his book, A Channel of Blessing, *Bob Ellis tells about Danny being inducted into the exclusive and prestigious Frankfort Community High School's Special Achievement Society in 1998. Apparently, only eighteen people (up to that time) had been honored in this way, even though thousands had gone through the high school. On the evening when the presentation was made, Danny told a friend that he didn't understand what all the fuss was about. Or why he was being honored. "It [3ABN] is all God's doing," he said, "not mine." The plaque with Danny's photograph and the following tribute can be seen in the FCHS Library. The text is included here because Bob Ellis had a great deal to do with this, and it does show what Danny and 3ABN have done for the community over the years.*

The story of FCHS alumnus Danny Shelton's success is remarkable. He was raised in well-below-average economic conditions. "Poor" would describe them. However, he now presides over and hosts a daily program with his wife, Linda, on a television network that he raised up from a cornfield in Thompsonville, Illinois.

Three Angels Broadcasting Network airs twenty-four-hours-per-day, seven-days-a-week. He has also built television studios in Russia and Romania. The signal that originates from the 3ABN Production Center, in Thompsonville, covers all of North America, parts of Central America, many islands, Europe, and North Africa. It is estimated that 3ABN currently covers three-quarters of the globe, and plans are being made to expand coverage to encompass the entire globe in the near future. This international expansion complements a huge network of over one hundred stations in the United States.

Although religion is the cornerstone of 3ABN's broadcasting, it would be a misnomer to use the word television "ministry" to describe the [sole] content of the broadcasts. The station's programming is untypical in the sense that the words "television ministry" mostly conjure up images of the more standard "beg-a-thons" where money is king. Above all else, 3ABN is dignified in its format. More importantly, the programming also delivers good health advice, cooking and clean living messages. It is a wholesome overall schedule. For example, shows on organic gardening, home schooling, and children's activities spice the schedule. These are regular programs along with preaching prophecy and poignant testimonies.

Specifically, as far as local achievement is concerned, 3ABN's signal shows "3ABN, West Frankfort, Illinois" to the world [flashed on the screen regularly, twenty-four hours a day]. Likewise, mail comes here from around the globe, as well as international visitors [once, the president of a foreign country] . . . all of whom take back with them a part of West Frankfort.

Mr. Shelton has shared his success locally in many ways. He has contributed both money and equipment for the use of [school] District 168, specifically through anti-drug use messages and programs. He has arranged for financing national TV coverage for our young people's sporting events. He has also made generous cash donations to local projects he deems worthwhile for the community. Most recently, he has been working with our community council to promote West Frankfort worldwide.

Danny Shelton is recognized internationally. However, he is modest in dress, demeanor, and attitude. In fact, large segments of this area's population are unaware that the multimillion dollar, internationally known entity of which he is president, is located in their midst.

Danny Shelton, inducted May 9, 1998

---

[1] 3ABN board members gave special donations for this (and other) community projects.

Jack Woolard, former mayor of West Frankfort

Jack Woolard

I was mayor of West Frankfort for a number of years off and on since 1975. When 3ABN was still a dream, Danny was building a house for my son. I remember sitting down on a pallet of two-by-fours as he told me about God impressing him to build a television station that would reach the world. He mentioned how a place out by Thompsonville was a perfect spot for a satellite uplink station. Well, to tell you the truth, I really didn't think too much of the conversation. We were both raised up poor kids, and I thought he was kind of out in la-la land!

Later when things started to happen, buildings were being built, and the station was operating, I said, "This guy wasn't just kidding me! This is really happening!"

Danny's always there if someone needs a helping hand. He has been highly involved in our community in so many different ways—in youth groups, in the schools with anti-drug programs, in sponsoring softball leagues, and in the parks. What he and 3ABN have done for this community has been greatly appreciated.

When I was finally able to receive the 3ABN signal in West Frankfort, I realized what a spiritual impact 3ABN was having on our community. 3ABN has also had an economic impact on West Frankfort and Franklin County, offering employment opportunities for our residents and stimulating businesses with the dollars 3ABN employees and guests spend here.

If the city has a need, we know we can depend on 3ABN. For a number of years, we've needed to tear down some old buildings and clean up our city, but we had no money. 3ABN owned a number of buildings in town that were not being used by them. Danny donated these to the city. They have now been sold, and the funds are earmarked for the city's renovation project. Generous acts such as this go above and beyond what might be expected.

Danny's quite a character and has a great sense of humor. He loves life. And he's fun to be around. He's a great friend of West Frankfort! And I highly admire him!

G. David Green, economic developer for the city of West Frankfort

Danny and I go back to the time when we were little kids playing together and then going to school together. Our mothers were good friends, and we lived only a few blocks from each other. We even played basketball together, but not now. Danny's too good! Most people, like me, slow down as they get older. Danny's as good now, or better, than he was in high school.

David Green and and his wife

Danny's inspiration, drive, and faith in the Lord to do what's right is an inspiration to me.

How thrilling to see Danny, through 3ABN, move forward to reach out to the parts of our world that have never been touched by the gospel.

I'm so proud to have 3ABN in our community. What a positive influence it has had in West Frankfort and Franklin County. Not only the full-time employees of 3ABN affect our economy but those who visit, as well. I'm impressed with Danny's philosophy of business. He hires people for their abilities and has people from all faith groups working for the ministry, not just Adventists.

But above the economic advantage of 3ABN, there is Danny's personal involvement in the community. It's amazing to me that Danny, who is responsible for running a corporation as large as 3ABN, can find time to serve on community committees and attend council meetings.

One year the National Girls Junior High School Fast Pitch Softball Tournament was held in West Frankfort. The community really wanted it televised. Danny arranged for McKee Foods to sponsor this national event on another network so that other communities would have access to it. He rented equipment and sent the signal up to a satellite. Without Danny, we would have never been able to make that happen.

When I was president of the chamber of commerce, I wanted a guest speaker for our annual membership dinner. I asked Danny for his ideas. He said, "What about getting Ellsworth McKee, of McKee Foods, famous for Little Debbie products?" When we called, the secretary said that he doesn't do that kind of speaking. But because of Danny, he agreed to come, and he did a phenomenal job.

Danny's not one to toot his own horn, so I do it for him. I'm proud of what has been accomplished at 3ABN. I enjoy bringing groups such as the community council, the economic board, and various corporate leaders out to tour the facilities. I like 3ABN's open-door policy. Someone is always available to show us around.

For many people, especially in the Thompsonville area, 3ABN has been an unknown. If only those who question this ministry would take time to visit, tour the facility, and hear some of the incredible things 3ABN is doing around the world, their perceptions would very likely change.

To me, 3ABN is a great success story. I believe that is because it stands for good and demonstrates integrity for God.

Note: G. David Green is from a family of eleven children. Danny remembers him always getting good grades. From the time he was a young boy, he delivered papers for the local newspaper, The Daily American. *Through the years, he worked his way up to managing editor and spent many years in the publishing business before running for city office. Danny highly admires him for the contributions he has made to the community.*

David Lee and grandson, Kyle David

Coach David Lee

Danny and I have a great friendship. It's so special, I couldn't put a price on it. I enjoy knowing someone who is as honest as he is. He's the same whether you see him on TV or off. He's easy to talk to. In this part of the country we'd say, "He's a good old boy!" We both love singing, and we both love sports. He has a very competitive and generous heart.

I was principal of the West Frankfort High School when I wanted to do something for our students to emphasize the antidrug program called Red Ribbon Week. So I contacted Danny. We got two hundred kids involved making posters, skits, and anti-drug slogans.

Danny, through 3ABN, gave eight to ten thousand dollars in prizes to the winners of the various categories. But even more, he brought out the cameras to publicize what the kids had done on television. It was a tremendous success.

Later, when my wife was superintendent of West Frankfort schools, the school council decided it wanted to do something for needy children at Christmastime. 3ABN gave a thousand dollars to buy gifts. Danny has always worked with our community to provide things for people who don't have what they deserve. Any time we have needed something, he has been there to help.

Let me share a couple of stories about Danny. First, I have to tell you that we both love basketball; we love to shoot. I've been a coach for thirty years. I played basketball at Southern Illinois University, where I was most valuable player for two years and in the hall of fame. And Danny can beat me!

He will come out to my house, where we have a basketball goal, and say, "Let's play a game of HORSE." We'll play two or three games—even in the middle of winter. My hands will be freezing. But that doesn't stop Danny. When I do beat him, he wants to play again and again. Danny's winning strategy is to take the ball way out of my range—thirty feet from the goal, close to the halfway line on the court—and he makes the shot! In addition, he has so many trick shots that it's very hard to beat him!

When I went over to Russia with Danny, we even taught the workers who were building the 3ABN Russian Evangelism Center how to play basketball. Danny asked them to find a goal. They rigged something up, but couldn't find a net. We finally made one out of a potato sack. Then Danny, the Russians, and I would play until well after midnight.

I've gotten Danny into golf. It's great exercise. It takes a lot of concentration, so it takes his mind off his many responsibilities and lowers his stress level. Danny loves cold weather, and we play golf all winter. Most of the time, Bob Ellis joins us and sometimes Mike Adkins. Most of the time we're all alone on the course.

One time last year, the ice was frozen over on one of the ponds. Danny's ball landed on the ice. I would have left it. Not Danny. So I helped him go out on the ice to get the ball, and I could just imagine the ice cracking and both of us falling in—for a golf ball that cost less than a dollar!

One year, Danny invited me out to 3ABN camp meeting. He asked people from the different states to stand. I couldn't believe it. All fifty states were represented! In front of all those people, Danny asked me to come up and say a word. All I could think of to say to the audience was, "I realize that you come from all over the country, and people are watching from all over the world, but I want you to know, Danny Shelton belongs to us here in southern Illinois. And you can't have him!"

Kenneth J. Gray

Congressman Kenneth J. Gray (retired)

Kenneth Gray first ran for the U.S. Congress when he was only twenty-seven years old and became the youngest member ever. He served for a twenty-year period between 1955 and 1975, and then, "at a weak moment," as he tells it, he decided to run again in 1985 and served two more terms.

He has known the Shelton family since childhood when he went to school with Danny's mother. Danny has always had a deep respect for Congressman Gray because of his willingness to help when his influence was needed.

The first occasion was when Danny's father, Tommy, became disabled because of a heart condition. Because of a technicality, Tommy was not given veteran's benefits. Congressman Gray went back into the files and proved that Tommy was eligible. It may have been a small act, but it was significant to Danny's family.

Years later, Congressman Gray proved to be in the right place at the right time to once again help Danny. 3ABN had applied to the FCC for a license and was waiting for a ruling. The building and plans for 3ABN could not go forward until the license was granted. Danny phoned his friend in Washington. Congressman Gray found the 3ABN application at the bottom of the FCC pile. Since the FCC depends on its appropriations from Congress, it was willing to fulfill Gray's request that 3ABN's application be put on the top of the pile. In record time, the license was issued!

What's this longtime congressman doing now that he is retired? One of his projects is the Presidential Museum on Highway 37 in

West Frankfort. It houses thirteen thousand items, from antique cars to rare pictures and memorabilia—some you can't even find in the Smithsonian.

When asked to comment on the influence of Danny and 3ABN on the West Frankfort community, Congressman Gray responded:

Ralph Waldo Emerson once said, "Make the most of yourself because that's all there is to you." Danny Shelton is the living epitome of that statement. Although raised in a poor family, Danny didn't let that fact dampen his dreams. I was surprised when Danny started 3ABN because I knew he was a poor kid and that starting a television network would take millions of dollars. But Danny has what I call "capable tenacity." When he starts something, he stays with it. He won't let anyone discourage him.

3ABN has helped millions worldwide, and at the same time, it has been a continual blessing to our own community. Few people give back to their hometown like Danny has. He's helped the schools. He has bought buildings and donated them back to the city to auction off and use the money for good purposes. He even bought an ambulance that West Frankfort was trying to sell and donated it to the little township of Thompsonville that needed it.

I compare the influence that 3ABN has had on the community to two different types of guns. First, the shotgun. That's the general effect. 3ABN provides jobs. It's an inspiration to people. It's a service to shut-ins and others who can't get to church. Then there's the ripple effect of 3ABN helping with specific community needs.

Our community is a better place to live because of Danny Shelton and 3ABN.

22
Changing the World One Miracle at a Time

" 'Assuredly, I say to you, if you have faith and do not doubt,
you will not only do what was done to the fig tree,
but also if you say to this mountain,
"Be removed and be cast into the sea," it will be done.
And all things, whatever you ask in prayer, believing, you will receive' "
—Matthew 21:21, NKJV.

Miracle: Noun 1. an extraordinary and welcome event attributed to a divine agency. 2. A remarkable and very welcome occurrence. ORIGIN: Latin *miraculum*, "object of wonder."

Although miracles can be defined as "extraordinary" events, they happen daily at 3ABN. Almost every employee has experienced God's direct intervention in some aspect of personal life or on the job. Callers relate miracles to prayer line-partners. Testimonials given on TV or radio almost always reveal some miraculous event. The task to round up these miracles and record them together in one place could be compared to the task of picking up the feathers of a pillow in a windstorm. But by hanging around the hallways at 3ABN and chatting with the volunteers and staff, a few of these precious happenings have been captured and deserve to be shared. Each is a testimony of God's intervention on some level. And each can be a faith builder for other people who are eager for God to work in their own lives. In describing 3ABN, it would be accurate to say that 3ABN is a place of miracles. Each miracle is, indeed, a "remarkable and very welcome occurrence."

Miracles of how God brought workers to 3ABN

Joe and Nancy O'Brien (in Joe's words)
I was working for Georgia Pacific in northern Minnesota. After twenty years with the company, I had five weeks paid vacation and

Joe O'Brien

two retirement systems to which the company contributed, I had good pay and seniority, and I liked my work. It would have been foolish to ever leave such a job!

So when I prayed, "Lord, I wish I could give eight hours a day to You," He knew I wouldn't quit. The very next Monday when I went to work, the plant was shut down. Pinkerton guards were at the gate. More than a hundred people had lost their jobs. Some were in tears; some were fearful. Others were angry and ready to fight. I went home and told my wife. "We'd better start packing. God has a plan!"

I was the personal ministries director of our local church, and since we had twenty thousand dollars saved toward building a UHF downlink for 3ABN and were waiting for an FCC window to open, I called 3ABN to check on the status. In talking to Mollie, I asked in passing, "You wouldn't have any job openings, would you?" She said there was an urgent need for someone to give technical support over the phone to people installing their own dish systems. 3ABN also needed help shipping the dishes. When Mollie heard my wife, Nancy, was a teacher, she told me about the school that was starting and asked for a résumé from each of us. We went for interviews and were hired.

Be careful what you pray. God can even close major companies when He wants to move you from your comfort zone into His zone!

Matthew Andrews

I had a great job, but the greatest job of all is when you're working full time for the Lord.

Matthew and Phyllis Andrews (in Matthew's words)

You really have to be careful when you ask the Lord to use you to His glory. In early 2002, I asked that very thing. Without searching, I was offered a job in a supporting ministry in northern New York. It required a considerable cut in pay, but we were committed to go. After a year, a downturn in the economy forced the ministry to cut back. I was out of work in an area that was terribly depressed economically. Since our home in Ohio had not yet sold, a number of friends felt it was God's will that we move back there. Someone even offered to pay our moving expenses.

As we prepared to move back to Ohio, I was impressed to write Danny Shelton at 3ABN. He had written several books, and I had acquired knowledge of saturation mailing programs that I thought might be useful. However, in the rush of moving, I had not enclosed complete information on how to contact me. As we started unpacking in Ohio, I felt impressed to call 3ABN to give someone our current contact information. Mollie, Danny's assistant, said she had my letter on her desk and was just about to write me to find out when I could come to 3ABN and talk to Danny! Phyllis and I immediately stopped unpacking and drove to southern Illinois—with my neatly prepared proposal for circulating books. As we were ushered into Danny's office, I marveled at the strange turn of events that had brought us to this point. But the real surprise was yet to come.

Without any mention of my proposal, Danny asked me if I would consider accepting the position of marketing director at 3ABN. It then struck me how mysteriously God moves. I had no idea how God might use me, but He had plans radically different from the proposal that still sits in my briefcase! After a few minutes of discussion, Phyllis and I both left Danny's office, employed at the place we so greatly admired but never dreamed that we would have the privilege of serving. When we pray the prayer, "Bless me so that I might be a blessing," the Lord is willing to answer in ways beyond our comprehension. Within a couple hours, we had found a suitable rental home and were on our way back to Ohio to pick up our things—most of which were still packed. We were thrilled that God had given us an opportunity of a lifetime to serve Him in this place. Our God is an awesome God!

Interesting ways people have found the 3ABN signal

How did 3ABN get over the mountain?

In 2001, the marketing department at 3ABN was busy trying various approaches to introduce 3ABN to potential viewers. Penny Turner, one of 3ABN's marketing managers, recalls that one Friday morning Mike called wanting to get 3ABN on cable in Rome, Georgia. Penny explained the process. But before he hung up, he told her this story:

He and his family were Christians and at times watched religious programming. One day, curious to see if there had been any changes in TV reception, he went outside to move his TV antenna. Perhaps there was a new channel or two. That's when he found 3ABN. He and his wife began watching. After quite some time, they became convicted that what they were hearing was Bible-based, so they started visiting the Adventist church in Rome, Georgia. When Mike called Penny, he told her that the next day, Sabbath, he, his wife, and teenage son were going to be baptized.

And now for the rest of the story. When Penny heard where Mike lived, she commented to him, "I don't think it's possible to receive the 3ABN signal from where you live. The downlink is too far on the other side of the mountains." But he assured her that he was, indeed, receiving the signal. When she talked to him a couple weeks later he said, "You won't believe this, but I no longer can get the signal."

God knew Mike and his family needed a miracle and provided that signal for them until they had found Bible truth and were safe in their new church family. When the signal wasn't absolutely essential, the miracle ceased!

Other impossible connections

There have been numerous calls to 3ABN from people receiving the 3ABN signal as a local channel in locations that, humanly speaking, it would be impossible to receive the signal. For example, a call from Racine, Wisconsin. The closest downlink station was channel 25 in Berrien Springs, Michigan, several hundred miles away. The maximum distance channel 25 reaches is twenty to twenty-five miles. Yet, the caller insisted he was getting 3ABN on channel 54! That channel doesn't exist!

Lightning struck

The father of a Catholic family with seven children worked from 4 P.M. until midnight. The children would watch television until 10 P.M. and then go to bed. The mother, however, would watch until her husband got home. One day lightning struck the system, and afterward the family could get only two channels—Disney and 3ABN. After the kids went to bed, the mother began tuning into

3ABN just as a Revelation seminar started. After a couple of weeks, she was so impressed with what she was learning that she told her husband she was going to take the children to a Seventh-day Adventist church. He considered Adventists to be a cult, so he said the only way that he would let the children go was if she would go with them. She started attending church; then Dad came along. Within a few months the entire family was baptized.

Seinfeld's prayer line

Although God has used many divine appointments to introduce people to the Bible truth found on 3ABN, here's one that is technically impossible. It happened in the spring of 1999 just after *Seinfeld,* the popular (and very secular) television series, was promoting its final episode. There was so much publicity concerning this show that millions of individuals were watching. It was late night; suddenly the 3ABN switchboard lit up with about twenty-five new calls—all of them from around the Nampa, Idaho, area where 3ABN is available on a local television station. The operator took the calls as quickly as possible. The first caller asked, "What is 3ABN?" The operator explained it was a religious television network called Three Angels Broadcasting Network. The caller seemed confused. "What's this telephone number doing on my television screen?"

"It's the number for the 3ABN prayer line."

"But why am I seeing it on my TV?"

"Because," replied the operator, "you are watching Three Angels Broadcasting Network."

"No, I'm not," the caller replied emphatically. "I'm watching *Seinfeld.*"

How did the 3ABN logo and telephone number get on the screen of another network's programming? It's impossible. That information is generated and placed on the screen at master control. The signal carrying the picture does not go out separate from the logo and telephone number. Yet God chose to defy physics and airwaves, and the impossible happened. A number of the callers were very interested in 3ABN and asked for literature to be sent to them. A few asked for special prayer.

Someday Danny will be walking down heaven's streets of gold when he will meet someone who will say, "I am here because I was watching *Seinfeld!*" And then that person will relate the rest of the story.

3ABN replaces a wicked channel

Robert called the 3ABN prayer line saying, "I need your prayers because my life is a total mess. I know better, but I've been involved in drugs and drinking. My marriage is falling apart, and our kids are being given up for adoption. My wife is with another man. I took a rifle and was going to shoot them, but they weren't there. As I was driving back, I was involved in an accident, and my pickup turned over several times. Looking back, I don't know how I lived through it." He went on to explain that in the days following the accident, he began to be impressed he should get back to the Lord. "Just now, I was watching a wicked channel, and your station came over that channel. It faded in enough that I noticed the prayer line number, and I'm calling for prayer. Please pray that God will give me the strength to straighten out my life."

Stuck dish stories

God fixes satellite equipment

In 1994, John Dinzey, who today is director of the 3ABN Pastoral Department and works with 3ABN Latino, arrived in Chicago after finding Christ while he was in the military, stationed in Germany. He had been told an excellent job was going to be coming his way. He waited for a couple of days, but the company never called. He didn't know his phone was out of order. The company had been trying to reach him but couldn't get through. During this waiting time, John became impressed about the miracles he was hearing as he watched 3ABN. *Wouldn't it be wonderful to work at such a place?* he thought.

The first week that John was working at 3ABN, he volunteered to answer phones during the live broadcast. That's when he received a praise report about a stuck dish. Here's what the woman said:

"One day, my satellite dish was stuck on 3ABN. I'd never seen this station before, but since it was the only channel coming in, I continued watching it for two or three months. I was loving it because the messages were from the Bible. I was still going to church on Sunday but was just about ready to make a change when my dish stopped working. I was greatly disappointed and got on my knees. "Lord," I prayed, "if Saturday is still the Sabbath, and You want me to keep it, fix my satellite equipment." I got up, turned the TV on, and it was working! I'm a leader in my church. I'm going there next Sunday and telling everyone what I've learned on 3ABN."

Another time when John was working master control, he received a call from a Spanish-speaking lady asking what was happening to her satellite equipment. She and her husband had been switching channels and found 3ABN. They started watching. Somehow the dish got stuck on 3ABN. Since her husband wanted to watch soccer and other international programs, they had the dish repaired, but the repair man didn't program 3ABN back into their system. Several weeks went by. They were beginning to miss 3ABN but didn't know how to find it. Then one day they were watching a soccer match; outside, it was raining with lightning and thunder. The lights in the room flickered. Suddenly, they weren't watching soccer; they were watching 3ABN! She and her husband got down on their knees and prayed, "Thank You, Lord, for bringing 3ABN back to us. And thank You for letting us know we should be watching it." They called back a number of times to give progress reports. The last time they called, they reported they were going to Mexico to tell their parents what they had learned on 3ABN.

Football, 3ABN, and a can of beer

In the early nineties, a man wrote to 3ABN with this story. He was a sports addict and for months had been looking forward to what he called "the godfather of all sporting events"—the Super Bowl. There he was, sitting in his comfortable recliner, drinking beer and enjoying the game. At halftime he decided to surf through the channels to see what was available. And wouldn't you know it, when he came to 3ABN, his dish got stuck. He was furious because he had to listen to the rest of the game on radio. Immediately, he called the satellite repair service, but he couldn't find anyone who could fix the problem in less than a week or two.

The man was so ingrained into his custom of coming home from his construction work, sitting in his comfortable recliner, and drinking a six-pack of beer while watching sports on TV that he decided he'd just watch 3ABN and get as much entertainment as possible out of it. Night after night, with a can of beer in his hand, he made fun of the speakers—the way they combed their hair, their mannerisms, or the things they said. Two weeks went by before someone came to fix the system. But the bad news was that something inside the receiver had burned out, and the part would have to be ordered, which meant another couple of weeks before the stuck dish could be fixed.

During this time, the man continued to watch 3ABN. Almost six weeks went by before the system was finally fixed. By that time, he had become convicted of the Bible truth presented on 3ABN. He wrote, "I'm attending a Seventh-day Adventist church for the first time. How thankful I am that my dish got stuck."

Bird keeps owner watching 3ABN

Although this next story might not be termed a "miracle," it is interesting. At a weekend program at the church in Fort Walton Beach, Florida, in 2003, a lady mentioned that her pet macaw had developed a real liking to 3ABN's lineup of inspirational programs.

Every day the macaw listens and watches 3ABN from its perch in the family room. When the macaw's owner comes home and tries to watch another channel, the macaw has a fit! It squawks and shrieks so much that the owner has had to give up watching anything else on that TV. As soon as she switches back to 3ABN, the bird instantly calms down. Could it be that God even uses pet birds to keep His people tuned-in to inspirational programming?

Lost and found

A man had been watching 3ABN for six to eight weeks and was really impressed with what he was learning about the Bible. He decided he wanted to attend a Seventh-day Adventist church, but there was no listing in his local phone book for the Adventist church. He asked a number of other people, but no one had any idea where an Adventist church might be.

His house was at the end of a long private driveway with a turnaround so narrow that when people drove down the drive by mistake and tried to turn around, they almost always ran over his flowers. It made him furious! Why couldn't people read the signs that said "PRIVATE DRIVE" and stay off his property?

One day while watching 3ABN, he began to pray that God would send him someone who could tell him where the nearest Adventist church was located. While praying, he heard an engine running and immediately knew a big truck had come down his drive by mistake. He was just about to give the driver a piece of his mind when he read the sign on the side of the truck, "Seventh-day Adventist Community Services." The driver began to apologize when he saw the man running toward him.

"Don't worry," the man said. "Are you a Seventh-day Adventist?"

"Yes," the driver replied.

"Can you tell me where the nearest Seventh-day Adventist church is?"

"It's about forty miles from here." And then he told him how to find the church.

What are the chances that a Seventh-day Adventist Community Services truck would come down a private drive just as the resident was praying for a Seventh-day Adventist contact? It had to be a divine appointment!

3ABN prayer line saves lives

Raised up from a coma

In 1998, Richard Umlauf was new at 3ABN. He was working the midnight to eight shift at master control, where the prayer line was answered at night. About one-thirty in the morning, Richard received a call from a distraught mother who was watching 3ABN in her twelve-year-old daughter's hospital room. The girl had been seriously injured in a car accident. She had been in a coma for two weeks. The doctors gave no hope of recovery. "I don't know where to turn," said the mother with tears in her voice. "Would you pray for my daughter?" Richard was touched with this mother's request. However, he felt inadequate to present such a lifesaving request to the Lord. He earnestly prayed and then said a few words of comfort. As he hung up, he prayed again, pleading silently, *Lord, You can do something for this lady; my hands are tied. Please heal her daughter!* Then the heaviness left him. He went on about his work and forgot about the call.

The next night, just minutes after midnight, he received a call. This time it sounded like the lady was at a party. Her voice was happy and excited. "Are you the fellow I talked to last night?"

"What was it about?" Richard asked. "I get many calls."

"Well, I'm the lady with the daughter in the hospital."

"I remember," he said gravely.

"Well, I called back to tell you what happened after you prayed. Within an hour, my daughter sat up in bed and said, 'I'm hungry. Can we go home now?' "

Years later, as Richard related the story, tears formed in his eyes. "What an awesome experience to have God use me to be an instrument to connect someone with His incredible healing power!"

Saved from suicide

A man was so discouraged he decided the only way out was to kill himself. He got a shotgun and aimed it at his head. He then realized it would make a terrible noise, which would attract people. So to mask the sound, he decided to turn on the TV as loud as possible. You guessed it, the station that came on was 3ABN. He listened for a while and was so interested that he decided to call the prayer line instead of killing himself.

Crank caller accepts Christ

Any organization publishing a toll-free number is likely to get some off-the-wall crank calls. Sometimes it's easy to forget there is a real person whom Jesus died for behind each one of the calls. When Charlie Swanson started working at master control—knowing he would be answering the published prayer line at night he determined that he would treat each call with courtesy and Christlike concern.

Sure enough, one night a woman called in saying foolish things that made little sense. Then she called again—and again. Each time the phone rang, Charlie had to answer it, because it could be someone in need. Six times he politely allowed the woman to talk without getting upset or frustrated. Instead, he remembers, after each call he "sicced" the Holy Spirit on her, pleading with God for her spiritual healing.

A week later, a very rational woman called in and asked, "Remember those six calls you got a week ago from a crank caller? Well, I'm that lady. And I want you to forgive me for the way I acted. Not only did she apologize, but when Charlie asked her if she wanted to give her heart to the Lord, she said she did. So he prayed with her, and she accepted Christ.

Lost and found stories

The place of Jacob's ladder

3ABN has been described by one employee as "the place of Jacob's ladder." The original ladder, of course, was in the Middle East at Luz (later called Bethel) somewhere between the ancient cities of Beersheba and Haran. It appeared to Jacob in a dream when he was scared his brother was going to kill him. By showing him a ladder on which angels were going up and down from heaven to earth, God reassured Jacob that He was in control and that Jacob had access to the whole angel army if he needed it. The Bible account in Genesis 28:16 (NKJV) says, "Then Jacob awoke from his sleep and said, 'Surely the Lord is in this place, and I did not know it.' And he was afraid and said, 'How awesome is this place! This is none other than the house of God, and this is the gate of heaven!' "

I'm not sure how many of the hundreds of employees and untold number of volunteers who have worked at the 3ABN headquarters over the years would say 3ABN was the "house of God" and the "gate of heaven." Many, however, feel they are, indeed, working on what they call "holy ground." With all the mending of broken people that's going on because God is blessing this work, it's not hard to believe that 3ABN is under attack by the enemy. Satan must be mad as a stirred-up hornet over all the things that are happening and all the souls that are being saved for God's kingdom. Can't you see the devil's demons scurrying around trying to stir things up, causing strife and confusion at the 3ABN headquarters—so the signal gets messed up, so production is delayed, so the employees get frustrated when things don't seem to be working out?

In the midst of it all, there seems to be a Jacob's ladder with angels going up and down, finding misplaced items and easing tensions. Here are a few interesting examples. They may seem trite after lifesaving miracles, but they are viewed by employees as miracles, nevertheless.

Just the right part

One day, Al Denslow, who volunteers at 3ABN, needed an LNB with two receiver ports, a piece of equipment that is necessary when sending a signal from a satellite dish to two different television sets. The part is about six inches long and three inches high and wide. It's big enough to spot quite easily. The request was urgent. Al needed to get a dish up in a nursing home facility that had two receivers, and he couldn't do it without that part. You have to realize that 3ABN isn't exactly located next to big city warehouses filled with electronic parts! So if the job were to get done that day, Al needed to find the part at 3ABN.

He asked Richard Umlauf, who was in charge of satellite downlink equipment. They knew there should be an LNB around somewhere, but they both looked and found nothing. Because they were in the process of moving the downlink supplies from Bos Auditorium to the new call center, Al decided to see if an LNB might be in one of the boxes along the back wall of the Bos. Nothing! Al needed to go to the administrative offices for something, so he walked across the empty floor of the Bos. When he returned, he noticed something familiar lying in the middle of the Bos Auditorium floor. He walked over and picked up the exact part he needed. How did it get there when it wasn't there before? It had to be those angels!

One in a hundred

One day Richard Umlauf got a call from a listener who had returned his receiver to have it repaired by 3ABN. The caller wanted to know if his receiver had been repaired yet. Richard was new on the job, the move from Bos Auditorium to the call center was in process, and it seemed impossible at the time to find one box out of hundreds. He searched Bos Auditorium and couldn't find it. He prayed as he walked to the end of studio B to a huge stack of boxes. Finding what he wanted was going to be like looking for a needle in a haystack! All of the boxes were stacked about eight deep, except one that was lying in the middle of the floor. He picked that box up to move it onto a stack—and it was the very box he needed!

The paper in the hallway

Another time, Richard had been looking for a lost customer sheet. Several days passed, and he couldn't find it anywhere. He was carrying a box down the hallway from the administrative area to studio B and was looking down, watching his feet so that he wouldn't trip. If there were something lying in the hallway, he would have seen it. When he made the return trip, he noticed a piece of paper in the middle of the hall. He picked it up. It was the exact customer sheet he needed. How it got there is a mystery—unless you believe in angels!

God inspires people to give

Two miracle stories that haven't yet been told deserve a place in this book: The first is how the Bos Auditorium came into being, and the second has to do with the production truck.

In 1997, Danny was impressed that God wanted 3ABN to produce a live evangelistic crusade, because the Seventh-day Adventist Church would not be doing Net 97. Danny knew he wanted Doug Batchelor to present the series, and Doug was excited about the prospect. But 3ABN had no auditorium that would be suitable for a live audience.

Danny went on the air—just once—and said that 3ABN was going to build an auditorium, although they did not yet have the money. Then he instructed the 3ABN construction team to start clearing the land.

A few days later, Danny received a call from Mrs. Lydia "Toots" Bos. "I have some money to give to 3ABN. My sister-in-law and I were married to brothers who did well in the trucking business. They have both died, and we were wondering if you have any needs." Danny mentioned the auditorium.

"How much do you need?"

"Honestly, I don't know. I've drawn up some plans, but I don't yet know what the project will cost."

"Call me back when you know, and we'll see what we can do."

When Danny called back, Mrs. Bos said, "I'm putting a check in the mail today."

It was for the entire amount. When Danny called to thank her, she asked, "Is there anything else you need?"

"Well," replied Danny, feeling a little chagrin, "I forgot to add the cost for heating and air when I told you the amount." When Danny mentioned the added amount, she responded, "I think we can handle that."

What a blessing the Bos Auditorium has been. It was used to tape live presentations, seminars, and concerts, until it was outgrown a few years ago. It now houses master control and is used for needed office and studio space, while the worship center is used for live studio audience productions.

Something very similar happened when 3ABN needed a production truck. Danny mentioned the need on television, and at just the right time, God inspired the people to give. The truck eventually cost

$1.3 million, but Danny likes to say they built the truck the same way you eat an elephant—one bite at a time.

The truck and chassis was ordered, even though 3ABN didn't have the $100,000 needed. "Could we have three months to pay?" Danny asked. And in three months the money was there. Then came the box on the back of the truck, which would cost approximately $200,000. Once again, ninety days was requested. And at just the right time, the money was there. Within a year, $250,000 was given for the equipment—much of which 3ABN was able to get at an incredibly low cost—and the crew did the wiring. The truck was completed without 3ABN having to go into debt!

At the end of the year, the auditors complimented Danny on his business leadership. "Few companies are able to grow 30 percent or more a year, budget for a major expense such as the $1.3 million needed for the construction of the production truck, and end the year in the black." Danny smiled and explained that 3ABN had no budget and no money in the bank. "But," the man said, "you paid for everything you did. How did you do that without a budget?" Danny commented that it was 3ABN's philosophy never to limit God. Of course, there is a plan, but if a need arises, 3ABN steps out and fulfills that need, and God has been faithful to provide.

The raccoon at the rally

Most of the miracle stories that have resulted from the influence of 3ABN have been because people have been blessed by the radio or television programming. But 3ABN rallies have experienced miracles as well. Danny and the 3ABN team assemble to minister to the people and to pray that God will give them a message, that God will impress them to sing the right song, and that everything that is said or done will reflect God's will. Then they allow the Holy Spirit to lead as to how everything comes together.

E. T. Everett, director of 3ABN's sound center, and her husband, David, were part of the team that went to Yakima, Washington, a number of years ago. The restaurant where they ate breakfast had some very lifelike stuffed animals for sale. When E. T. saw a raccoon, she had to have it. It reminded her of the little orphaned raccoons she had raised over the previous three summers. E. T. made such a fuss over the raccoon that Danny finally said, "David, go get fifty dollars and buy that woman the raccoon. She needs it!"

As E. T. and David were leaving their hotel room, E. T. picked up her raccoon. With tears in her eyes, she said, "God told me to take it to the meeting tonight."

That evening, Danny did something he had never done before. He didn't feel God had given him a sermon-type message. Instead, he asked each one of the team to give a testimony. When he called on E. T., she picked up the raccoon, sat it on the pulpit, and once again tears came to her eyes. "I don't know why, but God told me to bring this raccoon to church. I'm just trying to be obedient." There were a few sympathetic giggles in the crowd. After all, it *did* seem rather strange. She continued, "So God, here I am. I'm willing to look foolish if that's what You want from me." She quoted 1 Samuel 15:22, "To obey is better than sacrifice," and told how Saul had lost his anointing because he wasn't willing to be 100 percent obedient. She closed by saying, "If I can be obedient and bring a raccoon to church, you can do whatever God's asking you to do." And she sat down.

After the service, a young woman came up to E. T. with tears in her eyes. "I wasn't raised in a church and don't know much about God, but I was baptized a few months ago. Since then, I haven't felt any different; I began to doubt. On Wednesday, I told a friend that I wasn't going to come back to church. It might be good for her, but not for me. My friend begged me to come to the 3ABN rally on Friday. I finally said, 'OK, on one condition. You won't ask me to go to church again.'

"On Thursday morning, I prayed, 'God, I want to know if I'm Your child. If You are really real, let me see a deer today.' I saw several. But then I got to thinking, *I see deer often in this area. That could have happened whether God was real or not.*

"So Friday morning I prayed, 'Lord, if You're really God and I'm Your child, let me see a raccoon.' If I would see raccoon, it *would* be a miracle because they are nocturnal animals. When you sat that raccoon on the pulpit, I was shocked. Now, I know God hears my prayers. Now I know I'm His child."

A man came up to E. T. next. "I know you brought that raccoon for me. My last name is Coon. I've been needing to go talk with a couple who has marriage problems, but I've been reluctant. I think God was talking to me!"

Then another man said, "I was impressed to give a book to a family acquaintance, but I didn't want to interfere. Now I know for sure, I must do it, because the author's name is Coon!"

The next day, a young girl came up to E. T. with her grandmother. The grandmother commented, "When you were talking about that raccoon, I just didn't get it. I thought it was being a little disrespectful to bring it to church." E. T. told her about the three people who came up after the meeting. The lady replied, "Now I get it!"

When E. T. took the raccoon back to the hotel room, she named him OB to remind her that she must always be obedient to God.

Not long after this, Danny was under unfair attack by individuals who should have been supporting him. E. T. gave OB to Danny, saying, "I'm impressed to give OB to you to help you remember that you are to be obedient to God, regardless of what anyone says." A few weeks later, E. T.'s house burned to the ground. Nearly everything was lost, but OB wasn't! The next day, Danny brought OB back to E. T. as a sign that God cares.

By this time, E. T. was beginning to work with Bobby Bradley on the sound center. One day, she felt impressed to give OB to Bobby, but she didn't have OB at work with her at the time. Bobby didn't know about E. T.'s impression when he came home with David to spend the night. He immediately noticed the raccoon. "Man, that thing looks real!" he commented. E. T. told him the raccoon's story. She also mentioned that she was impressed to give it to Bobby to let him know just how special he was to God. Bobby held the raccoon like a baby. Later, E. T. led him to have a deeper relationship with the Lord.

A friend, after hearing the raccoon story and how God impressed E. T. to give OB away, happened to see a stuffed raccoon in a furniture showroom. When you squeezed the racoon's paws, it sang a song. Somehow, this friend talked the company into selling the raccoon, and she brought it to E. T.

Some time later, E. T. and David attended an ASI International Convention with Danny and the 3ABN staff. E. T. brought her raccoon along. The 3ABN team was asked to speak to a junior-high-school group. The kids had been sitting for a long time and weren't interested in any presentation. Instead of paying attention, many were talking to each other. One girl in particular completely ignored the speakers. She even got the kids around her to make a circle, so their backs were to the speaker. She opened her purse and spilled its contents, made noise, and got up in the middle of Danny's presentation to get a drink. It was very disrespectful. E. T. found herself glaring at this girl! When E. T. began to tell the raccoon story, she got the feeling that God was about to have her give the raccoon away.

She noticed a quiet girl in the back. She had learned the girl was going through a very difficult time since her parents were divorcing. She was about the only one who was paying any attention. She deserved to get the raccoon. Then accidentally, E. T. squeezed the raccoon's paws, and it began to sing. Everyone looked up—including the unruly girl.

As E. T. ended her testimony, she said, "There is something I have to do before I leave. You've heard stories all week from adults about what you should or shouldn't do, but actions speak louder than words." Then E. T. felt herself going over to stand directly in front of the unruly girl, saying, "God wants to honor you. You are special to God. He wants to get this message across to you through this raccoon," and she handed it to her. "It's yours!" The girl was so shaken, she began to weep.

E. T. was angry with herself that she had given the raccoon to someone so undeserving. She went out into the hall and had a little talk with the Lord: "I didn't want to give the raccoon to her, Lord. She was the biggest jerk in the whole room."

God said to E. T., *Yes, just like you have been at times. But you honored the least of these, like I honored you. For just a few seconds you were Me.*

E. T. responded, "You mean, I was *like* You."

God said, *I need people to represent Me to others, not just be* like *Me!*

That broke E. T.'s spirit.

Next, a friend gave E. T. a raccoon just like the "singing" raccoon—except it had no song. E. T. was impressed to give this one to a young fellow who gave up his vacation to do volunteer work on the sound center. He had such low self-esteem that his head hung down most of the time. E. T. told him the raccoon story as they were sitting in her office.

"Is that the raccoon?" he asked.

"This is the third raccoon," she replied.

He came alive as he reached to touch it. E. T. could just tell what was going to happen next. She said, "The Lord thinks you are very important. You have passed the test of obedience by coming here and working for God this last week. You are a child of God. Hold your head up. I think God wants you to have this raccoon." He left 3ABN with the raccoon—and a lot more confidence!

There have been more raccoons since then—one as big as a person! And each one leaves E. T. with a God-given message to someone. God works in incredible ways to let His children know that they are special and that He is their God. For the rest of the story, you'll just have to ask E. T. when you visit 3ABN's sound center!

3ABN builds friendships

A caller reported this story to Penny Turner who was working in 3ABN's marketing department: "When I used to see my neighbor in the grocery store, she never appeared very friendly. Then one day she seemed very excited to see me and called me by name. What made the difference? My neighbor had found 3ABN on her television set and had begun watching. Suddenly, she had a new appreciation for me because I'm an Adventist. Now, we walk together and pray for people—especially our neighbors when we pass their homes. One day I introduced her as my friend. 'Don't introduce me like that,' she chided. 'I am your sister in the Lord.' I'll always be grateful to 3ABN for helping this neighbor find a new appreciation for the Bible—and for me!"

Miracles on the road with 3ABN

August 1999: ASI Convention in Orlando, Florida

On the opening night of the live broadcast, a stage light bulb blew over a crowded section of the auditorium and the hot glass fell many feet into . . . an empty chair! This particular type of stage light isn't supposed to explode yet God dealt with the problem so that no one was hurt, and there was no interruption in the program.

On another evening, just before a live program, a forklift ran over a camera cable, causing the main center camera to lose power. Although the program began with no center camera, the crew was able to make some technical adjustments, allowing the camera to come back to life in record time. Viewers had no idea there had been a problem.

God changed the path of Hurricane Floyd for 3ABN

In September 1999, the 3ABN production truck traveled to Orlando, Florida, to videotape and broadcast La Red, the largest Spanish-language televised evangelistic series in the history of the world.

Pastor Alejandro Bullón began his series on Saturday evening. On Sunday, the 3ABN crew heard reports that Hurricane Floyd was heading straight toward Orlando. By Monday, people were being urged to buy extra food and water or to leave town. Since Floyd was predicted to hit Tuesday night, it was decided to videotape two meetings on Monday so that viewers around the world would have no interruption in the series.

By Tuesday, most houses and businesses had boards over the windows. Convenience stores had little on their shelves, and highways were completely jammed with people trying to leave Florida. After much prayer, the 3ABN crew decided to pack up their equipment and try to find a warehouse that could house the production truck during the storm. One of the crew saw a man in a parking lot picking up signs and asked him if he knew of a place where they could shelter the truck. Amazingly, the man knew of an ideal place and helped them make contact with the right people. That night, when Hurricane Floyd was supposed to strike, the 3ABN crew were safe in their hotel rooms while many throughout the world prayed.

The next morning, the newscasters reported that although the hurricane was headed straight for Orlando, a "cold front" hovered over the area, causing Floyd to be pushed in another direction. God's Word says it like this, "The Lord has His way in the whirlwind and in the storm, and the clouds are the dust of His feet" (Nahum 1:3, NKJV). One of the crew observed, "We've traveled nearly all summer taping On the Road events for 3ABN, and we never saw the devil work so hard causing technical problems as he has with this series." As a result of the meetings, there were two hundred baptisms in Florida and more than a thousand in Michigan—and that was just the beginning.

Angels hold 3ABN's trailer on the road

Greg Morikone has spent many hours on the road with the 3ABN production crew. One February night in 2002 he was driving a van full of exhausted production crew members and pulling a trailer full of equipment. Some of the crew were trying to sleep and were not buckled in properly. They were on their way to Minnesota for a shoot. It was blowing snow, but the roads were clear. The production truck had gone ahead. The minivan with lighting equipment and another employee was bringing up the rear. Greg recalls, "Suddenly, next to me there was a big boatlike car in the fast lane. Out of the corner of my eye, I realized that the car had either lost control or didn't see me. His front tire hit the front fender of my van, causing us to skid onto the snow-covered shoulder. I remember seeing the guardrail racing toward us. I thought, *We're going to have a terrible accident.* I tried to correct the van, but the trailer was pushing me, threatening to jackknife. All of a sudden, everything straightened out, and I was able to get back on the highway. Those who watched from behind, commented, 'When you hit the snow on the shoulder, it looked like white angels were pulling you back onto the road.' The car who hit us never slowed or stopped!"

A divine appointment in Canada

A number of years ago, Leonard and Lorraine Payne donated a motor home to 3ABN—if someone would pick it up in Washington. Danny asked E. T. and David Everett if they would be willing to make the trip. "Take a few extra days and have little vacation on your way back," Danny suggested. They decided to travel through Canada.

As they drove north into Vancouver, B.C., the weather turned cold, and the heater on the motor home wouldn't work. They piled on the blankets. That's when they discovered that their cell phones wouldn't work, either, and that the only credit card they had with them wasn't accepted in Canada. Would their two hundred dollars cash get them all the way to Illinois? Things obviously weren't looking good! To add to their problems, *BOOM!* A tire blew, nearly causing David to lose control of the motor home. He finally got the rig stopped just a few feet from a dangerous drop-off.

David found the jack, but it was too small to get the motor home high enough to take the tire off. He finally found a couple of boards to raise the jack. But then he couldn't get the spare off the back of the motor home. The wrench wouldn't fit the lug nuts. They prayed that someone with tools would stop and help them. Across the median, an old tow truck, pulling an antique pickup, slowed to a stop. But the trucker didn't have the wrench they needed either. Then he got an idea, headed back across the median, and rummaged around in a toolbox on the antique truck. Believe it or not, he found a wrench that would fit!

The trucker then warned David that he might need more than one tire and directed him to go thirty-five miles down the highway until he came to an old garage-junkyard that had some tires. After helping David put on the spare, the trucker got a call and left him to lower the jack himself. It wasn't until the tire hit the ground that he realized there was hardly any air in the tire. There was nothing more they could do but to limp down the highway at thirty miles per hour, bump, bump, bump, praying they would make it to a gas station to get some air. Then they hoped to find a junk yard where they could get a tire that would fit for a price they could afford.

Not long after they arrived at the tire place, an old man appeared. He assessed the problem and a few minutes later came out with the exact tire that was needed. Once it was in place, they found that another tire on the motor home had dry rot and was ready to explode. "Would you, by chance, have another tire?" David asked. All this time, he and E. T. were wondering how they were going to pay for the tires. A few minutes later, the little man came out rolling another tire. He had this funny grin on his face.

"Ya'all from Oregon?" he asked looking at the plates.

"No," replied David. "We work with a Christian television network. This motor home was donated to the ministry. We picked it up in Washington and are driving it to Illinois."

"Ya," he said, still grinning. "You're David, and you're E. T., aren't ya? I watched you play the piano on TV this morning. My wife has back problems and can't get out, so she watches 3ABN all the time. I'm Len Atrill. Come into the office here and let's give Marjorie a call. She loves your playing."

"Marjorie," the old man said excitedly, "you won't believe who I have here." He handed the phone to E. T. Among other things, Marjorie mentioned she had some money to donate to 3ABN but was having a difficult time finding someone from 3ABN who could tell her how to do so without losing anything in the exchange rate. E. T. assured her that an accountant from 3ABN would be in contact with her. E. T. promised Marjorie some cookbooks and then gave Len one of her CDs.

Len said, "Here's what I'm going to do. I'll let 3ABN have the tires for cost and send them an invoice." The Everetts didn't even have to admit that they were short on cash. God took care of everything.

As David and E. T. drove away, they marveled at God's perfect timing and attention to detail. The blowout happened at exactly the place the tow truck would stop. And even though the trucker didn't have the right wrench, he just happened to be towing a vehicle that had one in its toolbox. And then, what are the chances of the Everetts being recognized by someone in Spences Bridge, B.C.? What are the chances that E. T. would be featured on that particular Sunday morning's broadcast when the couple just happened to be watching and that Mr. Atrill would have not only one odd-sized tire that fit that motor home—but two?

To add to the story, the 3ABN signal was not yet widely available in Canada at the time. The Atrills picked up the signal from their home, but no one else in the area could! To add to this incredible set of circumstances, soon after the Everetts left Spences Bridge, the heater on the motor home started working, as did their cell phones. The closer they got to 3ABN, the better the motor home functioned.

The Everetts not only had new tires on the motor home—and a promised donation that would probably pay for their whole trip—but had one more incredible miracle story to tell, which they did at almost every stop they made across country! God is good!

The 1998 New Year's Eve special was designed by God

Miracles happen all the time in the production studio. One thing is planned; something else happens; and what works out is better than ever. On one such occasion the production team asked for God's leading prior to pre-taping a four-hour New Year's Eve program. Each hour was outlined as to what would be presented, except for the second half of the second hour. They seemed to draw a blank about this portion of the program. They decided, as they had many times previously, to just step into the water by faith. They began taping, but soon stopped, realizing that this was not the right direction. Instead, they decided to work on hour number four until the Lord made things a little clearer.

They had lunch, finished the fourth hour, and were preparing to do the second half of the second hour (again with no real direction in mind). Just then Danny came into the room and said, "You won't believe what just happened. I met a lady in the lobby who shared an incredible story. One evening several years ago, she was very upset and was planning to commit suicide. Flipping through the channels, she came across 3ABN and began watching. The messages she heard on 3ABN changed her heart and gave her a new outlook and direction for her life. She is now full of love for her Savior and is working in full-time ministry for Jesus Christ. She just felt impressed to come to 3ABN today to say Thank you."

It was as if neon lights flashed. They recognized immediately what God had in mind for the second half of the second hour! As always, God's timing was perfect! Although Betty Footen had been at 3ABN only for a few short minutes when she was asked to come on the program and share her testimony, she did not hesitate. Once again, God demonstrated that He is the Producer, the Director, and the One who is really making the programs happen at 3ABN!

Sometimes it takes a miracle to get 3ABN on cable

One of the primary objectives of the marketing department is to place 3ABN on as many cable outlets as possible. In the process, there have been a number of situations in which God was definitely working. Here are a few examples:

Comcast Cable comes through

When AT&T, which used to be the largest cable provider, ran into financial problems and sold the cable part of the company to Comcast in 1999, Comcast became the largest cable company in the world. At the beginning of this merger, 3ABN contacted Comcast and asked for an appointment.

When the time for the appointment came, there was a mix-up, and the gentleman who was supposed to be present was not there. He was known for his hard-line approach. The 3ABN marketing team knew that he would hammer them with tough questions, and they had prayed earnestly about the situation. The woman from Comcast who was present had not heard of 3ABN and was very congenial. She asked a few questions. When she found out how long 3ABN had been broadcasting and in what locations and that 3ABN wasn't in debt, she gave a favorable recommendation. That was followed up with four and a half months of their lawyers working on a corporate agreement that allowed 3ABN to be on the approved list of channels that Comcast Cable companies can air. 3ABN personnel know that God had a lot to do with the mix-up of that appointment.

Turning an enemy into an ally

In 1999, Annette Christian, who at the time was working in 3ABN's marketing department, told the story about how 3ABN had tried for a long time to get major cable companies to broadcast 3ABN.

In one company, there was a woman who had no use for 3ABN. She was with one of the industry giants, and regardless of what 3ABN did, it could not get past her. She was a bottleneck.

A suggestion was made that they should pray for this woman. They prayed she would be moved, promoted, or that the Lord would open up a way around her. At the time, she had no plans to change jobs. Shortly after they began praying for her, however, she became marketing advisor of an organization in which her job was to advise other organizations on how to get past the roadblocks of the cable companies. God answered 3ABN's prayers and turned an enemy into an ally. Instead of a roadblock, she became an escort vehicle!

The dream that initiated a donation

Danny had just spoken in the Knoxville, Tennessee, First Seventh-day Adventist Church when he received a call from a lady who said she had had a dream about 3ABN. She had not watched 3ABN very much at all, but in her dream she was looking at the map to see where 3ABN was located. Instead of seeing just the map, however, she saw the actual 3ABN buildings. She said it was unreal. She didn't think too much about it until 3ABN did a program that involved showing the buildings. They were exactly what she had seen in her dream. She was so impressed that she donated ten thousand dollars.

This chapter really has no end. The miracles shared are only a sample of the broad spectrum of "remarkable and very welcome occurrences" associated with 3ABN. Most were experienced with thanksgiving and joy but were never recorded. The chances are great that if you become a part of the 3ABN family, sooner or later you will experience some "remarkable and very welcome occurrences" because of 3ABN. When you do, so it won't be lost like feathers blowing in the wind, please take a minute and send a written account to 3ABN. Be sure to mark the top of your letter "MIRACLE." Date it, and give your name, address, and phone number so that if 3ABN needs to verify something, it can find you. Or just send your miracles via email to kaykuzma@3ABN.org.

Reading a yearly account of 3ABN miracles would be a wonderful way to strengthen your faith during these last days. Thank you for helping us.

Section VI
Words of Wisdom

"Happy is the person who finds wisdom
and gains understanding.
For the profit of wisdom is better than silver,
and her wages are better than gold.
Wisdom is more precious than rubies;
nothing you desire can compare with her.
She offers you life in her right hand,
and riches and honor in her left.
She will guide you down delightful paths;
all her ways are satisfying.
Wisdom is a tree of life to those who embrace her;
happy are those who hold her tightly"
—Proverbs 3:13-18, New Living Translation.

Life is to be lived for two reasons: to share God's love and to learn from our life experiences what God wants to teach us so we will become more like Jesus. Through the last twenty years, Danny has been busy sharing God's love, and he's also learned a lot! Danny shares his insights with a prayer that his words will make a difference in your life, as well.

Finally, Danny challenges us to step out in faith and become everything God has designed us to be. Here's perhaps the best advice of all:

"Reverence for the Lord is the foundation of true wisdom.
The rewards of wisdom come to all who obey him.
Praise his name forever!"
—Psalm 111:10, NLT.

23

Danny Shares Lessons
He Has Learned

"Listen to counsel and receive instruction,
That you may be wise in your latter days"
—Proverbs 19:20.

Life is a wonderful classroom—if we are willing to learn from the experiences the Master Teacher designs for us. In the past twenty years of ministry at 3ABN, Danny has learned many valuable lessons. In this chapter, Danny shares—in his own words—what he considers to be the five lessons that have been most influential in shaping his character and the decisions he makes as the president of 3ABN.

Lesson 1: Never underestimate the Lord

God pays electricity bills

It was November 1981. The weather had turned cold early that year, and our electricity bill had soared. I couldn't work because of a broken wrist, so we had no income. When the electricity bill came, I shuddered. It was for $164. Where were we going to get the money? The days ticked away, and still no money had come in. We were down to the wire. If the bill wasn't paid by Friday, our electricity would be cut off. We prayed and held on to the belief that God would somehow intervene.

That Thursday, I got a call from Pastor Hal Steenson. At the time, he had a little church down on Main Street, and they had prayer meeting on Thursday nights. "Why don't you and your family come over and sing for our prayer meeting?" he asked. "We'll take up a thank offering!"

"Sure," I said, "I'll be happy to!"

But when we arrived that night and I looked around at the "crowd" of about fifteen people—three men, nine or ten women, and two or three children—the Lord impressed me, *Don't let Pastor Hal take up an offering.* I began to argue with the Lord. *But we need the money.*

The Lord answered, *Who are you depending on, him or Me?* So as soon as the prayer was over, I whispered to Pastor Hal to not take up an offering.

As soon as church was over, the strangest thing happened. Steve Adkins was the first guy to shake hands with me, and I felt paper between his hand and mine. I looked down. It was a twenty-dollar bill. Wayne Griffin, the piano player, pressed another twenty dollars into my hand when he thanked me. The third man in that audience came by and shook hands, and there was another twenty dollars. I had felt the money each time it came, but hadn't looked down to see just how much had been given to me. Then Pastor Hal came up to me and said, "Brother, the Lord has impressed me that I should give you something for your time and ministry. But the amount God has impressed me to give is a very strange amount."

"Pastor Hal," I said, "if I'd wanted an offering, I'd let the people give it. I don't want any money."

"Brother," he said, "do you think it's right of you to rob me of a blessing? I already have the check made out. It's for eighty-four dollars! And here's another twenty dollars someone gave me." When I counted the money that had been given me that night, I realized it was the exact amount of our electricity bill—$164.

That very next Sabbath as we were sitting in church, the call was made for the offering. I looked in my wallet and saw two dollars. I started to put them in the plate. Then I thought, *I shouldn't be putting our last penny into the offering plate!* I looked to my wife, Kay, to see what she thought as I gestured that I was going to put the money in the plate. She was quiet, so I gave the whole thing. On the way home, we came to an intersection with a van waiting to pull onto our road. When the driver pulled out, our eyes locked momentarily. Then she motioned for me to pull over. As I stopped the car, she called out, "Danny, I'm so glad I saw you. I have something for you!"

"What's that?" I asked, now recognizing Eva Mae.

"Do you remember several years ago—in 1973—my electricity bill was going to be cut off, and I didn't have anybody to help me? I asked you for a loan, but you said you wouldn't loan it. Instead, you gave me the $109. For years, I've thought that I should give it back to you, but I haven't seen you until now." She immediately took $109 from her purse and gave it to me!

That incident was just one of hundreds I have experienced in my life. After I started the work with 3ABN, the miracles have multiplied.

We limit God when we say, "There are only so many pieces of the pie, and the more ministries that start, the thinner the funds become as they are divided among the ministries." I've gotten a lot of criticism during the first years of this ministry because some church administrators felt 3ABN would take all the money and there wouldn't be enough for the official church projects and mission work.

That is simply not so. Why are we talking about how many pieces there are in God's pie? God doesn't have just one pie. He has a refrigerator full. And if that's not enough, He has a universe of refrigerators filled with pies!

Thompsonville Christian School

God builds a school

About four o'clock one Sabbath morning in 1998, I was impressed that a Christian school needed to be built in Thompsonville for the children of church members and for 3ABN employees. I had known for a long time that there was a need but didn't want to get involved because I had too many irons in the fire—and no money designated for that project. But that particular morning, the impression was so strong that I couldn't get back to sleep. It stayed with me all day.

Saturday night after vespers, I attended a church business meeting. Dee Hilderbrand, the church treasurer and 3ABN's production coordinator, said that someone had put one dollar in the offering plate and had designated that it was for the church school. She proposed that since we didn't have a church school, the dollar be given to the church school in Marion, thirty miles away. It seemed like a sensible decision.

Just then, Ronnie Hogue, who had a Pentecostal background and was baptized after watching 3ABN, spoke up. "Just a minute, Sister. Maybe the Lord had someone plant this dollar as seed money for a 3ABN church school. If God had wanted it to go to Marion, He could have designated it for Marion." Everyone laughed. After all, it was only one dollar!

I raised my hand. "I've been thinking about this, and I've been impressed we should have a school. Maybe we should just keep the dollar as seed money."

By Sunday night, I was so pumped up about the school that I had already drawn up plans and called a local builder. "What would it cost to build a shell for a school building with a gym 80 x 120 feet and a kitchen and classrooms? It would be mostly metal with some wood so that the roof wouldn't be noisy. I'll need your bid soon."

My philosophy is that you build buildings the same way one might eat an elephant—one bite at a time. If the shell could be built, then the volunteer builders who come to 3ABN could finish the interior as time and finances permitted.

The bid came in: $70,282. It seemed reasonable.

Two or three days later as I was opening the mail, there was a letter from a previous donor, who I knew had little in the way of worldly goods and lived in a small camper at the end of a country road in the back hills of Tennessee. What a shock to open the envelope and find a check for $70,000. I immediately called him. "John,[1] I just got your check for $70,000. Where do you want this money to go?"

"Wherever . . ." he replied hesitantly.

"But you must have some idea. Where is your heart?"

"To tell you the truth," John replied, "this was my wife's money. She was a school teacher and would have loved to have it be used for kids. But I know you don't have anything for kids there, so use it wherever."

I realized once again that God's timing is perfect. What better place to use it for kids than to build a school!

"Wow," I exclaimed, "this is exciting!" Then I told him how the Lord had been impressing me for the last few days about a school—and about the dollar seed money. Once again, God had made what seemed impossible, possible.

So I went back to the contractor who had given me the bid. "Sorry," I said, "the bid is $281 too high. I had one dollar when I asked for the bid, and today $70,000 was given for the school. Since

God supplies all our needs—not just all except for $281—maybe I have the wrong builder."

"No, Danny, you don't have the wrong builder," he said. "We've already given you a very tight bid, but we'll do it for $70,000."

Because of the one dollar seed money and the unexpected $70,000 gift, there's now a beautiful new Christian school for the children to attend. Nearly $400,000 went into the building of this school—and we never had to borrow any money!

When the 2003 school year started, we expected ten or fifteen students. Thirty-two enrolled, and we had to quickly build a new classroom into what used to be the cafeteria and hire a new teacher! But God provided for that, too. The new assistant pastor's wife, Rochelle Stanton, was a certified teacher, and she willingly stepped in to fill the need—evidence once again that where God guides, He provides. You shortchange yourself if you underestimate God, second-guess His will, and count all the cost up front! The next lesson I have learned is an expansion of this concept.

Lesson 2: Use what God has given you—or lose it

In the area of health we know that if you don't use your muscles, you lose strength and flexibility. But I've found the same principle applies to the financial operation of God's projects! If you don't use the resources God gives you, you lose them! I've seen a lot of what I thought were great ministries fade out of existence because they "didn't have enough money." The problem was, they always had some money but weren't willing to step out in faith and use what they had to do the work that needed to be done, trusting that God would supply more when it was needed.

One day early in this ministry, my brother called me. He was really worried. "Danny, our money's really getting low."

"What do we owe?" I asked.

"Nothing. Everything is paid for."

"You mean we've got some money in the bank?" I asked.

"Well, we have a little bit," he said hesitantly.

"Tell the secretary to spend it," I responded. "God's not going to give us any more money until we get rid of what He's already given us."

Every time we start a new project, it literally looks like we are going to run out of money. The project appears that it's going to have to stop. Doubters predict failure. But there's no such thing as failure

Danny, Melody, and grandchildren on the set

in God's eyes, just lessons that He has for us to learn! The biggest one is that *Where He guides, He provides!* If you believe this fundamental fact, then you will use what God has provided for His work, rather than hoarding it for some unknown future need. You will trust God to provide for everything He wills you to do now—and put His money to work immediately.

At one point in the beginning of this ministry, we got down to only a couple of hundred dollars. We wondered, *What are we going to do? Should we move ahead and build the building—or wait?* Early that next Sunday morning we moved forward as if we had all the money in the world and staked out the original 3ABN uplink studio building. It doesn't matter if our need is a dollar or a million dollars. God will supply it.

I thought the financial miracles at the beginning of this ministry were big. I'm not saying they weren't, because every miracle is awesome. But $6,000 for a gravel driveway or $50,000 for a building were peanuts when you consider what God is providing now for His ministry every single month! As of 2004, our annual budget was more than seventeen million dollars. That's almost 1.5 million dollars each month—and it continues to grow! It amazes me how God keeps bringing in the funds—all this without begging, crying, and gnashing of teeth! This money pays the monthly transponder fees, all operational expenses, salaries for over 150 employees, building projects, monthly expenses for tower rentals, equipment, and other expenses associated with the growing number of 3ABN's radio and television stations, along with the new stations that we are in the process of buying. Plus, there are the expenses for the 3ABN Russian Evangelism Center and television production studio and the other missions and outreach work 3ABN sustains in countries around the globe.

This is a faith ministry. If the money is already sitting in the bank waiting for a project to be done, that's not faith. That's good secular business planning, but it's not the way God wants this ministry to operate. We are here to give glory to the Lord for what He's done, not to take the credit for ourselves. As Psalm 50:15 says, "And call upon me in the day of trouble: I will deliver thee, and thou shalt glorify me." That's God's way. He wants us to first have faith in Him and move forward. If we get into trouble and can't help ourselves, He wants us to call on Him. Then when things work out, who gets the credit? Not us. We were helpless. At that moment there is no doubt in anyone's mind—it had to be God. Then where does the glory go? To Him! Let me tell you about a series of miracles that illustrates how God works.

God knows what experiences we need at certain times to increase our faith. Early in the ministry God did it with the miracle of two Kleenex boxes. We were facing what seemed like the Red Sea! We had a transponder bill of $50,000 that was due, and we had fallen behind $50,000 in operations. At that time, $100,000 seemed like a billion dollars! How would we ever meet our obligations?

The staff prayed for deliverance. The phone rang. A lady from California explained that she and her husband had just started watching 3ABN and that they were impressed they should give 3ABN the money they had been saving since they had sold their beautiful home. She explained that they had $50,000 in cash and were afraid to send it in the mail. "Could you come and pick it up?"

"You have *how much?*" I questioned, not believing what I had heard. She repeated the amount.

I told her it would be a week or so before I was out in California, but 3ABN had a board member who was an attorney—and a pilot— who could fly to her home and pick up the money the next day. She agreed to the arrangement. Herald Follett had a hard time finding the address. He finally drove up to a camper trailer that was not more than ten by thirty feet. He knocked on the door. Was this really the place? And if it was, how would he be able to convince this couple that he was the person whom Danny had sent?

As the lady opened the door, the TV was on. And on screen, there was Herald speaking on 3ABN! She looked from the TV screen to Herald and had no trouble recognizing him. She and her husband brought out a Kleenex box. "Here, have a Kleenex," they said. When Herald took the Kleenex from the top, he saw the box was stuffed with money.

The next day, Herald delivered the box to 3ABN. We counted it, and there was $570 more than the promised $50,000. I called to thank the lady, telling her what a miracle it was that all of our operational needs had been met with their gift.

Then I said, "You miscounted the money, however."

"Oh, no!" she seemed quite worried.

"There's $570 more than you said there would be. Do you want me to return it to you?"

"It's yours," she said, "but we'd still like to meet you. So if you can stop by next week when you're in California, we have another Kleenex box for you."

"I guarantee, I'll be there," I promised.

The next week, I returned to 3ABN with another Kleenex box worth $50,000, just the amount that was needed to meet the transponder bill that was due. God had met all of our needs. And God's principle was reinforced. When God's people go forward for Him, He is faithful and will supply all their needs "according to his riches in glory through Christ Jesus." This experience led me to believe even more firmly that God had a lot more "Kleenex boxes" for 3ABN. And over and over again, I have found this to be true.

A few years ago 3ABN gave $250,000 to Romania for a production center. Around the end of November our accountant told me that unless the Lord really blessed, we were going to be about $250,000 short at the end of the year. I was thinking, maybe we shouldn't have put that money into Romania. Then I remembered the statement by Ellen White on page 465 of her book *Gospel Workers.* These words have shaped many of the decisions that we have made in this ministry. "To show a liberal, self-denying spirit for the success of foreign missions is a sure way to advance home missionary work."

That next Friday, I got a call from a man I'd never met before, "I'm Dr. Bob Ford from Chehalis, Washington. A few weeks ago I got a dish so that we could watch 3ABN to decide if this ministry was something to which we wanted to contribute. When your Uncle Olen came on, strummed his guitar, and sang "Life Is Like a Mountain Railroad," I was really impressed. My wife's father loved that song so much that it was sung at his funeral. I thought, *Where else would someone like him have an opportunity to witness to so many?* I believe God wants me to give a gift to 3ABN so that this type of ministry can continue. I'm curious, what are your needs?"

I was thinking about the $250,000 that was needed before the end of the year, but I replied, "God knows what our needs are better than I do. Ask God to impress you how much money to give."

"Well, that's different," Dr. Ford replied. "I've never done that before."

The next Monday, he called back, "I did what you said. For the first time ever, a figure came to my mind. I sent the check this morning."

"Great! I appreciate it," I responded.

"Don't you want to know how much?"

"I'm dying to, but I didn't want to be too forward."

"Well," he said, "the Lord impressed me to send $250,000."

Dr. Ford got involved with 3ABN, became a board member, encouraged his folks to start watching 3ABN, and his mom became our own Mom Ford.

Another experience: It was late October 1999. 3ABN needed $550,000 to meet our needs by the end of the year. Out of the blue, a strong 3ABN supporter from Dayton, Ohio, called the trust department and requested that Leonard Westphal come to visit him. He ended up transferring to 3ABN some Worthington Foods stocks, which were sold for $200,000.

Around the same time, another supporter of 3ABN living in Walla Walla, Washington, called the trust department to ask what to do with his Worthington Foods stocks that had appreciated so much in value. Leonard Westphal gave him three options: (1) sell the stocks and fund a charitable gift annuity, (2) fund a cash trust from the sale of the stocks, or (3) make an outright gift of the money to 3ABN.

The caller said, "I will transfer the stocks to 3ABN via Merrill Lynch, and you sell them. Then I will pray about it and decide what to do." The stocks were sold for $370,000. When asked what he wanted to do with the money, the donor said, "The Lord has impressed me to make an outright gift now."

Note: The need was $550,000. With these two gifts, God provided $20,000 extra!

Toward the end of the year 2000, 3ABN was short $930,000. A few weeks earlier, a lady from Nevada funded a $100,000 charitable gift annuity. Within a month she passed away.

We still needed $800,000. We fasted and prayed as we always do when there are special needs. Leonard Westphal, who is in charge of stewardship and trust services for 3ABN, called. "How much would you need to get caught up this year? Would $100,000 or $150,000 do it?"

"No," I admitted, "that wouldn't quite do it!"

"Well," he said, "I've just wired your bank $876,000 from a ninety-seven-year-old woman who had this amount in stocks and bonds, but decided she wanted to give it now." Immediately, I praised the Lord that this lady was living by my friend Richard Bland's philosophy, "I be givin' while I'm livin', so I'll be knowin' where it's goin'." Once again, God had provided more than enough.

In 2001, we were down $750,000. Mollie received two calls within three minutes of each other, both women wanting me to personally pick up some money they had for 3ABN. The first lady was eighty-seven years old and lived in northern California. I told her I didn't usually pick up money personally, and I was very busy. Couldn't she just send a check? She explained that the amount of money was too large to carry to the bank, and she didn't want anyone knowing she had it in her house.

I told her, "I need to know how large the amount is because on commercial airlines, if you carry on more than $10,000, they suspect you of being in the drug racket. In that case, I'd need to arrange for a private plane."

"You'd better get a private plane," she advised.

"Can you give me an idea of how much money?" I asked.

"I don't want to say over the phone. Someone could be listening." Finally she said, "It's five or six CMs."

"I'm not sure what that means," I commented.

"Well, think about it and call me back when you figure it out," she replied.

A few minutes later, I figured out she was probably talking about Roman numerals, with the C being one hundred and the M, one thousand. Could she be talking about $500,000 or $600,000? I knew it couldn't be that much, because she said she had the cash in her house. It was even unlikely that she had $50,000 or $60,000.

When I called back, I said, "I think I figured it out, but I'm confused about where the comma goes? Is there one zero or two before the comma?"

"Two," she replied. "And if you come this week, I'll give you seven CMs."

Suddenly, I wasn't that busy! I made arrangements for a private plane and was told we would have to overnight in Colorado on our way back—either at Grand Junction or near Denver. I made arrangements to leave the next day.

I then called the second lady. "My husband has been a very successful businessman. He left the church twenty years ago, but he's been watching 3ABN and has some gold coins worth about $30,000 or $40,000 that he wants to give to the Lord. He feels you can be trusted. But before he gives them to you, he would like you to personally come to talk with him and pray for him."

"Where do you live?"

"We're in Grand Junction, Colorado."

"I'm leaving for California tomorrow and have to stop in Grand Junction on my way home. We can meet you and your husband then," I said.

I was a little nervous about having to carry all that money back with me, so I took along the two biggest guys around: Dave Everett, who is six feet, five inches tall, and my hefty brother-in-law, Bruce Chance.

When we arrived in northern California, the lady met us at the airport and drove us out to her mobile home. As she finished handing us $700,000 in aluminum-foil-wrapped bundles of $50,000 each, she suddenly said, "Actually, I want to give you $800,000. Let me go to my bedroom and get it." Then she noticed a little safe. "Oh," she said, "you might as well take that, too. There's probably ten or twelve thousand dollars in gold and silver coins in there." I had brought along a huge suitcase for the money. It was completely full!

As we left her home, she exclaimed, "I have never been so glad to get rid of anything in my entire life." I thought that was an unusual statement for someone to make about money.

The pilot, not knowing what was in the suitcase, tried to talk me into putting it in the luggage compartment. *No way*, I thought. *What if the baggage door flies open! It's going to ride with me! We're going to make it together, or go down together!*

The next day in Colorado, we were given $30,000 or $40,000 more in gold coins.[2] We then flew back to Marion, Illinois. After I dropped off Bruce and David, I suddenly thought, *It's Friday afternoon. The bank is closing soon. I don't want this kind of money hanging around all weekend!* So I called Neal Patterson, the bank manager, and told him I was bringing in some money that needed to be counted before I deposited it.

"How much?"

Now, I was afraid to mention the amount for fear someone was listening on my cell phone and would take the money before I could get it into the bank. "A little more than eight CMs," I said.

"Oh," he replied. Then after a pause, "How much is that?" I later learned that as soon as we finished talking, Neal called Linda to ask her what CMs were.

I was paranoid. I began to worry about having an accident on my way to the bank. When I got to the bank, I was afraid someone might be there to steal the money. Before I took the money inside, I actually locked the suitcase in the car and checked to make sure there were no unsavory characters loitering around. When the money was finally counted and in the vault, I said, "I have never been so glad to get rid of something in my whole life!" And it hit me, how much better it is to store up "treasure in heaven" than to store it up on earth and have the burden of responsibility to see that it doesn't get lost, stolen, or consumed by bad investments!

Every year, 3ABN selects a focus for the year. As 2001 was closing, I was impressed that 2002 should be the "Year of Wills and Trusts." But as I thought about it, it seemed rather negative; it's like celebrating when people die. But indeed, 2002 did turn out to be the "Year of Wills and Trusts"—or, more accurately, the "Year of Charitable Annuities." When faced with mounting expenses of approximately two million dollars for the construction of the worship center, and at the same time, another two million for the new digital master control center, we began to pray that God would supply this incredibly large need that was above and beyond what had been budgeted. Someone mentioned the charitable-annuity fund. When we checked, we found that 3ABN could use a certain percentage of those funds, which turned out to be the four million dollars needed for these special projects.

God wants us to use what He has given us so that He can continue to meet the needs of His work in such incredible ways that we have no choice but to praise Him for His faithfulness! It's the same today as it was back in Elisha's day. If the starving widow hadn't been willing to pour out the only oil she had into other containers, she would have never experienced God's power to refill (see 2 Kings 4:1-7).

We must never forget, when it comes to meeting the needs of His work, God has a universe of refrigerators filled with pies!

Lesson 3: Be a channel of blessing, not a garbage collector

Since the beginning of 3ABN, the devil has worked overtime finding things that someone could criticize about me. I've tried to live above the negative comments, let them flow under the bridge of time, and hope that they will disappear. But I'm human. Some of the things I hear or read are such blatant lies or such a twisting of the facts that I feel a righteous indignation well up in my heart. It makes me want to run to the phone and blast the accuser with the facts or my perception of truth! Or at least I feel like writing a rebuttal!

One such occasion was when another television ministry's newsletter published some gross inaccuracies about 3ABN. What was said to the tens of thousands who received this letter was so far from the truth that I thought, *I can't let this go by!* So while Linda was upstairs praying, I was downstairs for an hour and a half, feverishly typing a rebuttal that would set that ministry straight.

A little while later, Linda came downstairs. "Are you sure you want to send what you're writing?" she asked, not even having read it. "The Lord impressed me that you can be only one of two things."

"What's that?" I asked curiously.

"Do you want to be a garbage collector or a channel of blessing?"

"A channel of blessing, of course."

"Then let the love of God flow through you," she counseled, "not the devil's garbage!"

I threw my response in the trash and deleted the file from my computer's hard drive.

I've tried over the years to follow Linda's advice. And I've found that given time, God redeems His own. God eventually sets the record straight. God is a mighty defender of His work. I don't have to be! In the process, I've experienced many blessings!

Lesson 4: God knows my heart's desire is to do His will; therefore, I don't have to be paralyzed with fear that I'll make a mistake

Several years ago, I began to consider the awesome responsibility I was carrying for the success of this ministry. God was blessing it so much. I began to feel that one of the reasons for His blessings was that I was following His will. He could trust me; therefore, He blessed. This led me to experience a heaviness in my heart, a burden too big to bear. I feared that somehow my actions would either make or break the ministry.

The more I considered this, the more frightened I became. What if I did something wrong? What if I took a wrong step? What if Satan tempted me in an area of weakness, and I failed? These thoughts of heavy responsibility almost paralyzed me for a while.

Then one day, I decided to take a break in the middle of the afternoon and check on my brother Tommy's registered quarter horse. Both Tommy and I had mares that were foaling at the same time. My horse had just had her colt, so I knew Tommy's horse would deliver any time. It usually happened in the middle of the night, so I wasn't really expecting anything as I drove to the end of the driveway. But when I went into the stable to check on the mare, I was shocked when I saw the way the mare was lying in the stall jammed up against the wall. The baby had come out, but was still in the sack. I could tell it was a beautiful sorrel with a blaze and four white socks. I jumped over the mare and ripped the sack off the colt and began pumping the colt's chest, but I couldn't get it to breathe. "God," I cried, "You have blessed me so much. Why can't this dead one be mine? Why does it have to be Tommy's? Please let Tommy's colt live!"

Jesus knew my heart! At that moment, I would have gladly given my brother the living colt. But God was good and didn't ask for the sacrifice. I pumped that colt's chest again and again, praying all the time. Eventually, it took a breath! An hour later, I called Tommy and told him he was the proud owner of one of the most beautiful colts I'd ever seen.

That might have been a little thing for some, but for me it was an indication from God that He knew my heart. I might at times make a mistake out of ignorance or faulty judgment, but God wouldn't allow my error to cut off the flow of His blessings to *His* television ministry. What a comfort to know that as long as I have a heart for others and put them first—and a heart to do what is right—God will continue blessing both me and this ministry. The realization that God was blessing 3ABN not because of me but because this was *His* work took the paralyzing pressure away from me. Once again, I was able to relax and enjoy the work that God had given me to do.

Lesson 5: God uses us in spite of our faults

God is the real CEO of 3ABN. He is the One who works through Danny Shelton in spite of my faults! I'm growing spiritually, and God is helping me to become the representative He wants me to be.

Some people are shocked to hear that God called me to this ministry while I was still eating meat! "How could that be?" they question. Isn't it wonderful God uses us, even though at the time we are not living up to all the knowledge He has given us? I've learned that God picks people who are honest and have potential, not necessarily those who are "perfect." When it comes to living the health message, Linda has been an important influence on my life.

Even though my family was poor, I grew up in a home where Pepsi Cola was the preferred drink of choice. And I loved steak, Big Macs, and Chicken McNuggets! My philosophy was that if the Bible allows me to eat clean meats, no one should tell me I shouldn't. After Linda became an Adventist, and before we were married, she would come over to our house and sometimes cook for Melody and me. She had no trouble accepting the healthy lifestyle promoted by Adventists and almost immediately became a vegetarian. Melody and I would eat the vegetables she would prepare, then jump in the truck and go to the nearest McDonald's to complete our meal. I was of the opinion that no one could ever make me quit eating meat, even though I believed God had spoken to His messenger, Ellen White, over a hundred years ago about the connection between eating flesh foods and spiritual health.[3]

Over a period of time, however, we just had less and less meat in our home, until I, too, became a vegetarian. But that didn't cure my addiction to sweets. When I traveled, I liked nothing better than getting a Mrs. Field's cookie or a cinnamon bun. At potluck meals or parties, I'd feast on desserts. There was nothing more satisfying than to dunk a freshly baked cookie in milk and savor the taste! I also knew that Ellen White said that if we were going to eat meat or sugar, it would be better to eat meat. She also said that the mixture of sugar, milk, and eggs was especially unhealthy![4]

I've always had a lot of faith in the power of God. But I never asked Him to change my taste buds. I liked eating what I ate! God, however, worked a miracle and changed me anyway—in spite of myself! Here's how it happened.

I became concerned after watching a video of independent churches baptizing people out of the Seventh-day Adventist Church and into their particular branch of "historic Adventism." They seemed so sincere, yet they were so wrong! It was really scary to me. How could so many people be deceived? I began to realize how subtle error could be. How easily a person, or a ministry, could get caught up with a wrong idea and misrepresent God's character. I prayed God would give me a clear mind for discerning truth and error. That same day, I went on a twenty-four-hour juice fast. I didn't want anything to come between God and me that would keep 3ABN from being a channel that God could use to spread His message to the world.

When my fast was over and breakfast time came, I went to get my usual cereal. It didn't look good. Instead, I had some fruit—some cantaloupe and a banana. I went to Wendy's for lunch for a baked potato. I started to order cheese and broccoli, but I said, "Just give it to me plain." When I started eating it, I commented, "How do they make these things taste so good?" Suppertime came and all I wanted was a salad. I used to drink lots of milk, but it didn't look good either.

The next day on a trip, because I fly so often, I got an upgrade to first class. The scrambled eggs and waffles with syrup didn't look good, so I ate my little plate of fruit. I thought about grabbing a cinnamon roll on my dash through the airport between connections, but I didn't.

A number of weeks went by before I realized that all this time I hadn't eaten anything with eggs, milk, cheese, or sugar in it. In fact, fruit tasted better than anything. I began to feel better. My cholesterol went down, and I became convicted that 3ABN must continue airing programs on health. A large number of people could care less about watching a preacher on TV, but they would like to feel better and live longer. When health programs grab their interest, God can lead them to watch programs that promote spiritual health as well. It works the other way, too. There are many who are interested in spiritual health who don't realize that health habits, including what we eat, affect our ability to discern the subtle differences between truth and error!

I realize my journey to better health is unique. I wasn't praying, "Lord, change my diet." I was praying that God would keep me from error or from anything that would prevent Him from being able to use 3ABN in spreading the Bible truth to the world. His answer was to change my diet. Interesting, isn't it?

There's another area in my life that I have considered a "fault" of mine. It's my use of the English language. As a kid, I learned English by modeling my family and friends. In the process, I picked up some incorrect speech patterns. I'm learning, but I still make mistakes.

Before God called me to the work of 3ABN, I wouldn't have dreamed I'd be giving sermons and speaking to thousands of people across the country almost weekly. I used to be intimidated because I knew I butchered the king's English. I was especially fearful if an English teacher was in the audience. So I began praying, "Lord, don't let the people hear me talk today. Let me be a channel of blessing for You. Do a miracle on the ears of these people so that no matter what I say, they will hear the message You have for them. Let Your words reach the hearts of the people, not my poor English!"

After I began praying that prayer, people began coming up to me and saying things I'd never heard before. "That sermon really blessed me." Or when I've made a comment about my poor English, someone would say, "I was so involved in what you said that I didn't even notice the grammar. I didn't hear any mistakes."

When I hear comments like that, I know God has performed a miracle. Whether it's the gift of tongues or the gift of "ears," I'm not sure. I just know that people have heard something more than what I have said.

One time when I gave a sermon at Pioneer Memorial Church at Andrews University, where they give graduate degrees in English and speech, I knew I wasn't qualified to speak to that highly educated audience. When the sermon was over and I was shaking hands, someone came up and said, "What you said today really changed my life. I had a book ministry and had become discouraged. But when you talked about passing out books like the leaves of autumn, that encouraged me to keep doing what I'm doing."

The strange thing was, I didn't remember saying anything about the leaves of autumn, so I went back and had Mollie and Mom Ford listen to the tape that had been made of the sermon. There was nothing on the tape about the leaves of autumn. Obviously, God performed a miracle and gave that person the exact message that was needed.

I am so humbled to think God is using me for His work—in spite of my faults!

---

[1] John is a pseudonym.

[2] Later this gentleman made 3ABN a significant part of his estate planning.

[3] Although you can find statements from Ellen G. White on diet and its relation to health in many publications, her most popular health book is *The Ministry of Healing*, first published in 1905. It is now published by Pacific Press Publishing Association. Here are just a few quotations that Danny was familiar with, but chose to overlook, until God changed his taste buds!

"Grains, fruits, nuts, and vegetables constitute the diet chosen for us by our Creator. These foods, prepared in as simple and natural a manner as possible, are the most healthful and nourishing. They impart a strength, a power of endurance, and a vigor of intellect that are not afforded by a more complex and stimulating diet" (p. 296).

"The effects of a flesh diet may not be immediately realized; but this is no evidence that it is not harmful. . . . Many die of diseases wholly due to meat eating, while the real cause is not suspected by themselves or by others.

"The moral evils of a flesh diet are not less marked than are the physical ills. Flesh food is injurious to health, and whatever affects the body has a corresponding effect on the mind and the soul. Think of the cruelty to animals that meat eating involves, and its effect on those who inflict and those who behold it. How it destroys the tenderness with which we should regard these creatures of God" (p. 315).

"Is it not time that all should aim to dispense with flesh foods? How can those who are seeking to become pure, refined, and holy, that they may have the companionship of heavenly angels, continue to use as food anything that has so harmful an effect on soul and body? How can they take the life of God's creatures that they may consume the flesh as a luxury? Let them, rather, return to the wholesome and delicious food given to man in the beginning, and themselves practice, and teach their children to practice, mercy toward the dumb creatures that God has made and has placed under our dominion" (p. 317).

[4] "Far too much sugar is ordinarily used in food. Cakes, sweet puddings, pastries, jellies, jams, are active causes of indigestion. Especially harmful are the custards and puddings in which milk, eggs, and sugar are the chief ingredients. The free use of milk and sugar taken together should be avoided. . . . Butter is less harmful when eaten on cold bread than when used in cooking; but, as a rule, it is better to dispense with it altogether. Cheese is still more objectionable; it is wholly unfit for food" (pp. 301, 302). *Note: She was not talking about cottage cheese or foods of a similar character when she made this statement.*

Here is Ellen White's statement about sugar versus meat. It can be found in *Testimonies for the Church*, vol. 2, p. 370: "I frequently sit down to the tables of the brethren and sisters, and see that they use a great amount of milk and sugar. These clog the system, irritate the digestive organs, and affect the brain. Anything that hinders the active motion of the living machinery affects the brain very directly. And from the light given me, sugar, when largely used, is more injurious than meat."

24

From Danny's Heart

"Through wisdom a house is built,
And by understanding it is established;
By knowledge the rooms are filled
With all precious and pleasant riches"
—Proverbs 24:3, 4, NKJV.

How better to end the story of twenty years of miracles that makes
up the history of 3ABN than to let Danny Shelton share a message
from his heart. May you be inspired, as I was, by the following words
from Danny as he continues the ministry of mending broken people.

When people hear about the miracles that have happened with the establishing of 3ABN, and the continuing miracles, they are amazed. But Acts 10:34 says, "God is no respecter of persons." What He did for us at 3ABN, He is willing to do for anyone. Each person has different talents and areas of influence. Each has a work to do that no one else can do in exactly the same way. And everyone could do more for the Lord if they were willing to step out and believe that God would fulfill all their needs.

We are living in a time when God isn't holding anything back from us. Good parents want to lavish gifts on their children. But at the same time, they don't want to spoil them. God is something like that. If we found out today that one of our children had only one week to live, we would pull out all the stops. We wouldn't hold anything back. We would meet all the child's heart's desires that we were able to meet.

We are God's children, and He knows our time is short. We don't have much longer to live in this world, so the Lord isn't holding anything back. If we can handle it and not become spoiled or self-centered, He'll give us everything—blessings, finances, miracles. He wants to lavishly

3ABN has grown from a vision planted in Danny's heart by God to a globe-encircling ministry as illustrated by the state-of-the art production center currently in use.

give every good thing to His children. It's available to everyone!

As I look back over the years, I definitely think the miracles have increased since the beginning of 3ABN. The beginning miracles were incredible, there's no doubt about that! But just as it was the daily miracle of manna that sustained the Israelites in the desert for forty years, it is the manna that falls every day that sustains this ministry. Look at the figures. Look at the phenomenal growth that is taking place right now, and any intelligent person would have to conclude that the Lord has to do a lot more now to keep this ministry running than it took in the beginning to get it started. But He has counted His resources and is not found wanting.

People will write to 3ABN and express their desire to do something big for the Lord then complain that God hasn't given them anything to do. The question is, Why would God give someone a big task if they haven't been willing to faithfully do the little ones? (See Matthew 25:21.)

Realistically, God will ask you to do the small things first—give a Bible study, teach a children's class, play the piano, read a poem, visit a friend, play games with the kids, donate to community services, or invite someone over for lunch. God comes to earth daily in the shape of people. He has said, "If you do it unto the least of these . . . you have done it unto me" (Matthew 25:40). In doing something small for someone, we are really doing something big for the mighty God of this universe! What an awesome thought!

God says, "Go ye!" He doesn't say, "Go ye, and do something big and important and impressive." He just says, "Go ye, and teach others to follow Me and do what I've asked." And by the way, we're all a "ye." That means God is commanding all of us to go to somebody! That's how His message is going to reach the world! (See Matthew 28:19, 20, KJV.)

And God doesn't say, "Go ye, who have lots of money and resources." Moses didn't think he had anything going for him when God asked him to free the children of Israel from the bondage of Egypt. God's reply was, "Moses, what's in your hand?" Moses said, "A rod." You can find the story in Exodus 4. But if you will read on, you'll find that God used Moses' rod—an ordinary stick—to do extraordinary things! God says, "Go ye, with whatever you have in your hand, and I will work through you to set people free from the bondage of sin, addictive habits, bitterness, heartache, and hopelessness. Through you, I will mend broken people!"

The Bible makes it plain: The way God sees things isn't the way we do. His ways aren't our ways (see Isaiah 55:8). The people who we think are the greatest now are going to be the least in His kingdom (see Luke 22:26). Those who are first now will be last then (see Matthew 19:30). Who are we to judge whether a work that God calls us to do is a big one or a small one? In God's point of view, there are no insignificant tasks!

The task of leading a worldwide satellite ministry with an annual budget of more than seventeen million dollars may boggle your mind. It does mine. Because 3ABN is not a part of what's referred to as the "organized work of the church" no regular or annual offerings are taken up by the church for this ministry. There are no committees to appropriate necessary funds should 3ABN get into financial straits. 3ABN does not participate in on-air "beg-a-thons" (commonly called praise-a-thons). We believe God has called us to give this message 24/7, and we trust Him to be our philanthropist. We have no savings accounts on earth. 3ABN's savings account is with the Lord.

Several other non-Adventist satellite ministries operate on an annual budget of over one hundred million dollars a year, yet we are now the second largest television network (as far as stations owned and operated) in the United States and possibly the world. But we eat and sleep like anyone else. There is nothing special about us. It's God and His Word who are special. There is nothing special about you either, but God working through you makes you and your work very special. What sets us apart from everyone else is doing the special work that God has called us to do.

The work differs, yes. But one piece of God's work is not more important than another—not in God's eyes. God's ministry on this earth shows that Jesus preached to and fed the five thousand, but He also stopped in the middle of a pressing crowd to heal a lady who had a continual discharge of blood and probably an offensive odor. His heart went out to all the miserable people trying to get into the pool of Bethesda, but He picked out one man who was suffering paralysis—probably caused by sexual immorality—and He healed him. Jesus gave some of His greatest sermons to an audience of *one!* The sermon about Christ being living water and our only source of eternal life was given to the Samaritan woman who had gone through five husbands and was currently shacking up with a live-in boyfriend. And the sermon on the importance of being spiritually born again, Jesus gave in the middle of the night to Nicodemus, a Pharisee who was too embarrassed to talk to Jesus during the day when others might see them! Was Jesus' mission smaller because He met the needs of individuals one at a time, rather than broadcasting the truth about God into billions of homes simultaneously? Of course not.

Whatever the work that God gives you to do, it's incredibly significant in God's overall plan for this planet. Don't hesitate to do it because you don't feel qualified. Don't hesitate to do it because it seems too insignificant. Don't hesitate to do it because you're afraid you don't have the resources. Remember, the water of the Jordan didn't part until Joshua commanded and the priests stepped into it. Your resolve, followed by your *actions* of faith in moving forward, gives God the permission to break through the evil forces that are trying to protect what they think is their territory from receiving the blessings of God.

If God blessed first and *then* His people did what He wanted them to do, can't you hear the accusations of Satan? "God, these people are doing what You want them to do only because You're blessing them so much. Stop the blessings, and they won't work for You anymore! They're only in it for what they can get out of it!"

How do we know Satan is making this accusation? Well, if he made this complaint about God's servant, Job (see Job 1 and 2), you can be sure he's still complaining today! Satan has put the character of God on trial in the universe. It's your stepping out in faith and getting your feet wet that shows the universe you're doing something not because of what God has done for you in the past, as if you have some obligation to work off before God is willing to bless you again. God doesn't play this kind of tit-for-tat game. Rather, it shows the universe that without any foreknowledge on your part, God will indeed, in His time, break open the windows of heaven and pour out so many blessings on you that you won't be able to receive them all. You will, in faith, move forward because of your relationship with God. You love Him and trust Him so much that if He asks you to do something, you'll do it! Regardless. You serve God, not for what you've gotten out of Him or what you're going to get out of Him, but because He is the mighty King of this universe who first loved you and gave His life for you. Period!

I am absolutely certain that the number and immensity of God's miracles are currently on the upswing! Some complain that the days of miracles are over—at least in North America. But that's *not* so! They are just beginning. Romans 5:20 says that where sin increases, grace increases all the more. There's no doubt that sin is increasing exponentially in these end times. If we believe Scripture, that means that God's grace is going to increase even more. If that's so, we need to hold on to our hats, for the most incredible show of God's mighty power is yet to come!

When you can abandon your self-centeredness, without thought for your own reputation, comfort, or financial security, and just do what God asks you to do, you better watch out because it's going to start raining. The showers of God's blessings are going to be more than you could have ever hoped for or even imagined. The greatness of the miracles will take your breath away. I know. I've experienced it.

So ...

• if you're hesitating on the back row and feeling you can't do anything for the Lord,

• if you're afraid of failure, thinking people will laugh at or criticize you if you were to start doing what you feel God is asking you to do,

• if you're trying to get out of God's calling because the vision He's given you seems impossible and the work too hard . . .

let me encourage you.

God wants to accomplish the impossible,
    the incredible, and the marvelous, through you.
So, stand up, step out, and look up in faith to God,
    for the greatest show of miracles on earth
is about to begin for you!

* * * * *

May God richly bless you abundantly more than you could ever ask or think.

Production truck

Worship center

Call Center

Mail room

Epilogue

" 'But he who endures to the end shall be saved.
And this gospel of the kingdom will be preached in all the world
as a witness to all the nations,
and then the end will come' "
(Matthew 24:13, 14, NKJV).

If you have read this far, you probably feel like exclaiming with me, *"What hath God wrought!"* It has, indeed, been an incredible twenty-year journey. Twenty years may have passed, but the journey is not over. Every year that the Lord tarries, 3ABN will continue to grow, stretching to reach more population groups, stretching to minister to people with different needs with more effective programming, and stretching to add many more languages to the visual satellite signal in order to reach all of God's lost sheep on the thousands of hillsides of the earth.

It's difficult to end a book that has no ending. For as we go to press, late-breaking news begs me tell you one more story—a story about how God uses whoever is willing to be used. In this case, the person is a successful businessman who for many years has not been active in the church. But God never rejected him. Instead, God placed this man in a key position to work out a contract with two major cable companies—Comcast and Cable One—making it possible for 3ABN to saturate the Washington, D.C., and Baltimore, Maryland, areas, as well as twenty-six other cities throughout the United States. All this for half the asking price! 3ABN had been working on this contract for years with no success. This man "just happened" to be part owner of a full-power station that was on a frequency that Comcast wanted. Therefore, they were willing to negotiate. And once more we celebrate a miracle.

You might ask, why did I write this book? That's a good question, because my ministry has been for families. If you watch 3ABN, you'll see me giving an occasional presentation or a parenting spot. My handle has always been the love cup and how love creates love. Perhaps that's why I reacted so strongly when I saw Danny, who has suffered incredible physical pain throughout the years, being hit by criticism that I considered to be emotionally painful.

Danny's optimistic response was, "We have had many ups and downs with different leadership over the years. God has shown me, however, that if He puts something on your heart, if it's in compliance with Isaiah 8:20 ('To the law and to the testimony . . . '), don't let anyone discourage you. Go forward. Know that if you go forward, God will supply your every need. He will pave the way before you. No matter what the odds, God does as He says. He finishes what He starts, that good work in you. Always keep your eye on His calling and the vision. Don't be deterred. And I promise that you and God will always be the majority."

Danny's faith has never wavered. He knew that his calling was sure. But I thought, *If only those who criticized could walk the 3ABN hallways, see the miracles that were happening in the employees' lives, and hear the testimonies from viewers whose lives have been changed. If those who are tempted to criticize could hear about all the miracles, certainly they would see that 3ABN is God's work, not Danny's. Thousands and thousands of people are now taking Bible studies, attending Seventh-day Adventist churches, and serving God because of the influence of 3ABN.*

And so I began to write. I wrote off and on for six years. As I began to see "the end of the road," my husband, Jan, and I literally moved to 3ABN for a number of weeks so that I could pull together all the loose ends. It was then that my family got caught in the great controversy between good and evil. I don't think the devil wanted this book to be finished! At 3ABN, the evidence for a lovingly powerful God who is actively involved in the daily lives of His children is overwhelming!

What would be the best way to keep this book from being completed? Attempt to destroy the one person on earth I love the most. On December 2, 2003, at 4:00 A.M., my husband had a stroke. Danny rushed us to the hospital in Herrin. Although Jan was weak on his left side, he had some movement. My children said they would come immediately so that I could continue writing.

I don't think the devil was happy with that decision! Thirteen hours later, Jan suffered a massive hit that paralyzed him completely on his left side. For the next two and a half weeks, I lived in the hospital with him. When he was strong enough to make the trip to Tennessee, Hal Steenson took him home to be nursed by our physical therapist daughter and her family. I stayed on a few more days, hoping to finish the first draft by Christmas.

But alas, the task was too big. I put my writing aside and traveled home for the holidays, home to my family and the wounded man I love. Was I discouraged? How could I be when we have a most awesome and powerful God who can move mountains *and* paralyzed limbs?

Over the next few months, Jan needed me to do for him what he couldn't do for himself. But by May, as my husband's strength and function began to return, I went back to the task of putting the finishing touches on the last few chapters of this incredible story. It was not until then that I realized that Danny was also going through a very difficult time.

As both Danny and I have traveled through the "valley of the shadow" these last few months, we have become even more convinced that we are living very, *very* close to the end of the great controversy between Christ and Satan. Just at the exact time God has put into place the technology, satellites, and programming to carry the gospel message to all the world, Satan has unleashed his forces with demonic fury to try *anything* to stop God from completing His plan for redemption.

Never forget that in 1984, 3ABN was God's dream—not Danny's. Danny caught the vision and became an instrument God used to fulfill His purpose. 3ABN was, and continues to be, God's ministry, not man's. It is going to go forward regardless of satanic attack!

Never forget that although God called one person to jump-start this ministry, He has called an ever expanding staff of highly committed and talented workers, many serving without pay, to carry the gospel forward. These workers are not just at 3ABN's headquarters in southern Illinois; they are located throughout the world, actively promoting God's media ministry. Plus, God has created an ever growing family of dedicated supporters and prayer partners who provide the resources and inspiration that empowers 3ABN's signal to reach the ends of the earth. This ministry is a result of God's united family of believers working together, believers who have claimed the promise that "this gospel of the kingdom will be preached in all the world as a witness to all the nations, *and then the end will come.*"

The 3ABN story—the story of God mending broken hearts through this worldwide ministry—is a powerful one. We should never be discouraged if we just remember how God has worked miracles for us in the past. Now is not the time to give up. Our salvation draws near. Let's look up, step out in faith, and expect God to continue working miracles for us as He has so faithfully done for twenty years for 3ABN!

Because God is in control, you have nothing to fear. Just as God has provided for 3ABN, He will provide for you. Take time out of your schedule to let His love warm you, comfort you, and sustain you through whatever challenges you may face in the future. He will be with you through whatever "valley of the shadow" you may be asked to travel. God is good, and as Danny would say, "May God bless you and do for you exceeding abundantly above all that you may ask or think" (see Ephesians 3:20).

Since there is no end to God's grace and miracles, I will end this book with these words:

To be continued. . . .

Appendix 1

A Brief Look at Twenty Years of Miracles

November 15, 1984

The Lord impressed Danny Shelton to build a television station that would carry the undiluted three angels' messages of Revelation 14 to a lost and dying world.

1984–1985

- God inspired a Pentecostal pastoral couple, Hal and Mollie Steenson, to give television equipment owned by their church, worth approximately $100,000, to help start this new television ministry.

- A Baptist engineer, Clarence Larson, told Danny where he thought an uplink television station could be built near Thompsonville, Illinois.

- Fonda Summers gave land in Thompsonville that was free from microwave interference and suitable for a satellite uplink television station.

- Three-phase power was found at the entrance of the driveway leading to this land.

- Danny and his family traveled from church to church on weekends singing and sharing about Three Angels Broadcasting Network (3ABN). Small donations were given.

- With two hundred dollars in the bank, Danny and his brothers rented a bulldozer and began making a road to the uplink facility. In faith, they ordered $6,000 worth of gravel for the road. God sent two checks—one for $2,000 and one for $4,000—at exactly the time it was needed to pay for the gravel.

- Marvin and Rosella McColpin, a retired couple, gave $50,000, the exact sum that was needed to build the shell of the uplink television station.

- After church, a small band of workers and supporters would gather at the construction site and sing, "We Are Standing On Holy Ground."

- In September 1985, at the ASI International Convention in Big Sky, Montana, an ASI couple donated $10,000 without knowing it was the exact sum needed for the cement floor of the building.

1985–1986

- 3ABN purchased a transmitter and built a 32-foot satellite uplink dish to get the signal onto the satellite. The dish and equipment cost $350,000. With only a $10,000 down payment, the equipment was sent, requiring no bank credit or collateral. Each time a payment came due, the Lord provided the funds.

- Gonzalo Santos, a Chicago area electrician, donated his time on weekends to wire the uplink building. He often brought a friend along to help him, but he accepted payment only for his traveling expenses.

- On November 23, 1986, broadcasting began from the tiny transmitter shack on both Monday and Thursday nights from eight o'clock to ten o'clock. This was before the uplink building was completed. It was just two years and one week after Danny's call to the 3ABN ministry.

1987

- During the month of March, the first *3ABN Presents* set was built.

- On April 1, 1987, 3ABN began broadcasting eighteen hours a day. All viewers had to have large, home satellite dishes to pick up 3ABN's signal. A few months later, the ministry began broadcasting twenty-four hours a day, seven days a week.

- "Mending Broken People" became the theme and mission for 3ABN.

1988

- 3ABN began to broadcast a few hours every week over a full-power station in Houston, Texas.

- Applications were made to obtain construction permits for downlink television stations in various places across the United States.

- Negotiations were begun with cable companies.

1989

- Salem, Illinois, became the site of the first downlink television station. It reached 50,000 potential viewers.

- Cox Cable in San Diego, California, began airing 3ABN programming during the night hours. A surprising number of viewers watched.

1990

- 3ABN broadcast the Seventh-day Adventist Church General Conference session from Indianapolis, Indiana.

- Five new television stations began broadcasting in the United States.

1991

- Seven new television stations went on the air, and 37 construction permits were obtained.

- 3ABN purchased property in Thompsonville, Illinois, to construct a twenty-two-thousand-square-foot building to house the production center and worldwide headquarters.

- 3ABN answered the call and began work on the Romanian production studio.

1992

- 3ABN broadcast Pastor John Carter's evangelistic meetings in Nizhny Novgorod, Russia, which resulted in over 2,500 people being baptized.

- 3ABN purchased an abandoned, partially completed, 100,000 square-foot building in Nizhny Novgorod and began work on the 3ABN Russian Evangelism Center that would eventually house two sanctuaries, offices for local church workers, television and radio studios, and more. It is now the largest Protestant evangelism center in all of the former Soviet Union.

1993

- A new transmitter was purchased.

- Three new television stations began broadcasting in the United States.

1994

- Thirteen new television stations began broadcasting in the United States.

- Eleven new construction permits were obtained.

- The first church service was held in the youth chapel of the new 3ABN Russian Evangelism Center.

1995

- Twenty-six new television stations began broadcasting, adding 7.8 million potential viewers to the network.

- The Net 95 evangelistic series with Mark Finley was broadcast by 3ABN in cooperation with the Seventh-day Adventist Church. 3ABN provided free air time and uplinked the series to homes and churches across the Americas.

- 3ABN broadcast the Seventh-day Adventist Church General Conference session from Utrecht, Netherlands.

1996

- Twelve new television stations were added, including one that covered the Cayman Islands.

- 3ABN began broadcasting to Europe and North Africa just in time for the Net 96 evangelistic series with Mark Finley. The series was simultaneously translated into eight different languages.

- 3ABN moved into the new production center and worldwide headquarters building.

- A new set was constructed for *3ABN Presents*.

- 3ABN's Web site went online offering program schedules, information, free offers, and sermons.

1997

- Nine new television stations began broadcasting in the United States.

- The program *3ABN Presents* was taped on a new set.
- Bos Auditorium in the new production center was completed.
- Satellite Seminar 97 with Pastor Doug Batchelor, a live evangelistic series, was produced at 3ABN. One thousand churches and home gatherings followed the series.
- The production truck was built, which allowed 3ABN to produce more On the Road programs.

1998

- Fifteen new television stations began broadcasting in the United States.
- Five new television series were produced by 3ABN.
- 3ABN began airing on Dominion Sky Angel, a Christian owned and operated direct-broadcast satellite service.
- 3ABN's television production truck began crisscrossing North America, traveling to camp meetings, conventions, and special events.
- 3ABN broadcast Pastor Dwight Nelson's Net 98 series in eight different languages across North and South America, Europe, and North Africa.
- On February 28, the 3ABN Russian Evangelism Center in Nizhny Novgorod was dedicated.
- The 3ABN Russian Evangelism Center began producing television programs in its own studios. Dozens of television stations asked for the programming and were willing to broadcast the programs without charge.

1999

- Four new television stations began broadcasting in the United States.
- Three new 3ABN-produced television series were started.
- 3ABN built a large gymnasium that would serve as an auditorium for camp meetings and large gatherings.
- As a service to the surrounding communities, a Christian school was established by 3ABN in cooperation with the Thompsonville Seventh-day Adventist Church.

- In the Philippines, 3ABN was awarded the last full-power television license for the city of Manila with a potential audience of twenty-plus million people.

- 3ABN was invited to build a television station in the capital city of Port Moresby, Papua New Guinea. Danny formally accepted a license to broadcast in that country when he met with the governor general, His Excellency, Sir Silas Atopare, who expressed his personal desire to have God lead his nation.

- 3ABN broadcast two live evangelistic series: La Red 99 from Orlando, Florida, with Pastor Alejandro Bullón, and Net 99 from New York with Pastor Doug Batchelor. Millions of viewers heard the gospel preached in their own language.

- 3ABN began broadcasting on the Hotbird satellite system in Europe, adding millions of potential viewers.

- On New Years Eve, 3ABN Radio Network began broadcasting.

2000

- 3ABN began production on six new television series.

- Twenty-six new 3ABN radio affiliates were added.

- The U.S. Federal Communication Commission (FCC) opened a window of opportunity to apply for low-power FM radio stations.

- Seventy-eight new cable systems began broadcasting 3ABN, increasing the demand for 3ABN materials and free offers.

- The new 3ABN Call Center was completed to answer calls and process thousands of orders for satellite dishes and other materials.

- A new satellite uplink truck was built, eliminating the need to rent equipment for On the Road productions.

- On June 28, 3ABN could be seen worldwide, except New Zealand, Greenland, and parts of Siberia. 3ABN was able to broadcast around the world by sending its signal from Illinois to AMC-4, a satellite that covered North and Central America. At the same time, 3ABN sent the signal to PAS 9 satellite that covered South America and Europe. In Rome, Italy, a teleport picked up the signal and sent it to Hotbird, the most-used satellite in Europe. In Jerusalem, another teleport downlinked the signal and sent it to the Thaicom 3 satellite that covered the area from west of Africa to east of Australia. With these four satellites, 3ABN's signal could be received almost anywhere in the world. The incredible thing was that it took only eight seconds for the signal to go from Thompsonville, Illinois, all the way to Australia!

2001

- 3ABN's theme for 2001 was the "*Year of Full-Power Television and Radio Stations.*"

- A record number of programs were produced in the studio. Programs on exercise, the Holy Spirit, the rapture theory, and *Kids Time* were started.

- 3ABN participated in the lay-evangelistic series in Ongole, India. Up to 4,000 people loaded into trucks and buses traveling several hours each way to come to this series, and 15,000 were baptized.

- Two new satellite dishes were built just behind the production center, eliminating the extra teleport 3ABN was renting to get the signal across the Atlantic Ocean.

- Twenty-six new cable systems were added in the United States.

- 3ABN-Russia programming reached millions on more than 125 full-power television stations across the former Soviet Union.

- On New Year's Eve, the 3ABN Sound Center was dedicated. A number of projects were completed, including Danny and Tommy Shelton's instrumental CD entitled *Songs of Inspiration.*

- Danny Shelton's book, *The Forgotten Commandment,* was published by Pacific Press® Publishing Association.

2002

- 3ABN's theme for 2002 was the "*Year of Wills and Trusts.*"

- In January, the 3ABN Philippine television station began broadcasting on channel 45 in the metro Manila area to over twenty million potential viewers.

- In February, construction began on the new master control facility. It would feature a large room for the automation system that would run the English and Latino feeds simultaneously.

- 3ABN produced several new television series: *Marriage Matters* with Harvey and Kathy Corwin, *Earth Talk* with Howard Lyman on the stewardship of God's world, a sermon series entitled *Faith Chapel, Tiny Tots for Jesus* for children two through four years of age, and a new Spanish-language children's program called *Amiguitos de Jesús.*

- The production of live broadcasts on location increased. 3ABN traveled to various Seventh-day Adventist colleges and universities for live broadcasts featuring local musicians, teachers, and students. 3ABN broadcast a record number of 3ABN weekend rallies featuring powerful testimonies, miracle stories, inspired music, and Spirit-filled sermons. The largest rally in 3ABN history happened in New York City.

- 3ABN Radio expanded:

  - 3ABN purchased WBLC, a full-power AM station in Lenoir, Tennessee. A new affiliate, WBIN-AM, started broadcasting in Benton, Tennessee. 3ABN Radio produced a new weekly program entitled *Your Family Health* with Cheryl Swanson.

- Pastor Owen Troy, 3ABN's director of international development, reported an expansion of international work.

  - Several radio and television stations were in various planning stages in Africa. Almost every country in Africa had a grass-roots network of viewers and supporters.

  - In Thailand, 3ABN was quickly becoming well-known among cable operators. Some had already added 3ABN programming.

  - India reported an increase in cable systems carrying 3ABN.

  - John and Rosemary Malkiewycz were installing dishes and spreading the word about 3ABN throughout Australia.

  - The equipment for the new television station in Port Moresby arrived and cleared customs in Papua New Guinea.

- 3ABN received 27 new construction permits for new downlink television stations across the United States.

- The book about 3ABN, *A Channel of Blessing*, by Bob Ellis was published.

- Danny Shelton's books *Does God Love Sinners Forever?* and *Can We Eat Anything?* were published by Pacific Press® Publishing Association.

2003

- 3ABN's theme for 2003 was the *"Year of Expansion."*

- 3ABN was the second largest owner and operator of low-power television stations in the United States.

- In August, 3ABN Latino—a twenty-four-hour network broadcast in Spanish and Portuguese—was launched. Four months after broadcasting began, 3ABN Latino was on cable stations in every Latino nation on earth except Cuba, Paraguay, and Uruguay.

- The shell of the worship center was built. On November 14, the first live telecast from the sanctuary was an eight-night series called *Victory of Life* with Pastor John Lomacang. This corresponded to the nineteenth anniversary of God's call to Danny to establish the 3ABN ministry.

- The new state-of-the-art, digital, fully automated master control center was completed.

- Funding was received for a downlink production studio in New York City to produce programs from the inner city.

- Ruben Carr, Jr., was successful in getting almost three million signatures to put 3ABN on cable in New York City.

- Funding was received to build a 3ABN studio in France to produce Arabic programs for Muslims on issues such as health and lifestyle that are important to the Muslim value system.

- Two new series for children began airing: *Tiny Tots for Jesus* for children two through four years of age, and *Amiguitos de Jesús* for the 3ABN Latino channel.

- Three new adult series programs were launched: *From Rags to Riches* hosted by Cynthia Prime, *Exalting His Word* with Shelley Quinn, and *Health Headlines* with Dr. Bernell Baldwin and Dr. Roby Ann Sherman.

- 3ABN aired eleven evangelistic series—a record number.

- John and Rosemary Malkiewycz, directors of 3ABN-Australia, installed more than 150 satellite dishes in Australia.

- 3ABN was added to cable systems in Denmark and Iceland.

- 3ABN-Africa was organized in Uganda with plans to build a downlink station and have it operational in 2004.

- 3ABN Radio expanded with two new low-power affiliate stations, two new full-power affiliate stations, and the purchase of a full-power FM station, WDQN in Du Quoin, Illinois. Three new foreign stations were being built: St. Lucia, Grand Cayman Islands, and St. Croix, Virgin Islands.

2004

- 3ABN's theme for 2004 was the "*You Haven't Seen Anything Yet.*"

- 3ABN-India signed a contract with Siti Cable, which makes 3ABN available in 45 of the largest cities in India, reaching a potential cable audience of a quarter to a half billion viewers, doubling 3ABN's potential viewing audience.

- 3ABN-Nigeria signed a contract with Trent TV, a small-dish direct-to-home (DTH) system, making 3ABN available to over eight hundred thousand homes in western Nigeria. In the next year, they will be expanding to southern and eastern Nigeria, reaching an additional one million homes!

- In March, Optus B3 started carrying 3ABN, which makes it possible to get a good signal in New Zealand and Australia.

- A cable contract was signed with Comcast, making it possible to reach the Washington, D.C., and Baltimore, Maryland, area viewers, a potential audience of 2.5 million.

- A cable contract was signed with Cable One, making 3ABN available on cable in 26 large cities in various states. The potential viewing audience is 2.5 million.

- A cable contract was signed with Time Warner, the largest cable company in the United States, making it possible for 3ABN to be available in any city in the United States (including New York City) that has the Time Warner Cable system.

- Taping of the new On the Road series, titled *3ABN Up Close,* was begun in various locations throughout the United States.

- After twenty years, *3ABN Presents* and *3ABN Presents Live* were retired. A new opening and a new format were designed to launch the new 3ABN flagship program—*3ABN Today* and Thursday night's *3ABN Today Live.*

- 3ABN launched a number of new programs:

  - *House Calls,* a weekly live Bible-answer program hosted by John Lomacang and John Stanton.

  - *Kids Time Praise* was added to the children's programming lineup.

  - 3ABN Latino added a new cooking program and began taping a Spanish equivalent of the *3ABN Today* program

  - 3ABN broadcast live from Chattanooga the *04 Revival* with Doug Batchelor from Amazing Facts and live from Sacramento, the General Youth Conference.

- 3ABN Music completed new CDs by Allison Speer, Danny Shelton, Maddy Couperus, Darrell Marshall and Annette Campbell, the Kids Time Singers, and a 3ABN Family Album.

- A record number of people, more than 1,500, attended 3ABN camp meeting on the last weekend of May, and for the first time, 3ABN held a fall camp meeting, September 30–October 2.

- 3ABN began planning a third television network—Urban Inspirational Television—which will target minorities in major cities.

- On July 1, 2004, 3ABN launched 3ABN Books in cooperation with Pacific Press® Publishing Association. The first two books published were: *Mending Broken People,* a book written by Kay Kuzma telling the story of twenty years of miracles at 3ABN and *The Antichrist Agenda* by Danny Shelton and Shelley Quinn.

- Construction on two new television production trucks was started in New York City and France.

- Twenty-five new radio stations came on the air for a total of 57 outlets.

- 3ABN began using "vitual sets" to cut costs and increase production.

- The new magazine *3ABN World* was launched, with a free monthly subscription available.

2005
- Theme for 2005: Revival and Reformation.

* * * * *

In just twenty years, God has fashioned a worldwide network of television and radio programming broadcasting the undiluted three angels' messages in many languages with the potential to reach billions. It is abundantly clear that God has carefully provided for each need. As you review the history and accomplishments of 3ABN, may you remember Philippians 4:19—"But my God shall supply all your need according to his riches in glory by Christ Jesus." Truly, God has guided and provided for 3ABN—and He will provide for you.

Appendix 2

Who Are Seventh-day Adventists, and What Do They Believe?

Seventh-day Adventists are Christians who base their faith on Jesus Christ and upon His Word, the Bible. All their fundamental beliefs are found in the Bible. Above all, Adventists believe in salvation by faith through Jesus Christ.

The Seventh-day Adventist Church was officially organized in 1863. Many of those early believers who formed the church were a part of the Millerite movement of Christians who believed Christ was coming in 1844. When they were disappointed, some turned against God, and others drifted back to their old churches, but a small group banded together and went to their Bibles to see where they had erred in their thinking.

Their study revealed a number of Bible truths that the established denominations either ignored or explained away without supporting Bible evidence. The first was the realization that the seventh-day Sabbath had never been changed by God. God established the Sabbath at the end of Creation week and commanded His children to keep it holy (see Exodus 20:1-17). Another important Bible truth they discovered was that death is an unconscious state, that there is no soul that lives apart from the body (see Ecclesiastes 9:5, 6). The resurrection of the body along with man's restored spirit at Christ's coming make up a living soul. And since the body is the "temple of the Holy Spirit" (1 Corinthians 6:19, NKJV), it is important to keep it healthy. That's why Adventists believe in living a healthy lifestyle and why health information is such a vital part of 3ABN's broadcasting.

Seventh-day Adventists are one of the fastest-growing Christian churches in the world. In 2004, membership approached the 14 million mark. When the Adventist Church was organized in 1863, it had a total of some 3,500 members, all of whom lived in North America. Today, nine out of ten of its members live outside North America—in 209 countries of the world.

Seventh-day Adventists have one of the most extensive centralized Protestant educational systems in the world and have one of the most comprehensive networks of healthcare providers. Adventists work in at least 725 languages and 1,000 dialects. In addition, Adventists have established 57 church-owned printing plants and editorial offices.

Twenty-Seven Fundamental Beliefs of Seventh-day Adventists

1. The Holy Scriptures

The Holy Scriptures, Old and New Testaments, are the written Word of God, given by divine inspiration through holy men of God who spoke and wrote as they were moved by the Holy Spirit. In this Word, God has committed to man the knowledge necessary for salvation. The Holy Scriptures are the infallible revelation of His will. They are the standard of character, the test of experience, the authoritative revealer of doctrines, and the trustworthy record of God's acts in history. (2 Peter 1:20, 21; 2 Timothy 3:16, 17; Psalm 119:105; Proverbs 30:5, 6; Isaiah 8:20; John 17:17; 1 Thessalonians 2:13; Hebrews 4:12.)

2. The Trinity

There is one God: Father, Son, and Holy Spirit, a unity of three co-eternal Persons. God is immortal, all-powerful, all-knowing, above all, and ever present. He is infinite and beyond human comprehension, yet known through His self-revelation. He is forever worthy of worship, adoration, and service by the whole creation. (Deuteronomy 6:4; Matthew 28:19; 2 Corinthians 13:14; Ephesians 4:4-6; 1 Peter 1:2; 1 Timothy 1:17; Revelation 14:7.)

3. The Father

God the eternal Father is the Creator, Source, Sustainer, and Sovereign of all creation. He is just and holy, merciful and gracious, slow to anger, and abounding in steadfast love and faithfulness. The qualities and powers exhibited in the Son and the Holy Spirit are also revelations of the Father. (Genesis 1:1; Revelation 4:11; 1 Corinthians 15:28; John 3:16; 1 John 4:8; 1 Timothy 1:17; Exodus 34:6, 7; John 14:9.)

4. The Son

God the eternal Son became incarnate in Jesus Christ. Through Him all things were created, the character of God is revealed, the salvation of humanity is accomplished, and the world is judged. Forever truly God, He became also truly man, Jesus the Christ. He was conceived of the Holy Spirit and born of the virgin Mary. He lived and experienced temptation as a human being, but perfectly exemplified the righteousness and love of God. By His miracles He manifested God's power and was attested as God's promised Messiah. He suffered and died voluntarily on the cross for our sins and in our place, was raised from the dead, and ascended to minister in the heavenly sanctuary in our behalf. He will come again in glory for the final deliverance of His people and the restoration of all things. (John 1:1-3, 14; Colossians 1:15-19; John 10:30; 14:9; Romans 6:23; 2 Corinthians 5:17-19; John 5:22; Luke 1:35; Philippians 2:5-11; Hebrews 2:9-18; 1 Corinthians 15:3, 4; Hebrews 8:1, 2; John 14:1-3.)

5. The Holy Spirit

God the eternal Spirit was active with the Father and the Son in Creation, Incarnation, and Redemption. He inspired the writers of Scripture. He filled Christ's life with power. He draws and convicts human beings; and those who respond He renews and transforms into the image of God. Sent by the Father and the Son to be always with His children, He extends spiritual gifts to the church, empowers it to bear witness to Christ, and in harmony with the Scriptures leads it into all truth. (Genesis 1:1, 2; Luke 1:35; 4:18; Acts 10:38; 2 Peter 1:21; 2 Corinthians 3:18; Ephesians 4:11, 12; Acts 1:8; John 14:16-18, 26; 15:26, 27; 16:7-13.)

6. Creation

God is Creator of all things and has revealed in Scripture the authentic account of His creative activity. In six days the Lord made "the heaven and the earth" and all living things upon the earth, and rested on the seventh day of that first week. Thus He established the Sabbath as a perpetual memorial of His completed creative work. The first man and woman were made in the image of God as the crowning work of Creation, given dominion over the world, and charged with responsibility to care for it. When the world was finished it was "very good," declaring the glory of God. (Genesis 1; 2; Exodus 20:8-11; Psalm 19:1-6; 33:6, 9; 104; Hebrews 11:3.)

7. The Nature of Man

Man and woman were made in the image of God with individuality, the power and freedom to think and to do. Though created free beings, each is an indivisible unity of body, mind, and spirit, dependent upon God for life and breath and all else. When our first parents disobeyed God, they denied their dependence upon Him and fell from their high position under God. The image of God in them was marred, and they became subject to death.

Their descendants share this fallen nature and its consequences. They are born with weaknesses and tendencies to evil. But God in Christ reconciled the world to Himself and by His Spirit restores in penitent mortals the image of their Maker. Created for the glory of God, they are called to love Him and one another, and to care for their environment. (Genesis 1:26-28; 2:7; Psalm 8:4-8; Acts 17:24-28; Genesis 3; Psalm 51:5; Romans 5:12-17; 2 Corinthians 5:19, 20; Psalm 51:10; 1 John 4:7, 8, 11, 20; Genesis 2:15.)

8. The Great Controversy

All humanity is now involved in a great controversy between Christ and Satan regarding the character of God, His law, and His sovereignty over the universe. This conflict originated in heaven when a created being, endowed with freedom of choice, in self-exaltation became Satan, God's adversary, and led into rebellion a portion of the angels. He introduced the spirit of rebellion into this world when he led Adam and Eve into sin. This human sin resulted in the distortion of the image of God in humanity, the disordering of the created world, and its eventual devastation at the time of the worldwide Flood. Observed by the whole creation, this world became the arena of the universal conflict, out of which the God of love will ultimately be vindicated. To assist His people in this controversy, Christ sends the Holy Spirit and the loyal angels to guide, protect, and sustain them in the way of salvation. (Revelation 12:4-9; Isaiah 14:12-14; Ezekiel 28:12-18; Genesis 3; Romans 1:19-32; 5:12-21; 8:19-22; Genesis 6–8; 2 Peter 3:6; 1 Corinthians 4:9; Hebrews 1:14.)

9. The Life, Death, and Resurrection of Christ

In Christ's life of perfect obedience to God's will, His suffering, death, and resurrection, God provided the only means of atonement for human sin, so that those who by faith accept this atonement may have eternal life, and the whole creation may better understand the infinite and holy love of the Creator. This perfect atonement vindicates the righteousness of God's law and the graciousness of His character; for it both condemns our sin and provides for our forgiveness. The death of Christ is substitutionary and expiatory, reconciling and transforming. The resurrection of Christ proclaims God's triumph over the forces of evil, and for those who accept the atonement assures their final victory over sin and death. It declares the Lordship of Jesus Christ, before whom every knee in heaven and on earth will bow. (John 3:16; Isaiah 53; 1 Peter 2:21, 22; 1 Corinthians 15:3, 4, 20-22; 2 Corinthians 5:14, 15, 19-21; Romans 1:4; 3:25; 4:25; 8:3, 4; 1 John 2:2; 4:10; Colossians 2:15; Philippians 2:6-11.)

10. The Experience of Salvation

In infinite love and mercy God made Christ, who knew no sin, to be sin for us, so that in Him we might be made the righteousness of God. Led by the Holy Spirit we sense our need, acknowledge our sinfulness, repent of our transgressions, and exercise faith in Jesus as Lord and Christ, as Substitute and Example. This faith which receives salvation comes through the divine power of the Word and is the gift of God's grace. Through Christ we are justified, adopted as God's sons and daughters, and delivered from the lordship of sin. Through the Spirit we are born again and sanctified; the Spirit renews our minds, writes God's law of love in our hearts, and we are given the power to live a holy life. Abiding in Him we become partakers of the divine nature and have the assurance of salvation now and in the judgment. (2 Corinthians 5:17-21; John 3:16; Galatians 1:4; 4:4-7; Titus 3:3-7; John 16:8; Galatians 3:13, 14; 1 Peter 2:21, 22; Romans 10:17; Luke 17:5; Mark 9:23, 24; Ephesians 2:5-10; Romans 3:21-26; Colossians 1:13, 14; Romans 8:14-17; Galatians 3:26; John 3:3-8; 1 Peter 1:23; Romans 12:2; Hebrews 8:7-12; Ezekiel 36:25-27; 2 Peter 1:3, 4; Romans 8:1-4; 5:6-10.)

11. The Church

The church is the community of believers who confess Jesus Christ as Lord and Savior. In continuity with the people of God in Old Testament times, we are called out from the world; and we join together for worship, for fellowship, for instruction in the Word, for the celebration of the Lord's Supper, for service to all mankind, and for the worldwide proclamation of the gospel. The church derives its authority from Christ, who is the incarnate Word, and from the Scriptures, which are the written Word. The church is God's family; adopted by Him as children, its members live on the basis of the new covenant. The church is the body of Christ, a community of faith of which Christ Himself is the Head. The church is the bride for whom Christ died that He might sanctify and cleanse her. At His return in triumph, He will present her to Himself a glorious church, the faithful of all the ages, the purchase of His blood, not having spot or wrinkle, but holy and without blemish. (Genesis 12:3; Acts 7:38; Ephesians 4:11-15; 3:8-11; Matthew 28:19, 20; 16:13-20; 18:18; Ephesians 2:19-22; 1:22, 23; 5:23-27; Colossians 1:17, 18.)

12. The Remnant and Its Mission

The universal church is composed of all who truly believe in Christ, but in the last days, a time of widespread apostasy, a remnant has been called out to keep the commandments of God and the faith of Jesus. This remnant announces the arrival of the judgment hour, proclaims salvation through Christ, and heralds the approach of His second advent. This proclamation is symbolized by the three angels of Revelation 14; it coincides with the work of judgment in heaven and results in a work of repentance and reform on earth. Every believer is called to have a personal part in this worldwide witness. (Revelation 12:17; 14:6-12; 18:1-4; 2 Corinthians 5:10; Jude 3, 14; 1 Peter 1:16-19; 2 Peter 3:10-14; Revelation 21:1-14.)

13. Unity in the Body of Christ

The church is one body with many members, called from every nation, kindred, tongue, and people. In Christ we are a new creation; distinctions of race, culture, learning, and nationality, and differences between high and low, rich and poor, male and female, must not be divisive among us. We are all equal in Christ, who by one Spirit has bonded us into one fellowship with Him and with one another; we are to serve and be served without partiality or reservation. Through the revelation of Jesus Christ in the Scriptures, we share the same faith and hope and reach out in one witness to all. This unity has its source in the oneness of the triune God, who has adopted us as His children. (Romans 12:4, 5; 1 Corinthians 12:12-14; Matthew 28:19, 20; Psalm 133:1; 2 Corinthians 5:16, 17; Acts 17:26, 27; Galatians 3:27, 29; Colossians 3:10-15; Ephesians 4:14-16; 4:1-6; John 17:20-23.)

14. Baptism

By baptism we confess our faith in the death and resurrection of Jesus Christ and testify of our death to sin and of our purpose to walk in newness of life. Thus, we acknowledge Christ as Lord and Savior, become His people, and are received as members by His church. Baptism is a symbol of our union with Christ, the forgiveness of our sins, and our reception of the Holy Spirit. It is by immersion in water and is contingent on an affirmation of faith in Jesus and evidence of repentance of sin. It follows instruction in the Holy Scriptures and acceptance of their teachings. (Romans 6:1-6; Colossians 2:12, 13; Acts 16:30-33; 22:16; 2:38; Matthew 28:19, 20.)

15. The Lord's Supper

The Lord's Supper is a participation in the emblems of the body and blood of Jesus as an expression of faith in Him, our Lord and Savior. In this experience of communion, Christ is present to meet and strengthen His people. As we partake, we joyfully proclaim the Lord's death until He comes again. Preparation for the Supper includes self-examination, repentance, and confession. The Master ordained the service of foot washing to signify renewed cleansing, to express a willingness to serve one another in Christlike humility, and to unite our hearts in love. The Communion service is open to all believing Christians. (1 Corinthians 10:16, 17; 11:23-30; Matthew 26:17-30; Revelation 3:20; John 6:48-63; 13:1-17.)

16. Spiritual Gifts and Ministries

God bestows upon all members of His church in every age spiritual gifts that each member is to employ in loving ministry for the common good of the church and of humanity. Given by the agency of the Holy Spirit, who apportions to each member as He wills, the gifts provide all abilities and ministries needed by the church to fulfill its divinely ordained functions. According to the Scriptures, these gifts include such ministries as faith, healing, prophecy, proclamation, teaching, administration, reconciliation, compassion, and self-sacrificing service and charity for the help and encouragement of people. Some members are called of God and endowed by the Spirit for functions recognized by the church in pastoral, evangelistic, apostolic, and teaching ministries particularly needed to equip the members for service, to build up the church to spiritual maturity, and to foster unity of the faith and knowledge of God. When members employ these spiritual gifts as faithful stewards of God's varied grace, the church is protected from the destructive influence of false doctrine, grows with a growth that is from God, and is built up in faith and love. (Romans 12:4-8; 1 Corinthians 12:9-11, 27, 28; Ephesians 4:8, 11-16; Acts 6:1-7; 1 Timothy 3:1-13; 1 Peter 4:10, 11.)

17. The Gift of Prophecy

One of the gifts of the Holy Spirit is prophecy. This gift is an identifying mark of the remnant church and was manifested in the ministry of Ellen G. White. As the Lord's messenger, her writings are a continuing and authoritative source of truth that provide for the church comfort, guidance, instruction, and correction. They also make clear that the Bible is the standard by which all teaching and experience must be tested. (Joel 2:28, 29; Acts 2:14-21; Hebrews 1:1-3; Revelation 12:17; 19:10.)

18. The Law of God

The great principles of God's law are embodied in the Ten Commandments and exemplified in the life of Christ. They express God's love, will, and purposes concerning human conduct and relationships and are binding upon all people in every age. These precepts are the basis of God's covenant with His people and the standard in God's judgment. Through the agency of the Holy Spirit they point out sin and awaken a sense of need for a Savior. Salvation is all of grace and not of works, but its fruitage is obedience to the commandments. This obedience develops Christian character and results in a sense of well-being. It is an evidence of our love for the Lord and our concern for our fellow men. The obedience of faith demonstrates the power of Christ to transform lives and therefore strengthens Christian witness. (Exodus 20:1-17; Psalm 40:7, 8; Matthew 22:36-40; Deuteronomy 28:1-14; Matthew 5:17-20; Hebrews 8:8-10; John 15:7-10; Ephesians 2:8-10; 1 John 5:3; Romans 8:3, 4; Psalm 19:7-14.)

19. The Sabbath

The beneficent Creator, after the six days of Creation, rested on the seventh day and instituted the Sabbath for all people as a memorial of Creation. The fourth commandment of God's unchangeable law requires the observance of this seventh-day Sabbath as the day of rest, worship, and ministry in harmony with the teaching and practice of Jesus, the Lord of the Sabbath. The Sabbath is a day of delightful communion with God and one another. It is a symbol of our redemption in Christ, a sign of our sanctification, a token of our allegiance, and a foretaste of our eternal future in

God's kingdom. The Sabbath is God's perpetual sign of His eternal covenant between Him and His people. Joyful observance of this holy time from evening to evening, sunset to sunset, is a celebration of God's creative and redemptive acts. (Genesis 2:1-3; Exodus 20:8-11; Luke 4:16; Isaiah 56:5, 6; 58:13, 14; Matthew 12:1-12; Exodus 31:13-17; Ezekiel 20:12, 20; Deuteronomy 5:12-15; Hebrews 4:1-11; Leviticus 23:32; Mark 1:32.)

20. Stewardship

We are God's stewards, entrusted by Him with time and opportunities, abilities and possessions, and the blessings of the earth and its resources. We are responsible to Him for their proper use. We acknowledge God's ownership by faithful service to Him and our fellow men and by returning tithes and giving offerings for the proclamation of His gospel and the support and growth of His church. Stewardship is a privilege given to us by God for nurture in love and the victory over selfishness and covetousness. The steward rejoices in the blessings that come to others as a result of his faithfulness. (Genesis 1:26-28; 2:15; 1 Chronicles 29:14; Haggai 1:3-11; Malachi 3:8-12; 1 Corinthians 9:9-14; Matthew 23:23; 2 Corinthians 8:1-15; Romans 15:26, 27.)

21. Christian Behavior

We are called to be a godly people who think, feel, and act in harmony with the principles of heaven. For the Spirit to recreate in us the character of our Lord, we involve ourselves only in those things that will produce Christlike purity, health, and joy in our lives. This means that our amusement and entertainment should meet the highest standards of Christian taste and beauty. While recognizing cultural differences, our dress is to be simple, modest, and neat, befitting those whose true beauty does not consist of outward adornment but in the imperishable ornament of a gentle and quiet spirit. It also means that because our bodies are the temples of the Holy Spirit, we are to care for them intelligently. Along with adequate exercise and rest, we are to adopt the most healthful diet possible and abstain from the unclean foods identified in the Scriptures. Since alcoholic beverages, tobacco, and the irresponsible use of drugs and narcotics are harmful to our bodies, we are to abstain from them as well. Instead, we are to engage in whatever brings our thoughts and bodies into the discipline of Christ, who desires our wholesomeness, joy, and goodness. (Romans 12:1, 2; 1 John 2:6; Ephesians 5:1-21; Philippians 4:8; 2 Corinthians 10:5; 6:14-7:1; 1 Peter 3:1-4; 1 Corinthians 6:19, 20; 10:31; Leviticus 11:1-47; 3 John 2.)

22. Marriage and the Family

Marriage was divinely established in Eden and affirmed by Jesus to be a lifelong union between a man and a woman in loving companionship. For the Christian a marriage commitment is to God, as well as to the spouse, and should be entered into only between partners who share a common faith. Mutual love, honor, respect, and responsibility are the fabric of this relationship, which is to reflect the love, sanctity, closeness, and permanence of the relationship between Christ and His church. Regarding divorce, Jesus taught that the person who divorces a spouse, except for fornication, and marries another, commits adultery. Although some family relationships may fall short of the ideal, marriage partners who fully commit themselves to each other in Christ may achieve loving unity through the guidance of the Spirit and the nurture of the church. God blesses the family and intends that its members shall assist each other toward complete maturity. Parents are to bring up their children to love and obey the Lord. By their example and their words they are to teach them that Christ is a loving disciplinarian, ever tender and caring, who wants them to become members of His body, the family of God. Increasing family closeness is one of the earmarks of the final gospel message. (Genesis 2:18-25; Matthew 19:3-9; John 2:1-11; 2 Corinthians 6:14; Ephesians 5:21-33; Matthew 5:31, 32; Mark 10:11, 12; Luke 16:18; 1 Corinthians 7:10, 11; Exodus 20:12; Ephesians 6:1-4; Deuteronomy 6:5-9; Proverbs 22:6; Malachi 4:5, 6.)

23. Christ's Ministry in the Heavenly Sanctuary

There is a sanctuary in heaven, the true tabernacle which the Lord set up and not man. In it Christ ministers on our behalf, making available to believers the benefits of His atoning sacrifice offered once for all on the cross. He was inaugurated as our great High Priest and began His intercessory ministry at the time of His ascension. In 1844, at the end of the prophetic period of 2,300 days, He entered the second and last phase of His atoning ministry. It is a work of investigative judgment which is part of the ultimate disposition of all sin, typified by the cleansing of the ancient Hebrew sanctuary on the Day of Atonement. In that typical service the sanctuary was cleansed with the blood of animal sacrifices, but the heavenly things are purified with the perfect sacrifice of the blood of Jesus. The investigative judgment reveals to heavenly intelligences who among the dead are asleep in Christ and therefore, in Him, are deemed worthy to have part in the first resurrection. It also makes manifest who among the living are abiding in Christ, keeping the commandments of God and the faith of Jesus, and in Him, therefore, are ready for translation into His everlasting kingdom. This judgment vindicates the justice of God in saving those who believe in Jesus. It declares that those who have remained loyal to God shall receive the kingdom. The completion of this ministry of Christ will mark the close of human probation before the Second Advent. (Hebrews 8:1-5; 4:14-16; 9:11-28; 10:19-22; 1:3; 2:16, 17; Daniel 7:9-27; 8:13, 14; 9:24-27; Numbers 14:34; Ezekiel 4:6; Leviticus 16; Revelation 14:6, 7; 20:12; 14:12; 22:12.)

24. The Second Coming of Christ

The second coming of Christ is the blessed hope of the church, the grand climax of the gospel. The Savior's coming will be literal, personal, visible, and worldwide. When He returns, the righteous dead will be resurrected and together with the righteous living will be glorified and taken to heaven, but the unrighteous will die. The almost complete fulfillment of most lines of prophecy, together with the present condition of the world, indicates that Christ's coming is imminent. The time of that event has not been revealed, and we are therefore exhorted to be ready at all times. (Titus 2:13; Hebrews 9:28; John 14:1-3; Acts 1:9-11; Matthew 24:14; Revelation 1:7; Matthew 24:43, 44; 1 Thessalonians 4:13-18; 1 Corinthians 15:51-54; 2 Thessalonians 1:7-10; 2:8; Revelation 14:14-20; 19:11-21; Matthew 24; Mark 13; Luke 21; 2 Timothy 3:1-5; 1 Thessalonians 5:1-6.)

25. Death and Resurrection

The wages of sin is death. But God, who alone is immortal, will grant eternal life to His redeemed. Until that day death is an unconscious state for all people. When Christ, who is our life, appears, the resurrected righteous and the living righteous will be glorified and caught up to meet their Lord. The second resurrection, the resurrection of the unrighteous, will take place a thousand years later. (Romans 6:23; 1 Timothy 6:15, 16; Ecclesiastes 9:5, 6; Psalm 146:3, 4; John 11:11-14; Colossians 3:4; 1 Corinthians 15:51-54; 1 Thessalonians 4:13-17; John 5:28, 29; Revelation 20:1-10.)

26. The Millennium and the End of Sin

The millennium is the thousand-year reign of Christ with His saints in heaven between the first and second resurrections. During this time the wicked dead will be judged; the earth will be utterly desolate, without living human inhabitants, but occupied by Satan and his angels. At its close Christ with His saints and the Holy City will descend from heaven to earth. The unrighteous dead will then be resurrected and with Satan and his angels will surround the city; but fire from God will consume them and cleanse the earth. The universe will thus be freed of sin and sinners forever. (Revelation 20; 1 Corinthians 6:2, 3; Jeremiah 4:23-26; Revelation 21:1-5; Malachi 4:1; Ezekiel 28:18, 19.)

27. The New Earth

On the new earth, in which righteousness dwells, God will provide an eternal home for the redeemed and a perfect environment for everlasting life, love, joy, and learning in His presence. For here God Himself will dwell with His people, and suffering and death will have passed away. The great controversy will be ended, and sin will be no more. All things, animate and inanimate, will declare that God is love; and He shall reign forever. Amen. (2 Peter 3:13; Isaiah 35; 65:17-25; Matthew 5:5; Revelation 21:1-7; 22:1-5; 11:15.)

Appendix 3

How You Can Help Get 3ABN Into Your Community

3ABN's uplink facilities in southern Illinois broadcast its programs via satellite. The signal beams from earth to a satellite in geosynchronous orbit 22,300 miles above the earth. If 3ABN is to be a blessing to you and those in your community, there must be some way to downlink the signal.

There are three possible ways to get 3ABN into your community: (1) persuade cable companies to add 3ABN to their listing, (2) encourage individuals to purchase satellite dishes, (3) establish downlink stations. (Note: Options 1 and 3 bless thousands!)

1. Getting 3ABN on local cable

Almost all local cable companies have empty channels that are available for future broadcasting possibilities, depending on consumer demand. 3ABN's marketing department will help you develop a successful plan for your community to get 3ABN on cable, based on postcard canvasses to residents. (For the story of how New York City was able to get over three million signatures, see Ruben Carr's story in chapter 15.)

Launch a church campaign to get 3ABN on cable in your community.

Before starting your 3ABN campaign, obtain the following materials:

- *Informational video.* 3ABN provides a five-minute informational video about 3ABN. It shows the kind of programming 3ABN offers and the evangelism potential in a church district.
- *Informational flyers.* Flyers are available to give people when you ask them to write a postcard request. People need to know what they are requesting. The flyer can also be used as a bulletin insert on the day you launch the 3ABN campaign. Encourage every member to give a flyer to other subscribers or potential subscribers in the community when they ask them to write a postcard. *The flyers are not to be distributed house-to-house without asking for requests on the postcards.*
- *Postcards.* Purchase postcards at the post office. Write by hand the address of the local cable company on the cards before asking people to write their request. *(Do not use labels to address these postcards!)*

Conducting a "Campaign 3ABN" in your church

- *Show the video the day you introduce the 3ABN campaign to your church family.* Be sure all persons who will be making the requests are current cable subscribers or could become cable subscribers if 3ABN were available. The informational flyers about 3ABN can be given out at this time. Hand out postcards and have members write their request immediately and drop the card in the offering plate. Encourage members to take additional postcards and flyers to their neighbors, coworkers, or friends who are cable subscribers or potential subscribers, asking them to fill out a postcard request. Be sure members drop these in the mail, rather than relying on others to do so. The note should say, "I want 3ABN!" Include a "thank you" along with the person's name and address on the postcard.
- *During the church service each week, share stories from church members* who have had an interesting experience the past week while asking friends and neighbors to fill out a postcard request. Plan who will share stories in church the following week. These exciting experiences help keep up the motivation and momentum of the campaign. They also create a good opportunity to remind members each week to take home a few more postcards and flyers to use in the community!

- *In church, encourage members who have not yet written their postcards to do so* during the announcement time and to place the postcards in the offering plate.
- *Continue to remind church members of the 3ABN campaign* by placing the following announcement in the church bulletin each week: *Campaign 3ABN: Write a note requesting 3ABN be put on local cable service. Send to: [address of cable company]. Pre-addressed postcards are available. Ask your neighbors and friends to do the same.*

What to say when asking your neighbors and friends to fill out a postcard request:

Here is a sample of what you can say at the door when asking someone to request the local cable company to include 3ABN:

Hi, my name is _____. I know about Three Angels Broadcasting Network (3ABN). I believe it would be a benefit to our community if the _____ cable company would add 3ABN to the cable lineup. [Show him/her the flyer and point to what you're describing.] *3ABN has really good children's programs, a lot of health education shows, and different inspirational programs. The cable company needs to hear from people in the community who would like a channel like this. So I was wondering if you would be willing to write a note on this postcard to the cable company.* [Hand the postcard and pen to the person. He/she may ask you what to write.] *You can just write "I want 3ABN" with your name and address. That is all the cable company wants to know.*

Note: 3ABN Latino may also be requested if suitable for your area. Tell the individual to write: "I want 3ABN English and 3ABN Latino" with his/her name and address.

When the person is done writing, you can continue: *Thank you for your request. I'll be happy to mail the postcard for you.* [Take the postcard and hand him/her the flyer.] *This reminds you of the programming to which you have to look forward. I hope you have a wonderful day.*

2: Encourage individuals to purchase a satellite dish

When 3ABN is not available on a local cable or television channel, or you don't have computer Internet service, the only way to get 3ABN is by a satellite dish. You may want to consider helping others obtain and install satellite dishes, as John and Rosemary Malkiewycz have done in Australia (see chapter 15).

For the latest satellite information, check 3ABN's Web site, <www.3ABN.org>. As of 2004, 3ABN was received worldwide through eight different satellites.

In North and Central America and some of the Caribbean islands, 3ABN offers a dish system that uses a *free* to air satellite receiver. This allows the viewer to receive almost every Seventh-day Adventist satellite channel—3ABN English TV; 3ABN Latino TV; 3ABN Radio, Hope Channel, Loma Linda Broadcasting Network, Radio 74 (France); and Life Talk Radio, plus a number of non-SDA channels. The suggested dish size is thirty-six inches. The entire equipment package—including the dish—is available for a one-time fee of only US$200. Prices are subject to change, of course. Contact 3ABN or any of the above networks.

In North America, Dominion Sky Angel offers a monthly subscription or lifetime membership package of religious and family oriented programming. The suggested dish size is eighteen to thirty-six inches.

3. Consider starting or buying a downlink station in your area

3ABN's downlink stations consist mostly of low-power unmanned television or radio stations. These VHF and UHF television stations rebroadcast 3ABN's satellite signal in a twenty- to thirty-mile radius. The low-power radio stations rebroadcast the signal in an eight- to ten-mile radius. They are controlled and monitored by computers via telephone lines.

Many of the downlink stations are owned and operated by 3ABN; others are affiliated with the network and run by independent organizations. Occasionally, full-power stations do come up for sale. To find out if a station is for sale in your community, check the following Web sites: for television, <www.thelptvstore.com>, for radio, <www.buysellradio.com> or <www.radiobroker.com>.

You might also call local stations and inquire if they are interested in selling, as Gonzalo Santos did (see chapter 13). If you are interested in purchasing a station, regardless of location, contact 3ABN. There may be a station that 3ABN would like to purchase if the funding were available.

Please be aware that downlink stations are becoming more and more difficult to obtain because only a few frequencies are left. Applications for low-power frequencies can be submitted only when the Federal Communication Commission (FCC) opens a low-power application window. The last time the FCC opened an application window was August 2000. No one knows if or when another window will be opened. (Please contact 3ABN for more information.) That is why 3ABN encourages people to call their local cable companies and ask them to carry 3ABN channels on their system. This is the best and least expensive way to get 3ABN in most communities.

Note: There is one way you can get 3ABN programming to your local community if your local cable company is not carrying the 3ABN Network. Every cable system has a local access channel on which local individuals can provide programming without a charge. If there is time available on this channel, you can tape 3ABN programs and take them to the station. Contact your local cable system to learn more about this possibility.

Appendix 4

How You Can Be a Part
of the 3ABN Family

3ABN exists because of the dedication and support of thousands and thousands of individuals worldwide who are inspired by the Holy Spirit to give financially. Perhaps you, too, feel God calling you to become a part of the 3ABN family of supporters. If you choose to give a large gift, a special project donation, or set up a trust or annuity, you will most likely talk to 3ABN's director of stewardship and trust services. As this book goes to press, Leonard Westphal holds this position. Leonard, however, did not come to 3ABN to do a job. Rather, he responded to a call from God. Here is his story in his own words:

May Chung had been after me for a number of years to help 3ABN develop a stewardship and trust-services department. At first, I knew nothing about the ministry and wasn't interested. When my wife and I moved to Loma Linda, California, May urged me to visit 3ABN. I agreed. After Danny gave me a tour, I heard a voice in my head telling me, This is God's work. You must join it. At this very time and without my knowledge, 3ABN's board of directors had voted to ask me to organize and develop a stewardship and trust department. When Danny conveyed the action of the board to me, I gladly accepted.

That very day, a family visiting from a southern state asked to speak with someone in the trust department about their desire to donate their estate to 3ABN upon their demise. I was amazed that God would bring someone to me so soon. I had heard God's call; now I felt God was con-

firming it. The next day, I drove to this couple's home and helped them develop a trust agreement leaving their entire estate to 3ABN. They then handed me a check for $125,000 along with the deeds to two beautiful southern mansions! The timing of this encounter brought me the assurance and confidence to know God wanted me to do this work.

Leonard ends his story by saying, "I look upon 3ABN as one of the greatest wonders and miracles of the twenty-first century. Please come along and join our family."

If you accept Leonard's invitation, you might consider one of the following possibilities:

Regular monthly and annual commitments

Although large gifts are essential to making large projects happen—such as the Russian Evangelism Center or the worship center—the lifeblood for 3ABN is the thousands of donors who have committed to help 3ABN with a monthly or an annual gift, whether ten dollars or ten thousand dollars. This broad base of donor support not only sustains the ministry but gives it financial stability. With a large number of regular donors, if something happens and a few donors cease giving, the operation of 3ABN is not threatened.

Special project donations

Special project donations are Holy Spirit-inspired gifts—not that the others aren't. But if you are inspired in a special way that you should give a larger gift of a specific amount, almost always it's because the Lord is moving on His people to fund another one of His projects. You can be a special channel of blessing in this way.

Gifts of quality goods and vehicles

3ABN has a wonderful donation center, managed by Tammy Chance, where donations of various items are displayed and sold in various ways, including over the Internet. Cars, boats, guns, antiques, collectibles—all kinds of valuable items—have been donated to 3ABN. These items are then sold, and the funds go to help support 3ABN. If you have something valuable and don't have a use for it, consider donating it to 3ABN and receiving a receipt that may help you reduce your income taxes! You can initiate this process by calling 3ABN's donation center.

A charitable gift annuity

A gift annuity is a unique way through which you may make a substantial gift to enhance the soul-winning ministry of 3ABN while also receiving a fixed income for life for you and/or other family members. It might also reduce your income tax.

For example, you may fund an annuity for an older relative or friend who will benefit from its income for life while you will receive a charitable income tax deduction in the year the gift is made.

Annuities can be funded with cash or stocks. If the annuity is funded with stock or real property that has increased in value, there is an additional benefit because of the partial bypass of capital gains tax. The annuity rate can be as high as 11.3 percent depending on the age of the beneficiary(ies). The rate is fixed and will not change regardless of current investments or market conditions.

A gift annuity is an irrevocable document. This means that once it is executed it cannot be changed or revoked. You may fund a gift annuity with as little as $5,000 for a single-life or $10,000 for two. For more information on this type of giving, contact 3ABN Stewardship and Trust Services, P.O. Box 7148, Loma Linda, CA 92354. Call 909-796-7800 or, toll free, 800-886-4800. Fax to 909-796-8611 or send email to threeabntrust@verizon.net.

Stewardship and Trust Services team. (L to R) Rita Westphal, Trenton Frost, Leonard Westphal, Oriana Frost, and Hope LeBrun

3ABN Family Photos

3ABN today

Camp meeting

Danny's parents

Danny and Tammy

Danny and Ronny

Danny's family

Shelton boys

The Shelton extended family

Shelton siblings

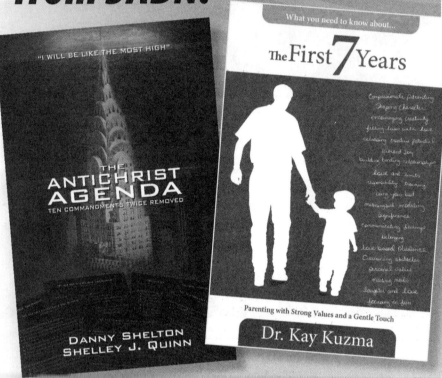